The Historical–Critical Method

A GUIDE FOR THE PERPLEXED

T&T CLARK GUIDES FOR THE PERPLEXED

T&T Clark's Guides for the Perplexed are clear, concise and accessible introductions to thinkers, writers and subjects that students and readers can find especially challenging. Concentrating specifically on what it is that makes the subject difficult to grasp, these books explain and explore key themes and ideas, guiding the reader towards a thorough understanding of demanding material.

Guides for the Perplexed available from T&T Clark:

The Historical Jesus: A Guide for the Perplexed, by Helen K. Bond
Martyrdom: A Guide for the Perplexed, by Paul Middleton
New Testament and Jewish Law: A Guide for the Perplexed,
    James G. Crossley
The Origin of the Bible: A Guide for the Perplexed,
    Lee Martin McDonald
Paul: A Guide for the Perplexed, Timothy G. Gombis

A GUIDE FOR THE PERPLEXED

The Historical– Critical Method

A GUIDE FOR THE PERPLEXED

DAVID R. LAW

continuum

Published by T&T Clark International
A Continuum imprint
The Tower Building, 11 York Road, London SE1 7NX
80 Maiden Lane, Suite 704, New York, NY 10038

www.continuumbooks.com

British Library Cataloguing-in-Publication Data
A catalogue record for this book is available from the British Library.

ISBN: HB: 978-0-567-11130-2
PB: 978-0-567-40012-3

Library of Congress Cataloging-in-Publication Data
A catalog record for this book is available from the Library of Congress.

Typeset by Newgen Imaging Systems Pvt Ltd, Chennai, India
Printed and bound in India

To my Grandmother
Eileen Muriel Law

CONTENTS

Preface viii

1 Introduction 1

2 A Brief History of Historical Criticism 25

3 Textual Criticism 81

4 Source Criticism 113

5 Form Criticism 140

6 Redaction Criticism 181

7 The End of the Historical–Critical Method? 216

Appendix 238

Notes 242

Bibliography 288

Bible References 313

Index 318

PREFACE

The historical–critical method has developed over the past 300 years or so as a means of making sense of the Bible. Its employment by leading scholars of the day has led to original, stimulating and nuanced insights into the different writings that make up the Bible and has shed light on the processes by which they have come into existence. This book is a conscious attempt to simplify these methods as much as possible in order to give the reader a foothold in what are complex ways of reading the Bible that require a high degree of technical expertise on the part of the interpreter. For the sake of providing the reader with as clear an introduction as possible to the different methods employed in historical criticism, I have simplified and 'streamlined' the presentation of the methods in four ways.

(1) The methods of textual criticism, source criticism, form criticism and redaction criticism belong together and are usually employed in conjunction with each other by the biblical scholar. It is thus somewhat artificial to separate them in the way I have done in this study, especially with regard to the separate application of the four methods. For the sake of clarity and to enable the reader to grasp the distinctive features of each method, however, I have treated them as far as possible independently of each other.

(2) Chapter 2 provides a brief history of historical criticism and focuses on the scholars who have played a role in the development of historical approaches to the interpretation of the Bible. Chapters 3 to 6 contain sections sketching the history of textual criticism, source criticism, form criticism and redaction criticism, respectively. Since these methods are the outcome of the historical approach to the Bible, it is again to some extent artificial to separate them from the general development of historical criticism. Nevertheless, such separation is helpful in order to highlight what is distinctive about the different historical methods that have come into existence to interpret the Bible.

(3) The Old Testament and New Testament are distinct bodies of literature raising their own particular problems of interpretation. Treating them together thus risks homogenizing them and failing to do

justice to their distinctiveness. To give the reader as straightforward an introduction as possible, however, and for reasons of limitation of space, I have attempted to identify the common features of the different historical methods and to show how they can be applied to both Old and New Testaments. The reader should bear in mind, however, that the distinctive character of the two testaments as well as the different types of literature they contain raise genre-specific questions of interpretation that cannot be addressed in a work of this kind.

(4) To highlight the distinctive features of textual criticism, source criticism, form criticism and redaction criticism, we shall apply them to the same two biblical texts, namely Gen. 2.4b–3.24 and Matt. 15.21–28, which can be found in the appendix. The aim of applying the methods to the same two texts is both to highlight what is distinctive about each method and to show their interdependence. As we shall see, the different methods often take as their point of departure the results of the other methods or are attempts to resolve issues inadequately addressed by the other methods.

Biblical references are to the New Revised Standard Version Bible: Anglicized Edition, copyright 1989, 1995, Division of Christian Education of the National Council of the Churches of Christ in the United States of America. Used by permission. All rights reserved.

Like all authors I am indebted to family, friends, colleagues, and students in a multitude of ways. I am grateful to my colleague Professor George Brooke for allowing me to draw upon his expertise in textual criticism. Above all, I have been blessed by the constant support of my wife Claudia (Prov. 31.29). This book is dedicated to my grandmother as a small token of my affection and esteem on the occasion of her ninety-fifth birthday.

David R. Law
Manchester 2011

CHAPTER ONE

Introduction

'Historical criticism' and 'the historical–critical method'[1] are generic terms given to a cluster of related approaches which all focus in some way on the *historical* character of the Bible. History in one form or another plays an important role in the Bible. The 'historical' books of the Old Testament such as Joshua, Judges, Samuel, Kings and Chronicles relate the history of Israel, while the prophetic works contain frequent references to contemporary events and persons. The same is true of the New Testament. The Gospels and the Acts of the Apostles are organized in what appears to be a chronological sequence, and these works contain references to contemporary Jewish and Roman history. The importance of history in the Bible is further evident in the fact that both Judaism and Christianity claim that God has revealed his will in a series of historical events that are recorded in the Bible. Judaism and Christianity are sometimes said to be 'historical religions' precisely because they are based on historical events in which God is said to have revealed himself and his purpose for humankind. The Old Testament describes how God selected Israel as his chosen people, led them out of Egypt and gave them the land of Canaan, while the New Testament tells the story of Jesus of Nazareth, a first-century Palestinian Jew in whom Christians believe God has revealed himself in a new and definitive way. The Bible also contains a distinctive understanding of history. In the Old Testament, Israel's history is determined by its covenant with God and successes and misfortunes ascribed to whether Israel has fulfilled or broken its side of the agreement. The apocalyptic works of the Bible such as Daniel in the Old Testament and the Revelation of St. John in the New Testament present a vision of history moving towards a dramatic climax, culminating in the end of the world, divine judgement and the dawning of the kingdom of God. If we wish to understand the nature and meaning of the Bible, then it is necessary to be attentive to its historical character.

A question of importance to communities who base their faith on the Bible is that of the *historical trustworthiness* of the Bible. There are, however, numerous episodes in the Bible which modern readers may find difficult to accept at face value. How was Cain able to find a wife and father children if he was the only human being alive in his generation, as the Bible seems to imply after he had murdered his brother Abel (Gen. 4.17)? How could Moses have written the *entire* Pentateuch, which is the traditional view, in light of the fact that it relates his own death (Deut. 34.5–8)? What was the point of Jesus commanding the witnesses of his healing of Jairus' daughter to conceal the miracle (Mark 5.43) since it was already common knowledge that the girl had died (Mark 5.38–40)?

The problem of historical improbability becomes even more acute with those biblical accounts that describe supernatural occurrences. To the modern reader whose understanding of the world has been moulded by the natural sciences, biblical accounts of prophetic visions, miracles, visitations by angels and demonic possession seem inherently implausible.

Other problems concern what appear to be inconsistencies between different books of the Bible. Why are there different accounts in Kings and Chronicles of what appear to be the same events? Why does the date of the crucifixion differ in John's account from that stated in Matthew, Mark and Luke, and whose account is correct? How is the chronology of Paul's missionary journeys as related in Acts to be reconciled with the information Paul himself provides of these journeys in his letters? A good example of the problems created by variant parallel accounts in the Bible is provided by the three versions of the parable of the wicked husbandmen (Matt. 21.33–46; Mark 12.1–12; Luke 20.9–19), which, despite their similarities, have different endings. In Matthew's version, Jesus' hearers answer his question what the owner of the vineyard would do to the tenants who had murdered his son (Matt. 21.40–41), while according to Mark and Luke Jesus himself answers the question (Mark 12.9; Luke 20.16). Luke diverges from both Matthew and Mark in telling us that the crowd responded to the parable with the exclamation 'Heaven forbid!' (Luke 20.16), while there is no mention of this response in either of the other two Gospels. Another example of parallel but divergent narratives is provided by the accounts of the first missionary journey of the disciples. According to Mark, Jesus commanded the disciples to take nothing but a staff on their travels (Mark 6.8), while in the Gospels of Matthew and Luke, the disciples were not permitted even this small concession (Matt. 10.10; Luke 9.3).

The *order* of biblical narratives may also diverge, raising questions about the veracity of the chronology of the events depicted in the Bible. In Matthew, Jesus heals a leper (Matt.8.1–4), before later healing Peter's mother-in-law and the people brought to him by the crowds who have flocked to see him (Matt. 8.14–17). Mark, however, places these events in the opposite order (Mark 1.29–31, 40–45). Another example of divergence of order is provided by the story of the stilling of the storm. Matthew places this event some time before Jesus' teaching in parables (Matt. 8.23–27; 13.1–52), while Mark has Jesus preach his parables immediately before the stilling of the storm (Mark 4.1–41).

Such parallel but divergent accounts prompt us to raise the question: which account is the most accurate? Which of these accounts gives us the most reliable description of the events they purport to relate? And how do we account for the divergences that exist between such parallel accounts? It is such questions that prompt historical investigation into the biblical writings in the hope of constructing the most plausible historical account of the events the Bible describes.

Historical investigation of the biblical texts is also prompted by conflict between the biblical and secular accounts of the same historical events, or when discrepancies arise between biblical accounts and archaeological evidence. An example of such a discrepancy is Luke's statement that Quirinius was governor of Syria when Augustus held his census (Luke 2.1–2). This conflicts with the account of the Jewish historian Josephus, who tells us that Quirinius' governorship and census did not take place until 6 CE, several years after Jesus' birth.[2]

Further historical questions emerge when we reflect on the role of the communities in which the biblical writings were formed and handed down. Those responsible for passing down the literature of the Bible such as the followers of the Old Testament prophets and the early Christian communities had their own theological agendas. What appears at first sight to be a historical account may in reality be a construction of a community or an individual writer in order to further their theological, ecclesiastical and political interests. To understand the meaning of biblical texts, it is thus necessary to identify the interests of the author(s) and to consider to what degree these interests have moulded and modified the formation of the text. This will help us to establish to what degree the text we have before us has been written for historical or theological purposes. For example, if we can ascertain that a passage in one of the Gospels is strongly influenced by the evangelist's theological assumptions, then we will be inclined to interpret the text as a reflection of the theological development of the early Church rather than as an objective account of an event in the life of Jesus.

Historical questions are also posed by the literary genre of biblical texts. Is a particular text a historical account or does it belong to a different category such as poetry, liturgy or pious embellishment? Are such passages as the description of Jesus' temptations by the devil (Matt. 4.1–11; Luke 4.1–13) or the rending of the veil in the temple (Matt. 27.51/Mark 15.38) to be understood as accounts of historical events or are they rather symbolic expressions of the overwhelming significance of the person at their centre? To interpret the stories of the Good Samaritan and the Prodigal Son as historical records rather than as parables would be to misunderstand them. Clearly our understanding of the Bible and the events it relates will be affected by whether we interpret biblical texts as the literal accounts of historical events or as symbolic representations or literary constructions.

Historical criticism is a method that has developed in order to address the historical questions posed by the Bible. In this book, I aim to provide an outline of the most significant features of this method, to sketch its history, to consider the various approaches it has developed to make sense of the Bible and to consider its strengths and weaknesses. In this chapter, however, we shall be concerned to consider the critique that has been levelled at the term 'historical–critical method' before going on to consider the senses of Scripture with which the historical–critical method has been understood to be concerned. This will be followed by a sketch of the presuppositions of historical criticism.

The disputed status of the historical–critical method

On the basis of our discussion so far, the character of historical criticism would seem to be fairly straightforward. The terms 'historical criticism' and 'historical–critical method' refer to approaches which are concerned with the history of the Bible both with regard to the history of the text and the events which the text recounts. Each element in the phrase 'historical–critical method', however, has been challenged in the late twentieth and early twenty-first centuries. Indeed, some commentators have argued for the abandonment of the term 'historical–critical method' and its replacement by some other term such as 'biblical studies' or 'biblical criticism'. Other commentators have disputed the appropriateness of the methodology of historical criticism to the Bible and have called for it to be supplemented or even replaced by other methods.

Problems with the term 'historical' in the historical–critical method

Several scholars have questioned whether 'historical criticism' and 'historical–critical method' are appropriate terms to describe the work of the biblical critic. James Barr prefers to avoid the term 'historical criticism', since in his opinion it 'is much too narrow and limited a term to indicate how scholars handle and interpret the Bible'. Furthermore, biblical criticism is not 'necessarily primarily historical in character', since 'the basis of biblical criticism seems . . . to be essentially literary and linguistic, rather than historical in character'.[3] John Barton has similar reservations, asking, 'How far is a concern for *history* a defining characteristic?'[4] Barton rightly points out that critical approaches to the Bible need not be historical in character and that scholars of the Bible have been concerned with many other issues, such as biblical theology, the literary forms of the Bible and particular types of material in the Old and New Testaments such as wisdom, prophecy, apocalyptic, Gospels, epistles and so on.[5] As Barton puts it, 'a great deal of their [i.e. biblical scholars'] time is not spent in reconstructing history anyway, and to call biblical criticism the historical–critical method skews our awareness of this'.[6] Barton further observes that, 'biblical criticism is essentially a literary operation, concerned with the recognition of genre in texts and with what follows from this about their possible meaning'.[7] It is textual issues such as literary genre and internal inconsistencies in the text rather than historical concerns that prompt the work of the biblical scholar. Thus the quest to identify the sources of the Pentateuch and the Gospels, for example, was motivated by the awareness of incompatibilities *in the text*, which is first and foremost a literary rather than a historical concern and predates the concern to reconstruct the history of Israel or the life of Jesus. To describe biblical criticism as *historical* criticism thus fails to capture the *literary* character of the study of the Bible. For these reasons, Barton has 'reservations about building a historical quest into the very name of the discipline and for that reason prefer[s] the older name',[8] by which he means 'biblical criticism'.

A further difficulty in describing the work of the biblical scholar as the '*historical*–critical method' stems from the difficulty of pinning down the meaning of 'history'. The problem here is that there are four different senses in which the term 'history' has been employed in biblical studies.

Firstly, the 'history' with which the historical–critical method has been said to be concerned is the *historical truth of the events recounted in the Bible*. The historical–critical method is 'historical' in that it is concerned with identifying and reconstructing the historical events that underlie the biblical text. Understood in this sense of history, the historical–critical method is concerned with the reconstruction of the history of Israel, the life of Jesus and the history of the early Church.

Secondly, the historical–critical method may be concerned with the *history of the biblical text*. Here the focus of the biblical scholar is on the development of the text itself and on identifying the sources from which it has been constructed. This involves identifying the different layers of the text and tracing which go back to the originator of the text and which are later additions.

A third sense of history to which 'historical' could refer is the 'historical meaning' of texts, i.e. 'the meaning that [biblical] texts had in their original historical context'.[9] Here the task of the historical–critical method consists in identifying how biblical terms were used by the original authors of the biblical texts.

Finally, 'historical' in 'historical–critical method' can denote the use of secular historical methods in interpreting the text. The historical critic notes that the age in which the biblical texts were composed was a superstitious age that lacked scientific knowledge and attributed what were probably natural events to supernatural agency. Assuming that the past was like the present and that what is impossible in the present was also impossible in the past, the historical critic searches for alternative, 'natural' explanations for the supernatural events described in the Bible. If it is this secular meaning of history that is intended, then the historical–critical method comes to be identified with historicist and reductionist ways of interpreting the Bible. Secular historical–critical study of the Bible is sceptical of the historicity of the events described in the Bible, particularly those which describe supernatural agency and divine intervention.

In short, the term 'historical' in historical–critical method can denote different things according to how 'history' is understood, each understanding of which has different consequences for how the method of historical criticism is considered to operate. Consequently, 'historical–critical method' is an unreliable and confusing term to describe the scholarly study of the Bible.

It is such considerations that prompt Barton to offer 'an alternative approach'.[10] Barton holds that although 'history has been a considerable part of what some biblical critics have been interested in', 'it is not part of the definition of biblical criticism'.[11] For Barton, 'the *defining* marks of biblical criticism do not include an interest in history, but come down to three features, which are linked in a logical chain'.[12] These defining marks are a concern with semantics and genre, both of which are *literary* concerns, and a refusal on the part of the reader of the Bible to be 'constrained by prior convictions about the text's meaning, drawn from an interpretative tradition'.[13] Because of the primary literary and critical character of biblical studies, Barton advocates replacing the term 'historical–critical method' with 'biblical criticism', which he believes captures more adequately the type of work in which biblical scholars are engaged.[14]

There are two responses that could be made to Barton's argument. Firstly, Barton is right to draw attention to the fact that the term 'historical–critical method' gives undue prominence to the *historical* element in biblical criticism and obscures the central role played by *literary* considerations in biblical studies. This is an argument, however, not for the removal of the term *historical*, but rather for a greater consciousness of the *literary* basis of this emphasis on history. The distinctive feature of the historical–critical method is that it addresses the internal inconsistencies of biblical texts by looking to history to solve these problems. Thus the historical–critical method is differ-ent from other methods such as, for example, harmonizing and synchronic approaches, which do not turn to historical solutions to explain the internal tensions and contradictions of the Bible. It is therefore perfectly legitimate to use the designation '*historical* criticism', for it captures something essential about this approach to interpreting the Bible. Furthermore, the anomalies the biblical scholar recognizes in the text raise not only literary questions but also *historical* questions. What were, for example, the historical circum-stances that prompted the editor(s) of the Pentateuch to combine a variety of different sources into a continuous narrative? Perhaps the most accurate term would be historical-literary-critical method. It is, however, the phrase 'historical–critical method' that has established itself and it is this phrase which we will continue to employ in this study.

Secondly, Barton's critique is valid only if historical criticism is regarded as a synonym for biblical criticism as such. Barton's argument excludes only using 'historical criticism' and 'historical–critical method' to denote *all* critical approaches to the Bible. It does not rule out these terms to denote a specific type of biblical interpretation, namely as a designation of a subdivision within biblical criticism that is concerned above all with the *historical* questions, problems and issues arising from the biblical texts. That is, 'biblical criticism' should be considered to be a broader term than 'historical–critical method' and should be reserved for a generic approach that employs critical methods of a variety of different kinds to make sense of the Bible. The phrase 'historical–critical method', on the other hand, should be employed to denote critical methods employed with reference to the historical questions raised by the Bible.

In my opinion, it lends clarity to the study of the Bible and makes clear the role the historical–critical method, if we establish a hierarchy of terms to describe the different ways in which readers may engage with the Bible. The term 'biblical studies' should arguably be applied to all types of reading of the Bible, both critical and non-critical. It is a broad, generic term encompassing the work of the scholar, the activities of church bible study groups and the individual's private meditation on the Bible. Barton's preferred term of 'biblical criticism' should be reserved for all forms of engagement with the Bible from a *critical* perspective of some sort. Thus understood, 'biblical criticism' includes canonical criticism, reader-response criticism, rhetorical criticism, feminist criticism, libera-tion exegesis, structuralist and poststructuralist interpretation and so on. Finally, the phrase 'historical–critical method' should not be identified either with biblical studies or biblical criticism but reserved for a particu-lar type of criticism, namely the critical study of the Bible with an eye to the historical questions raised by the text and employing a cluster of his-torical techniques to address these questions.

We might think of biblical studies in terms of an axis suspended between the two extremes of literary and historical concerns. The approach of individual scholars could be plotted at different points on this sliding scale according to the prominence they give to either of these elements. Some scholarly approaches such as rhetorical criticism, reader-response criticism and poststructuralist interpretation will be situated more closely to the literary pole of the literary-historical axis, whereas source criticism will be located nearer to the historical pole. We could also perhaps express this idea in terms of *direction*. All approaches to understanding the Bible are in some sense literary, since *they all begin with the text*. The question is what is to be done with the text. This can be understood in terms of the *direction* of interpretation. More historically minded interpreters move from the text to the historical questions it poses. More literary-minded interpreters move from the text to its role within the community of readers and its interrelationship with other texts.

Problems with the term 'critical' in the historical–critical method

The terms 'criticism' and 'critical' have negative connotations in everyday speech. 'To be critical' or 'to criticize' normally means to find fault with someone or something. This is not intended to be the meaning the term has when applied to the study of the Bible. Reinhart Kosellek points out that, 'The terms *critique* and "criticism" (and also "criticks") established themselves in the seventeenth century. What was meant by them was the art of objective evaluation – particularly of ancient texts, but also of literature and art, as well as of nations and individuals'.[15] The *Oxford English Dictionary* puts it still more succinctly, defining criticism as 'the art of estimating the qualities and character of literary or artistic work'. The term 'critical' does not mean that the scholar is hostile towards the Bible and is hell-bent on picking holes in it. Nor is 'criticism' synonymous with 'scepticism' or 'unbelief'. The terms 'criticism' and 'critical' do not refer to the personal disposition and motives of the scholar towards the Bible, but to the approach he or she is employing to make sense of the text. In Barr's words, 'criticism means the freedom, not simply to *use* methods, but to follow them wherever they may lead. Applied to theological problems, this means: the freedom to come to exegetical results which may differ from, or even contradict, the accepted theological interpretation'.[16] 'Criticism' denotes the application of reason to the Bible, irrespective of where this may take the human being and a refusal to allow the understanding of the Bible to be dictated by tradition, the Church, the academy or any other supposed authority.

This view of the openness of and suspension of judgement by the biblical scholar, however, has been questioned by some scholars. For Gerhard Maier in his *The End of the Historical–Critical Method*, it is not the 'historical' element that is controversial and revolutionary, for the use of the term 'historical' 'obviously has justifiable support in historical change and in man's experience of God'. It is rather the word 'critical' in the historical–critical method that is the problem, for it commits the interpreter in advance to a secular interpretation of the Bible. As Maier puts it, 'a critical method of biblical interpretation can produce only Bible-critical propositions'.[17] Far from being open and unprejudiced, the historical–critical method 'represents a prejudgement in the sense of an a priori decision concerning the outcome'.[18] We shall deal with Maier's critique in more detail in the final chapter. Here it suffices to note his challenge to the impartiality of the historical–critical method and his claim that the method is prejudiced by its alleged commitment to a secular world view. Treating the Bible critically and freely as if it were like any other book is not an unbiased approach but implicitly treats the Bible as a human work rather than as the Word of God. In doing so, it rules out in advance the truth of the doctrinal content of the Bible and the reality of the God of whom it speaks. The historical–critical method is thus not objective and ideologically neutral, but is the biased application to the Bible of an implicitly secular world view.

This challenge to the impartiality of the historical–critical method is often accompanied by the argument that criticism is an inappropriate attitude towards divine revelation. In subjecting the Bible to the historical–critical method we are guilty of imposing human judgement on the Divine Word. This is a point made by Christopher Seitz with reference to the Old Testament:

> The basic challenge of the Old Testament is not historical distance, overcome by historical–critical tools, or existential disorientation, overcome by a hermeneutics of assent or suspicion. The Old Testament tells a particular story about a particular people and their particular God, whom in Christ we confess as our God, his Father and our own, the Holy One of Israel. We have been read into a will, a first will and testament, by Christ. If we do not approach the literature with this basic stance – of estrangement overcome, of an inclusion properly called "adoption" – historical–critical methods or a hermeneutics of assent will still stand outside and fail to grasp that God is reading us, not we him.[19]

On this view, in applying historical criticism to the Bible, we are presumptuously measuring the divine contents of Scripture according to our human judgement and are guilty of presupposing a notion of what the Word of God should be. Furthermore, human reason is subject to sin, and is therefore unable to make judgements concerning revelation. In view of our human limitations, the proper response to divine revelation is thus not critique but obedience. It is not our task to correct God's revelation but to allow ourselves to be corrected by it. As Maier puts it, 'He who is to be redeemed has about as much right to stand in judgement about redemption as a patient has the right to change the prescription of his physician according to his own whim'.[20]

Barton, however, claims that the objectivity attacked by critics of historical approaches to Bible is 'something of a straw man'.[21] He claims: 'Few biblical critics have ever claimed the degree of objectivity they are being accused of. What they have argued for is reasonable objectivity, that is, a refusal simply to read one's own ideas into the text or to have no sense of detachment from it even for the purposes of study.'[22] Furthermore, treating the Bible like any other work can arguably highlight how it *differs* from other works. One of the consequences of historical criticism may be to show that the Bible is *not* like any other book. A truly impartial reading will neither favour nor rule out the possibility that the Bible may be more than merely a collection of ancient texts. The historical–critical method need not necessarily be sceptical towards the Bible being the Word of God. Its critical spirit consists in attentiveness to the character of the text, particularly to its problematic features. As Barton puts it, 'the critical spirit . . . consist[s] in the observation that the text contains difficulties'. In this usage, 'Criticism . . . is understood to be any attempt to deal rationally with such difficulties'.[23] The term 'critical' in the phrase 'historical–critical method' thus does not presuppose the application of a secular world view to the Bible but rather refers to the attempt to be open to the meaning of the text without prejudice or regard to what the consequences of our critical investigation might be.

Problems with the term 'method' in the historical–critical method

Finally, some commentators have questioned the appropriateness of describing historical criticism as a *method*. In his *Discerning the Mystery*, Andrew Louth argues that the term belongs in the natural sciences and its use in the phrase 'historical–critical method' is an attempt to smuggle the criteria of a secular world view into the study of the Bible. He regards the historical–critical method as an example of what George Steiner calls the 'fallacy of imitative form',[24] which Louth defines as that 'whereby humane culture relinquishes to a scientific method, depending upon the non-verbal, non-humane language of mathematics, concern for what is true'.[25] The humanities have taken scientific method as their ideal and have attempted to develop an analogous method in the hope of producing results as empirically convincing as those of the natural sciences. According to Louth, they have achieved this and have developed a pseudo-scientific method by developing the notion of *historical consciousness*, by which is meant the theory that to grasp the meaning of texts we must imaginatively enter into the mind of the author and attempt to understand the text in the light of that author's historical context. Passages in the text which are problematic from the modern perspective can be attributed to the historical epoch in which the author was writing, which naturally conditioned the thought forms and vocabulary in which he was able to express himself. According to Louth, this notion of historical consciousness provided the basis of a method which some believed was appropriate to the humanities, namely the historical–critical method.[26]

In Louth's opinion, however, the historical–critical method smuggles in assumptions that are inappropriate to the humanities, namely, 'the notion of objective and subjective truth' and 'a privileged position being ascribed to the present, or what is thought to be the present'.[27] The natural sciences attempt to eliminate the subjectivity of the scientist in order to achieve the objective truth, that is, 'truth that inheres in the object, independent of the one who knows this truth'.[28] The historical–critical method allows this principle to be applied to the humanities by conceiving of there being an objective meaning embedded in texts which the skilful interpreter can extract and which is independent of the subjectivity of that interpreter.[29] For Louth, such a method is inappropriate to theology, for in theology the individual does not stand over against the object of study in an objective relationship, but is personally addressed by it. We do not know God by treating him as an object of investigation but only by entering into a relationship with him. The historical–critical method is thus utterly inappropriate to the 'object' with which theology is concerned.

Barton also questions historical criticism's status as a method, albeit on different grounds from those of Louth. Barton points out that the methods that comprise historical criticism, namely source criticism, form criticism and textual criticism, do not follow the procedures we would normally expect of a genuine method. Barton's argument is based on a distinction he makes between method and understanding. If I have understood him correctly, Barton holds that a 'method' is a neutral tool or technique that can be applied to the object of study in order to elicit objective information, which can then become the basis for 'understanding' that object of study. Those who hold source criticism to be a method, for example, do so because they consider it 'to be a procedure involving no "understanding" of the texts, but only the application of a quasi-scientific technique based on observations about word frequencies and distributions, and perceptions of inconsistencies between passages on a superficial, literal-minded level'.[30] This, however, Barton points out, 'is a caricature of the approaches of source critics. What comes first in source analysis is always an act of understanding, or rather of *attempted* understanding. Source criticism did not arise from a theoretical idea about how the biblical text should be studied. It arose from an attempt to understand the biblical narratives, especially in the Pentateuch, as finished wholes, an attempt that the texts themselves seemed systematically to frustrate'.[31] As Barton puts it in *Reading the Old Testament*, 'source analysis did not really begin with the application of a "scientific" technique to the text of the Pentateuch, but with an intuition about the text, springing from an attempt to read it with understanding, to grasp it as a coherent whole'.[32] On similar grounds, Barton claims that form criticism is not a method, but 'a set of hypotheses'. Classifying verses according to their genre, he claims, 'is not best characterized as the application of a method'. This is because 'One cannot set out rules that will generate the identification of literary forms; one comes upon them serendipitously in reading the Bible with a certain kind of openness to its literary character'.[33] Barton also denies that textual criticism is a method: 'Such a basic text-critical principle as preference for the harder reading – far from being a piece of method that can be applied without any entering into the meaning of the text – makes sense only if it can be assumed that the critic already understands what the text means, for only so can one judge a particular reading to be "harder," that is, less intuitively probable in its context and therefore less likely to have been introduced by a copyist.'[34]

The reason Barton denies that the various approaches of historical criticism are *methods* is that the person employing these methods already has an understanding in place before he or she begins to apply them to the text. Rather than the understanding of the object of study arising from the application of method, a prior understanding of the object of investigation dictates the character and the application of the method. Those who regard these approaches as *methods* are thus mistaken in their belief that they are applying a set of neutral techniques to the Bible. They fail to realize that source criticism, form criticism and textual criticism are based on a prior understanding of the text and that these are placed in the service of this understanding.

The conclusion Barton draws from these considerations is 'that *biblical criticism is not correctly seen as any kind of method*, and as such does not rightly attract the kind of critique leveled at it by Louth'.[35] Barton prefers to see biblical criticism as 'the application, not of method, but rather of a sort of intuition. One cannot establish through any method what a text means: one has to grasp it by an intuitive appropriation of the combination of words that make it up'.[36] For Barton, then, it is not by means of a method but rather by intuition that the biblical critic engages with the text.

The validity of the arguments of Louth and Barton hinges on what we mean by 'method'. Their denial of the appropriateness of the term 'method' to historical criticism is based on the use of the term in the natural sciences to denote an allegedly neutral set of procedures aimed at eliciting objective facts about the object of study. Scientific method, however, is arguably less 'objective' than it is often taken it to be, for it consists not in the neutral, theory-free application of an objective and universally accepted set of techniques,[37] but is a procedure emerging from a particular understanding of the object to be investigated. As Thomas Kuhn has argued, scientific method takes place within a paradigm that generates certain research questions, the solution of which constitutes the everyday work of the scientist. The scientist does not apply a set of procedures to the object of investigation and then arrive at 'facts', which can be combined into a theory. Rather, he or she begins with a theory, i.e. a potential understanding of the object of study, which generates testable research questions.[38] In the attempt to resolve its research questions, the theory either proves its mettle, as Popper puts it,[39] or it is shown to be inadequate, for example, by being unable to answer the research questions generated by the paradigm or by arriving at results which do not fit the initial theory. The response to such a state of affairs is to modify the theory to accommodate the results, or – in extreme cases – there may take place a paradigm shift, where a new theory replaces the inadequate older theory, and the whole process begins again. It seems to me that a similar procedure is at work with historical criticism. An initial theory or understanding is proposed to explain the anomalies in the text, namely that, to take source criticism as our example, the tensions in the text can be explained by theorizing that the text has come into existence through the conflation of multiple sources. The theory is then tested by attempting to separate out the constituent elements of the text and considering whether this results in the identification of coherent sources. If this procedure is able to explain the presence of tensions in the text, then it can be accepted as a plausible way of understanding the text. If the theory is only partially successful, then it must be modified to account for the data unaccounted for by the initial theory. If it fails completely, then the theory must be abandoned and the search begun for a more adequate way of accounting for the data. There is arguably a procedural coherence involved in the work of the biblical critic that merits the description of 'method'.

Barton's own description of the procedure of biblical criticism implies that – even if it is not a method in the scientific sense of the word – it can nevertheless be *methodical* in its approach to the biblical texts. He states: 'Like science, biblical criticism appeals to evidence; it weighs probabilities; it judges between what is more and what is less probable. But there is no divide between the sciences and the humanities in this respect; both are intellectually rigorous.'[40] He further points out: 'Criticism is a semantic operation, and grasping the macrosemantics of entire texts is not a task for which there is any method; it requires empathy and imagination.' He emphasizes, however, that, 'this does not mean on the other hand that it is simply a manner of unfocused emotion. Detailed attention to questions of language, historical context, and authorship is required. But these questions in turn cannot be settled by method; they too require informed judgement'.[41] To my mind this emphasis on intellectual rigour and on criticism as an empathetic, imaginative semantic operation implies a type of method. To be intellectually rigorous, the humanities must have a set of procedures acknowledged by experts in the field to be adequate to the subject matter under investigation. Furthermore, to avoid empathy degenerating into unfocused imagination it is surely necessary to determine the means for focusing the empathy and imagination necessary for engaging with biblical texts. If historical criticism is indeed intuition – and I would not wish to deny that intuition plays an important role in reading the Bible – then it is *guided* intuition. Indeed, 'guide' might be a better description of historical criticism than method. Nevertheless, there is a degree of guidance in historical criticism that in my opinion legitimates its description as a method. As Barton points out, biblical criticism is an 'attitude towards texts'. But this attitude can arguably be formulated as a series of guidelines or principles, i.e., a sort of method.

The sense of Scripture

The historical–critical method is concerned with the 'meaning' or 'sense' of the Bible. This raises the question of with what type of 'meaning' or 'sense' of Scripture historical criticism is concerned. There are five meanings or senses that have been regarded as the goal of the historical–critical method.

(a) The original sense

It is often said that historical criticism is concerned with the *original sense* of the Bible. There is indeed evidence to support this view, for much of the work of historical critics has been concerned with getting back to the earliest form of the text and then tracing how the final, canonical version was built up through additions and modifications until it came to be fixed in its final literary form. One of the tasks of the historical–critical method has been to peel back the layers of interpretation the text has accumulated in the attempt to recover the original meaning of the very earliest form of the text. Commenting on the biblical scholarship of the past hundred years Robert Alter describes this approach as 'what we might call "excavative" – either literally, with the archeologist's spade and reference to its findings, or with a variety of analytic tools intended to uncover the original meanings of biblical words, the life situations in which specific texts were used, the sundry sources from which longer texts were assembled'.[42] Historical criticism has an archaeological character in the sense that it resembles the work of the archaeologist who painstakingly strips away layers of soil to reveal the original form of, say, a bronze age village lying beneath the modern city.

This concern with the original sense has been criticized for privileging the earliest form of the text, thereby ignoring the fact that it is the *final* version of the text which is canonical and which is used by synagogues and churches. Furthermore, this privileging of the original sense leads to a disparaging of the later stages of the text's development. It sets up an opposition between what the text meant and what it now means, and gives the former precedence over the latter. Focus on the original sense also leads to the fragmentation of the text into primary and secondary and 'authentic' and 'inauthentic' elements.

To avoid such problems the meaning of 'original sense' has been broadened to denote not the first form a text might have had but the meaning the text – including its subsequent layers of modification – may have had in its *original setting*. That is, the notion of the original sense applies not only to the earliest level of the text but also to its subsequent layers, all of which can be properly understood only if we can identify their meaning in their original historical setting. Here the focus on the original sense is motivated by the concern to avoid reading the biblical text anachronistically and imposing upon it meanings that do not do justice to the text.

(b) The intended sense

Closely connected with the 'original' sense is the notion of the 'intended' sense. That is, biblical interpretation should be concerned with identifying the meaning the authors of the biblical texts had in mind. The search for the intended sense need not be restricted to the originator of a text, however, but can be extended to those involved in its later modifications and adaptations. Indeed, to·understand the original sense, it is important to identify the meaning intended by later adaptors in order to differentiate their meaning from the one intended by the originator of the text.

Historical criticism's concern with the intended sense of Scripture has been criticized on several grounds. Firstly, Barton questions whether understanding biblical criticism to be concerned primarily with the intended sense of Scripture does justice to the work of biblical scholars. He points out that scholars such as Mowinckel, Noth and von Rad were certainly biblical critics, and yet they were not concerned with the 'intended meaning' in their work on the Psalms and the Pentateuch, but were interested 'in tradents rather than authors'.[43] Describing biblical criticism as concerned with identifying the intended sense of the biblical texts thus does not do justice to the work of these scholars. Secondly, some biblical texts owe their existence not to a single author or even group of authors but to the community as a whole. Texts such as the Pentateuch, Psalms and Proverbs are the products of the life of a community and embody the folk memory, worship and wisdom of that community, all of which developed over a long period before finally coming to be set down in writing. In the case of such texts, it is questionable whether we can speak of a sense *intended* by the 'original' author. A further significant point, Barton points out, is that 'much biblical writing was produced in a culture that placed less emphasis on the intention of authors in any case. Ancient authors were often producing something more like a score for performance than a distillation of their thoughts for appropriation, and expected that readers would bring to the text an element of interpretation that went beyond the ideas the author had consciously had'.[44] If we are to continue to speak of the intended sense, then it is arguably better to speak of the *work's* intention rather than that of the author.

A serious challenge to the concept of 'intended sense' has come from a different quarter, namely, from the notion of the 'intentional fallacy' that has played an influential role in modern literary studies. The 'intentional fallacy' denies that authorial intention is definitive for understanding the text. The author has no right to determine the meaning of the text,[45] for the act of writing sets the text free for interpretation by its readers. There is an important insight contained in the 'intentional fallacy', namely, that once a text enters the public domain, the meaning supposedly intended by the original author can no longer dictate the way the work is appropriated by its recipients. It is furthermore the case that the text may contain possibilities of meaning of which the author him/herself was not conscious. While, however, acknowledging the importance of such insights and the way they can liberate the text for a wealth of new readings and meanings, it seems to me to be an exaggeration to condemn the search for the intended sense as 'the intentional fallacy'. The intended sense is *one* of the senses we should take into account when embarking on our interpretation of a text. It is not, however, the *only* sense, nor is it necessarily the most important one. It is, however, one of the meanings we should take into account if we wish the text to address us and if we wish to avoid our simply imposing our own agenda upon the text. Historical criticism can play an important role here, for it can help us to identify the intended sense. In doing so, it provides the checks and balances that are needed to do justice to the reality of the text.

(c) The historical sense

Another sense with which historical criticism has been concerned is what has been described as the *historical* sense. The meaning of texts is historically and culturally conditioned. Texts arise in a particular time and place, and naturally reflect the mode of thought, vocabulary and cultural assumptions of the particular time and place in which they came into existence. Consequently, knowledge of the historical and cultural context of a word, phrase or text is essential for understanding a text's meaning. Words can change in meaning over time and if we are to do justice to a text, we must be aware of how the terminology it uses was used in earlier historical and cultural settings and how the meaning of these terms may have shifted in their current usage. Umberto Eco provides a good example of this with reference to Wordsworth's *I wandered lonely as a cloud*, which contains the verse that 'a poet cannot but be gay'. Eco points out that, 'a sensitive and responsible reader is not obliged to speculate about what happened in the head of Wordsworth when writing that verse, but has the duty to take into account the state of the lexical system at the time of Wordsworth. At that time "gay" had no sexual connotation, and to acknowledge this point means to interact with a cultural and social treasury'.[46] That is, before we begin speculating on Wordsworth's sexuality we should first establish whether the term 'gay' had the same connotations in the early nineteenth century as it does in the twenty-first century. To avoid misunderstanding terms such as 'gay' in nineteenth-century literature, it is necessary to investigate the way these terms were used in the past. The historical investigation of the text is thus an essential activity, for it is the means by which we ensure that we are giving the text its due and not subordinating it to the interests of its current readers. It secures the text's status as a genuine dialogue partner.

The importance of establishing the historical sense of the text does not necessarily mean, however, that the historical–critical method is *historicist*, although some of its proponents have been. Nor need it mean that historical criticism is motivated by merely antiquarian interest. Concern to identify the historical sense of a text does not commit the reader to the view that its past meaning is the only meaning there is in the text. Nor does it shut out other, non-historical meanings that can emerge from the text. To be concerned to establish the historical sense of a biblical term entails only that if we wish to understand the text it is necessary to investigate how the text was understood in its historical and cultural context. This historical sense is not the definitive meaning of the text, but is one of the factors that must be taken into account when attempting to ascertain the text's meaning for us today. Literature is open to future interpretations, but not to *all* interpretations. The text must control the range of interpretations if these are indeed to be interpretations of the text and not instances of modern readers reading their own agendas and ideologies into the text.

(d) The literal sense

It might be said that concern with the historical sense of the text stems from a concern to establish the *literal* meaning of the text. This may come as a surprise to some, since historical criticism has sometimes been criticized for not being true to the literal meaning of the text. For example, reading the creation accounts of Gen. 1-2 as mythology rather than as a literal account of God's creation of the universe has long been a contentious issue between conservative evangelical Christians and advocates of the historical–critical method. The crucial issue here is what constitutes the *literal* meaning of the text. The term 'literal' should not be equated with 'literalist'. A literal understanding of the Bible means understanding the *letter* of the Bible. But understanding the letter of the Bible means being attentive to the types of literature the Bible contains. We misunderstand the Bible if we do not take literary genre into consideration when interpreting a text. A literal reading of a metaphor, for example, means respecting the metaphor as a metaphor. If we interpret the proverb 'the grass is always greener on the other side of the fence' in a literalist way and take it to be an objective statement concerning the superiority of my neighbour's lawn to mine, then we have fundamentally misunderstood the proverb. Attempting to prove the truth of the proverb by doing tests to show the superior greenness of my neighbour's grass or to insist on its superiority simply on the grounds of the authority of the proverb indicates merely that we have not grasped its true meaning. Understanding the statement 'the grass is always greener on the other side of the fence' will consist of recognizing its literary genre, namely that it is a proverb. This will give us the key to grasping the *literal* meaning of the text, namely that it expresses the insight that human beings have the tendency to be dissatisfied with what they themselves have and envy what others have. Similarly, only by being attentive to the types of literature the Bible contains will we be able to ascertain the *literal* sense of the Bible.

Others have argued that it is the *Church* which determines the literal sense of Scripture. Thus Childs argues that the literal sense is not identical with the historical sense, but is determined by the Christian understanding. He points out that for the Reformers the *sensus literalis* is the *Christian* meaning of the text.[47] There are, however, both literary and theological reasons for questioning whether a reading determined by the Church or the academy can really be said to be the *literal* sense of the biblical text. The task of the interpreter is surely to allow the Bible to speak for itself and not to impose an official interpretation upon it. The text should be examined on its own merits and we should not impose an a priori meaning upon the text. This does not mean that we should rule out ecclesiastical readings of the text. To do so would again be to come to the text with an a priori agenda. Rather the first task of the interpreter is to allow the text to speak for itself, as far as this is possible and while recognizing that the interpreter's assumptions and world view will always play a role in the act of interpretation, even when the interpreter attempts to allow the text to speak for itself. There is also a theological reason for not allowing the Church to determine the literal sense of Scripture, namely that to do so fails to respect the autonomy of the Bible as the Word of God. If the Bible is indeed in some sense the Word of God, then it will always confute all attempts – including those of the Church – to place limitations upon its meaning. Respect for the Bible means recognizing that the Bible stands over against the Church, both inspiring the Church but also standing in judgement of it. For the Church to determine the meaning of the Bible is for the Church to consider itself the master of the Divine Word rather than its servant. The literal sense of the Bible should therefore not be determined by the Church or any other non-biblical reality, but should be allowed to emerge from the text itself. This is where historical criticism can play an important role, for – if done properly – it can allow the *biblical* meaning of the text to become apparent.

(e) The plain sense

Because of the difficulties faced by the notions of the original, intended, historical and literal senses of Scripture, Barton's own preference 'is to use the term "plain sense" to refer to the sense that biblical criticism is interested in, a sense not colored by any particular prior confessional attachment to the truth of Scripture or its self-coherence'.[48] His thesis is that 'biblical criticism, in its quest for this plain sense, is a semantic or linguistic and a literary operation first and foremost, only indirectly concerned with the original, the intended, the historical, or the literal meaning'.[49] We can go along with Barton's emphasis on the 'plain' sense in the way that he uses the term. The problem is that 'plain sense' is a loaded term which has non-critical connotations such as 'obvious', 'straightforward', 'simple', 'self-explanatory' and 'easy to understand'. The 'plain sense' with which biblical criticism is concerned, however, may be none of these things. Nevertheless, as defined by Barton, the phrase 'plain sense' captures the type of meaning with which the biblical criticism in general and historical criticism in particular is concerned, namely, with a meaning that arises from careful engagement with the linguistic and semantic character of the text. Only by paying careful attention to this plain sense will we be able to respect the integrity of the text and allow the Bible to speak to us as a genuine dialogue partner.

The presuppositions of historical criticism

The question of the presuppositions of historical criticism is a controversial one. Its classic proponents have regarded it as a presuppositionless, objective, scientific method concerned with the 'facts' that can be elicited from the text. Its critics, about whom we shall say more in the concluding chapter, regard it as an ideological method of interpretation employed in the service of the interests of white, middle class Western males.

Consideration of the presuppositions of historical criticism raises some profound and difficult philosophical and theological questions concerning how we know the past, the character of historical truth and the relation between faith and history. The following is an attempt to provide a survey of some of the presuppositions that have been held to underlie historical approaches to the Bible and which distinguish the historical–critical method from other ways of reading the Bible.

1. Probability

We base our judgements of the past on probability, on what is 'likely' to have happened. Troeltsch describes this as the first of the three principles of the historical method, namely, what he calls the 'principle of historical criticism'. This principle 'indicates that in the realm of history there are only judgements of probability, varying from the highest to the lowest degree, and that consequently an estimate must be made of the degree of probability attaching to any tradition'.[50]

2. Analogy

Our understanding of what is probable is based on the principle of *analogy*, i.e. the principle that the experiences, actions and events of the past are analogous to the experiences, actions and events of the present. As

Troeltsch puts it: 'On the analogy of the events known to us we seek by conjecture and sympathetic understanding to explain and reconstruct the past.'[51] Analogy is the second of Troeltsch's three principles for understanding history.[52] Van Harvey describes Troeltsch's principle of analogy as meaning 'that we are able to make such judgments of probability only if we presuppose that our own present experience is not radically dissimilar to the experience of past persons'.[53] We can break down the principle of analogy into two aspects:

(a) The past is like the present

Put in its most simple form, the principle of analogy is the principle that things did not happen in the past which do not happen today. What is known to be possible in the present is made the criterion for what is likely to have happened in the past. If texts report events which are now considered to be improbable or even impossible, then they should not be regarded as historical accounts and the interpreter should look for other explanations such as, for example, that the text reflects a now outmoded world view or is a literary embellishment. The consequence of making the present the criterion for understanding the past is that natural explanations are preferred over supernatural explanations. Historians thus do not (usually) accept at face value accounts of divine intervention, miracles, talking animals and so on, but look for what they consider to be rational explanations for these events. This results in the attempt to accommodate ancient accounts of past events to what is compatible and consistent with modern experience and the modern perception of reality. Thus the Assyrian army was not defeated by the angel of the Lord (2 Kings 19.35; Isa. 37.36), but by disease breaking out among the Assyrians camping outside Jerusalem. New Testament miracles such as casting out demons were healings of psychological problems or of epilepsy.

(b) Analogy between societies

Human societies are similar. Therefore what applies in one society will be analogous to what occurs in other societies. This conviction allows the knowledge of better known societies to be used to interpret less well-known societies. Thus the more firmly established knowledge of certain ancient societies and what we know about how societies function today can be employed to understand ancient societies about which we have only meagre information. For example, accounts have come down to us of the titles of the court officials in the courts of David and Solomon such as 'recorder' and 'secretary' (2 Sam. 8.16–17; 20.24–25; 1 Kings 4.3), but these accounts say little about the duties of these officials. Assuming that the practices of ancient Israel were analogous to those of contemporary societies, historians draw on the court records from Israel's neighbours to construct a plausible account of how the court in Israel is likely to have functioned.

3. The principle of correlation

The third of Troeltsch's principles of historical method is what he calls 'correlation' (*Korrelation*),[54] namely, 'the interaction of all phenomena in the history of civilization'.[55] This principle states that historical events should be understood as part of a nexus of antecedents and consequences, cause and effect. Historical events cannot be isolated from the broader historical context in which they occur and must be understood in terms of their relation to this context. As Troeltsch puts it: 'This concept implies that there can be no change at one point without some preceding and consequent change elsewhere, so that all historical happening is knit together in a permanent relationship of correlation, inevitably forming a current in which everything is interconnected and each single event is related to all others.'[56] Van Harvey again provides a helpful summary of this principle, stating that by correlation Troeltsch 'meant that the phenomena of man's historical life are so related and interdependent that no radical change can take place at any one point in the historical nexus without effecting a change in all that immediately surrounds it. Historical explanation, therefore, necessarily takes the form of understanding an event in terms of its antecedents and consequences, and no event can be isolated from its historically conditioned time and space'.[57]

4. Anti-supernaturalism

The principles of probability, analogy and correlation account for the *anti-supernaturalism* of classical historical criticism. Underlying historical criticism is the scientific world view which conceives of the world as ordered according to the laws of nature and the law of cause and effect. In the Bible, however, we read of many occasions where God suspends or overrides the laws of nature. God parts the waters of the Red Sea to allow the Israelites to escape from the Egyptians. He appears to Moses in the burning bush, he raises people from the dead. Historical criticism, however, cannot take such accounts of supernatural intervention at face value, because to do so would be a violation of the laws of historical study, namely acceptance of the laws of nature as understood by modern science and the operation of the law of cause and effect *within* history. There is thus a prejudice in favour of natural explanations over supernatural explanations among modern historians. Establishing 'what really happened' thus means searching for an account of the events described in the Bible that is compatible with the modern scientific and historical understanding of reality.

5. The bracketing out of inspiration

Although some scholars have indeed rejected the notion of inspiration, it is probably more accurate to say that historical criticism is methodologically indifferent to the question of the inspired status of the Bible. The question is put to one side, 'bracketed out' and plays no role in the historical critic's examination of the text. Historical critics tend to leave God as the author or inspirer of the Scriptures out of consideration and treat the Bible as a historical work, or rather a collection of works, to be interpreted by means of the historical methods appropriate to all historical texts.

The methods of historical criticism

Historical criticism is not one single approach or method, but employs a cluster of related methods that seek to answer questions concerning the historical origins of biblical texts, the historical factors that gave rise to those texts and the historical events which underlie and/or are described by those texts.

The first task is to establish as accurate a text as possible. After all, a faulty or corrupt text will hinder the interpreter's attempts to understand the meaning of the text. The concern to establish the most original and authentic form of a text gave rise to *textual criticism* or 'lower criticism', as it has sometimes also been known. The second task is to identify the sources from which biblical texts were constructed. Many biblical texts were not written at one sitting by one single author, but came into existence through the combining of a variety of different sources. The concern to identify these sources led to the development of *source criticism* or 'higher criticism'. A third approach has been to attempt to identify the smallest units from which a biblical text was built up. This is the task of *form criticism*, which attempts to identify the oral units in which the biblical texts were passed down before they were put down in writing. This also requires the study of the means by which these units were transmitted, which led to the study of the history of tradition. The fourth type of historical criticism is *redaction criticism*, which is the consideration of how the final authors/editors of the text edited and wove their sources into the final version of the biblical text.

These methods are not hermetically sealed but are usually employed in combination. For example, the redaction critic will employ source criticism and form criticism in order to identify the redactional elements that will be the focus of his or her study. Similarly, the form critic will need to identify and exclude redactional elements from consideration, if he or she is to isolate the pre-literary forms from which a biblical text has been constructed. To make clear the distinctiveness of these different approaches to the text, however, we shall treat them as far as possible in isolation from each other, although we shall indicate points of contact and mutual dependence where appropriate.

CHAPTER TWO

A Brief History of Historical Criticism

The conventional view is that historical criticism originated as a result of the revolution in human thinking known as the 'Enlightenment' or 'Age of Reason', which began in the seventeenth century.[1] Those who subscribe to this view argue that it was the Enlightenment's rejection of dogma and its emphasis on reason as the bar at which all beliefs, ideologies, authorities and claims to truth had to justify themselves that created the context in which the historical–critical method could emerge.[2]

Other scholars, however, have traced the origins of historical criticism to the Reformation. Thus although he holds that the rise of the historical–critical method was made possible by the collapse of traditional Western metaphysics in the Enlightenment, Gerhard Ebeling 'venture[s] to assert that the Protestantism of the nineteenth century, by deciding in principle for the critical historical method, maintained and confirmed over against Roman Catholicism in a different situation the decision of the Reformers in the sixteenth century'.[3] Wolfhart Pannenberg ascribes the importance which historical–critical investigation acquired in the history of Protestant theology to the Lutheran doctrine of the clarity of Scripture.[4] The doctrine of *sola scriptura*, i.e. the view that the Bible alone and not the Church and its dogmas is the authority for the Christian, loosened ecclesiastical control over the interpretation of the Bible and created the freedom for believers to interpret for themselves the meaning of Scripture rather than having this meaning dictated by the Church. Rudolf Bultmann, Ebeling and Ernst Käsemann (1906–1998) also link the development of the historical–critical method with the Lutheran doctrine of justification by faith alone.[5] The historical scepticism resulting from the application of historical criticism makes clear that faith does not rest on historical knowledge, but is a response to God's gracious gift of justification to human beings in the person of his Son Jesus Christ.

Another group of scholars traces the origins of historical criticism still further back, namely to the Renaissance. Troeltsch claims that three of the four 'movements' leading to modern historiography, namely, the modern conception of nature, the new conception of history as a closed causal nexus and what he calls 'the modern ethics of humanity' 'sprang from the Renaissance'.[6] The fourth movement Troeltsch identifies comprises 'the new conditions of social life on its economical and industrial sides, and the sociological mode of thought issuing from them', which he sees as a product of the Enlightenment.[7] For Barton, 'the intellectual pedigree' of biblical criticism is also to be found in the Renaissance rather than the Enlightenment. He writes: 'What we are looking for is essentially a source for philological, literary-critical, and noncommittal approaches to texts; and the Renaissance is a more obvious candidate than either the Enlightenment or the Reformation.'[8]

It is thus mistaken to identify the origins of the historical–critical method exclusively with the Enlightenment period. Its roots lie much deeper and both the Reformation and above all the Renaissance laid the foundations which would make possible the development of the historical–critical method in the modern period. As Krentz puts it, the Renaissance and Reformation were the 'first rustles of criticism'.[9] The historical–critical method is therefore not a purely modern phenomenon but has a long history behind it. This becomes evident when we examine the history of the historical–critical method, for, as we shall see, the concerns that have occupied modern historical critics of the Bible were also known to the early Church Fathers.[10]

Traces of historical criticism in the early Church

The dominant method of biblical exegesis in the early Church was *allegorical interpretation*. The term 'allegory' is derived from the Greek words *allos*, meaning 'other', and *agoreuein*, meaning 'to speak in the market place', i.e. to speak publicly. 'Allegory' thus means speaking publicly, but meaning something other than what one's public speech appears to mean. As Pseudo-Heraclitus puts it, 'saying one thing and signifying something other than what is said is called allegory'.[11] In short, allegory is saying one thing and meaning another.[12]

For the allegorical interpreter all texts, regardless of whether they are overtly allegorical or not, comprise two levels, namely the surface meaning and a deeper spiritual meaning concealed beneath the surface meaning of the text. Allegorical interpretation is the means by which this deeper spiritual meaning of the text is made apparent. A good example of allegorical interpretation is provided by the early Church's treatment of the story of how Israel crossed the Red Sea. The surface meaning of this text is a historical description of how the Israelites escaped from Egyptian captivity. For the Church Fathers, however, the text also refers to Christ's passing through the waters of death in order to free human beings from the powers of evil.

For the allegorical interpreter, the tensions, inconsistencies and contradictions in the text are signposts alerting the reader to a deeper level of spiritual meaning underlying the surface meaning of the text. It was thus unnecessary to search for historical factors in the production of the biblical texts to account for the problematic material of the Bible, since to do so would be to remain at the surface level of the text and constitute a failure to break through to the spiritual sense. Indeed, to remain at the surface meaning of the text was a sign of an unspiritual nature and was appropriate only for simple believers incapable of grasping deeper spiritual truths. The spiritually advanced, however, endeavoured by means of allegorical interpretation to advance beyond the literal meaning of the text to the divine mysteries concealed within it.

Although the dominance of the allegorical method retarded the development of historical criticism, there were some hints of historical approaches to biblical interpretation in the early Church. Firstly, despite the dominance of allegorical interpretation, there was also awareness of the danger of it not doing justice to the reality of the text. Thus although Jerome made free use of allegorical interpretation, he was conscious of its risks and in a letter to Paulinus emphasized that it was important 'not to distort expressions and wrest reluctant Scripture into agreement with one's fancies'.[13] In his *Prologue to Isaiah*, he criticizes Origen, who 'mistook his own subjectivity for ecclesiastical mysteries',[14] while in his commentaries on Galatians and Jeremiah he condemns allegorical interpretation as cloud and shadow.[15] On another occasion, he states his desire to allow Scripture to speak for itself,[16] and voices his regret at having failed to grasp the historical sense of the text in his earlier commentary on Obadiah.[17]

Secondly, the need to decide on the status of disputed writings led some early Church Fathers to address issues that we would today associate with historical criticism. In a letter to Origen, Julius Africanus wrote of his doubts concerning the authenticity of the story of Susanna, which he felt was inconsistent with the rest of the Daniel,[18] and advanced what we would now regard as a series of critical points to support this view.[19] Origen himself doubted on stylistic grounds that Paul had written Hebrews,[20] while Dionysius of Alexandria was sceptical that the author of the Gospel of John was also the author of Revelation.[21] We also know from Jerome that there was widespread doubt that the Apostle Peter was genuinely the author of 2 Peter.[22]

Jerome himself showed unusual critical acumen for his time.[23] He questioned the authenticity of the Letter of Aristeas and argued that it was only the Pentateuch, not the entire Hebrew Bible, which was translated under Ptolemy I. Jerome was also sometimes prepared to criticize the biblical authors,[24] and pointed out problems with Paul's style.[25] He also points out that Paul's argument in Gal. 3.15–18 is dependent on taking the Hebrew term *berîth*, covenant, as equivalent to 'will', a meaning which the Hebrew term, however, does not have.[26] Jerome draws back, however, from following these critical insights through to their logical conclusion and fails to take the historical–critical step of arguing that these problematic features in the text stem from Paul's historical and cultural context. Instead, he searches for reasons for Paul's use of such dubious arguments and comes to the conclusion that Paul must be accommodating himself to the foolishness of the Galatians.

There are also hints of a historical approach to the Bible in the thought of Augustine (354–430).[27] In the preface of his *De Doctrina Christiana* [On Christian Teaching], Augustine advocates the use of secular learning in studying the Bible and rejects the arguments of those who claim to be able to interpret the Bible exclusively by means of their alleged divine illumination. In Book XV of *The City of God*, he notes the presence of discrepancies between the Hebrew Bible and the Latin Old Testament with regard to the age of the Patriarchs. Some of the methods he employs to address these difficulties resemble the approaches of modern biblical scholars such as, for example, comparing one biblical passage with other passages elsewhere in the Bible and appealing to external evidence.[28] He resorts to historical explanations to account for questionable passages in the Bible. Thus he attributes the polygamy of the Old Testament to the primitive state of Israelite society and claims that accounts of such immoral behaviour as David's adultery are included in Scripture as a warning to us. Augustine also warns against interpreting texts in isolation,[29] although he often does so himself in his own writings. He notes the presence of a human element in Scripture,[30] and attributes problematic biblical texts to this human contribution,[31] although he could also assert that the biblical writers were 'pens of the Holy Spirit'.[32]

So there is nothing new about observing irregularities in the Bible. As the awareness of Jerome and Augustine of such irregularities indicates, they are not the invention of modern scholars. Barton suggests that, 'Rather than saying that these are unusual *precursors* of biblical criticism among precritical commentators, it seems to me better to acknowledge that biblical criticism as we now know it genuinely does go back into the remote past'.[33] He points out, however, that 'criticism was often neutralized, and its insights ignored or discouraged, because of a commitment to the religious authority of the biblical text'.[34] This is evident in Origen's response to Africanus. Origen, who lists a series of other problematic passages he has discoverd in Scripture, argues against Africanus not on the basis of a critical analysis of the text but by appealing to the Church's acceptance of the canonical status of Susanna, which for Origen takes precedence over Africanus' reservations.

It is, however, above all the Antiochenes who have been regarded as having the greatest affinities with modern historical approaches to the study of the Bible.[35] The Antiochene School,[36] members of which were Diodorus of Tarsus (d. 393), Ephraem Syrus (c. 306–373), Eusebius of Emesa (c. 300–c. 360), St. John Chrysostom (347–407), Severianus (fl. c. 400), Theodore of Mopsuestia (350–428), and Theodoret (393–457), criticized the allegorical interpretation practised by the Alexandrians for not doing justice to the literal sense of the text and for undermining its historical meaning. Theodore is particularly scathing in his criticism of allegorical interpretation, commenting that, 'There are some people who make it their business to pervert the meaning of the divine Scriptures and to thwart whatever is to be found there. They invent foolish tales of their own and give to their nonsense the name of "allegory"'.[37] In reply to the Alexandrian argument that allegorization is legitimized by Paul's use of allegory in Gal. 4, Theodore argues that there is a great difference between Paul's use of the term in the Epistle to the Galatians and the way the Alexandrians employ allegory. Paul, Theodore points out, is not disputing the historicity of the events he is discussing in Gal. 4, but is citing these events as examples to further his argument. The Alexandrians, on the other hand, rob Scripture of its basis in history, thereby undermining God's saving actions. If Adam was not really Adam, but an allegory for something else, Theodore argues, then it was not necessary for Christ, the second Adam, to repair the damage done by the first Adam. Far from being a means of unlocking the true meaning of Scripture, allegorical interpretation was for Theodore a distortion of Scripture, for it undermined its literal meaning. The Antiochene rejection of allegorical interpretation was accompanied by a method of biblical exegesis that paid attention to the literal and grammatical meaning of Scripture, emphasized the importance of interpreting a text in its context and did not follow the Alexandrian tendency to atomize the text.

Theodore's emphasis on the literal meaning of the text led him to understand the persons depicted in the Bible as historical figures, not merely as types or allegories. Theodore does not reject typology, but holds that the function of a biblical person as a type is based on his or her historical role. This means that Theodore can identify two levels of meaning in the biblical text: (1) the literal, historical level and (2) the typological meaning. But with Theodore the typological meaning is much more firmly connected with the literal, historical level than was the case with Alexandrian interpretation. It is precisely because of the *historical* role played by a particular person that that person can function as a type. Furthermore, typological and allegorical senses are permissible only when the Bible itself permits their use, such as in Gal. 4, but these senses are always subordinated to the literal sense. Such insights prompted Theodore to provide a historical reading of the Psalms and to refrain from interpreting them as referring wholesale to Christ. He argued that at the literal, historical level the Psalms were written by David for the people of Israel. If we wish to understand this level, we must attempt to understand David as prophet and ruler of Israel. But the Psalms also have a typological meaning, which refers to Christ and to the redemption of human beings he has accomplished.

Thus Theodore accepted that some Old Testament passages were fulfilled in Christ, but denied that these were originally written *specifically* about Christ. For example, Theodore holds that although Ps. 22 is ultimately about Jesus, it was originally written by David during his struggle with Absalom. The passage was later, quite rightly in Theodore's opinion, understood to be about Christ's Passion. Similarly, Joel 2.28 was not originally written by Joel with reference to Pentecost, but was only later, as Peter rightly noted, fulfilled in the coming of the Holy Spirit upon the Church. In contrast to the Alexandrians, however, Theodore does not find references to Christ everywhere in the Psalms and recognizes only four Psalms as messianic, namely Pss. 2, 8, 44 and 109. Theodore also denied that Isa. 53.7 was originally understood by the author as a reference to the crucifixion, even though it later came to be understood in this way by Paul and others. Later Christian, even New Testament understandings of an Old Testament passage do not indicate that the respective Old Testament text was *originally* understood in the way the New Testament understands it.

Their supposed affinity with the historical approach to biblical interpretation is the reason why the Antiochenes tended to receive a good press in nineteenth- and twentieth-century theology. An example of such positive assessment is provided by Frederic Farrar, who writes that 'the School of Antioch possessed a deeper insight into the true method of exegesis than any which preceded or succeeded it during a thousand years'.[38] Indeed, for Farrar, 'their system of Biblical interpretation approached more nearly than any other to that which is now adopted by the Reformed Churches throughout the world',[39] and if the insights of the Antiochenes had been followed instead of being condemned, 'the study of their commentaries, and the adoption of their exegetic system, might have saved Church commentaries from centuries of futility and error'.[40] This preference for the Antiochene approach over that of the Alexandrians continued well into the twentieth century. In their history of biblical interpretation, R. M. Grant and David Tracy state that Antiochenes insisted on the historical reality of the biblical revelation and firmly grounded their understanding of Scripture on the literal meaning of Scripture. In contrast to the

Alexandrians, the Antiochenes were unwilling to lose the historical reality of the biblical revelation 'in a world of symbols and shadows'.[41] Frances Young, however, has challenged the view that Antiochene exegesis can be regarded as a forerunner of modern biblical criticism. She questions whether the Antiochene concern with history is really as paramount as modern admirers of the Antiochenes have held and points out that the problems with this view lie 'in the assumption that Antiochene literalism meant something like modern historicism'.[42] She further observes that 'explicitly locating revelation not in the text of scripture but in the historicity of events behind the text . . . is anachronistic'.[43]

The consequence of Theodore's condemnation at the Council of Constantinople in 553 was that his biblical exegesis did not gain the influence that it might otherwise have had. His condemnation for Nestorianism inhibited the spread of his understanding of biblical interpretation, though the Antiochene approach continued to survive in Nisibis and Edessa. Despite this setback, some works influenced by Antiochene exegesis may have permeated into the West.[44] The Pelagian bishop Julian of Eclanum (c. 386–455), who sought refuge with Theodore, may have been a conduit for Antiochene influence in the Western Church.[45] Julian wrote a commentary in Latin on Hosea, Joel and Amos, in which he emphasizes the literal sense of scripture and criticizes the allegorical interpretation of Origen and Jerome and their failure to take context into consideration when interpreting Scripture. Junilius Africanus (c. 550), who spent some time in Nisibis, which was under Antiochene influence, translated into Latin an introduction to the study of the Bible written by Paul of Nisibis, which may have played a role in communicating Antiochene ideas to the West.[46] In his study of Antiochene influence on Western theology, however, M. L. W. Laistner notes: 'In the theological writers of the ninth century and after there are very few discernible traces of Junilius.'[47] Beryl Smalley concludes: 'Much of the Antiochene material was irretrievably lost to the medieval Latin student. He never at any time had an opportunity to soak himself in the works of Theodore. On the other hand, enough material existed in the early Middle Ages to enable a Latin reader to learn at least the principles of Antiochene exegesis and to experiment with them for himself if he wished.'[48] It was, however, Smalley points out, only a few early Irish scholars who availed themselves of this opportunity. The result was that, 'We have seen an entire school of exegesis fall into an oblivion so profound that its successors remind us of men building on the site of a buried city, unaware of the civilization lying beneath their feet'.[49] Despite the efforts of the Antiochenes and an awareness on the part of some of the Fathers of the historical issues arising from the biblical texts and the need to anchor interpretation to a literal reading of the text, allegorical interpretation continued to dominate biblical interpretation up until the late

Middle Ages. There were, however, a number of developments in medieval theology which would eventually lead to the decline of the use of allegorical interpretation.

Intimations of historical criticism in the Middle Ages

Several factors in the Middle Ages led to the loosening of the grip allegory had on the interpretation of the Bible. One important influence was the rise of the universities. These had begun life as cathedral schools, but in the twelfth century became independent of the monasteries. This detachment of the universities from the monasteries marks the beginning of the liberation of scholarship from the control of the Church.[50] Smalley and others argue that modern study of the Bible has its origins in this development and created an environment which made possible a movement away from the allegorical exegesis that had dominated biblical interpretation since the Fathers.

Another influence on Christian biblical scholarship during the Middle Ages came from the literal exegesis practised by such Jewish scholars as Rashi (1040–1105).[51] If the literal meaning is the most important meaning a text possesses, then it becomes necessary to study the Scriptures in the original languages in order to ascertain the literal meaning of the text as precisely as possible. This insight prompted some medieval theologians to learn Hebrew and Greek, and to acquire philological skills.[52] One of the leading Christian scholars of the Middle Ages, Hugh of St. Victor (c. 1096–1141), had contact with Jewish scholars and took the trouble of acquiring the necessary linguistic skills to study the Old Testament in Hebrew.[53] He argued that to do justice to the Old Testament, it should be studied in its original languages and that to facilitate biblical exegesis, the interpreter should acquire knowledge of the cultural context in which the biblical texts were written. In his *On the Scriptures* and *Didascalion*, Hugh emphasized the need to pay greater attention to the literal meaning of the biblical text, although he still saw literal interpretation only as a springboard for the use of allegorical interpretation, which remained necessary in order to unlock the deeper spiritual resources of Scripture.[54]

Perhaps the most important development in biblical scholarship in the Middle Ages, however, was the influence of Aristotle. Since Augustine, the dominant philosophy within Western Christianity had been Platonism, which understood universals to possess real existence, independent of the particulars in which they appear in the concrete world. The consequence of this view was that the world of experience was regarded merely as a shadow of the real world of universals. Applied to the Bible, this meant that the interpreter should look beyond its surface meaning to the deeper truths of the transcendent world of universals which lies behind the particularities of the biblical text. The means of achieving this was the allegorical interpretation developed by Origen and refined by subsequent theologians.

Aristotle's philosophy, however, placed in question the philosophical basis of allegorical exegesis. The philosophy developed from Aristotle came to be known as 'nominalism', i.e. the view that universals are abstractions arrived at by means of logical deduction on the basis of the resemblances between the things themselves. They are not realities that exist independently of the particularities to which they are applied, but are merely names. The implication of this for biblical interpretation is that the truth of the Bible is to be found in the biblical texts themselves, not in a reality which lies partially obscured and partially revealed in the biblical texts. Despite this philosophical shift, however, allegorical exegesis was so firmly part of the Church's tradition of biblical interpretation that the rise of Aristotelianism did not result in the immediate decline of allegorical exegesis. Nevertheless, the impact of Aristotelianism increasingly prompted scholars to focus more on what the Bible itself actually said rather than seeing it as a collection of symbols of deeper realities beyond the text. A good example of this shift in focus is provided by Albertus Magnus (1200–1280), who emphasized the literal sense of the text and the importance of authorial intention.[55] Thus he rejected the common contemporary interpretation of Jesus' temptation to turn stone into bread as an allegory of the Law or the heart of the sinner with the comment: 'I think it an absurd exposition, and contrary to the mind of the author.'[56] Only by means of logical deduction based on the literal meaning of the text is it possible and legitimate to proceed to allegorical interpretation.

Thomas Aquinas (1225–1274) also played an important role in the shift away from allegorical to literal interpretation. Thomas emphasized the literal meaning of the text, but understood this literal meaning to include allegories, similes and metaphors, if these were clearly intended by the author. This acceptance of metaphorical language, however, is very different from allegorizing a text in violation of the author's intention. For Thomas, theology is concerned with deriving concepts by logical deduction from the literal sense intended by the author, which limits the scope for the exegesis of allegorical interpretation. Nevertheless, Thomas permitted the use of allegorical exegesis as an aid to prayer.

Another factor that led to the decline of allegorical interpretation was the increasing consciousness of the distinction between the teaching of the Church and what was contained in the Bible. The apocalyptic interpretation of Joachim of Fiore (1132–1202), although insignificant in the development of formal methods of biblical interpretation, is important because it clashed with the official interpretation of the Church. It thus made people conscious of the possibility of interpreting the Bible in ways that did not conform to the teaching of the Church. In short, there arose the possibility of interpreting Scripture *against* the Church. This awareness of the difference between the tradition of the Church and the teaching of the Bible was also hinted at by Henry of Ghent (1217–1293) and William of Ockham (1285–1349). Henry pointed out that Church teaching and biblical truth are not identical and thus could theoretically differ from each other, while William's nominalism led him to deny that theological propositions can be derived from Scripture by means of logical deduction. He concluded from this that it is the tradition of the Church rather than the Bible that provides the basis of the Christian faith. The interpretations of Henry and William are important because they drive a wedge between Church tradition and the Bible. This increasing awareness of the difference between tradition and Scripture was coupled with an increasing consciousness of the discrepancy between the Gospel and an allegedly corrupt Church, so that the Bible increasingly came to be used as the basis not for supporting but criticizing the official teaching of the Church. There was growing awareness that the literal meaning of Scripture could conflict with official Church doctrine and practice.

The Renaissance: laying the foundations of historical criticism

It was in the Renaissance that allegory began to lose its dominant position and be replaced by early forms of historical criticism. According to Erike Rummel, 'Two features of Renaissance Humanism had a direct bearing on the course of biblical studies in early modern Europe: the privileging of classical antiquity over the "dark" Middle Ages and a preference for rhetoric and language studies over the traditional academic core subject, Aristotelian logic'.[57] This concern with classical antiquity prompted Renaissance scholars to attempt to recover the sources of ancient literature. A distinctive feature of Renaissance scholarship is thus the principle of *ad fontes*, 'back to the sources'. With regard to the Bible, this concern with the sources motivated an interest in the Bible in its original languages rather than resting content with the Latin translation of the Vulgate. This concern with getting back to the sources of classical antiquity had two consequences which would be important for subsequent biblical scholarship. Firstly, it prompted the collection of manuscripts. Secondly, it motivated a concern to establish the authenticity of the manuscripts, the consequence of which was the production of critical editions of ancient writings. The Renaissance arguably laid the foundations for the historical approach to biblical interpretation.

The rediscovery of classical literature in the Renaissance period encouraged a critical attitude which was also applied to the Bible. Lorenzo Valla (1406–1457) employed linguistic and historical arguments to demonstrate the inauthenticity of the Donation of Constantine.[58] Valla's employment of such methods makes him one of the forerunners of historical criticism. He also wrote a work entitled *Annotations on the New Testament*, published by Erasmus in 1505, in which he exposed the differences between the Vulgate text and the original Greek text of the New Testament, and pointed to the dependence of some aspects of scholastic theology on the Latin translation. This marked the beginnings of the philological approach to the Bible.

Erasmus of Rotterdam (1466–1536),[59] Cardinal Cajetan (1469–1534)[60] and John Colet (1467–1519)[61] held that the interpreter's task is to identify the literal sense of the text, an approach which is just as applicable to the Bible as it is to any other literature. Scholars of this period also showed an interest in literary sources, which expressed itself in the collection of ancient manuscripts and the learning of the original languages. Christian scholars, notably Johann Reuchlin (1455–1522), studied the Old Testament in Hebrew.[62] Hebrew grammars were published and editions of parts and eventually the whole of the Hebrew Bible were printed. Interest developed in the study of the Greek New Testament. In 1516 Erasmus published his edition of the New Testament under the title of *Novum Instrumentum omne*, in which he laid out the Greek original and a modified version of the Vulgate on opposite pages. He also provided extensive notes on textual problems. This critical attitude towards texts and the collection of ancient manuscripts were accompanied by the development of printing, which made the dissemination of texts easier. Texts became more readily available and therefore more accessible to scholars.[63]

The Reformation and the rise of literal exegesis

An important factor in the transition from allegorical interpretation to historical criticism was the attempt from the fourteenth century onwards to translate the Bible into the vernacular. The official Bible of the Western Church was the Vulgate, a Latin translation made by Jerome in the late fourth and early fifth centuries. Latin was the language of the educated elite and its use as the language of Scripture made the Bible inaccessible to ordinary people. Awareness of the divergence between the Vulgate and the Greek New Testament, the text of which was now becoming increasingly available, motivated scholars to try their hands at new translations into the language not of the educated elite but of the common people. In England, John Wycliffe (c. 1328–1384) produced a translation in the 1380s, which was followed by translations by William Tyndale (c. 1494–1536), Myles Coverdale (c. 1488–1569), and others, before culminating in the King James Bible of 1611.[64] In Germany, Martin Luther translated the Bible into German, publishing his translation of the New Testament in 1522 and the entire Bible in 1534. These early vernacular translations went hand in hand with the critique of the Church. When the Bible became intelligible to all, it became apparent how far short the Church fell of the biblical ideal. Another reason why vernacular translations were important was that they constituted an implicit attack on the exegetical monopoly of the Church. The continuation of allegorical interpretation into the Middle Ages had meant that interpretation was concentrated in the hands of an educated elite who possessed the hermeneutical skills to make sense of the Bible. This partly explains the medieval Church's resistance to vernacular translations of the Scriptures. It was felt that to make the Scriptures freely available to the common people would result in a misunderstanding or misuse of the Scriptures. This view was confirmed for many in the Church hierarchy by the fact that scholars who attempted to provide vernacular translations, such as Wycliffe, frequently held views which the Church considered to be heretical. The availability of the Bible in the language of the people also encouraged individualism in interpretation. If the people could read the Bible in their own language, there was no need for a priest to interpret it for them. The notion of the expert, authoritative interpreter of the Bible was thus gradually being undermined and with it the allegorical interpretation employed by such experts.

The Reformers still conceived of interpretation as a relationship between Scripture and the self-understanding of the Church. Where they differed from the Roman Catholic Church was in how they understood this relationship. For the Reformers, Scripture was the dominant partner in the relationship, and the Church was understood be 'under' or subservient to Scripture. This meant that it became important to identify the meaning of Scripture in itself and independently of the Church's interpretation. The result of this emphasis on scripture was that exegesis became a central concern of the Reformation churches.[65]

This shift in emphasis led to the displacement of allegorical interpretation as the dominant method of interpretation and to increasing focus on the literal meaning of Scripture. This in turn strengthened the return to the original languages that had begun in the Renaissance. The need to ascertain the literal meaning of Scripture made it necessary to study Scripture in the languages in which the Bible had originally been written, which weakened the status of the Vulgate as the definitive text of the Bible.

If the Church stands under Scripture and is not its definitive and authoritative interpreter, this naturally raises the question of the legitimate method of interpreting the Bible. How do we identify the true, i.e. literal meaning, of Scripture and how do we avoid imposing our own meaning upon Scripture? It is such concerns that led Luther to consider the problem of exegetical method.[66]

Although Luther occasionally made use of allegory for devotional purposes, he eventually came to reject it as an inappropriate method of biblical interpretation. As he puts it in his *Table Talk*, 'I know [allegories, tropologies, and analogies] are nothing but rubbish. Now I've let them go, and this is my last and best art, to translate the Scriptures in their plain sense. The literal sense does it – in its there's life, comfort, power, instruction, and skill. The other is tomfoolery, however brilliant the impression it makes.'[67] For Luther, allegorical interpretation is permitted only where Scripture clearly intends a metaphorical or figurative meaning. It should not be employed as a universal method of interpretation. Luther also challenged the right of the Church to determine the understanding of Scripture. His doctrine of *sola scriptura* affirmed Scripture as the sole authority for the Christian, an authority to which the Church and its dogmas are also subject. This can be regarded as the first step to the division between biblical interpretation and Church doctrine that would become influential from the Enlightenment onwards.

Luther replaced the allegorical method with an exegetical method organized around the notions of the *sensus literalis*, *grammaticus* and *historicus*, that is, the literal, grammatical and historical sense of the Bible. A scriptural passage has one basic meaning, which is to be established not by allegorization but by means of grammatical study and by paying attention to the setting of the passage. The guide for interpretation should be the literal meaning of the text. For Luther, the literal meaning of the text *is* its spiritual meaning.

Like Luther, Calvin rejected allegorical interpretation. Far from enabling the interpreter to extract spiritual meaning from the Bible, for Calvin allegorical interpretation obscured the sense of Scripture intended by the Holy Spirit. Calvin's commentaries are devoted to eliciting the literal sense of the biblical writings. The task of the literal, historical interpretation of Scripture is to enable Scripture to function as an instrument of the Holy Spirit. Literal interpretation is not in itself the goal, however, but is necessary to prepare the ground for the activity of the Spirit. The Spirit itself witnesses to and authenticates the biblical message in his internal testimony in the believing reader or hearer of Scripture, a notion which Calvin described as *testimonium spiritus sancti internum*.[68]

The Reformers' emphasis on the literal sense of Scripture resulted in a shift in the task of interpretation. The task was no longer to pass beyond the literal meaning to an allegedly higher, spiritual meaning, but to trace how the literal meaning of the text expresses and mediates Christ's saving work. This led to an increasing consciousness of Scripture as the witness to God's acts in history rather than as a compendium of spiritual truths.

Among Luther's successors Matthias Flacius Illyricus (1520–1575) is important in the development of a more historical approach to the interpretation of Scripture.[69] His *Clavis scripturae sacrae* (1567) marks an important contribution to the development of Protestant hermeneutics. Written in response to the Council of Trent, Flacius's work sought to counter the Roman Catholic rejection of the Protestant principle that Scripture alone is the sufficient source of divine revelation. In responding to the Catholic challenge, Flacius lays down a series of important and influential rules for the interpretation of the Bible.

The reader, Flacius argues, should 'exert himself to comprehend the simple and original sense of the sacred writings, and, in particular, of the passage he happens to be reading'.[70] Consequently, the starting point of exegesis must be the grammatical sense of the text. For Flacius, this means two things. Firstly, it entails establishing how the original readers of a text understood the individual words of that text. This necessitates mastering the biblical languages, for, as Flacius puts it, 'Without that, O Reader, you are necessarily dependent on the judgment of others, or you must guess at the meaning'.[71] Secondly, it means establishing 'how [the readers] understand the sense of the passage that is imparted by the words of the individual sentences'.[72]

The next principle of interpretation, which Flacius describes as the 'theological treatment of Scripture', is to establish 'how the hearers understand the spirit of him who speaks' and, following from this, the purpose of the text in question. 'Without this knowledge', Flacius comments, 'even he who understands the words and the meaning of the language still understands too little in Scripture'.[73]

Finally, the interpreter should strive to ascertain 'how the application of any given passage of Scripture is to be understood'. This method, which must be accompanied 'by assiduous and devout reading and especially by meditation', is for Flacius 'the most important function of reading Scripture'.[74]

Flacius' approach meant the rejection of the principle of the multiple meanings of Scripture and the repudiation of allegorical approaches to Scripture. Allegorical interpretation is permissible only when all possible literal interpretations have been excluded and if the passage in question 'is manifestly an allegory and the literal sense in general is useless, or even absurd'.[75]

The Enlightenment: the rise of the historical study of the Bible

In 1543, Copernicus' *De Revolutionibus Orbium Coelestium* was published, which argued for the heliocentric understanding of the solar system. The observations of Galileo and the mathematical proofs developed by Kepler in the seventeenth century lent weight to the Copernican theory. The increasing plausibility of heliocentrism raised the problem of reconciling the new discoveries with the apparently geocentric teaching of the Bible.

There were also important philosophical developments that contributed to the growth of the critical spirit that would ultimately give rise to the historical–critical approach. An important figure in the development of this critical spirit was Descartes, whose *Discourse on Method* (1637) made doubt the starting point of rational thinking. Many of Descartes' followers and successors had no reservations in applying the principle of radical doubt to the Christian faith. This contributed to the view that only those elements of religion that could prove their validity in the face of critical doubt were acceptable.

During these developments, scholars continued to develop historical approaches to interpreting the Bible. Flacius' grammatical approach was continued by Joachim Camerarius (1500–1574) in his commentary on a selection of New Testament texts (1572).[76] In this work, he argued that the writings of the New Testament must be interpreted from the perspective of its authors. It is only when we understand the world in which the New Testament authors were writing that we will be able to grasp the meaning of the text as each New Testament writer intended it. It is the knowledge of the context of the biblical authors and not the opinions of the early Church Fathers that provides the key for interpreting the New Testament.

Like Camerarius, Hugo Grotius (1583–1645) held that the New Testament needed to be interpreted in its ancient setting. In his *Notes on the New Testament* (1641) he interpreted New Testament texts in the light of classical, Jewish, Hellenistic and early Christian literature. In doing so, he paved the way for the development of comparative approaches which draw on contemporary non-biblical sources as resources for the interpretation of the biblical literature. Also of importance for the future study of the New Testament were Grotius' attempts to explain problematic biblical passages by arguing either that the traditional views concerning identity and date of authorship were untenable or that the present state of the text does not correspond to the text's original form.

A further impulse to the historical study of the Bible was provided by the Anglican priest and scholar John Lightfoot (1602–1675), who argued in his *Horae Hebraicae et Talmudicae in Quattuor Evangelistas* [Hebrew and Talmudic Hours on the Four Gospels] (1658–1678) that the New Testament could be adequately understood only when its Jewish background is taken into account. This led him to study rabbinic literature, which he believed provided insights into the language of the New Testament and thus gave assistance in interpreting obscure and difficult passages. What is important here is that Lightfoot interprets the New Testament not by following the views of the Church Fathers but on the basis of contemporary Jewish literature.

An important feature of the Enlightenment was the rise of the idea of *method* as the means by which we arrive at truth. Descartes was important not so much for the specific method he employed in his thinking, but for his view that method was the essential way of establishing truth. Method is the means by which the human being progresses from ignorance and doubt to knowledge and truth. The use of method seemed to be justified by its successful use in the sciences. The success and explanatory power of the sciences increasingly led to science being seen as *the* model for obtaining knowledge, and prompted attempts to apply scientific method to the interpretation of the Bible. Baruch Spinoza (1632–1677) provides an early example of this in his *Tractatus Theologico-Politicus* (1670), in which he argues 'that the method of interpreting Scripture is no different from the method of interpreting Nature, and is in fact in complete accord with it'.[77] For Spinoza, just as the method of interpreting nature consists in deducing definitions on the basis of a detailed empirical study of nature, so too 'in exactly the same way the task of Scriptural interpretation requires us to make a straightforward study of Scripture, and from this, as the source of our fixed data and principles, to deduce by logical inference the meaning of the authors of Scripture'.[78] On the basis of this 'scientific' approach to the study of Scripture, Spinoza concludes, firstly, that 'the universal rule for the interpretation of Scripture, [is] to ascribe no teaching to Scripture that is not clearly established from studying it closely'.[79] Secondly, we should make no doctrinal assumptions concerning Scripture but seek the meaning of Scripture 'simply from linguistic usage, or from a process of reasoning that looks to no other basis than Scripture'.[80] Finally, 'our historical study should set forth the circumstances relevant to all the extant books of the prophets, giving the life, character and pursuits of the author of every book, detailing who he was, on what occasion and at what time and for whom and in what language he wrote'.[81] That is, Spinoza is arguing for the development of what would later come to be known as 'introduction', i.e. the investigation of the historical background of the Bible and the historical questions raised by the individual biblical writings.

Spinoza is also important for making a distinction between what is of permanent value in Scripture and what is historically conditioned. The question of the 'divinity of Scripture' can be answered only by distinguishing the 'teachings of eternal significance' in the Bible from 'those which are of only temporary significance or directed only to the benefit of a few'.[82] For Spinoza, the criterion for making this distinction is whether Scripture 'teaches true virtue'. Only careful historical study will enable us to establish this and to distinguish between what is eternally significant in Scripture and what is historically conditioned and therefore of only temporary significance.

Deism played an important role in furthering the development of new methods of biblical interpretation. The most significant contribution of English Deism was arguably its suspicion towards and criticism of much of the Church's traditional dogma, a suspicion which encouraged the non-dogmatic, purely historical study of the Bible. John Locke (1632–1704) in *The Reasonableness of Christianity* (1695), John Toland (1670–1722) in *Christianity not Mysterious* (1696) and Matthew Tindal (1653–1733) in *Christianity as Old as Creation; or, The Gospel, a Republication of the Religion of Nature* (1730) put forward the view that Jesus had taught 'natural religion', an undogmatic faith which had been corrupted, distorted or diluted by the Church.[83] This critique was important for driving a wedge between Scripture and religious truth, thereby giving impetus to the historical analysis of the Bible. If Scripture contained only partial truth, then it became necessary (a) to isolate what is true and (b) to explain how the distortion of Christianity had come about. This necessitates historical study. Although English Deism was not concerned with biblical exegesis as such, its critique of orthodox Christianity provided important impulses for the development of a historical approach to the Scriptures, especially as English Deism became known and influential on the continent.

Another factor in the development of historical criticism was the rise of Pietism, despite the fact that Pietism was in part a reaction against the rationalist ideals of the Enlightenment and was suspicious of the critical study of the Bible.[84] In his *Pia Desideria* (1675), Philipp Jacob Spener (1635–1705) identified as one of the reasons for the lamentable state of the contemporary Lutheran Church its neglect of the study of the Bible and its dependence on Aristotelianism. To remedy this state of affairs, Spener called for a return to 'proper biblical theology', the criterion of which should be 'the proper simplicity of Christ and his doctrine'.[85] Spener emphasized the Bible's role in deepening faith and fostering Christian brotherhood in the community of believers. The highly intellectualized and systematized treatment of Scripture by Protestant Orthodoxy failed to cultivate this deepening of Christian life. Thinkers influenced by Pietism, notably August Hermann Francke (1663–1727) and Johann Albrecht Bengel (1687–1752), attempted to return to the original meaning of biblical texts.[86]

On being appointed in 1691 professor of Greek and Oriental Languages and later in 1698 of Theology at the newly founded University of Halle, Francke together with like-minded colleagues embarked on a reform of the theology curriculum, which placed the philological and historical study of the Bible at its centre. Francke distinguished between the 'husk' and the 'core' of Scripture. Historical, grammatical and philological study of the Bible is concerned with the husk and aims at eliciting the literal meaning of the text. Such study can be undertaken by anyone with the necessary philological skills. Francke warns, however, that such study should not become a goal in itself but is only an introductory discipline which serves the understanding of the core. The 'core' of Scripture, however, is available only to those who have been born again, who alone are capable of perceiving the spiritual meaning intended by the Holy Spirit.[87] In view of this mixture of Pietistic and critical elements in Francke's understanding of the Bible, Reventlow holds that overall Francke can be considered to be 'a transitional figure who unites orthodox Lutheran, typically Pietistic aspects, but also some critical aspects (as far as the literal meaning of Scripture is concerned)'.[88]

In the eighteenth century, rationalism played a significant role in spurring on the development of historical approaches to the study of the Bible. In his *Concerning the Methods of Interpreting Holy Scripture* (1728), the Swiss theologian Jean Alphonse Turretini (1671–1737) attacked conventional and traditional methods of biblical exegesis and argued for their replacement by a method founded on reason and on an awareness of the distinctiveness of each biblical book. The interpreter must not impose his or her conceptions upon the text, but must attempt to adopt the perspective of the author of the biblical writings. Turretini sees this principle as being 'of the greatest importance for the understanding of Scripture',[89] but one which has for the most part been ignored by theologians and interpreters. Only by adopting the perspective of the biblical writers will one be able to understand their writings and to establish which of the Church's dogmas are valid. Turretini also emphasized the importance of interpreting individual passages in the context of the text as a whole. He prefigured many aspects of the historical–critical approach to Scripture, but his work had only a limited impact during his lifetime.

It was with Johann August Ernesti (1707–1781) that the ideas espoused by Turretini began to gain in influence. Two features of Ernesti's argument in his *Institutio Interpretis Novi Testamenti* [*Instruction for the Interpreter of the New Testament*] (1761) were important for subsequent development.[90] Firstly, Ernesti made clear the necessity of studying the Old and New Testaments not as a homogeneous whole but as distinct bodies of literature. Secondly, he applied to the New Testament the philological-historical method that had been developed in the interpretation of classical texts. Ernesti's emphasis on exegesis as the establishment of the grammatical sense of the text constituted an implicit critique of the dogmatic interpretation of Scripture and implied the necessity of replacing it with a historical approach. Ernesti, however, failed to follow these insights to their logical conclusion and, affirming the doctrine of inerrancy, continued to hold a conservative view of Scripture.

Although in many respects a conservative scholar, especially with regard to the authorship of the Old Testament books, Siegmund Jakob

Baumgarten (1706–1757) played a role in the development of biblical criticism by distinguishing between the 'natural' understanding of the Bible, which permitted the use of philology and historical criticism, and the 'supernatural' understanding that treated the Bible as a divine communication. The former is accessible to all who wish to concern themselves with it, but the latter is the exclusive province of the believer.

Johann Salomo Semler (1725–1791) was a pupil of Baumgarten and took the next logical step by dropping Baumgarten's notion of the supernatural understanding of Scripture and arguing for a biblical interpretation free of doctrinal presuppositions. It was with Semler and his contemporary Johann David Michaelis (1717–1791) that the historical study of the New Testament came into its own. Indeed, Semler is sometimes described as the 'father of historical–critical research'.[91]

In his *Historical Introduction to Dogmatic Theology* (1759–1760),[92] Semler distinguishes between 'outward' and 'inward' religion. Outward religion is the public form of religion practised by a community of faith and includes its rituals, clergy and traditions. For Semler, this outward, public religion is characteristic of all religions, including faiths such as Judaism, Islam and Hinduism. Religious differences are due merely to the local, historical traditions which have moulded the distinctive practices of the outward religion of a particular faith. Private religion on the other hand is 'inward' and 'moral'.[93] This distinction between outward and inward religion and his view that outward religion is historically conditioned allowed Semler to treat the Bible as a historical artefact. The Bible should not be treated as a unified work containing timeless truths, but as a collection of works which bear the mark of the historical period in which the biblical writings were composed. This insight opened up the possibility of treating the books of the Bible independently of the interpretative framework provided by the canon into which they had been incorporated by the Church. This was a task Semler undertook in his most important work, the four-volume *Treatise on the Free Investigation of the Canon* (1771–1775),[94] which contained two arguments of particular importance in the development of historical criticism. Firstly, Semler distinguished between 'Scripture' and 'the Word of God'. The term 'Scripture' refers to writings that are relevant only to the distant past in which they were written, but no longer speak to modern human beings. The phrase 'Word of God', on the other hand, refers to those biblical texts which contain insights of permanent value. The criterion for distinguishing between 'Scripture' and 'the Word of God' is moral edification. The biblical writings can be classified according to whether they cultivate and foster virtue in the believer or speak of historical events and concerns relevant only to the biblical authors and the communities for which they were writing. As Semler puts it, the question is which texts 'help such a discriminating reader to become more skilful and capable of doing all good works and cultivating all virtues and merits, which is the goal and consequence of all soundly based and rational religions, and thus all the more so with Christianity'.[95] This differentiation determines for Semler what elements of the Bible are the Word of God and which are merely historically conditioned texts, and allows Semler to impose a hierarchy upon the biblical texts. He regards much of the Old Testament as lacking in ethical content and therefore of only historical interest. Thus Ruth and Esther make no contribution to moral insight, but contain merely information concerning ancient Israelite affairs which are of no significance to non-Jews.[96] Semler asks with reference to the historical books of the Old Testament, 'just because the Jews consider these books to be divine, holy books, must then other nations also regard their content as divine and much more worthy than the account of the history and events particular to other nations?'.[97] Semler thus drives a wedge between history and theology. What is of theological value in the Bible is its moral teaching. The historical events described in the Bible belong to the sphere of secular history, just as does the history of other peoples and nations. What we have with Semler, then, is the partial historical relativization of the Bible. The Bible is a historically conditioned work and contains much that is no longer significant. Only the biblical writings which contain inward moral truths are of permanent value.

Semler's second important insight was that the question of the canonical status of biblical writings is a historical rather than a doctrinal issue. The canon is merely the collection of writings accepted by the Church as authoritative as a result of a series of historical decisions taken by the early Church for the conduct of its worship and regulation of its life. On the basis of these arguments, Semler pleads for the 'free investigation' of the canon, i.e. an investigation that is not determined by dogmatic considerations. Such a free investigation requires the interpreter to put aside his/her conceptions concerning the writing under consideration and to undertake a grammatical study of the biblical text. This in turn entails identifying the writing's historical context and interpreting the text as a witness to that context.

This emphasis on establishing the meaning of a biblical text in its historical context independently of any dogmatic considerations marked a watershed in biblical interpretation and set the scene for subsequent developments. By arguing that biblical writings should be interpreted as historical documents, Semler opened the door for the differentiated study of the Old and New Testaments. He also opened up the possibility of appealing to historical and literary considerations to explain problematic features of the biblical text. A good example of this is his argument that the absence of Rom. 15 and 16 from Marcion's Bible indicates that these two chapters were later additions to the Epistle to the Romans. This practice of attempting to explain anomalies in the text on the basis of secondary emendations has become common and accepted practice in biblical scholarship since Semler.

His historical studies of the New Testament also led Semler to posit different historical contexts for the various New Testament writings. Thus he argues for a division in the early Church between Jewish and Gentile Christianity, and argues that this division is reflected in the writings of the New Testament. Early Christianity, he claimed, was characterized by a struggle between Petrine and Pauline Christianity. This recognition that the New Testament is not a homogeneous whole but contains differences and distinctions that reflect tensions in early Christianity marks an important stage in the historical investigation of the New Testament.

Johann David Michaelis (1717–1791) first published his *Introduction to the Divine Scriptures of the New Covenant* in 1750, but it was the extended fourth edition of 1788 that was important in the development of the historical study of the New Testament, for this version was the first example of the *New Testament Introduction*. 'Old Testament Introduction' and 'New Testament Introduction' are the terms used in biblical scholarship for the historical study of the individual writings of the two Testaments and the historical questions they raise.[98]

Michaelis is also significant for the development of historical arguments concerning the canonical status of certain New Testament writings. He makes a connection between apostolic authorship, canonicity and the 'divinity' or 'inspiration' of the New Testament writings. Only texts written by apostles are canonical, possess divinity and are inspired. This led him to deny the canonical status of Mark, Luke and Acts on the grounds that they were not written by apostles.

Another concern that developed during the eighteenth century was with the life of Jesus and its relation to the teaching of the Church. An important impulse in what would later come to be known as the quest of the historical Jesus was the publication of the *Fragmente eines Ungenannten* [Fragments of an Anonymous Author] by G. E. Lessing (1729–1781). These fragments, which became known as the *Wolfenbüttel Fragments* after the library where Lessing was librarian, consisted of a selection from the writings of Hermann Samuel Reimarus (1694–1768).[99] Reimarus had been a teacher of oriental languages in Hamburg. Under the influence of English Deism, he wrote a lengthy critique of Christianity entitled *Apologie oder Schutzschrift für die vernünftigen Verehrer Gottes* [Apologia or Defence for the Rational Worshippers of God], which, however, he refrained from having published during his lifetime. After Reimarus' death, Lessing published seven 'fragments' from the work, which caused considerable controversy. The identity of the author of the 'fragments' became known only in 1813, when Reimarus' son made it public knowledge. It was thus Lessing who had to bear the brunt of public indignation at the publication of such a controversial book.

Of particular importance is the seventh and final fragment, which deals with the purpose of Jesus and his disciples. In this fragment, Reimarus makes a distinction between what Jesus actually taught and how Jesus is portrayed in the New Testament. According to Reimarus, Jesus was a political messiah who hoped to win political power. When he failed and was executed, the disciples stole his body and began to proclaim that Jesus had been raised from the dead. This subterfuge was carried out for wholly worldly motives: the disciples did not wish to return to Galilee but wished to continue to enjoy the status and privilege they had enjoyed as members of Jesus' movement. In order to ensure the survival of the Jesus movement and their privileged places within it, the disciples invented the idea of a spiritual, suffering saviour of the human race. This idea of Jesus as a spiritual redeemer, Reimarus claims, has heavily overlaid and distorted the accounts of Jesus' life, but traces of the historical Jesus can still be detected in the Gospels. Because of this distinction between the allegedly real Jesus and the Jesus invented by the disciples and recorded in the New Testament, Reimarus has been described as the instigator of the quest of the historical Jesus. Schweitzer, for example, writes that, 'Before Reimarus, no one had attempted to form a historical conception of the life of Jesus'.[100]

Reimarus' interpretation of the Gospels made clear the independence of historical criticism from Christian commitment. It became evident that historical criticism need not be in the service of Christian theology but could exist quite independently of it and indeed could be employed in opposition to the interests of the Church. Reimarus thus contributed to the development which would lead to the historical study of the Bible being governed solely by rational criteria and rejecting all deference to tradition. Historical criticism became the handmaiden of a belief in rational religion and the history of religion became understood in terms of the moral and religious progress of humankind. An increasing gulf began to open up between the tradition of the Church, Church doctrine and historical method. Reimarus' controversial work prompted a response from Semler and made necessary critical engagement with the Gospel record in order to refute Reimarus' arguments.

Lessing's contribution to historical criticism was to raise in an acute form the problem of the relation between faith and history.[101] Lessing's position in 'On the Proof of the Spirit and of Power' (1777) is that the historical events of Christianity are insufficient for faith.[102] His argument in his essay is based on Leibniz's distinction between 'necessary truths of reason' and 'contingent truths'. A necessary truth is a truth that *must* be true. There are no circumstances under which it cannot be true. As Leibniz puts it, 'truths of reasoning are necessary and their opposite is impossible'.[103] A necessary truth is not dependent upon its appearance at a particular point in history. It is *always* true. Such truths are obtainable not through observation of the empirical world, but only by means of the exercise of pure reason. As Leibniz puts it, 'The fundamental proof of necessary truths comes from the understanding alone, and other truths come from experience or from observations of the senses'.[104] A contingent truth on the other hand is a truth derived from our experience of the world. These are *not* necessary, for it is possible to conceive of them being otherwise and, in addition, it is possible for such truths not to be valid in all places at all times; in Leibniz's words, truths 'of fact are contingent and their opposite is possible'.[105] The significance of this is that Christianity would seem to be based on a confusion of necessary and contingent statements. God, if he exists, must exist necessarily. If God is God, then he is eternal and there can never be a time or a place where and when he did not exist. Christianity makes the claim, however, that God has entered into time at a specific point in history. There are, however, several problems with this claim.

(1) The historical events that gave rise to Christianity are contingent, precisely because they are historical. They could have turned out differently. They are therefore arguably inadequate vehicles to carry necessary, i.e. non-contingent, non-historical truths. Furthermore, if God is eternal and omnipresent and therefore accessible to all people at all times by the exercise of reason, he does not need to reveal himself definitively at a particular point in history. The 'revelation' that allegedly takes place in Jesus Christ cannot bring new knowledge that is not accessible to human reason alone.

(2) There is the problem of the gap between the present and the religiously significant events of the past. Why should we accept past events as significant for the present? To put it in Lessing's language, what proof do we have of the spirit and the power of these events? One reason for accepting the claims about Christianity is that which is advanced by Origen, namely that the truth of Christianity is indicated by the miracles with which it was accompanied. Lessing is prepared to accept the validity of this argument for Origen. His was an age in which miracles still took place 'among those who lived after Christ's precept'.[106] Consequently, if a person 'was not to deny his own senses he had of necessity to recognize that proof of the spirit and of power'.[107] Origen could see the proof of the power of Christianity because in his day miracles were still taking place in the name of Jesus.

Unfortunately, however, this is no longer the case in the eighteenth century. Miracles no longer happen, and therefore the Christian appeal to miracles as evidence for the truth of Christianity fails. One way around this problem is to turn to the *testimonies* to the miracles of Christianity that have come down to us. That is, we have the Bible. The problem is that even if it is accepted that 'the reports of these miracles and prophecies are as reliable as historical truths can ever be', such reliability is not sufficient for faith.[108] According to Lessing, because we are basing a relationship with God on these reports, they should not be *just as* reliable but *infinitely more* reliable than general historical reports. The fact that they are no more reliable than any other historical reports means that we are going far beyond what the New Testament reports warrant when we attempt to base our relation with God upon them. As Lessing puts it, 'something quite different and much greater is founded upon them than it is legitimate to found upon truths historically proved'.[109] Lessing's conclusion is that 'accidental truths of history can never be the proof of necessary truths of reason'.[110]

(3) There is a discrepancy between the historical facts alleged about Christ's life and the theological claims based on these alleged facts. Lessing asks, 'if on historical grounds I have no objection to the statement that this Christ himself rose from the dead, must I, therefore accept it as true that this risen Christ was the Son of God?'[111] For Lessing, these two assertions, namely that Christ was raised from the dead and that he is the Son of God, belong in different classes. The first is a historical claim which (Lessing assumes for the sake of argument) can be verified historically. The second assertion is a theological claim. It is an expression of faith and allegiance. It is therefore of a different order from the historical claim that Christ was raised from the dead. The problem is that there is no natural or necessary transition from a historical statement to a theological statement. To posit such a transition is to be guilty of a *metabasis eis allo genos* – a leap from one class to another. It is not enough to say that Christ was raised from the dead, therefore he is the Son of God. For this claim to be accepted, it must be shown that there is a necessary connection between resurrection and divine Sonship. This cannot be done. We might also add that the Church implicitly admits this by not claiming divine Sonship for those other individuals the Bible reports to have been raised from the dead.

History and faith, historical truths and religious truths, are thus fundamentally different. There is no continuity between the two. We cannot begin with history and arrive at faith. Lessing writes that this division between historical and religious truths 'is the ugly broad ditch which I cannot get across, however often and however earnestly I have tried to make the leap'.[112]

So why should we accept the teaching of Christ? We cannot be bound to it by miracles, for since miracles no longer occur in the present age, they are no longer convincing as proofs of the truth of Christianity. Furthermore, the historical reports of these miracles are insufficient, for they are no more reliable than any other historical reports. Yet they ought to be infinitely more reliable than other historical reports, if we are to commit ourselves in faith to the theological claims made on their basis. Does this mean that there is nothing that can make us accept Christ's teaching? Lessing's answer is as follows: 'What then does bind me? Nothing but these teachings themselves'.[113] What counts are the fruits of these teachings, not the myths, legends and dogmas that surround it. That is, it is the moral content of Jesus' teaching that remains significant. We can recognize the worth of this teaching and continue to follow it today.

Lessing made a further contribution to historical approaches to the Bible in his *The Education of the Human Race* (1778). The arguments he advanced in 'On the Proof of the Spirit and of Power' appeared to make revelation redundant, since the revelation that supposedly took place in Christ contained nothing that was inaccessible to reason. Lessing deals with this problem by arguing that revelation is a shortcut God employs to introduce human beings to ideas they would eventually reach by means of reason. He writes: 'Education gives man nothing which he could not also get from within himself, only quicker and more easily. In the same way too, revelation gives nothing to the human race which human reason could not arrive at on its own; only it has given, and still gives to it, the most important of these things sooner'.[114] Also of importance in this work was Lessing's division of world history into three ages, a division which he derived from Joachim of Fiore. Lessing divided history into the epochs of Israel, Christianity and the 'eternal Gospel', each of which is a stage in God's education of the human race. In the first, Israelite period, God educated the human race by giving the Mosaic law to the people of Israel. In the second, Christian epoch God educated the human race to a more noble form of morality by motivating human beings to moral behaviour not on the basis of temporal rewards and punishments but on the basis of the immortality of the soul, the first reliable and practical teacher of which was Christ.[115] The third stage in the education of the human race is when the human being 'will do right because it *is* right, not because arbitrary rewards are set upon it'.[116] This age of the 'eternal Gospel' still lies in the future.

Such an understanding of history allowed the diverse forms of literature found in the Bible to be interpreted as different stages in the education of the human race. It thus provided a positive way of interpreting the problematic material in the Old Testament rather than writing it off as absurd or immoral. By means of this philosophy of history Lessing contributed to the growing tendency to locate the significance of biblical texts in the age in and for which they were written.

A further important stage in the development towards the historical criticism of the Bible was the introduction of the concept of *myth* into biblical scholarship. The term 'myth' was employed by Christian Gottlob Heyne in his study of classical philology. For Heyne, myths are summaries of the beliefs of primitive people in the pre-literary period, who were incapable of abstract thought, lacked knowledge, and were naively reliant on what was evident to their senses. These myths were subsequently taken up and reworked by the classical poets such as Homer and Hesiod. For Heyne, myths are not fanciful inventions but the forms of expression of the infancy of humankind and should be interpreted as such. He distinguishes between two types of myth, namely historical myths, which have some genuine historical event at their core such as the foundation of a city or the acts of a hero, and philosophical myths, which contain an ethical principle or an attempt to explain some feature of the world.[117] Heyne's concept of myth was taken up and applied to the Bible by Johann Gottfried Eichhorn (1752–1827), Johann Philipp Gabler (1753–1826) and Georg Lorenz Bauer (1755–1806).

In 1779, Eichhorn published anonymously his *Urgeschichte* [Primitive History] a study of Gen. 1.1–2.4 and 2.4–3.24. Between 1790 and 1793 Eichhorn's pupil Gabler republished the work together with extensive introductions and notes. Eichhorn and Gabler are considered the founders of the 'mythical school' of biblical interpretation, although, as Reventlow points out, 'this applies more strongly to Gabler than to Eichhorn'.[118]

Contemporary advances in geology were making clear that the creation of the world must have take place over a much longer period than the six days described in Gen. 1.1–2.4. The Bible's apparent conflict with the discoveries of geology together with such logical contradictions in the creation account such as the creation of light (Gen. 1.3–4) before the creation of the sun and the moon (Gen. 1.14–18) raised questions concerning the authority of the Bible. The application of Heyne's notion of myth provided a way of addressing these problems. Such stories as the account of God's creation of the world and the fall of the first human beings are biblical myths which came into existence in the human race's infancy when human beings had not yet developed abstract modes of thought. Moses, whose authorship of the Pentateuch Eichhorn did not question, was simply telling the account of God's creation of the world from the mythical perspective typical of the age in which he lived. The mythical character of the creation story does not mean, however, that it should now be rejected as having nothing to say to enlightened human beings, for it contains an important truth, namely, as Gabler sums up his teacher's view of the passage, 'Everything comes from God'.[119] It is this that is the great truth that Moses wishes to convey to his readers and which remains as relevant today as when it was written by Moses. To do justice to those texts in the Bible which seem incredible from the modern perspective, then, it is necessary for the interpreter to take as his/her starting point the insight that they are couched in the primitive thought-forms and modes of expression of the human race in its infancy.

In short, the interpreter must take into consideration the historical context in which the biblical texts were written if he or she is to grasp their meaning. The fact that the oldest parts of the Bible are myths should not lead us to disparage them, but to recognize them as belonging the history of human development.

Another important contribution Eichhorn made to the historical study of the Bible was his development of the 'introduction'. Indeed, Eichhorn is considered to be the founder of this discipline of biblical studies.[120] In 1780–1783, Eichhorn's *Introduction to the Old Testament* appeared in three volumes and went through four editions, culminating in the five-volume fourth edition of 1823–1824. In this work, Eichhorn applies to the Old Testament a philological and historical method based on Heyne's concept of myth. He thus consciously employs a non-theological approach to the interpretation of the Old Testament and in doing so, Reventlow comments, 'thereby ushers in the historical criticism of the nineteenth century'.[121] Eichhorn also wrote an *Introduction to the New Testament*, which appeared in five volumes between 1804 and 1827.

Gabler followed Eichhorn's example and applied Heyne's concept of myth to the interpretation of the Bible.[122] Where Gabler goes further than Eichhorn is in his attempt to place the application of myth to the interpretation of the Bible on a more adequate theoretical basis and his clarification of the theological principles that underlie the biblical myths. To achieve this, he distinguishes between historical, poetical and philosophical myths. Historical myths relate real events of the ancient world in the ancient language and thought-forms of the age in which they were written. Poetical myths are the result of historical myths having been embellished by didactic additions and expansions or through the combination into a whole of earlier, originally disparate ancient myths by a poetic genius. Philosophical myths originated from pure speculation about the cause of things or about moral issues, but have clothed this speculation in the form of a story.[123]

Gabler also distinguishes between two types of exegesis. Firstly, there is grammatical exegesis, which is concerned only with establishing what the author meant by a particular passage. This form of exegesis is not sufficient in itself, however, for modern human beings are no longer able to rest content with the author's understanding of the passage. Consequently, we must employ a second type of exegesis, namely what Gabler terms 'historical and philosophical criticism'. This form of exegesis consists in illuminating the meaning of a passage by identifying its underlying theological principle. Thus in the case of the Temptation Narrative (Matt. 4.1–11/ Luke 4.1–13), it is not sufficient for the interpreter to establish how the evangelists understood this myth, for modern human beings can no longer accept their understanding. To understand this narrative, the interpreter of the Bible has to ascertain why the evangelists constructed the story of Jesus' temptation by the devil. This entails the interpreter asking after the real events lying behind the story, which have been expressed in mythical terms by the evangelists. Applying this approach leads Gabler to conclude that the Temptation Narrative should be understood as an account of a real struggle with sensual desires that Jesus rejected on firm rational principles. As a result of the contemporary belief that evil originated with the devil, this struggle was expressed by the evangelists as the myth of the devil's temptation of Jesus.

Gabler's analysis is also important for distinguishing between biblical and dogmatic theology. The title of Gabler's inaugural lecture as Professor of Theology at Altdorf in 1787 was 'On the proper distinction between biblical and dogmatic theology and the correct establishment of their boundaries'. In this lecture, Gabler argued for the separation of biblical and dogmatic theology, which until then had tended to be conflated. This separation of biblical and dogmatic theology into distinct disciplines requires reflection on what is distinctive about these two ways of doing theology. In his preface to Part 1 of Eichhorn's *Urgeschichte* [Primitive History] (2 vols. 1790–1792) he writes: 'Dogmatics must depend on exegesis and not inversely exegesis depend on dogmatics.'[124] Gabler assigns to biblical and dogmatic theology different natures and tasks. The task of biblical theology is to ascertain the ideas of the biblical writers and then to consider which ideas are historically conditioned and therefore no longer relevant to the present, and which are of permanent value. The task of dogmatic theology, on the other hand, is for the theologian to 'philosophize', i.e. reflect upon these permanently significant and relevant biblical ideas. Because dogmatic theology is the result of the theologian's own deliberations, it is subject to changes and developments like any other human discipline.

In pursuit of his goal of collating and establishing the nature of the 'sacred ideas' of the biblical writers, Gabler argued for a differentiated understanding of biblical history, namely an acknowledgement of the distinctive perspectives of the biblical writers, and a sensitivity to the different literary forms employed in the Bible. Gabler, however, did not follow through with this insight. His work constitutes a preparation for biblical theology rather than an articulation of biblical theology.

The work of Eichhorn and Gabler was continued by Georg Lorenz Bauer, who published a compendium of the myths of the Bible entitled *Hebrew Mythology of the Old and New Testaments* (1802).[125] In this work, Bauer drew comparisons with non-biblical myths in order to throw light on such texts as, for example, Abraham's near sacrifice of Isaac, Jacob's struggle with God and the birth of Jesus.

The nineteenth century to the mid-twentieth century: historical criticism as the status quo

The lines of development laid down in the Enlightenment continued into the nineteenth century. Two works that influenced the application of historical method to biblical interpretation were Barthold Georg Niebuhr's *Römische Geschichte* [Roman History] (1811–1832) and Leopold von Ranke's *Geschichte der romanischen und germanischen Völker von 1494 bis 1535* [History of the Roman and German Peoples from 1494 to 1535] (1824). By means of a detailed study of the available sources, Niebuhr (1776–1831) strove to distinguish historical truth from poetry and falsehood and thereby to construct a plausible account of the history of Rome. Also of importance was his analysis of the *bias* (*Tendenz*) of the sources, which enabled him to gain historical insights that went beyond the surface meaning of ancient texts.

The work of the historian Leopold von Ranke (1795–1866) was important for laying the foundations of what has come to be known as 'historicism'. In his *History of the Roman and German Peoples* and subsequent works von Ranke strove to achieve as objective a representation of history as possible. In the preface of his book, he states as his aim that 'he merely wishes to show how it really was'.[126] He is not concerned to consider the relevance of historical events for the present, but is concerned solely with a supposedly objective portrayal of the past. Ranke's notion of the possibility of achieving an objective understanding of the past would influence the nineteenth-century study of the Bible, where it became a goal of biblical scholarship.

In the second volume of his *Contributions to the Introduction to the Old Testament* (1806–1807), Wilhelm Martin Leberecht de Wette (1780–1849) provides a summary of the principles of historical criticism.[127] The motto of this volume is 'Truth is the first great law of history, love of truth the first duty of the historian'.[128] De Wette identifies three principles of historical criticism. Firstly, the source of knowledge of history is the report. The historian must recognize, however, that a report is not identical with the historical event it describes, but is only an *account* of that event. The initial task of the historian is thus to comprehend what the report relates. To achieve this it is necessary to understand the perspective of the report's author. The second task of the historian is to test the credibility of the report. For de Wette, the credibility of the report and the historicity of the events it relates must be placed in doubt if it contains miraculous elements such as God or angels speaking directly to human beings or when it describes events which violate general human experience or the laws of nature. De Wette's application of these principles led him to the conclusion that the Pentateuch 'is useless as a source of historical knowledge or rather is simply not a source of history at all'.[129] For de Wette, however, this does not mean that the Pentateuch is of no value, but that its significance lies not in the events it describes but in what it tells us about the community that produced it.[130] De Wette's reasons for claiming this is his conviction that the Pentateuch is a 'product of the national religious poetry of the Israelite people, in which their spirit, patriotism, philosophy, and religion are reflected, and is thus one of the first sources of the history of culture and religion'.[131] What is significant here is de Wette's recognition of the Pentateuch not as a historical account of the events it relates, but as a source for the knowledge of the history of Israel's culture and religion.

De Wette drew on the philosophy of Jakob Friedrich Fries (1773–1843) to address the problems raised by the Old Testament. Fries understood religion in aesthetic terms. Great art mediates eternal values. Religion, too, is an intuitive grasping and subsequent institutionalization of eternal values. Of particular importance for de Wette was Fries' view that spontaneous and unforced experiences and the expressions of these eternal values were of more value than their developed dogmatic forms. Indeed, the dogmatic formulations of organized religion actually constitute a loss of something essential and powerful from the spontaneous forms in which they originated. De Wette applied these ideas to the Old Testament. The Old Testament expresses eternal values in a way that retains their liveliness and spontaneity, in contrast to dogmatic formulations. This view contains an implicit critique of progressive views of religion, according to which later forms of religious belief are superior to earlier forms.

This approach allowed de Wette to construct an understanding of the religion of the Old Testament that differed from that portrayed by the Old Testament itself. He argued that Mosaic religion had originally been very simple, but that it had increased in complexity and ritual as the centuries wore on. Judaism developed after the Babylonian Exile and was inferior to the more spontaneous religion that had existed prior to that period. In this way, de Wette was able to treat the Old Testament in its own right and not merely as a compendium of doctrine.

In his New Testament work, de Wette distinguished between the teaching of Jesus and the apostolic interpretation of Jesus, the latter of which, he argued, is not identical with the former. On the contrary, much of the apostolic interpretation constitutes a mythologizing and dogmatizing of Jesus' message. De Wette also made contributions to the study of the New Testament in his *An Historico-Critical Introduction to the Canonical Books of the New Testament* (1st edition, 1817) and *Kurzgefasstes exegetisches Handbuch zum Neuen Testament* [A Brief Exegetical Manual on the New Testament] (1836–1838).[132] De Wette argued for the presence in the New Testament of three distinct theological strands according to which the significance of Jesus was interpreted, namely the Jewish-Christian strand, consisting of the Synoptic Gospels, Acts, James, Peter, Jude and Revelation; the Alexandrian strand, which comprised the Gospel of John and the Epistle to the Hebrews; and the Pauline strand.

The early decades of the nineteenth century were characterized by the growing awareness of the need for historical study of the New Testament. The pioneers in this regard were Heinrich Eberhard Gottlob Paulus (1761–1851) and Karl Hase (1800–1890). Paulus sought to apply Kantian epistemology to the New Testament with the aim of defending the plausibility of the biblical witnesses and defending the rationality of the Christian faith against its rationalist critics. In his *Philological, Critical, and Historical Commentary on the First Three Gospels* (1800–1802), Paulus states his assumption 'that his readers wish him to treat his subject matter pragmatically and historically'.[133] This necessitates, firstly, focusing on 'the meaning intended by the narrator', which Paulus regards as 'the most important principle of all historical research'. Secondly, it entails drawing 'a clear distinction . . . between what is narrated and what happened'.[134] Paulus does not deny that such events as the miracles took place, but argues that they have been misinterpreted as miraculous occurrences because of the inadequate understanding of the Gospel writers, whose understanding of the laws of cause and effect was not as developed as that of modern human beings. By acquiring knowledge of the culture in which the biblical texts were written the reader will be able to distinguish what really happened from the narrator's historically conditioned understanding of what happened. As Paulus puts it, this will enable the reader 'to separate everything from the narrative that was not fact but the narrator's own view, interpretation, and opinion and to find out what happened in part more fully than is customarily described in any narrative, in part less adulterated with extraneous matter and more in accordance with its original form'.[135] Paulus followed up his commentary with his later *The Life of Jesus, as the Foundation of a Purely Historical Study of Primitive Christianity* (1828),[136] in which he attempted to provide a rationalist account of the life of Jesus, and his *Exegetical Manual on the First Three Gospels* (1830–1833).[137]

The lack of a genuine historical study of the life of Jesus prompted Karl Hase in 1829 to publish a textbook on the life of Jesus.[138] Hase, however, places John on a par with the Synoptics and fails to practise genuine and rigorous source criticism. Hase's significance lies in his argument for an inner development in Jesus' thinking away from a political to a moral and spiritual conception of messiahship. Although it is difficult to sustain this argument on the basis of the meagre textual evidence available, the introduction of the conception of *development* was important, for it paved the way to treating Jesus as a human being subject to the laws of psychological development. It was not only the historical Jesus, however, that was the subject of scholarly attention. Leonhard Usteri (1799–1833) had prior to the publication of Hase's life of Jesus attempted to provide a historical account of the development of Pauline thought. Prior to Usteri, Paul had been treated primarily from the perspective of dogmatic theology.[139]

The development of a historical approach to the interpretation of the Bible was accompanied by reflection on the nature of biblical hermeneutics. In 1788 Karl August Gottlieb Keil (1754–1818) had argued in his inaugural professorial lecture in Leipzig that there is only one valid method of interpretation, namely, grammatico-historical interpretation, whereby the interpreter should strive to establish as accurately as possible the meaning intended by the author of a text. This means leaving to one side questions of inspiration and the truth or falsity of the claims made by an author. Keil gave his fullest account of this understanding of biblical interpretation in his *Manual of the Hermeneutics of the New Testament according to the Principles of Grammatical-Historical Interpretation* (1810).[140] In his introduction to this work, he describes 'what it means to understand the meaning of a text' as being to understand the same thing the writer thought when writing it and what he wanted his readers to understand when they read it.[141]

This conception of hermeneutics as a purely grammatico-historical exercise was taken up by many subsequent scholars in the nineteenth century. In his *Commentary on the Letter of Paul to the Romans* (1831), Leopold Immanuel Rückert (1797–1871) demands of the interpreter of Paul, firstly, that he be free from doctrinal and emotional prejudice.[142] The interpreter must be completely neutral. Secondly, the interpreter should refuse to draw any conclusions concerning the truth or falsity of the claims made in the text he or she is interpreting. A similar approach was adopted by Heinrich August Wilhelm Meyer (1800–1873), whose sixteen-volume *Critical-Exegetical Commentary on the New Testament* is concerned only to establish the meaning of the text of the New Testament and leaves to one side all dogmatic and philosophical questions.[143] In 1829 Meyer published an edition of the text of the Greek New Testament together with a translation. These two volumes were followed by the first commentary (1832), which was devoted to the Synoptic Gospels. Meyer was responsible for the commentaries on the Gospels, Acts of the Apostles, and the major letters of Paul. Other scholars were appointed to write commentaries on the remaining New Testament writings, notably Friedrich Düsterdieck (1822–1906), who wrote an influential commentary on Revelation.[144] In 1873–1885, T & T Clark published an English translation of Meyer's commentary.[145] The commentary has continued to be updated up to the present

day. Meyer focused on the grammatical and historical questions raised by
the New Testament text, deliberately excluding theological questions as
outside the sphere of the exegete.[146]
There were, however, objections in some quarters to the purely historical conception of biblical hermeneutics. An attack on the grammatico-historical conception of interpretation was made in 1807 by Carl
Friedrich Stäudlin (1761–1826) in his inaugural address as Rector of
the University of Göttingen. In his lecture, which he entitled 'That the
Historical Interpretation of the Books of the Old and New Testaments is
not the Only True One', Stäudlin argued that precisely because the teaching of Jesus was concerned with eternal, divine truths, a purely historical
approach to the interpretation of Scripture must inevitably prove inadequate. In order truly to understand the Scriptures, the interpreter must
adopt an attitude appropriate to the character of Scripture. Since Jesus'
teaching contains eternal, unchangeable, divine truths, it cannot be fully
understood by an exclusively historical approach. The interpreter must
rather allow the Bible to speak to and elevate his spirit in order to make
it intelligible to others. Consequently, the writings of the Bible must be
interpreted not only grammatically and historically, but also morally, religiously and philosophically.[147]
     Friedrich Daniel Ernst Schleiermacher (1768–1834) is important in the
history of biblical scholarship for his concern to examine the philosophical foundations that underlie the act of interpretation. It is not sufficient
merely to justify the use of specific methods of interpretation. If we wish
to understand what is involved in interpretation it is necessary to examine
the philosophical structures that underlie these methods. In other words,
Schleiermacher goes beyond the interpretation of texts to the philosophical theory of interpretation, beyond *exegesis* to *hermeneutics*. Since no
such hermeneutical theory was available, Schleiermacher undertook to
provide one himself. Schleiermacher examined the processes by which
human beings arrive at an understand texts in his *Hermeneutics and
Criticism*, published posthumously in 1838. Schleiermacher was critical
of the contemporary approach to biblical interpretation. Although the
historical approach is important for understanding the text, it is not in
itself enough. If we are to cross the gulf that exists between us and the
author, we must undertake to emulate and empathize with the creative
act of the author. This means trying to recreate the selfhood of that
author: 'The task is to be formulated as follows: "To understand the
text at first as well as and then even better than its author." '[148] It is
because Schleiermacher recognized the importance of laying philosophical foundations for an understanding of interpretation before embarking
on exegesis that he has frequently been described as 'the father of modern hermeneutics'.[149]

1835 was a crucial year for the development of historical approaches to the Bible. Indeed, Theobald Ziegler has described it as a revolutionary year and a year of destiny which saw the birth of modern critical theology.[150] Ziegler's reason for this assessment is the publication in 1835 of Wilhelm Vatke's *Religion of the Old Testament*[151] and, above all, David Friedrich Strauss' *The Life of Jesus, Critically Examined*.[152]

Vatke (1806–1882) made use of Hegel's philosophy, particularly as expressed in the latter's lectures on the philosophy of religion. In these lectures Hegel distinguishes the concept of religion from the historical forms in which the concept manifests itself. Historical religions are the results of the self-unfolding of Spirit in ever higher forms. This view enabled Vatke to interpret the Old Testament in terms of *development*. He attempted to identify the inner essence of Old Testament religion and to trace the way it had manifested itself in progressive stages in the history of Israel.

It was, however, *The Life of Jesus, Critically Examined* of David Friedrich Strauss (1808–1874) that had the most profound impact on nineteenth-century theology. Indeed, according to Ziegler, it set the theological agenda for the next seventy years.[153] Ziegler describes the effect of the book as 'like a terrible earthquake or a violent revolution, and on its account the year 1835 has with good reason been called the great revolutionary year of modern theology'.[154] The book caused uproar and destroyed Strauss' hopes of finding an academic position.

Strauss' book was revolutionary in its thoroughgoing employment of the category of myth as the hermeneutical key to the interpretation of the life of Jesus. He recognized that this concept had been employed by earlier scholars, but these had failed to apply the concept consistently in their interpretation of the New Testament. What is new about Strauss' approach is his application of myth to the entire history of Jesus as related in the Gospels. Strauss holds the view that 'the mythical appears *at all points* in the history of Jesus' life'.[155]

Strauss carries out his examination of the mythical character of the Gospel narrative in dialogue with the two dominant ways of interpreting the Gospels in contemporary theology, namely, supernaturalism and rationalism. As representatives of these two positions he takes Hermann Olshausen (1796–1839) and Heinrich Eberhard Gottlob Paulus (1761–1851), respectively.

Strauss distinguishes between two types of supernaturalism and rationalism, namely a crude and refined form of each approach. The crude form of supernaturalism, as represented by Olshausen, treats the Gospels as literal, factual accounts of the life of Jesus and simply opposes the negative work of historical criticism with bald assertion: you can say what you want, it all happened in the way it says in the Gospels down to the smallest detail. For the supernaturalist, the Gospels are literal factual accounts of the life of Jesus and the miracles are instances of divine intervention. According to Strauss, this approach demands belief in the incredible. In view of our knowledge of how the world works we cannot take, for example, Jesus' walking on the water as literally true.

Refined supernaturalism, which Strauss identifies with Schleiermacher, acknowledges the insights of criticism and is prepared to give up some of the beliefs of supernaturalism. Refined supernaturalism remains committed, however, to a fundamental belief over which it refuses to allow criticism to have any power, namely that the historical individual Jesus Christ was the absolutely perfect human being.

The rationalists, on the other hand, regard miracles as misunderstandings of natural events and attempt to find natural explanations for the various miraculous occurrences depicted in the Gospels. Like supernaturalism, rationalism has both a crude and a refined form. As a representative of crude rationalism, Strauss cites Paulus, who made a sustained attempt to find natural explanations for the miraculous events described in the Gospels. To take one example of a rationalist interpretation, in Matt. 14.22–33 the rationalist might argue that Jesus did not really walk on the water but was simply walking on a ledge just beneath the surface of the lake. Once this negative work of demolishing the literal truth of the Gospel narrative had been carried out, the positive content remaining consisted in Jesus' significance as a teacher of moral values. According to Strauss, however, the rationalists are guilty of going to extreme and improbable lengths to find natural explanations for the events depicted in the Gospels. Furthermore, they reduce the miracle stories to trivialities. As John Macquarrie points out with reference to the rationalist explanation of Jesus' walking on the water, 'This would make the story credible, but it would at the same time deprive it of any point. For then it would mean only that the disciples in their ignorance and stupidity thought they were seeing a miracle worked by the *theios aner* [divine man] when in fact he was doing what anyone could do, if he knew the topography of the lake'.[156]

According to Strauss, the refined form of rationalism developed out of this crude form. Strauss takes as his representative of refined rationalism de Wette, who understands the 'facts' of the Gospels as symbols of dogmatic ideas. Strauss approves of this approach but criticizes de Wette for an inadequate concept of symbol. Thus Strauss feels that de Wette's interpretation of the death of Jesus as a symbol of resignation fails to do justice to the significance of Jesus' death. De Wette fails to achieve a more satisfactory interpretation because, like all rationalists, he does not have an adequate concept of spirit. Such a concept is essential for a genuinely scientific treatment of the Gospels.

According to Strauss, if we are to understand the Gospel narrative, the supernatural and rationalist explanations have to be synthesized in a third factor, namely myth. Like Vatke, Strauss draws on Hegelianism and advances an understanding of myth as a primitive stage in the Spirit's self-development. According to Hegel, religious language employs 'representations', i.e. pictorial and sensual images, which it is philosopher's task to bring to conceptual clarity by uncovering and articulating more fully the philosophical concepts partly revealed and partly concealed by religious imagery. This distinction allowed Strauss to understand the myths of the New Testament as representations of philosophical truths. Myth is an expression of religious imagination, which functions not at the level of *Begriff* (concept) but of *Vorstellung* (representation).

To aid him in his interpretation of the Gospels, Strauss distinguishes between three types of myth, namely what he terms 'evangelical', 'pure' and 'historical' myth. By 'evangelical myth', he means 'a narrative relating directly or indirectly to Jesus, which may be considered not as the expression of a fact, but as the product of an idea of his earliest followers: such a narrative being mythical in proportion as it exhibits this character'. 'Pure myth' has two sources, namely, 'the Messianic ideas and expectations existing according to their several forms in the Jewish mind before Jesus, and independently of him; the other is that particular impression which was left by the personal character, actions and fate of Jesus, and which served to modify the Messianic idea in the minds of his people'. Finally, historical myth 'has for its groundwork a definite individual fact which has been seized upon by religious enthusiasm, and twined around with mythical conceptions culled from the idea of the Christ'.[157]

For Strauss, this mythologization of the person of Jesus took place during a process of oral tradition in which the early Christians took the basic framework of Jesus' life and filled it with mythological elements drawn from the Old Testament in order to express their conviction that Jesus surpassed Moses and the prophets, and fulfilled the messianic prophecies. This process of applying Old Testament material to Jesus is hinted at in the New Testament itself in such passages as Luke 24.27: 'Then beginning with Moses and all the prophets, he interpreted to them the things about himself in all the scriptures.' Strauss believed that this interpretation of the Old Testament in the light of Jesus and the application of the Old Testament to Jesus continued for a generation after Jesus' death and was the means by which the disciples reconciled their faith in the crucified Jesus with the Jewish hope of a messiah.[158] In this way, the Gospels built up a fuller picture of the life of Jesus.

For example, the Old Testament prediction that the messiah would come from Bethlehem was a factor in the development of the birth stories

(Micah 5.2; Matt. 2.6). Also, the Gospel accounts of Jesus' life were influenced by Old Testament passages that seemed to fit. For example, the Passion Narrative has been influenced by Ps. 22. Thus Strauss reversed the traditional approach. Ps. 22 is not a prophetic prediction of the coming of the messiah and the fate that awaited him. Rather, the account of Jesus' death is moulded in such a way that it corresponds to Ps. 22. Strauss thus undermines one of the traditional proofs for the validity of Christianity, namely, its fulfilment of Old Testament prophecy.

Strauss posits negative and positive criteria for detecting myth. The negative criterion is, 'That an account is not historical – that the matter could not have taken place in the manner described. . .'.[159] The non-historical and therefore mythical character of a Gospel passage can be recognized by two features. Firstly, a text contains mythical elements, 'when the narration is irreconcilable with the known and universal laws which govern the course of events'.[160] Secondly, 'An account which shall be regarded as historically valid, must neither be inconsistent with itself, nor in contradiction with other accounts.'[161] The positive criterion for recognizing myth consists in the correspondence of a Gospel text to the mythical world-view of the New Testament period. Strauss writes: 'If the content of a narrative strikingly accords with certain ideas existing and prevailing within the circle from which the narrative proceeded, which ideas themselves seem to be the product of preconceived opinions rather than of practical experience, it is more or less probable, according to the circumstances, that such a narrative is of mythical origin'.[162] For example, the darkness and earthquake accompanying the crucifixion in Matthew is in line with similar descriptions of significant events in the ancient world.

For Strauss, then, the presence of myth in a text constitutes the criterion of that text's unhistoricity. Nevertheless, Strauss believed that a historical kernel underlies the Gospels, namely that Jesus existed, believed himself to be the messiah, had disciples, and was crucified. He also claims that the accounts of Jesus' teaching are mostly correct. Strauss was also significant in being one of the first to question the reliability of the Gospel of John as a historical source for the life of Jesus. Strauss's view was that the Gospel of John marks a more developed level of mythologization than is present in the Synoptics.

Strauss' *Life of Jesus* seemed wholly negative to many of his contemporaries. What made Strauss' book so shocking was that he regarded as myth much of what orthodox Christians regarded as essential to the faith. Strauss himself attempted to fill the gap by turning to idealist philosophy. At the end of the book, he briefly sketches a 'speculative Christology',[163] according to which he interprets Christ as a universal principle of divine-human unity, which has now become part of the general human consciousness. This was a solution that satisfied neither his contemporaries, nor ultimately Strauss himself. By the time he came to write his later *A New Life of Jesus* (1864), he had abandoned Hegelianism as a solution to the theological problems raised by his earlier works.[164] Strauss' one-time teacher F. C. Baur is important for attempting a critical study of the Gospels by applying insights drawn from Niebuhr's source critical study of Roman history and for arguing that John's Gospel is not an eyewitness account but a later theological work on the significance of the incarnation. Baur was the first to establish on critical grounds John's distinctiveness from the Synoptics. Baur is also significant for striving to construct a historical understanding of primitive Christianity. As we saw earlier, Semler had argued that early Christianity was characterized by a struggle between Petrine and Pauline Christianity. Baur undertakes a critical and comprehensive study of this issue in his essay 'The Christ Party in the Corinthian Congregation' (1831).[165] The Petrine party, which was made up of Jewish Christians, wanted to retain the Jewish law and impose it on converts to Christianity, while Pauline Christianity, which comprised Christians of pagan origin, argued for a Christianity freed from the law. Baur held that the conflict between Pauline and Petrine Christianity can be traced in the New Testament, but that attempts to impose a harmony on the history of the early Church are also visible. This is particularly apparent in Acts, which plays down the tensions between Peter and Paul. Subsequent study led Baur to the conclusion that the Pastoral Epistles (1 and 2 Timothy, Titus, and Philemon) cannot have been written by Paul, but were the product of the struggle against Gnosticism, which belonged to a later age than that of Peter and Paul.[166]

Baur adopted Hegel's conception of history as the self-unfolding of Spirit and made use of the latter's dialectic of thesis-antithesis-synthesis as a framework for his construction of the history of early Christianity. In his *Christianity and the Christian Church of the First Three Centuries* (1853), Baur argues that the opposition between Petrine Christianity (thesis) and Pauline Christianity (antithesis) is resolved in the synthesis of postapostolic Christianity, which Baur identified as early Catholicism.[167] Seeing the New Testament in terms of dialectical development allowed Baur to deal with the tensions and apparent contradictions between the New Testament writings. These tensions can be regarded as earlier stages in Christian development that were taken up into the synthesis that was early Catholicism.

In his later work on the Gospels, namely his *Kritische Untersuchungen über die kanonischen Evangelien* [Critical Investigations into the Canonical Gospels] (1847), Baur takes issue with Strauss and attempts to replace the latter's 'negatively critical' approach to the New Testament with a genuinely historical understanding of Jesus. The isolation of the historical content of the Gospels necessitates 'tendency criticism' of each of the Gospels. Only when we understand the 'tendency' or bias of the evangelists and how this has influenced their composition of the Gospels will we be able to separate the historical from the non-historical. The identification of bias in all of the canonical Gospels means that we can accept none of them as an objectively accurate historical report. This does not mean, however, that the Gospels possess no historical content. On the contrary, Baur argues that the Synoptic Gospels possesses greater historical value than that of the Gospel of John.

Despite the important insights of Baur, further progress in historical criticism of the New Testament could be made only when the question of sources was addressed more adequately. Only when this issue was resolved, would it be possible to construct an accurate history of early Christianity. Someone who rose to this task was the philologist Karl Lachmann (1793–1851). In his essay 'On the Order of Narratives in the Synoptic Gospels',[168] Lachmann made a significant contribution to the study of the Synoptic Gospels by arguing for Markan priority. Lachmann proposed that the order of the three Gospels is best explained if we assume that Matthew and Luke have used Mark as a source. Independently of Lachmann, Christian Gottlob Wilke (1786–1854) proposed a similar argument for the priority of Mark in his The First Evangelist (1838).[169]

In the same year in which Wilke's book appeared, Christian Hermann Weisse (1801–1866) published his The History of the Gospels, Critically and Philosophically Examined (1838).[170] In this book, he sought to recover a picture of the historical Jesus. Weisse's importance lies in his insight that such an undertaking necessitates an examination of the relationship between the Gospels. Weisse undertook such an examination, the result of which was that he came to the conclusion that Mark is the earliest of the canonical Gospels on grounds of order and more primitive style. Weisse also argued that Matthew and Luke have inserted into the Gospel of Mark a collection of Jesus' sayings that originated with the apostle Matthew.

From c. 1850, with the decline of Hegelianism, historical study became increasingly positivistic. The aim of the historian was increasingly understood as being that of establishing as objective an account of historical events as possible. These developments had an influence on biblical scholarship. Just as secular historians laid aside questions of the purpose, unity and guidance of history, so too did scholars of the Bible increasingly part company with any idea of supernaturalism in the interpretation of the Bible.

It took some time for historical criticism to establish itself in Britain. In 1846 Strauss' Life of Jesus was translated by George Eliot, but it was above all the publication in 1860 of *Essays and Reviews* that made historical criticism a burning issue.[171] Although these essays did not contain any new scholarship, their approval of historical criticism and their willingness to employ it in their interpretation of the Bible provoked controversy among the general public. In his essay 'On the Interpretation of Scripture', Benjamin Jowett argued that the object of the interpreter is to 'read Scripture like any other book'.[172] Scholars such as Joseph Barber Lightfoot (1828–1889), Brooke Foss Westcott (1825–1901), John Anthony Hort (1828–1892) and Samuel Rolles Driver (1846–1914), however, did much to establish the new critical methods. Resistance continued in some quarters, however. In 1881 William Robertson Smith (1846–1894) was tried for heresy by the Free Church of Scotland, of which he was a minister and professor of divinity.[173] An important event in introducing historical-critical thought into Anglican thinking was the publication in 1889 of *Lux Mundi*, a collection of essays edited by Charles Gore.[174] It was Gore's own contribution that caused the greatest controversy. In his essay 'The Holy Spirit and Inspiration', Gore attempted to develop an understanding of inspiration that did justice to the insights of the historical–critical method. Gore's essay provoked considerable opposition, but it marked the first stage in the gradual acceptance in Anglican circles of the historical approach to the interpretation of the Bible.

By the end of the nineteenth century, the historical–critical method had established itself as the accepted method of interpretation. This had significant consequences. Firstly, the biblical writings came to be understood as historical documents that could and should be examined and studied just like any other documents. The same criteria employed for the interpretation of any ancient text were to be applied to the Bible. Secondly, the dominance of historical criticism had theological consequences. The rise of the allegedly more 'scientific' approach of historical criticism was accompanied by the decline of revelation as a category of biblical interpretation and the increasing abandonment of notions of inspiration and any other form of supernatural input. At the same time, historical criticism appeared to some to provide the basis for a more viable theology by piercing through the centuries of dogma that had obscured our vision of Jesus to what was of permanent value in his ministry. This enabled liberal Protestant theologians such as Albrecht Ritschl (1822–1889), Willibald Herrmann (1846–1922) and Adolf von Harnack (1851-1930) to locate Jesus' significance in his ethical teaching and in the ethical community he founded.[175] The Old Testament was interpreted in terms of the evolution of an ethical monotheism which culminated in Jesus, while the Gospels were considered to be biographies of Jesus the moral teacher of the fatherhood of God, the brotherhood of humankind and the eternal value of the human being. The concern with recovering the Jesus of history also accounts for the large number of lives of Jesus that were written in the latter half of the nineteenth century, the most influential of which were those of Ernest Renan (1823–1892) and F. W. Farrar (1831–1903).[176] The use of historical criticism as the basis for an ethical interpretation of Jesus' significance was undermined, however, by several developments at the end of the nineteenth and beginning of the twentieth centuries.

For Franz Overbeck (1837–1905), historical criticism exposes the untenability of Christianity. In his *How Christian is our Present-Day Theology?* (1873) and *Christianity and Culture* (1919),[177] Overbeck argued that primitive Christianity was eschatological and apocalyptic in character. The first Christians had expected Christ to return immediately and usher in the kingdom of God. Primitive Christianity, then, was *not* historical precisely because it was predicated on the notion of the *end* of time, not on its continuation. History, however, has proved Christianity wrong. The sheer fact that Christianity has not brought history to an end but has continued to exist in and be part of history constitutes the utter refutation of Christianity. As Overbeck puts it: 'Christianity's advanced age is for serious historical reflection a fatal argument against its eternal nature. Christianity has always known this and, in so far as it is alive, still knows it today.'[178] To avoid facing up to this fact, Christianity invented theology, which is the means by which it has been able to accommodate itself to the world. Primitive Christianity, however, was the renunciation of the world, not accommodation with it. Theology is thus a falsification of Christianity.

For Overbeck, then, historical criticism thus does not provide the basis for doing theology but proves that Christianity has been utterly refuted by history. The task is indeed to recover the true character of Christianity, but for Overbeck this means exposing the historical character of Christianity and in doing so show that it has been proved wrong by history. Historical criticism is exclusively a historical task which reveals only that Christianity belongs to the past and should now be left to die in peace.

In his *Jesus' Proclamation of the Kingdom of God* ([1]1892, [2]1900),[179] Johannes Weiss (1863–1914) drew attention to the apocalyptic features of Jesus' preaching concerning the kingdom of God, which liberal Protestant theology had tended to play down or ascribe to outmoded views Jesus had inherited from his Jewish background. Weiss showed that 'Jesus' idea of the Kingdom of God appears to be inextricably involved with a number of eschatological-apocalyptic views', which makes it necessary 'to inquire whether it is really possible for theology to employ the idea of the Kingdom of God in the manner in which it has recently been considered appropriate'. The way in which the concept has been applied in contemporary theology raises the question of 'whether it is not thereby divested of its essential traits and, finally, so modified that only the name still remains the same'.[180] For Jesus, the notion of the kingdom of God was not merely an ethical notion gradually unfolding itself ever more fully in history, but was a transcendental reality which Jesus had expected to break into history and usher in a new age.

Weiss' uncovering of the apocalyptic dimension of Jesus' teaching and self-understanding raised questions concerning the validity of Ritschlian theology. Ritschl's theology had become influential because its strong ethical basis seemed to provide a way of doing theology that avoided the apparently insoluble metaphysical issues that dominated mid-nineteenth century theology, especially kenotic Christology, whose heyday in Germany was between 1840 and 1880. It also seemed to offer a way of understanding Jesus that was free of dogma. The discovery of the apocalyptic character of Jesus' understanding of the kingdom of God, however, placed in doubt the validity of the ethical interpretation of Jesus' life and mission.

The connection between Jesus and apocalyptic was made forcefully by Albert Schweitzer (1875–1965) in his *The Mystery of the Kingdom of God* (1901).[181] He returned to this theme in his *The Quest of the Historical Jesus* (1906). Schweitzer claimed that much of the historical research on Jesus had 'forced him into conformity with our human standards and human psychology'.[182] As evident in the Lives of Jesus written since the 1860s, this research was guilty of watering down Jesus' 'imperative world-denying demands on individuals, so that he did not come into conflict with our ethical ideas, and so to adjust his denial of the world to our acceptance of it'.[183] A genuinely historical–critical assessment of the evidence, however, reveals that Jesus is a much more alien figure than liberal Protestantism recognizes. As Schweitzer puts it, 'theology was forced by genuine history finally to doubt the artificial history with which it had thought to give new life to our Christianity and to yield to the facts, which, as Wrede strikingly said, are sometimes the most radical critics of all'.[184] History, then, itself places in question all efforts to modernize Jesus and make him palatable to modern taste and understanding, and compels theology to find new ways of speaking of Jesus.

A further significant critique of the attempt to recover the historical Jesus was made by Martin Kähler (1835–1912). In his *The So-Called Historical Jesus and the Historic, Biblical Christ* (1892), Kähler argued that it is not the historical Jesus who is significant but the Christ of faith: 'The risen Lord is not the historical Jesus *behind* the Gospels but the Christ of the Apostolic proclamation, of the entire New Testament. The real Christ, that is to say, the living Christ, the Christ who strides through the history of peoples, with whom millions have fellowship in childlike faith, with whom the great heroes of faith have had fellowship in struggle, in response, in victory, and in evangelism – *the real Christ is the Christ who is preached*.'[185] Consequently, we are missing the point if we look only for the historical Jesus in the New Testament and overlook the Christ of faith. Indeed, 'The historical Jesus portrayed by modern authors conceals from us the living Christ.'[186] This insight prompted Kähler to call for opposition to the historical approach to biblical interpretation. 'The task of the dogmatic theologian, in representing simple Christian faith', he writes, is 'to enter the lists against the papacy of historical scholars'.[187] A similar point was made some years later in Pope Pius X's condemnation of Catholic Modernism. The encyclical *Pascendi dominici gregis* (Sept 8, 1907) states: 'When they write history, they bring in no mention of the divinity of Christ; when preaching in churches they firmly profess it . . . Hence they separate theology and pastoral exegesis from scientific and historical exegesis.'[188]

The work of Wilhelm Wrede (1859–1906) was significant for the historical study of the Gospels and the attempt to reconstruct the life of the historical Jesus because it undermined the long-held belief that Mark provided a historically reliable account of the life of Jesus. In his book *The Messianic Secret* (1901), Wrede argued that Mark had not written 'objective' history but had moulded his material according to his theological interests.[189] According to Wrede, it was only after the resurrection that the followers of Jesus became convinced that Jesus was indeed the messiah. This conviction made it necessary to explain why Jesus had not been recognized as the messiah during his lifetime. According to Wrede, the early Church dealt with this problem by inventing the idea of the messianic secret, namely that Jesus deliberately concealed his messiahship during his earthly life. The doctrine of the messianic secret was thus a construction by the Church to explain why Jesus had not spoken of his messiahship during his earthly life. The early Christians then read this notion of the messianic secret back into the accounts of Jesus' life that had been handed down. Mark's Jesus was thus not a purely historical Jesus but was a dogmatic Christ that could not be employed to construct an objective historical account of the life of Jesus.

An influential approach at the end of the nineteenth century and beginning of the twentieth century was the *History of Religions* School, which studied the Bible in the context of its environment and in the light of the contemporary thought-world of the biblical writings. Scholars who adopted this approach attempted to trace the influence of near Eastern religions on the Old Testament and the impact of Hellenism, mystery religions and Gnosticism on the New Testament. This aim of studying the Bible in the context of its contemporary thought-world was stated as early as 1868 by Adolf Hausrath (1837–1909), whose aim was 'to fit New Testament history back again into the contemporary context in which it stood . . . to see it as . . . part of a general historical process'.[190]

One of the principles of the History of Religions approach is to put aside the doctrinal claims of Christianity. This is clearly stated by Otto

Pfleiderer (1839–1908) in his Berlin lectures of 1904 on the origins of Christianity. He comments:

> If Christianity has its origins in the descent of the second person of the Trinity from heaven to earth, in his becoming man in the womb of a Jewish virgin, in his bodily resurrection after his death on the cross and ascension into heaven: then the origin of Christianity is a complete miracle that escapes all historical explanation. For understanding a phenomenon historically means understanding its causal connections with the circumstances obtaining at a particular time and place in human life.[191]

Pfleiderer's aim was to interpret the history of Christianity 'according to the same principles and methods as any other [history]'. This means putting to one side doctrinal presuppositions. The only presuppositions Pfleiderer accepted were 'the analogy of human experience, the likeness of human nature in past and present, the causal connection of all external events and all internal spiritual experience, in brief the regular order of the world, which has determined all human experience for all time'.[192]

One of the most significant practitioners of the History of Religions School was Hermann Gunkel, who commented that 'history-of-religions research must take the fact seriously . . . that *religion*, including *biblical religion*, has its history as does everything human'. Consequently, 'the history-of-religions point of view [consists] . . . in paying constant attention to the historical context of every religious phenomenon'.[193] Of particular importance was Gunkel's *On the History-of-Religions Understanding of the New Testament* (1903). In this work, Gunkel argues that 'in its origin and development the New Testament religion stood at a few even essential points under the decisive influence of foreign religions and that this influence on the men of the New Testament came by way of Judaism'.[194] Gunkel claims that the Judaism of Jesus' day was a syncretistic religion formed from the fusion of the Old Testament and oriental religions. It is in this syncretistic Judaism that Christianity has its origins and from which Christianity gains its syncretistic features, which were in turn fused with elements from Greek thought. According to Gunkel, this syncretistic religion is particularly evident in the writings of Paul and John. Jesus, however, Gunkel claims, was not influenced by syncretistic Judaism. It was only after Jesus' death that oriental religious ideas percolated into the Church and moulded its understanding of Jesus. Such considerations led Gunkel to make a clear distinction between Jesus and early Christianity.

Other important practitioners of the History of Religions approach were Richard Reitzenstein (1861–1931) and Wilhelm Bousset (1865–1920).

Reitzenstein argued for the influence on Christianity of Hellenistic mystery religions. In his *The Hellenistic Mystery Religions* (1910) and *The Iranian Mystery of the Redemption* (1921), Reitzenstein claimed that Christianity had been influenced by a 'Hellenistic myth of a divine man', and that the impact of Hellenistic mysticism is visible in the Gospel of John.[195] In his *Kyrios Christos* (1913), Bousset argued for the influence of Hellenistic religions on early Christianity, and proposed that it was in the Hellenistic Church that worship of Jesus as Lord came about.[196] This worship of Jesus as Lord, he claims, was influenced by pagan worship, which customarily referred to its deities as 'Lord'. The conception of the Lordship of Jesus eventually displaced the earlier Son of Man theology, which had its origins in Jewish eschatology, thereby allowing Jesus to be worshipped as a present reality rather than be conceived of as a future eschatological figure. For Bousset, Paul's doctrine of redemption also had its roots in Hellenism, for Paul's notion of redemption from sin parallels the Hellenistic conception of liberation from the transitoriness of existence. Like Reitzenstein, Bousset held that the Gospel of John had its origins in Hellenistic mystery religions.

Two other important biblical critics who were influenced by the History of Religions approach were Martin Dibelius (1883–1947) and Rudolf Bultmann (1884–1976). Dibelius studied the Pauline conception of a world of spirits in relation to rabbinic literature and in his work on John the Baptist argued that the origins of baptism could be established only on the basis of the history of religions. The early Bultmann examined Paul's style of preaching by comparing his letters with the philosophical sermons of the Cynics and Stoics and the ethical teaching of Epictetus.[197]

The aim of interpreting the New Testament against the background of its cultural, linguistic and social environment brought with it consequences of which the early proponents of the History of Religions School were not fully aware. Firstly, by drawing out the connections between the New Testament and its environment, and by making the New Testament appear to be an instance of the ancient thought-world in which it had come into existence, the History of Religions approach weakened the claims for the uniqueness of the New Testament. Secondly, by interpreting the Bible primarily in terms of its cultural background the Bible was reduced to the status of a record of ancient religiosity. This raised the question of the relevance of this ancient record to modern human beings. Thirdly, the growing awareness of how Christianity was conditioned by contemporary culture and its now outmoded world view widened the gap between between the past and the present.

The result of these developments was a change in the way historical criticism was applied. Rather than forming the basis for the *theological* task of constructing an understanding of the Bible that could speak to modern human beings, it increasingly became a purely descriptive task which aimed to account for the world of the Bible but bracketed out questions concerning its theological significance. According to Krister Stendahl, this descriptive study of the Bible differed from earlier forms of historical criticism in three ways.[198]

Firstly, 'the strait jacket of doctrinaire evolutionism in Darwinistic as well as in Hegelian terms – was considerably loosened'.[199] Although attention was still given to development in the Bible, 'the later stages were not preconceived as progression (e.g., from priest to prophets) or regression (e.g., from Jesus to Paul)'.[200] The aim was to describe each of the biblical periods on its own terms rather than to fit them into a scheme of religious development and progression.

Secondly, 'The question of fact – i.e., whether, e.g., the march through the Red Sea or the resurrection of Jesus had actually taken place as described – was not any more the only one which absorbed the historian.'[201] The focus shifted to what 'the function and the significance of such an item or of such a message as "He is risen" might have been to the writers and readers (or hearers) of the biblical records'.[202] Such concerns lay behind the rise of form criticism and its emphasis on interpreting biblical texts in the light of their *Sitz im Leben* [setting in life].

Thirdly, 'The question about relevance for present-day religion and faith was waived, or consciously kept out of sight.'[203]

The result of this shift of historical criticism towards the descriptive study of the Bible was, Stendahl claims, that the History of Religions School 'had drastically widened the hiatus between our time and that of the Bible, between West and East, between the questions self-evidently raised in modern minds and those presupposed, raised and answered in the Scriptures'.[204] The result of this widening gap between the past and the present was that 'a radically new stage was set for biblical interpretation. The question of meaning was split up into two tenses: "What *did* it mean?" and "What *does* it mean?" '[205] The greater separation between these two questions created by the History of Religions School meant that the descriptive task could be carried out for its own sake and on its own terms. It was possible to focus wholly and exclusively on what the Bible *meant*. This raises acutely the problem, however, of how the Bible can speak today. How is the gulf between what the Bible meant and what it means to be bridged? This issue would become of increasing concern as the twentieth century wore on.

Much of the History of Religions study of the New Testament prior to the First World War had focused on the Hellenistic background of early Christianity and neglected contemporary Judaism. This was rectified by a number of scholars after the First World War, who undertook to trace out the connections and relations between Jesus and early rabbinic Judaism. Scholars such as Paul Billerbeck (1853–1932),[206] Gerhard Kittel (1888–1948)[207] and Julius Schniewind (1883–1948)[208] made use of post-biblical Jewish literature in order to show both similarities and differences between early Christianity and rabbinic Judaism, and thereby to highlight the distinctiveness of Christianity.

Accompanying this concern with Christianity's Jewish background was an interest in the relationship between Judaism and its broader religious environment. This interest led to a concern to identify the oriental roots of the Jewish Gnosticism that allegedly underlies such New Testament writings as Revelation. Bultmann,[209] Walter Bauer (1877–1960),[210] Ernst Lohmeyer (1890–1946)[211] and Hans Windisch (1881–1935)[212] argued that the oriental myth of the heavenly primal man, which is prominent in the Mandaean and Manichaean writings, has coloured Jewish and consequently Christian thinking. The influence of oriental mythology on Christianity was, however, denied by Karl Holl (1866–1926), who argued that Jesus' radically new message concerning God can be attributed to Jesus' own innovation and thus requires no recourse to explanation by external sources.[213]

The concern to identify similarities and differences between Christianity and its religious environment led Gerhard Kittel (1888–1948) in the 1930s to begin work on the *Theological Dictionary of the New Testament*.[214] This multi-volume work discussed New Testament terms by examining not only a word's use in the New Testament, but also the term's equivalent in the Old Testament, early Judaism and in Greek and Hellenistic usage.

The First World War had a significant impact upon the understanding of the Bible. The collapse of pre-war optimism and belief in human progress gave way to a more pessimistic spirit that created the context for a return to more overtly theological approaches to the interpretation of the Bible. This did not mean, however, that pre-war trends in biblical scholarship ceased after 1918. On the contrary, many of them continued to be developed and refined. They would, however, be supplemented by a renewed and vigorous concern for a *theological* interpretation of the New Testament. The key figure in the call for a specifically theological interpretation of the Bible was the Swiss Reformed theologian Karl Barth (1886–1968). It was above all the publication of his *The Epistle to the Romans* in 1919 and the second revised edition of 1922 that placed the issue of theological interpretation on the agenda.[215] Barth called for historical criticism to be placed at the service of theology and to go beyond mere historical investigation. Barth was not hostile to historical criticism, as is sometimes claimed, but wished to make clear what he believed to be its proper use. Historical criticism has its place, for the Bible is a human book. But this is not the whole story, for through the human words of the Bible speaks the Divine Word. Therefore biblical interpretation should not stop with historical problems, but go beyond them to elucidate the divine revelation present in the biblical texts.

These views led Barth to regard historical criticism as an introductory discipline that prepared the way for genuine theological interpretation.

The task of the interpreter of the Bible is to see beyond history in order to enter the spirit of the Bible. In pursuit of this aim, Barth interpreted the Epistle to the Romans not according to its historical context but in terms of its message for human beings *today*. Barth, however, did not develop a coherent method of interpretation. His emphasis on revelation and his suspicion of historical criticism hindered him from developing a method that both took the historical nature of the biblical texts seriously and yet allowed the theological significance of these texts to become apparent.

Attempts at providing the basis for a theological interpretation of the Bible were made by a number of scholars. Karl Girgensohn (1875–1925) addressed the problem by arguing that historical interpretation should be accompanied by what he termed 'pneumatic exegesis', a type of interpretation which focuses on the Bible as Holy Scripture and on the meaning of the Bible for faith and the individual's salvation.[216] This distinction between two types or levels of interpretation enables the interpreter to transcend the merely historical and penetrate to the spiritual core of Scripture.

Like Barth, Bultmann was concerned to recover the Divine Word present in the Bible. For Bultmann, this had to be recovered in a way that was intelligible to modern human beings. Bultmann attempted to deal with the problem of the relation between historical and theological interpretation by arguing that historical criticism is a *theological* activity. For Bultmann, historical criticism allows us to understand the Word that Scripture contains,[217] for it enables us to penetrate behind the historically and culturally conditioned thought-world of the New Testament to its underlying message. Of particular importance is Bultmann's notion of 'demythologization', which is the attempt to penetrate through the mythological language of the Bible to the existential meaning of the text. In order to uncover this existential meaning, i.e. the meaning the biblical texts have for the life of the individual human being, Bultmann drew extensively on Heidegger's existential philosophy. If we remain satisfied with a purely historical exposition of the meaning of Scripture, Bultmann argues, we have failed to carry through our historical research properly, for true understanding means conducting a dialogue with history. It means recognizing that history has a claim on us and has something new to say to us. This entails being open to the existential possibilities that the text contains and considering them as possibilities for our own lives. By this means Bultmann was able to achieve a synthesis of historical criticism and the theological interpretation of the New Testament.

Its combination of detailed philological and historical analysis with theological interpretation made Bultmann's exegesis influential in the 1950s and 1960s. During this period, however, developments took place which challenged Bultmann's approach and would lead ultimately to the development of such new approaches as the New Hermeneutic and the new quest of the historical Jesus.

The New Hermeneutic builds on insights from Bultmann, Dilthey and Heidegger. Two important figures in the New Hermeneutic were Ernst Fuchs (1903–1983) and Gerhard Ebeling (1912–2001). In his *Studies of the Historical Jesus* (1960),[218] Fuchs argued that the correct interpretation of Scripture entails the proclamation of the Word of God, with the aim of awakening faith in the hearer. Thereby the language of Scripture becomes a 'language occurrence' (*Sprachereignis*). In his *The Nature of Faith* (1959),[219] Ebeling speaks of the proclamation of Scripture as a 'word event' (*Wortgeschehen*) that takes place here and now in evoking faith in the hearers of God's Word.[220] James M. Robinson played an important role in introducing the New Hermeneutic into American theology.[221]

The new quest of the historical Jesus was in part a reaction to Bultmann's historical scepticism and to his attempt to cut loose the significance of the Gospel from its historical moorings. For Bultmann, if faith is dependent on history, then faith becomes subordinate to historical research and may therefore be undermined by future historical discoveries. Furthermore, if faith is dependent on history, it jeopardizes the doctrine of justification by faith. To rely on history is a form of works-righteousness, for dependence on history is parallel to relying on doing good works as the basis for one's relationship with God. If history is given too much prominence, then our God-relationship is no longer a free gift graciously bestowed upon us by God, but is dependent on the work of the historian. Bultmann thus sees the historical scepticism arising from his application of the historical–critical method not as undermining faith, but as liberating it from its historical dependency.

Those engaged in the new quest of the historical Jesus, however, were concerned that Bultmann's approach ultimately undermined Jesus' significance for faith. Why is Jesus necessary for the existential decision that constitutes faith? Why could this role not be performed by some other figure? A further problem is that Bultmann's insistence on the importance of the crucified Jesus would seem to be inconsistent with his insistence on the insignificance of history for faith. The result of these criticisms is that some of Bultmann's own disciples attempted to close over the division between the Christ of faith and the Jesus of history opened up by Bultmann. An important impulse in prompting the new quest was Käsemann's lecture on 'The Problem of the Historical Jesus' at a student reunion in 1953 at Marburg, in which he argued that a grounding of faith in the historical Jesus was necessary to avoid docetism.[222] This initiated a debate that has come to be known as the 'new quest' or 'second quest' of the historical Jesus, the major contributors to which were Günther Bornkamm (1905–1990),[223] Ernst Fuchs,[224] Ebeling,[225] Hans Conzelmann (1915–1989)[226] and in the English-speaking world James M. Robinson.[227]

Historical criticism and Roman Catholicism

The Roman Catholic Church resisted historical criticism until the twentieth century. The possibility of adopting a historical approach to the Bible was ruled out at the Council of Trent in 1546, which affirmed the Church as the only legitimate interpreter of the Bible and fixed the Vulgate as the authoritative text of the Bible. The Council decreed:

> Furthermore, to restrain irresponsible minds, [the Church] decrees that no one, relying on his own prudence, twist Holy Scripture in matters of faith and practice that pertain to the building up of Christian doctrine, according to his own mind, contrary to the meaning that holy mother the Church has held and holds – since it belongs to her to judge the true meaning and interpretation of Holy Scripture – and that no one dare to interpret the Scripture in a way contrary to the unanimous consensus of the Fathers, even though such interpretations not be intended for publication.[228]

This decision was reiterated at the First Vatican Council in 1869–1870,[229] where the proclamation of the doctrine of papal infallibility left even less room for Roman Catholic scholars to engage in historical criticism.

Despite the Church's condemnation, there were some attempts by Roman Catholic scholars to apply historical criticism to the Bible. Richard Simon (1638–1712), a member of the French Oratory, made use of a form of historical criticism to expose the inadequacies of Protestantism and to affirm the essential role of the Church in guaranteeing the right understanding of Scripture. Simon aimed to undermine Protestantism by showing the untenability of the central Protestant principle of *sola scriptura*. The sheer diversity of the biblical writings means that relying solely on Scripture leads to a variety of different interpretations, many of which are incompatible with each other and with the Christian faith. Consequently, the interpretation of the Bible needs the guidance of the Church in order to determine which readings of Scripture are correct. Simon, then, employed a form of biblical criticism in order to critique the Protestant doctrine of the clarity of Scripture and the claim that Scripture alone is sufficient for faith.[230] Despite this pro-Roman Catholic aim, however, Simon's critical approach to the Bible led to his expulsion from the Oratory and to the condemnation of his writings.

Over 200 years later, a similar fate awaited the Catholic Modernists Alfred Loisy (1857–1940) and George Tyrell (1861–1909). On 3 July 1907, Pius X condemned historical criticism of the Bible in his decree *Lamentibili*,[231] and on 8 September 1907 issued his encyclical *Pascendi*

Dominici Gregis, which proscribed 'the doctrines of the modernists'.[232] In the mid-twentieth century, however, the Roman Catholic Church shifted to a more positive view of historical criticism. In 1943 historical–critical exegesis was officially recognized as a legitimate form of biblical interpretation by Pope Pius XII in his encyclical *Divino afflante Spiritu*.[233] In 1964 the Pontifical Biblical Commission confirmed the validity of historical criticism in its *Instruction on the Historical Truth of the Gospels* (21 April 1964).[234] This more positive appreciation of historical criticism was confirmed by the Second Vatican Council (1962–1965). The Constitution on the Word of God, Twelfth Article, affirmed the importance of research into the original intention of the biblical texts and their authors as 'preparatory study' in the understanding of the Church's doctrine. The article states:

> It is the task of exegetes to work according to these rules toward a better understanding and explanation of the meaning of sacred Scripture, so that through preparatory study the judgment of the Church may mature. For all of what has been said about the way of interpreting Scripture is subject finally to the judgment of the Church, which carries out the divine commission and ministry of guarding and interpreting the word of God.[235]

Historical criticism remains subject to the authority of the Church, but the Church is more positively disposed towards its results in so far as these are compatible and can integrated with and contribute to the understanding of doctrine. This acceptance of historical criticism was reiterated on 23 April 1993, when the Pontifical Biblical Institute presented to Pope John Paul II a report entitled *The Interpretation of the Bible in the Church*.[236] The result of the shift in attitude towards historical criticism on the part of the Roman Catholic Church has been that historical criticism is no longer an exclusively Protestant discipline. As a result, there have been some significant Roman Catholic contributors to biblical scholarship, notably Rudolf Schnackenburg (1914–2002), Raymond Brown (1928–1998) and Joseph A. Fitzmyer (b. 1938).[237]

The late twentieth and early twenty-first centuries: the crisis of historical criticism?

Since the 1970s there has been increasing critique of historical criticism. For Fernando Segovia, historical criticism dominated the first three-quarters of the twentieth century, but has been 'in broad retreat during its last quarter'.[238] Writing in 2000 Segovia claimed that in the United States the decline of the historical–critical method was well advanced and that although it continued to exercise dominance in Europe, even here 'dangerous cracks' were beginning to appear. As evidence for these cracks, Segovia points to Brill's launching in 1993 of a new journal entitled *Biblical Interpretation: A Journal of Contemporary Approaches*, an outlet for new, alternative methods of interpretation.[239] The growing awareness of the threat to the dominance of the historical–critical method can be seen in two works published in the mid-1970s. In his *Historical Criticism and Theological Interpretation of Scripture*, first published in Germany in 1975, Peter Stuhlmacher observed that although the historical–critical method has found acceptance in Roman Catholicism, 'the Protestant exegete who labours in historical–critical fashion today sees himself involved in a war on many fronts'.[240] These fronts he identifies as the profound mistrust of historical criticism in fundamentalist and Pietist circles, the call for the 'transfer of the once radical historical criticism to a socio-critical political hermeneutic', and the attempts at mediation of a third diffuse and disunited group occupying the middle ground between these two extremes.[241] The result of these pressures is that the relevance of historical criticism 'is in part subject to serious doubt in theological and ecclesiastical circles'.[242] In 1978 the American scholar Norman R. Petersen similarly noted that the mood in biblical scholarship was shifting. In his *Literary Criticism for New Testament Critics* (1978) he drew attention to the beginnings of 'a process of potentially revolutionary change', which placed in question the future of the historical–critical method.[243]

The alleged crisis of the historical–critical method is due to two major developments. Firstly, there was in the late twentieth century an increasing shift away from historical interpretation towards literary approaches to the Bible. According to Segovia, these new literary approaches 'first began to dislodge traditional historical criticism from its position of dominance in the 1970s, rapidly establishing itself as a solid alternative through the 1980s and into the 1990s'.[244] The rise of the 'New Criticism' placed in question the way historical critics handle texts and their identification of textual meaning with its original, historical or intended meaning, while postmodernist approaches raised doubts about the very concept of 'meaning'. These developments have been accompanied by a shift to the *reader* in the process of interpretation, which has resulted in greater consciousness of the role played by the reader in the creation of meaning. Readers are much more than merely excavators of a meaning supposedly buried in the text, but are themselves involved in the production of a text's meaning. Meaning arises through the reader's creative interaction with the text and cannot be prescribed by the imposition of a supposedly objective method. From the perspective of modern literary theory, historical criticism's attempt to identify an 'original', 'historical' and 'literal' sense of scripture is based on a naive understanding of texts. The second factor in the crisis of historical criticism is that the development of new literary approaches to the Bible has been accompanied by a critique of the presuppositions of historical criticism. This criticism has come above all from liberation and feminist theologians, who see historical criticism as another example of the Western, patriarchal marginalization of minority groups. Far from being an impartial, neutral, 'scientific' approach to the Bible, the historical–critical method is in reality the affirmation of the Western male's interests. All readers of the Bible are situated in a specific social, political, economic and religious context, which affects the way they receive and interpret the Bible. This means that no interpretation of the Bible is free of ideological influence. Each act of interpretation is an ideological and political act. It is necessary that readers become aware of this and factor it into their interpretation of the Bible. The failure of historical critics to recognize that their own historical and social situation influences their reading of the texts means that they unconsciously read their own political, ideological and class interests into the texts they claim to be interpreting scientifically and objectively. This insight extends the notion of interpretation in two ways. Firstly, it means becoming attentive to the way ideology and political concerns have shaped the biblical texts. Secondly, it means extending criticism to biblical interpretation itself and bringing to the fore how ideological concerns have influenced acts of interpretation, particularly the way they have been employed in support of oppression. On these grounds Elisabeth Schüssler Fiorenza has called for biblical scholarship to 'reconceptualize . . . its task and self-understanding as engaged rhetoric rooted in a particular-historical situation'.[245] There is need for 'a paradigm-shift in the conceptualization of biblical studies from a scientistic to a rhetorical genre, from an objectivist-detached to a participatory ethos of engagement'.[246] This means that biblical interpretation needs to be grounded in an *ethics* of interpretation. In her 'Ethics of Biblical Interpretation', Schüssler Fiorenza calls for a *double ethics* that takes into account the social location of the interpreter and the plurality of textual meaning. This double ethics comprises 'an ethics of historical reading' and 'an ethics of accountability'. For Schüssler Fiorenza, 'An *ethics of historical reading* changes the task of interpretation from finding out "what the text meant" to the question of what kind of readings can do justice in its historical contexts',[247] while 'an *ethics of accountability* . . . stands responsible not only for the choice of theoretical interpretive models but also for the ethical consequences of the biblical text and its meanings'.[248] The failure of historical criticism to take into account its ethical consequences and its impact on those outside the privileged scholarly guild of white, Western males undermines its claim to be a universal, objective and neutral way of reading the Bible.

The ethical interpretation of the Bible means integrating the 'other' into the act of interpretation, which entails becoming attentive to the voices of the minorities both in the texts themselves and in contemporary society. Segovia describes the recovery of minority voices as the *liberation* and *decolonialization* of biblical studies. In the last decades of the twentieth century, he observes, 'the colonial powers of the Northern Hemisphere have lost their sociopolitical grip – though by no means their socioeconomic grip – on the colonized peoples of the Southern Hemisphere'.[249] There is, he claims, 'an analogous process at work in the classical theological disciplines, including biblical criticism', which is now undergoing 'a process of liberation and decolonization, away from the Eurocentric moorings and concerns of the discipline, not in complete abandonment of such discourse but in search of other discourses heretofore bypassed and ignored'.[250]

As a metaphor for the new situation that has arisen as a result of these developments Segovia draws on the description in Acts of the Apostles of men and women of every nationality speaking in tongues when filled with the Holy Spirit at Pentecost (Acts 2.4–5). According to Segovia, 'The result of such "speaking in tongues" is no longer a discourse controlled by the center . . . but a discourse with no center or with many centers.'[251] Segovia speaks of 'the state of anomie – permanent anomie, perhaps – that has come to characterize the discipline at this critical though enormously creative juncture in its life'.[252] The result, he claims, has been the end of the dominance of the historical–critical method.

Defenders of historical criticism, however, argue that its critics make too radical a break between the historical–critical method and the forms of interpretation employed in the last decades of the twentieth century and first decades of the twenty-first century. Writing in 1985, Edgar McKnight argued: 'A literary approach to the Bible has grown logically out of the recent history of biblical criticism.'[253] In his *The Bible and the Reader* he attempts to show 'how literary criticism may be grafted onto the historical approach',[254] and argues that, 'careful attention to the nature of the biblical text has caused scholars to see the necessity of genuine literary criticism to complete the historical task'.[255] For McKnight, then, literary approaches to interpreting the Bible do not undermine or replace historical criticism, but rather supplement and correct it, and supply a further set of tools to achieve the historical critic's aim of doing justice to the text. Odil Steck makes a similar point, arguing that some of the new methods can be integrated into historical criticism and claiming that feminist and sociohistorical questions 'can find their place entirely within the frame of the existing methodological perspectives'.[256] Heikki Räisänen likewise sees postcolonial and feminist readings of the Bible as 'a welcome broadening of the (historical-) critical enterprise' and stresses 'the continuity of the liberationist approach with the classical critical paradigm, of which historical criticism should be seen as a part'.[257] Schüssler Fiorenza, however, holds that the lecture in which Räisänen argued this point was 'a subtle attempt by an esteemed colleague to safeguard the center which he rhetorically marked as historical criticism and to misrepresent the margins'.[258] His stress on the continuity of the liberationist approach with the classical critical paradigm 'makes it clear that the center not only seeks to incorporate and swallow up approaches different from its own but also that it does so by setting the terms under which they can be accommodated'.[259]

As a result of these developments biblical interpretation has tended since the late 1960s and early 1970s to move in two distinct directions.[260] Firstly, there has been an explosion of new ways of reading the Bible. On the one hand, a plethora of new literary approaches has entered the arena such as narrative criticism, structuralism, rhetorical criticism, psychological criticism, reader-response criticism and deconstructionism. On the other hand, there has been a growth in liberationist methods of interpretation such as Marxist or materialist interpretation, liberation theology, feminist, gay and lesbian readings of the Bible.

Secondly, there has been a renaissance of History of Religions approaches to the study of the Bible, and the attempt to correct the alleged excesses of previous generations of historical–critical interpretation. The discovery of the Nag Hammadi Library in 1945 and the Dead Sea Scrolls in 1947 as well as the application of anthropological and social-scientific methods of interpretation have provided new insights and given fresh impetus to attempts to interpret the Bible in terms of its contemporary thought-world.[261] The application of sociology, which Rogerson describes as 'an extension and refinement of form-critical work begun by Gunkel and Gressmann',[262] combined with insights from liberation theology, has led to studies of class conflict in ancient Israelite society.[263] In Old Testament studies, the application of sociological and anthropological insights bore fruit in John Rogerson's *Anthropology and the Old Testament* (1978), Frank Crüsemann's *Resistance against the Kingdom* (1978) and Norman K. Gottwald's *The Tribes of Yahweh* (1979), while in the study of the New Testament there have been sociological studies of early Christianity by Gerd Theissen,[264] Wayne Meeks,[265] Bruce Malina[266] and others. The problem of the sources of the Pentateuch has also continued to exercise the minds of some Old Testament scholars, as is evident from Blum's *Studies on the Composition of the Pentateuch* (1990).

In New Testament studies, the Jewish background of Paul has been a major concern and has led to publications by E. P. Sanders,[267] Heikki Räisänen,[268] Francis Watson[269] and others. Research has continued into the historical Jesus and has led to what is sometimes called the 'third quest of the historical Jesus'. The 'second quest' ebbed in German scholarship during the 1960s, but interest in the historical Jesus continued to flourish in English-language scholarship, leading in 1985 to the founding of the controversial Jesus Seminar by John Dominic Crossan and Robert Funk. The result of the 'third quest' has been the publication of several important studies of the historical Jesus since the 1970s, notably those of E. P. Sanders,[270] Geza Vermes,[271] Gerd Theissen,[272] John Dominic Crossan,[273] Raymond Brown,[274] N. T. Wright,[275] John P. Meier,[276] J. D. G. Dunn,[277] Richard Bauckham[278] and Dale C. Allison,[279] to name but a few.

Historical criticism has continued to be employed even by those who have been critical of it. Despite the reservations of James A. Sanders and Brevard Childs concerning the way historical criticism has been applied, they do not reject it outright but subordinate it to the needs of faith communities.[280] Furthermore, the 'canonical criticism' or 'canonical analysis' practised by Sanders and Childs can be read as an extension of redaction criticism, for like redaction criticism canonical analysis is concerned with how units of tradition were combined into larger wholes. The difference between canonical analysis and redaction criticism is that the former is interested in how these larger wholes became Scripture and how they function as canonical texts in faith communities.

Similarly, feminist theologians have drawn on historical criticism to recover women's voices in the Bible, which had been overlooked by male scholars, while liberation theologians have employed historical–critical methods to highlight the Bible's opposition to oppression and its power to liberate the poor and downtrodden. It is thus questionable whether historical criticism is in crisis. It would arguably be more accurate to claim that classical historical criticism has been expanded, corrected and complemented by the introduction of new methods.

The current state of biblical studies is thus highly diverse. Biblical scholarship is divided into various camps. One camp comprises those who continue to use historical methods to interpret the Bible. Another camp consists of those who draw on various forms of literary theory. A third camp employs liberation theology, feminism and gender theory as hermeneutical keys for unlocking the meaning of Scripture. These different emphases in biblical studies are not mutually exclusive, of course, and many scholars combine different aspects of the various approaches in their study of the Bible. The current situation in biblical studies is thus arguably a fruitful one in which new voices are being heard and new insights acquired into the meaning of the Bible.

CHAPTER THREE

Textual Criticism

Strictly speaking, textual criticism (also known as lower criticism) is not a method or a theory of interpretation, but is concerned with providing the foundation upon which interpretation can take place.[1] The interpreter obviously needs a text to interpret, and the task of the textual critic is to ensure that the interpreter has an authentic and accurate text to work with. The purpose of textual criticism is to establish as far as possible the original wording of the text.

The problem that makes textual criticism necessary is that we do not possess the original manuscripts or 'autographs' of the biblical writings. Most of the writings of the Christian Bible were probably composed by the end of the first century CE, but we do not have any manuscripts that date back to that period. So the present text of our Bible is based not on the originals but on the copies that have come down to us. These copies, however, are not identical. They contain variations in their wording and some copies contain passages absent from other copies of the same text. These variations have arisen through the process of copying the biblical writings. The books of the Bible were written in an age long before the invention of the printing press and it was only with the advent of printing that it became possible to reproduce texts to a very high level of accuracy. Even in printed books, however, mistakes can creep in, and we sometimes discover typographical errors and omissions despite copy-editing, proof-reading and other checks to which printed books are subjected. In the ancient world, the opportunity for mistakes to creep into texts was still greater. Manuscripts were laboriously copied out by hand and a long process of hand-copying lies behind the texts as we now have them. What we have are copies of copies of copies of the original manuscripts of the Bible. Even the oldest of the manuscripts that have come down to us are copies of much earlier documents.

The result of this long process of copying manuscripts by hand is that there exists a large number of manuscripts of the biblical writings, none of which is identical in all respects with the others. Many variations are trivial and do not affect the meaning of the text. Such variations are differences in spelling or the omission of words and sometimes even whole verses by careless copyists, which can usually be easily corrected. But some variations are significant and may have important exegetical and theological consequences. An example of a significant variation is the ending of Mark's Gospel. Some manuscripts end at Mark 16.8 with the statement that the women were afraid when they discovered that Jesus' tomb was empty. Other manuscripts, however, include a description of Jesus' resurrection appearances and a brief account of his ascension (Mark 16.9–20). Other important variations in the New Testament are the story of the woman taken in adultery (John 7.53–8.11), which does not appear in the earliest manuscripts of John's Gospel, and the so-called 'Johannine comma' (1 John 5.7–8), which is the only passage in the entire New Testament that overtly affirms the orthodox doctrine of the Trinity. These variations raise the question of which versions are the most original and authentic – those which contain these disputed passages or those which do not have them. It is this that makes textual criticism necessary. The task of the textual critic is to sift through the manuscripts that have come down to us and to attempt to establish which reading of a disputed text is most likely to be the original.

A brief history of textual criticism

The reliability and trustworthiness of their scriptures has naturally been of concern to both Jewish and Christian scholars. For these reasons, fore-runners of textual criticism can be found in both early Rabbinic Judaism and in the early Church.

The history of the textual criticism of the Old Testament

It was Jewish scholars who were responsible for transmitting the Hebrew Bible, i.e. the Hebrew text of the Old Testament. The Old Testament of the early Church was the Septuagint, a set of early Greek translations of the Hebrew Bible, but one which included texts not contained in the Hebrew original. It was only with the Reformation that Christian scholars came to take the *Hebrew* text as the basis for their interpretation of the Old Testament. The Lutheran doctrine of *sola scriptura*, namely that Scripture alone is the authoritative source of doctrine, led to an interest among Protestant scholars in the Hebrew original of the Old Testament.

A form of textual criticism was practised by the Rabbis, who were concerned to safeguard the purity of the Hebrew Bible. This prompted them to address the problem of variant readings in the manuscripts available to them and from c. 100 CE they embarked on the task of producing a standard version of the Hebrew Bible. Their work can be regarded as an early attempt at textual criticism, although they followed different principles from those of modern text critics in their formation of a standard text of the Bible. They were above all concerned with editing the text in the light of the traditions they had received from previous generations of Rabbis. It is because of the central role played by tradition in their work that these scholars have come to be known as 'Masoretes', a term derived from the Hebrew *māsōrāh* or 'tradition'. The Hebrew text that the Masoretes produced has come to be known as the 'Masoretic' text, a text which had stabilized probably by the end of the second century CE and which had reached its final form by c. 1000 CE. Thereafter the task became that of transmitting the standard text as accurately as possible.

Of particular importance were the Tiberian Masoretes. The dominance of Christianity in Palestine prompted Jewish scholars to seek more favourable conditions for their work in Babylon, where several academies for the study of the Hebrew Bible came into existence between the third and the tenth centuries. The Islamic conquest of Palestine in 638, however, resulted in greater freedom for the Jewish population than they had enjoyed under Christian rule and led to the establishment of schools of Jewish learning, the chief of which was that of the city of Tiberias.[2] It was the Tiberian Masoretes who developed what was to become the standard system for writing vowels in Hebrew and it was their work on the text of the Hebrew Bible that would form the basis for subsequent editions.[3] The separation of the Tiberian Masoretes from Babylon, however, led to the development of divergences in the transmission of the Hebrew Bible. These are noted in the critical apparatus of the *Biblia Hebraica Stuttgartensia* by the abbreviation 'Occ', i.e. 'occidental', which refers to the Western Masoretes of Tiberias, and 'Or', i.e. 'oriental', which refers to the Eastern Masoretes of Babylon.[4]

The production of the Masoretic text led to other versions of the Hebrew Bible being suppressed, the consequence of which was that the Masoretic edition of the Hebrew Bible established itself as the standard Hebrew Bible and became the basis for subsequent editions.

Modern textual criticism of the Hebrew Bible was prompted by several factors. Firstly, despite the care taken in compiling the Masoretic text, centuries of copying and recopying have led to variant readings. It thus became necessary to compare the different versions of the text in order to establish which readings are the most authentic. Secondly, the discovery of manuscripts of the Hebrew Bible in the Cairo Genizah and in the caves near the Dead Sea has provided scholars with much earlier manuscripts than those that had previously been available.

Until the discovery of the Dead Sea Scrolls, the oldest manuscripts of the Hebrew Bible dated from the tenth century. In their 1884 preface to the Old Testament in the Revised Version of the Bible, the revisers remark in a footnote that 'the earliest MS. of which the age is certainly known bears the date A.D. 916'. Other important manuscripts of the Hebrew Bible are held in the Leningrad collection, which contains a codex of the entire Hebrew Bible that can be dated back to the early eleventh century. It was upon this text that the third edition of Kittel's critical edition (1929–1937) of the Hebrew Bible and the *Biblia Hebraica Stuttgartensia* (1968–1977) were based. Another codex which originally contained the entire Hebrew Bible, but which has now lost most of the Torah, is the Aleppo Codex, which dates from c. 925 CE. This is the text upon which the Hebrew University Bible Project is based. Two other manuscripts worthy of note are Heb. 24,5702 (formerly known as Sassoon 507), housed in the National and University Library of Jerusalem, which contains most of the Torah, and Sassoon 1053, which contains the bulk of the Hebrew Bible. The manuscript evidence from the twelfth century onwards is much more extensive. These manuscripts, which are called 'medieval', vary little from their tenth- and eleventh-century predecessors.

The discovery of the Cairo Genizah has added to the manuscript evidence for the transmission of the Hebrew Bible by providing insight into the state of the Hebrew Bible prior to 900.[5] When texts became worn through age they were buried in consecrated ground. Before their interment, the texts were stored in a 'genizah' or 'hiding place', which was a room in the synagogue set aside for the storage of documents that were no longer in use. A synagogue in Cairo, however, failed over a period of several hundred years to inter the documents stored in its genizah. These documents were discovered in the second half of the nineteenth century and have become an important source of knowledge for the text of the Hebrew Bible. The Cairo Genizah contains texts predating the other extant manuscripts of the Hebrew Bible, including the Masoretic edition, and provides insights into the state and transmission of the Hebrew Bible prior to the tenth-century manuscripts that had previously been the earliest witnesses to the text of the Hebrew Bible.

The discovery of the Dead Sea Scrolls in 1947 pushed back the manuscript record of the Hebrew Bible still further. In the caves near the Dead Sea where the Qumran community had concealed the scrolls, manuscripts of all the books of the Hebrew Bible apart from Chronicles and Esther were discovered, providing witnesses to the state of the text that go back as far as the second century BCE.[6] Of particular interest is the fact that the Dead Sea Scrolls provide evidence of the existence of traditions of transmission different from that of the Masoretic text. While 60 per cent of the manuscripts seem to be closely related to the Masoretic tradition and are considered to be 'proto-Masoretic' or 'proto-Rabbinic' texts,[7] other texts bear a closer resemblance to the textual traditions upon which the Septuagint and the Samaritan Pentateuch appear to be based.[8] In addition, there is a group of what Tov has called non-aligned manuscripts, which seem to be independent of the other witnesses.[9] Hendel, however, has suggested that Tov's terminology is best replaced by positing two groups, which he names 'texts of unknown affiliation' and 'texts of mixed affiliation'.[10] The discovery of the Scrolls has thus made clear that the Masoretic text was only one of several versions of the books of the Hebrew Bible in circulation in antiquity and that rival versions should not be downgraded to the level of corrupt or unreliable witnesses.[11]

The Dead Sea Scrolls are also important for placing in question the conventional understanding of textual criticism and the notion of the 'original text'. Traditional textual criticism is based on the assumption that the scribes were mere copyists and not creative contributors to textual transmission. Textual variants were thus attributed to scribal error. The evidence from Qumran, however, indicates that this does a severe injustice to the scribes and fails to take into account their role as co-authors of the Hebrew Bible. According to Eugene Ulrich, it is evident from Qumran that 'the scribes and their predecessors were at work along two lines. First, they often simply copied the individual books of the Scriptures as exactly as humanly possible. But secondly, sometimes the scribes intentionally inserted new material that helped interpret or highlight for their contemporary congregation in a new situation the relevance of the traditional text'.[12] Ulrich describes this process as 'composition-by-stages',[13] in which the scribe is 'a minor partner in the creative literary process'.[14] Such scribal intervention is not a corruption but an enrichment of the text and an important contribution to handing on the tradition the scribes had inherited. For Ulrich, this scribal co-composition is evidence of a 'period of pluriformity in the biblical text', which probably came to an end in the second half of the first century CE.[15] This pluriformity means that we should conceive of the biblical writings not in terms of an 'original text' written by a single author, but see textual formation as an organic development in which a text has been gradually built up through contributions from several generations of scribes. The organic character of the composition of many of the writings of the Hebrew Bible places in question the distinction made between 'lower criticism' and 'higher criticism', since the scribal contribution to the development of the text blurs the division between composition and copying. It also changes the status of textual variants. As George Brooke points out, 'in place of the old assumption of the text critics on the low road [i.e. lower criticism] that all variants should be understood as errors until shown otherwise, the dominant assumption should be that scribes have played an active part in their enterprise'.[16]

It is not only the texts from the Cairo Genizah and the Dead Sea that provide sources for the work of the textual critic of the Hebrew Bible. Manuscripts dating from the Bar-Kochba rebellion of 135 CE have been found near Wadi Murabba'at, which lies to the south of the site at which the Dead Sea Scrolls were discovered. These texts show close parallels with the Masoretic text and are evidence for the increasing dominance of this line of textual transmission. Other important witnesses to the state of the Hebrew text in the early Rabbinic period are provided by quotations of the Hebrew Bible in the Mishnah (c. 200 CE), the Palestinian Gemara (c. 350 CE), the Babylonian Gemara (c. 500 CE), the fragments of Origen's Hexapla (c. 240 CE) and the paraphrases and translations in the Aramaic Targums.

With regard to the Pentateuch, the Samaritan Bible is an important source of information. The Samaritan Bible became known to European scholarship through the discovery of a manuscript of the text by Pietro della Valle in Damascus in 1616. An important question is the date at which the separation and the transmission of the Jewish and Samaritan texts of the Torah began. It might have been as early as the sixth-century BCE, when it is possible that the Samaritan temple at Gerizim was established. If this was the case, then the Samaritan edition may provide evidence for the state of the Torah that predates the Septuagint.

There are 6000 readings in the Samaritan Pentateuch that differ from the Masoretic edition. Nineteen hundred of these are in agreement with the Septuagint.[17] Most of these variations are trivial and do not significantly affect the meaning of the text. The most significant differences can be attributed to the points of contention between the Jews and the Samaritans. The Samaritan version highlights the central role of Shechem and Mt. Gerizim, which were central to Samaritan worship, whereas the Jewish version tends to play down the roles of these two cultic centres. This is evident in the variation of Deut. 12.5 in the two texts. The Masoretic text has Moses speak of 'the place which the LORD your God *will choose* out of all your tribes to receive his name that it may dwell there'. The future tense indicates that the choice of the dwelling place of God's name has not yet been made. For Jewish readers, the passage is a prophecy of the establishment of the temple at Jerusalem. The Samaritan text, on the other hand, uses the *past tense*: 'the place which the LORD your God *has chosen* . . . .' The Samaritan version implies that Moses is referring to Mt. Gerizim, which is stated in Deut. 11.29 as the place where the Israelites are 'to set the blessing' once they have entered Canaan. Furthermore, whereas the Hebrew Bible's version of Deut. 27.4 cites Mt. Ebal at the place where God commands the Israelites to establish a place of worship, in the Samaritan version the reference is to Mt. Gerizim. This alternative reading is incorporated in the Samaritan versions of Exod. 2 and Deut. 5, thereby making clear the Samaritan belief that Moses received the Ten Commandments not on Mt. Sinai but on Mt. Gerizim. The question is whether the Samaritan Pentateuch is a modification of the original text or whether it preserves the earlier reading with the Masoretic text making the adjustment.

Although some of the first European scholars who encountered the Samaritan Pentateuch rated it very highly and sometimes considered it superior to the Masoretic text, most scholars declared it to be inferior to the Masoretic version. Wilhelm Gesenius (1786–1842) held the Samaritan Bible to be of little help in establishing the original text of the Pentateuch, a view which dominated Old Testament textual criticism for the rest of the nineteenth century. In 1915, however, Paul Kahle (1875–1964) argued against Gesenius for a more positive assessment of the variant readings of the Samaritan Bible, which in some cases are to be preferred over those of the Masoretic text.[18] His reason for arriving at this view was the support for the Samaritan readings that seemed to be provided in some apocryphal works, the Septuagint and the New Testament. Further weight was lent to Kahle's evaluation of the Samaritan Bible by the discovery of the Dead Sea Scrolls, some of which support the Samaritan Bible's variant readings against the Masoretic text.

Other sources for the knowledge of the history of the text are the various translations that have been made of the Hebrew Bible. The Septuagint provides evidence for the state of the Hebrew text in the last three centuries before Christ. What is of interest for the study of the transmission of the Hebrew Bible is that the text of the Septuagint frequently agrees with the Samaritan Bible *against* the Masoretic text. This may indicate that the Septuagint was translated from a different version of the Hebrew Bible from that of the Masoretic text. Because it is a *translation*, however, the evidence provided by the Septuagint must be treated with caution. It also suffers from the same text critical problems as other ancient texts, namely that its manuscripts are not the originals but are copies which themselves contain textual variants. Before we can use it as a witness to the Hebrew text, we must therefore establish by means of textual criticism the most reliable form of the Septuagint text. This compounds the difficulty of using the Septuagint as a witness to the state of the Hebrew Bible. Other translations that may provide information about the state of the Hebrew text from which they were translated are the Greek editions of Aquila, Theodotion and Symmachus. The confusion prompted by these multiple Greek translations of the Old Testament and the question of which reflected most accurately the Hebrew original prompted Origen to compose his 'Hexapla'. This enormous work consisted of the Hebrew text, a Greek transliteration and the four Greek translations laid out in parallel columns. Unfortunately, much of this work has been lost, but it marks an important attempt to address the confusion arising from multiple versions of the Old Testament.

Other translations that may shed light on the Hebrew text from which they were made are the *Peshitta*, a Syriac translation of the Old Testament, and various Latin translations such as the *Itala* or *Old Latin*, and the Vulgate. Although the *Itala* contains some preferable readings, caution should be exercised when using it, because it is a 'daughter translation', i.e. a translation made from a translation, namely the Septuagint. The Vulgate is Jerome's translation into Latin of the Hebrew original and thus provides information about the state of the Hebrew text in the fifth century CE. Jerome's references to Old Testament passages in some of his other writings also give us some indication of the Hebrew text with which he was working. He thus provides evidence for the state of the Hebrew Bible several centuries before the completion of the Masoretic edition. Other translations of limited usefulness are the Coptic, Ethiopic, Armenian and Arabic versions, all of which are daughter translations of the Septuagint.

The invention of printing led to the publication of the first printed editions of the Hebrew Bible. In 1477, an edition of the Psalms was published, probably in Bologna. This was followed by publication of the Prophets in Soncino in 1485–1486, the Writings in Naples in 1486–1487 and the Pentateuch in Lisbon in 1491. The first printed edition of the *entire* Hebrew Bible seems to have been published in 1488 in Soncino, which was followed by further editions in Naples in 1491–1493 and Brescia in 1494.[19] In areas which the new technology of printing was slow to reach, scribal copying by hand continued and indeed was still being practised in Yemen until the modern period.[20]

1516–1517 marked the publication of the first of the 'Rabbinic Bibles', Hebrew Bibles consisting not only of the text but also additional material such as Targums and Rabbinic commentaries. This edition, which was edited by Felix Pratensis, a Jewish convert to Christianity, was considered unsatisfactory and was succeeded in 1525 by a new edition edited by Jacob ben Chayyim (c. 1470 to before 1538). Ben Chayyim's edition was, however, based on manuscripts no earlier than the fourteenth century. This edition came to be known as the 'Received Edition' and was the foundation for many subsequent Rabbinic Bibles. It was the text upon which the first (1906) and second editions (1909) of Rudolf Kittel's *Biblia Hebraica* of the Hebrew Bible were based.[21] There are currently three different projects underway to produce new critical editions of the Hebrew Bible: the Hebrew University Bible Project (established in 1955); the *Biblia Hebraica Quinta* (established in 1991), which is intended to replace the *Biblia Hebraica Stuttgartensia*; and the recently founded Oxford Hebrew Bible Project.[22]

The history of the textual criticism of the New Testament

Although a version of the Greek text of the New Testament was published in Spain in 1514, it was the edition published by Erasmus in 1516, which later became known as the *textus receptus* ('the received text'), that gained the wider circulation and consequently had the greater impact.[23] Erasmus' edition, however, was based on inadequate and faulty manuscripts. It was this edition from which vernacular translations such as the King James Bible were made and which remained the standard edition of the Greek New Testament until the eighteenth century. Erasmus and other early editors of the Greek New Testament such as Stephanus (1503–1559) and Theodore Beza (15119–1605), however, had not yet developed a method for deciding between variant readings.[24]

An awareness of what would later be called textual criticism is evident in Spinoza's discussion of the interpretation of Scripture in his *Tractatus Theologico-Politicus*, where he writes that it is important to 'discover whether or not [a biblical book] may have been contaminated by spurious insertions, whether errors have crept in, and whether these have been corrected by experienced and trustworthy scholars'.[25] It is with the French Roman Catholic scholar Richard Simon (1638–1712), however, that we can arguably see the beginnings of the textual criticism of the New Testament, for in his works he addressed the problem of identifying the original form of the New Testament. He did this by comparing variant manuscripts of the New Testament and by studying the comments of the Church Fathers on the biblical text. Despite this employment of critical methods, however, Simon's study of the Bible was motivated by doctrinal considerations, namely his concern to show the untenability of the Protestant principle that Scripture alone was the sufficient source of revelation. He attempted to undermine the principle of *sola scriptura* in two ways. Firstly, he sought to show that the text of the Bible was untrustworthy because its transmission had introduced numerous corruptions, so that the text that has come down to us cannot be that originally penned by the authors of the biblical writings. The unreliability of the text is an indication of the necessity of the tradition of the (Roman Catholic) Church, without which the truth of the Christian faith would have long since been lost. Secondly, Simon attacks the Protestant principle of the perspicuity of Scripture. The variety of views held by Protestants in itself refutes the Protestant claim that Scripture's meaning is plain to the unprejudiced reader. Both points – the unreliability of the transmission of the biblical text and the lack of clarity of the meaning of Scripture – make clear the need for the tradition of the Church in order to guide the reader in the correct understanding of Scripture. Despite his use of critical methods in service of the Roman Catholic Church, Simon was too radical for the Catholic authorities. J. B. Bossuet (1627–1704) endeavoured to destroy Simon's *Critical History of the Old Testament* before its publication and Simon was expelled from the French Oratory.[26] This was a setback from which Catholic exegesis would not recover until the twentieth century.

While Simon was developing his text-critical approach in France, the Anglican theologian John Mill (1645–1707) was busy in England collecting variant editions of the Greek New Testament, which led in 1710 to the publication of his *Greek New Testament with Variant Readings* (1710).[27] The text of the New Testament which Mill published was the *textus receptus*. What is significant about this work is its publication of an apparatus beneath the *textus receptus* of the variant readings found in all the available manuscripts.

Mill's work was important in providing impulses for further study of the text of the Greek New Testament. One of those to take up the challenge was Johann Albrecht Bengel (1687–1752), whose faith in the inspired status of the New Testament had been undermined by the large number of alternative readings he had encountered in Mill's edition of the Greek New Testament. Bengel's studies of the text of the New Testament were undertaken in the hope of restoring his confidence in the divine status of the New Testament.[28] In 1734 he published his edition of the Greek New Testament.[29] Like Mill's edition, this version of the Greek New Testament contained a critical apparatus alerting the reader to alternative readings, which Bengel ordered according to their importance. Bengel's work was also significant for: (1) grouping manuscripts into families; (2) discussing such issues as which reading is most likely to have given rise to the variant readings; (3) and for advancing the principle that 'the more difficult reading is to be preferred to the easier'.[30] Bengel, then, is important for developing rules for classifying and organizing variant readings of the New Testament.

Johann Jakob Wettstein (1693–1754) of Basel was also interested in the text of the Greek New Testament and worked at producing a critical edition of the New Testament. Initially Wettstein seems to have wished to revise the *textus receptus* in the light of what he regarded to be the more authentic readings he had discovered through his study of the manuscript evidence. When this intention became known and sample pages of his new edition of the New Testament became available, he was dismissed from his position as pastor and migrated to Amsterdam. There he published his critical edition of the Greek Testament in 1751–1752.[31] This work comprised the *textus receptus*, which Wettstein was now wary of revising, but was accompanied by critical apparatuses that included not only manuscript evidence for variant readings but also relevant citations from ancient Jewish and classical literature. It was Wettstein who introduced the reference system for manuscripts that is still in use today. Also contained in his edition of the Greek New Testament was an essay 'On the Interpretation of the New Testament', in which Wettstein argued that the New Testament should be interpreted from the perspective of the age in which it was written.

Johann Jakob Griesbach (1745–1812) added further manuscript evidence to the work of Mill and Wettstein and published in 1774–1775 a new edition of the Greek text of the New Testament based on what he considered to be the most authentic readings of the variant manuscripts together with an extensive critical apparatus. Griesbach made a significant contribution to textual criticism in three respects. Firstly, the text of the New Testament which he published was not the *textus receptus*, but a text of his own construction based on what he considered to be the best and most reliable manuscripts. This marked the beginning of the end of the supremacy of the received text. Secondly, in his critical study of the Greek New Testament Griesbach introduced a categorization of the manuscript evidence that has continued to be used up to the present day. Griesbach divided the manuscripts into three major groups, namely what he termed the Alexandrian, Western and Constantinopolitan recensions. Of these he held only the Alexandrian and Western groups to be significant for the textual criticism of the New Testament. Thirdly, in the second edition of his Greek New Testament, Griesbach laid down guidelines for the study of the New Testament that were to be highly influential on subsequent scholarship. He argued that critical study of the New Testament should consist of: (1) establishing which manuscripts provide the most valuable witness to a text; (2) consideration of the internal evidence of a text, e.g. examination of the text's style and context. By these means the original text – or at least a close approximation to it – could be achieved.

Although he did not doubt Griesbach's contribution to the textual criticism of the New Testament, Karl Lachmann (1793–1851) felt that Griesbach had showed too much reverence towards the received text. The correct approach should not be merely to make adjustments to the *textus receptus* where a traditional reading was untenable, but should be to attempt to establish the earliest possible reading on the basis of the most ancient manuscripts. Lachmann, then, set New Testament scholarship on the road to the replacement of the *textus receptus* with a new text based on the oldest manuscripts. This approach led to his publication in 1831 of the first critical edition of the New Testament.[32] In the second edition of this work (published 1842–1850), Lachmann added scholarly apparatus and guidelines on the interpretation of the New Testament.[33] Lachmann's attempt to construct the earliest possible version of the New Testament, however, was hindered by his not having access to the best manuscripts.

The gap in the manuscript evidence was something Constantin von Tischendorf (1815–1874) endeavoured to fill. Tischendorf devoted his life to collating manuscripts of the New Testament and to this end travelled widely throughout Europe and the Middle East. The most famous of the manuscripts Tischendorf uncovered was the Codex Sinaiticus. Tischendorf employed the manuscript evidence he had collected together with the witness provided by the Church Fathers to construct a critical edition of the Greek New Testament (1841),[34] the most important edition of which is the eighth, which he published in three volumes between 1869 and 1872.[35]

In Britain, the two Cambridge scholars, B. F. Westcott and F. J. A. Hort, cooperated to produce a critical edition of the Greek New Testament. Of particular importance was their revival of Griesbach's insight into the necessity of grouping manuscripts into families. Only by such means would it be possible to arrive at an understanding of what constitutes the earliest and most reliable manuscripts. By means of careful examination and grouping of the available manuscripts and by examining the New Testament text cited by the Church Fathers, they arrived at the conclusion that what they termed the 'Syrian text' was an unreliable family of manuscripts. Since Westcott and Hort were able to show that the *textus receptus* belonged to this family of texts, their discovery of the inadequacies of the Syrian text meant that the version of the New Testament that had been in use since Erasmus finally had to be abandoned and replaced with a text based on the best manuscript witnesses. For Westcott and Hort it was above all the Codices Vaticanus and Sinaiticus that provided the most reliable versions of the text of the Greek New Testament. The text they derived from these two manuscripts they named 'neutral', although it is now recognized that this text too is a recension.

In the twentieth century, two significant developments took place in textual criticism. Firstly, on the basis of his text critical work, B. H. Streeter (1874–1937) posited the existence of a fourth important family of manuscripts, namely the Caesarean recension, which was used by Origen in the third century.[36] Secondly, the twentieth century saw the discovery of new manuscripts of the New Testament, which have enabled text critics to trace the transmission of the New Testament text back further than ever before.

The approach currently favoured in modern textual criticism is the 'eclectic' method. This method recognizes that no one manuscript or group of manuscripts fully reproduces the original text of a biblical writing and that each variant reading must be treated on its own merits. This means that the textual critic should choose whichever text critical criteria seem to be most appropriate to the text under discussion. Aland, however, dislikes the term 'eclecticism' and prefers to speak of the 'local-genealogical method'.[37]

There are two types of eclecticism, namely 'rigorous' or 'thoroughgoing' eclecticism and 'general', 'impartial' or 'reasoned' eclecticism. The term 'rigorous eclecticism' refers to textual criticism conducted exclusively on the basis of internal criteria, namely on the basis of the author's style and the sorts of mistakes scribes are prone to make. That is, it is concerned to establish what the author is likely to have written in view of his style of writing and theological interests, and how it may have come about that scribes have altered the author's original text.

'General' or 'reasoned eclecticism', on the other hand, includes not only internal evidence but also *external* evidence in assessing the authenticity of variant readings. The task is to reconstruct the history of each individual variant reading, whereby the 'best manuscript' version is only one of the readings to be taken into account. The change from classic textual criticism, then, is that the 'best manuscript' is not privileged. The status of each variant must be determined on the basis of a whole range of criteria, of which appearance in the 'best manuscript' is only one. It is possible, for example, that internal criteria might lead us to doubt the authenticity of a reading in the best manuscript. This will then lead to the next problem of thinking through why the best manuscript has reproduced what seems to be an inauthentic reading.

In the late twentieth and early twenty-first centuries, developments have taken place that may lead to a revolution in textual criticism. In his study of New Testament textual criticism (2008), D. C. Parker cites four causes for the dramatic changes that have taken place in the quarter century prior to his publication of his book, namely, (1) 'the introduction of the computer'; (2) the insight that 'the examination of manuscripts and of the variant readings which they contain . . . has also a part to play in the study of the development of Christian thought and in the history of exegesis'; (3) 'the publication of new manuscript discoveries continues to challenge traditional views of textual history and of the copying of texts'; (4) 'a number of research tools have been published which place far larger and better resources at the scholar's disposal than were ever available before'.[38] Nevertheless, despite these developments, Parker points out, there is still need for traditional textual criticism, and the following is an attempt to sketch its methods.

The method of textual criticism

Textual criticism has been applied both to the Old Testament and the New Testament. There are, however, differences in the way textual criticism is conducted in relation to these two bodies of literature. Whereas a large number of Greek manuscripts of the New Testament have come down to us, which contain variant readings, the number of available manuscripts of the Old Testament is much smaller and contains fewer variant readings. The limitation of the number of Hebrew manuscripts available means that, unlike his New Testament counterpart, the Old Testament text critic cannot always turn to alternative versions to establish the original reading and meaning of what appear to be faulty passages in the text. Barr points out that the high uniformity of manuscripts of the Hebrew Bible means that textual criticism proceeds along different lines in Old Testament studies from the way it is practised by New Testament scholars. Whereas the point of departure for New Testament textual criticism is the comparison of the versions of a problematic passage in multiple manuscripts, in Old Testament textual criticism such a comparison is usually not possible. Consequently, the starting point is not the comparison of variant readings but a 'difficulty' which the reader encounters in the text, such as when the text does not make sense, contains incorrect grammar or anomalous terminology, contradicts what is said elsewhere in the same work or conflicts with knowledge gleaned from other sources.[39] As Barr puts it, 'With a non-uniform text we may find variant readings, and textual discussion begins from these variant readings, even if all of them "make sense". With a text of high uniformity, however, textual discussion will more frequently begin from the feeling that there is a "difficulty"; the procedure will be more independent of the existence of variant readings, and conjectural emendation will take a larger place in the discussion'.[40] Thus whereas conjectural emendation is not usually necessary in New Testament textual criticism because there are usually variant manuscript readings that can be used to check questionable passages and the faulty transmission of the manuscript that led to such passages coming into existence, in the Old Testament such opportunities are much rarer. Barr points out that, 'it is quite normal experience to find that a reading is almost unanimously supported by Hebrew manuscripts but that scholars turn to emendation to find a text which seems to be viable'.[41] As an example Barr cites Ps. 2.11–12, the Hebrew of which 'reads materially alike in all Hebrew manuscripts'.[42] The literal meaning of the text appears to be, in the Authorized Version's translation, 'Serve the Lord with fear, and rejoice with trembling. Kiss the Son . . .' Because of the strange sense of the passage scholars have argued that some letters of the text have been lost in the process of transmission and have suggested the following emendation: 'Serve the Lord in fear; in trembling kiss his feet'. This emendation makes good sense of the text, but it is not attested in any of the extant manuscripts of the Psalms. Thus in the case of the Old Testament, Barr observes, 'the beginning of a textual discussion arises not primarily from the existence of variant readings but from the perception of difficulties in the Hebrew text'.[43]

To give an indication of the full range of techniques employed by the textual critic we shall focus on the textual criticism of the New Testament, but shall include discussions of the Old Testament where appropriate.

1. List variants with their manuscript support

The first task facing the textual critic is to collect the evidence. There are several sources upon which the construction of the text of the Bible is based, namely manuscripts, translations, Targums and quotations by the Rabbis and Church Fathers.

The manuscripts

Over 5360 New Testament manuscripts have survived, ranging from fragments to collections of the whole of the New Testament. These manuscripts fall into three types.

(a) Papyri

The papyrus is a plant native to southern Europe and North and Central Africa, from which a type of paper can be made. The term 'papyrus' has thus come to designate, firstly, the paper produced from the plant 'papyrus', and secondly, an ancient manuscript written on such paper. Papyrus was cheap, but did not preserve well, particularly in damp climates. It is for this reason that papyri have been found primarily in the dry climate of Egypt.

There are approximately 100 papyri of the New Testament that have come down to us, most of which are mere fragments. One of the oldest of these is P^{52}, a fragment containing John 18.31–33, 37–38, which dates from the first half of the second century. Modern textual criticism designates papyri by the letter P, written in Gothic script, followed by a number. These numbers refer not to the age of the papyrus but to the order in which it was registered. The most important papyri are P^{45} (the Chester-Beatty papyrus), which contains the Gospels; P^{46}, which contains the letters of St. Paul; and P^{47}, which contains the Revelation of St. John. All of these date from sometime in the third century. Also of importance are the well-preserved Bodmer papyri, of which P^{66} (c. 200 CE, containing the Gospel of John) and P^{75} (c. 200 CE, containing Luke and John) are the most important.

(b) Uncials/Majuscules

The bulk of manuscripts are codices made of parchment, which is more enduring but also more expensive than papyrus, and was used by Christian communities when they had grown more affluent. Of particular importance are the 'uncials' or 'majuscules'. These are manuscripts in which the text is written in capital letters, a common practice until the ninth century. The best known codices have traditionally been designated by Latin and Greek letters, and in the case of the Codex Sinaiticus by the Hebrew letter א (aleph). However, a new numeration has been introduced which denotes majuscules by Arabic numerals prefixed by a zero in order to distinguish majuscules from minuscules, which are not prefixed by a zero. That is, majuscules are denoted by 01, 02, 03, etc., whereas minuscules are denoted by 1, 2, 3, etc.

The most important majuscules
א = 01: the Codex Sinaiticus; fourth century CE
A = 02: Codex Alexandrinus; fifth century CE
B = 03: Codex Vaticanus; c. 350 CE
C = 04: Codex Ephraemi rescriptus, fifth century CE

(c) Minuscules

From the ninth century onwards, manuscripts were written in lowercase letters, which were easier to write, and they also saved space. Manuscripts written in lowercase letters have come to be known as 'minuscule manuscripts' or simply as 'minuscules'. Like majuscules, these were written on parchment or vellum. Of the three types of manuscript available, these are the latest and thus would seem to be of limited use in the attempt to construct the earliest possible version of the biblical text. Most minuscules stem from the tenth and eleventh centuries or later, and for this reason are generally not as important as the papyri and majuscules. Nevertheless, they cannot be ruled out of consideration, for it may be the case that they in some instances preserve earlier readings that have been lost or corrupted in the papyri and uncials that have come down to us. There are approximately 3000 minuscules that have survived into the present. The best known is Minuscule 33, the so-called 'queen of the minuscules', the text of which is close to that of the Codex Vaticanus, while Miniscule 1739 is significant for the Pauline epistles. As noted above, in the text critical apparatus miniscules are denoted by Arabic numerals.

Translations

Translations of the Bible may provide information on the state of the biblical text when the translation was made. As mentioned above, early translations of the Hebrew Bible exist in Greek, Latin and several other languages. The same applies to the New Testament, of which translations exist in Latin, Syriac, Coptic, Ethiopic, Armenian, Georgian and Gothic. Some of these translations were made at a date prior to the earliest Greek manuscripts that have come down to us and may thus shed light on the state of the Greek text from which the translation was made. That is, by translating the translations back into Greek, it may be possible to see which reading of a disputed text was current at the time the translation was made. There are, however, problems with the use of translations as a check on Greek manuscripts. Ancient translations suffer from the same problem as all ancient manuscripts, namely, that they are copies of copies of copies. They are thus prone to similar errors of transmission as the manuscripts they are being used to check for faulty transmission. Furthermore, there is the problem of the accuracy of the translation. Is what appears to be a variant reading evidence of a different manuscript tradition or the result of a poor translation or due to the translator merely paraphrasing a passage rather than fully translating it? As Barr points out with regard to the Hebrew Bible, 'The translators may have misunderstood the original Hebrew, so that their version is not a good, but a very bad, guide to what the original text said.'[44]

Quotations by the Rabbis and the Church Fathers

The Rabbis and the Church Fathers frequently quote the Bible and attempts have been made to reconstruct the text of the Bible on the basis of their quotations. Such citations are important in providing knowledge of which readings of a biblical text were in use at the time and place in which the Rabbis and the Fathers were writing. Furthermore, with regard to the Church Fathers, it is easier to fix their dates than those of the manuscripts of New Testament, so the Fathers' citation of particular readings gives us an insight into when those readings were current. The usefulness of the Fathers' quotation of the Greek New Testament is limited, however, by the fact that their works have come down to us through being copied by scribes and are thus prone to the same problems of transmission encountered with manuscripts of the New Testament. Indeed, the manuscripts of the Fathers have often been handed down in a poorer state than those of the New Testament. The scribes responsible for copying the works of the Fathers frequently altered the biblical text cited by a Church

Father to correspond to the version with which they were acquainted. So the problems encountered with biblical texts are present still more severely with patristic manuscripts. Furthermore, the Fathers may simply have been paraphrasing a biblical passage or quoting it from memory, and thus do not in fact provide evidence of the genuine reading of a disputed biblical text.

The task facing the textual critic is to order the evidence provided by the manuscripts, translations, and quotations by the Rabbis and Church Fathers into a hierarchy of authenticity and reliability. This is achieved by applying the following principles.

2. The criterion of best witness

The easiest way to establish the authenticity of a disputed reading might seem to be simply to count the manuscripts that support each of the variants of the text. On this basis, it can be concluded that the variant which appears in the largest number of manuscripts is likely to be the correct one. This criterion, however, should be used with caution, for we should remember that many manuscripts were not independent of each other. Many of the manuscripts that have come down to us may be copies from a single earlier manuscript. If this earlier manuscript contained an error, then the later copies would reproduce that error, thus perpetuating the error and creating the impression that it is the standard, authentic reading. There may have been many copies made of an earlier faulty manuscript, but only a few copies of a more accurate copy. Alternatively, through the vagaries of history more copies of the faulty manuscript may have survived than copies of the more accurate text. It may be the case that a single copy has come down to us of an earlier, more accurate manuscript which did not reproduce the error of the much better attested manuscript. In that case, although we would have only one witness to reading A against several witnesses to reading B, it would be A and not B that had the correct reading. Consequently, the rule for sifting manuscripts is *manuscripta ponderantur non numerantur* (manuscripts are evaluated, not counted). That is, the number of manuscripts of a particular version is not decisive for identifying the most original text. The status of individual text witnesses arises from the text's history of transmission. In the case of Old Testament textual criticism, this means that the Masoretic text has precedence except at those points where the text can be shown to be defective. This is because, as we saw earlier, the Masoretic text is the product of a careful process of editing and transmission by the Masoretic scribes.

3. The criterion of genealogical relationship

In order to employ the criterion of best witness, it is necessary to ascertain whether the manuscripts are independent witnesses or whether some manuscripts are dependent on others. That is, it is necessary to establish a 'family tree' or 'genealogy' of manuscripts. Text-critical studies have revealed that some manuscripts seem closely to resemble each other. This has led textual critics to place manuscripts into 'families' of texts and to draw up 'genealogies' tracing the history of related texts. The aim of this is to establish which group of manuscripts is likely to be the most reliable. By tracing the 'family tree' of a manuscript, we may be able to identify which of the extant manuscripts is the earliest. Since early manuscripts are closer in time to the original, it is argued, they may give us a more reliable picture of the original text.

Because of the lack of manuscripts, the construction of a genealogy of the Hebrew Bible is much more difficult than it is for the New Testament. Frank Cross, however, has argued for the existence of three distinct textual families,[45] namely, Palestinian, Babylonian and Egyptian, although his theory has been questioned by Shermaryahu Talmon and Emanuel Tov.[46] According to Cross, the Babylonian version became the basis of the Masoretic text, with the exception of the Latter Prophets for which the Palestinian text was used. It was this hybrid form of the Hebrew Bible that ultimately became the standard version. The Egyptian version, which Cross holds to have developed from the Palestinian text sometime in the fourth century BCE, formed the basis of the Septuagint translation, while the Palestinian version of the Torah seems to have provided the text upon which the Samaritan Bible was based.[47]

With regard to the New Testament, comparison of the various extant manuscripts has enabled scholars to group them into the following three groups or 'families'.

(a) The Alexandrian family

This group, which is regarded as the most important of the three families, contains such manuscripts as the Codex Sinaiticus, Codex Vaticanus and Codex Ephraemi Rescriptus. A large part of the Codex Alexandrinus also belongs to this group, though the Gospels belong to the Byzantine family. Minuscule 33 is also considered to belong to the Alexandrian family. These manuscripts are regarded as the best witnesses to the New Testament text on the grounds of their age and quality.

(b) The Western family

This title is a misnomer, since this group contains not only Western manuscripts but also some from the East. It appears to have acquired the name 'Western' because it contains Latin translations, but this family of manuscripts probably originated in Syria and was also known in Egypt, as is indicated by P[38] and P[48]. The main witnesses for this family of texts are the Codex Beza Cantabrigiensis (D[e]) and the Codex Claromontanus (D[p]). There is dispute over the reliability of the Western group. The Western version of Acts contains some significant variations, while the tendency with regard to the Gospels is to harmonize the narrative.

(c) The Byzantine family

The Byzantine group is also known as the 'imperial text' or simply as 'Koine' (Greek: common). This group contains most of the manuscripts that have come down to us and includes the majority of the later uncials and minuscules.

These divisions of the manuscript evidence into Alexandrian, Western and Byzantine groups are not rigid divisions, however, and some manuscripts appear to be a mixture of different categories. Thus the version of the Gospels contained in the Codex Alexandrinus seems to belong to the Byzantine group, whereas its version of the other New Testament writings seems to belong to the Alexandrian family. Particularly puzzling is the fact that that John 1-8 in the Codex Sinaiticus appears to belong to the Western group, whereas the remainder of the Gospel and of the codex as a whole belongs to the Alexandrian family of texts.

The general consensus is that the Alexandrian family of manuscripts is more reliable and should be followed when there are differences between the Alexandrian and Western texts. The Byzantine family of texts is generally regarded as containing more deviations than the Alexandrian and Western manuscripts, and is considered to be an unreliable guide to the authenticity of a variant reading. Most Byzantine variations can be explained as additions and attempts to improve the original text. If a reading is supported by all three manuscript families, however, then it is likely to be authentic.

4. The criterion of reliability

Texts that can be shown to be reliable with regard to certain readings are also likely to be reliable with regard to other readings. Where the evidence is not clearly in favour of either of two variant readings, we should follow the reading of the manuscript that has been shown to be more reliable in other areas.

5. The criterion of antiquity

The older the manuscript, the more likely it is to reproduce the original form of the text, for it will have passed through the hands of fewer copyists than a later text. Therefore there are likely to be fewer mistakes. Although this criterion is useful, it also has its problems, however, for it is possible that later manuscripts are copies of a manuscript that predates the earlier witness. In other words, we cannot know whether a fifth-century manuscript has been copied from a second century manuscript which predates the apparently 'older' manuscript from the third century. If an early copy was inaccurately made, then all subsequent copies of that early copy would reproduce the early copy's error. A later copy made from a more reliable, but now lost earlier manuscript may thus be more accurate even though it is less ancient that the inaccurate early copy.

6. The criterion of geographical diversity

If manuscripts from a particular region (e.g. Italy) support a variant reading, but manuscripts from other regions (e.g. Africa, Syria, Alexandria and other parts of the Roman Empire) do not support the variant reading, then the variant reading is likely to be due to the copyists in that particular region rather than its having been present in the original text. The fact that one reading was widespread across the Roman Empire while the other was restricted to a particular region is evidence for the authenticity of the widespread version.

7. The criterion of transcriptional probability

The criterion of transcriptional probability classifies variant readings according to the probability of their being the result of scribal error. If it can be shown that variant reading A is more likely than reading B to have arisen from a scribal error in transcribing the text, then we can consider reading B to be probably the more authentic version. The criterion of transcriptional probability is made up of two approaches. Firstly, the text critic must identify the reasons for errors having entered the text. Secondly, the text critic must employ a set of criteria for establishing which readings are likely to be the most authentic.

(a) The identification of error

The text critic tries to work out why the scribe may have changed the original form of the text into the reading we now find in the manuscript. If we are trying to decide between two rival versions of the same text, the reading which cannot be explained on the basis of scribal alteration is likely to be the more authentic reading. Identifying transcriptional probabilities allows us to establish which variant readings are scribal corruptions and which belong to the original text. There are two forms of scribal intervention that may lead to variant readings, namely unintentional error and deliberation alteration.

(1) Unintentional error

Many variant readings can be accounted for on the basis of scribal error.[48] It is easy to make mistakes when copying a text by hand and a variant reading may simply be due to the scribe making a mistake when copying the text. The textual critic's task is to identify such mistakes and to account for how they may have come about. The main errors are misspellings and omissions.

In the Hebrew Bible, confusion of similar letters is a common cause of variant readings. For example, the letters ד (d) and ר (r) are easily confused,[49] especially if the scribe was working in less than ideal conditions such as a poorly illuminated scriptorium or was simply tired at the end of a long day. An example of a likely confusion of ד and ר, is provided by Gen. 10.4, which lists among the descendants of Noah 'the sons of Javan: Elishah, Tarshish, Kittim, and *Dodanim*'. This genealogy appears again in 1 Chron. 1.7, where it is written: 'the sons of Javan: Elishah, Tarshish, Kittim, and *Rodanim*'. The Samaritan Pentateuch and the Septuagint versions of Gen. 10.4 both give the text as 'Rodanim', which is a more plausible reading since it appears to be a reference to the people of Rhodes, whereas the reference to *Dodanim* is obscure. It seems likely then that *Rodanim* is the authentic reading and that *Dodanim* has arisen as a result of a scribal confusion between two similar Hebrew letters.[50] Another error of this type is 'metathesis' or transposition, which is the term used to designate the scribe's inadvertent reversal of two letters.

Mistakes are even more probable with the New Testament in view of the difficulty of reading Greek manuscripts. Early Greek manuscripts of the New Testament do not contain punctuation and run words together, presenting the reader with a continuous line of letters without gaps to break up the words, a practice known as *scriptio continua*. When writing practices later changed and words were no longer run together but written separately, errors may have arisen simply from a scribe dividing up words incorrectly when copying a manuscript written in *scriptio continua*. A good English example of this is provided by the phrase *Godisnowhere*. Does this mean 'God is now here' or 'God is nowhere'? Clearly the way we divide the letters into words makes a significant difference to the meaning. Although *scriptio continua* does not seem to be have been practised in Hebrew, similar problems can arise through the crowding of letters due to a scribe attempting to fit too many words on a single line.[51]

Other errors may have crept into the text as a result of the scribe looking back and forth from the manuscript he was copying to the page on which he was making his copy. In doing so, it would have been easy for the scribe's eye to jump to another instance of a word he was copying. This unintentional writing once of a word that should have been written twice is call *haplography*, the literal meaning of which is 'single writing'. This can result in two types of error. Firstly, if the scribe's eye jumps from an earlier to a later instance of the same word, he will omit to copy the text between the two instances of the same word. A good example of this type of error can be found in the Codex Sinaiticus, which omits v. 32 in its version of the parable of the Good Samaritan (Luke 10.25–37). The omission of this verse can be accounted for by the fact that, like the previous verse, v. 32 ends with the phrase 'passed by on the other side'. It is likely that having copied the first use of this phrase in v. 31, the scribe's eye has jumped from the first to the second appearance of the phrase, which has resulted in the omission of v. 32.

The second type of error that can occur in the copying process is when the scribe's eye jumps to an *earlier* instance of the word he is copying, the result of which is that he will repeat material he has already transcribed into his copy. This phenomenon is known as *dittography* (double writing), i.e. the inadvertent *repetition* of letters or words when copying a manuscript. Similar errors can occur as a result of *homoioteleuton* and *homoioarcton*. *Homoioteleuton*, from the Greek for 'similar ending', is omission of text through the scribe's eye jumping from the first to the second of two words with *similar endings*. A related, but much less common error is omission by *homoioarcton*, which occurs when the scribe's eye has skipped from the first to the second of two words with *similar beginnings*. Errors of this type are usually easy to detect and can be easily corrected.

The problem of errors creeping into the text through the copying process is compounded still further by the fact that copies are made of earlier copies of the original. The distance between the copy and the original increases with every new copy made of an earlier copy. This in turn increases the possibility of errors entering into the text, for the second copyist will reproduce not only the mistakes of the first copyist, but may well add some new errors of his own. The situation is made still more confusing by the fact that a later copyist may spot a mistake in the text from which he is copying, and try to correct it. If the copier does not have the original manuscript, which is unlikely since it would then not be necessary to copy from a copy, then he has no way of ascertaining whether his correction is the right one. For example, if the copyist notices that a word is missing from the text which he is copying, he may incorporate into his copy the word he believes to have been omitted. He may, however, have guessed wrong, and by incorporating the wrong word may have distorted the original meaning of the text still further.

(2) Deliberate alterations

Deliberate alterations to the text arise from the copyist's improving an awkward passage, adding explanatory comments, and removing offensive passages. An example of a deliberate alteration can be seen in Mark 7.31, which in Alexandrian and Western manuscripts tells us that Jesus 'left Tyre and came through Sidon to the Sea of Galilee'. This is geographically unlikely, for the route from Tyre to the Sea of Galilee would not naturally pass through Sidon and would involve a considerable detour. It is likely that the geographically more plausible version of this verse found in Byzantine manuscripts ('Jesus left Tyre and Sidon and came to the Sea of Galilee') is due to scribal correction of what is otherwise an improbable route.

Sometimes deliberate alteration occurs for the sake of clarification. Thus the Codex Bezae Cantabrigiensis has reformulated Luke 3.16 from 'John answered, saying to all of them' to 'John, knowing what they were thinking, said . . .' This alteration can be explained as a scribal clarification of what prompted John to answer the people, since they had not actually asked the question to which John is replying, namely whether or not John was the messiah. Alterations may also have been made for theological reasons. Thus there are several manuscripts that have altered Matt. 24.36 by omitting 'nor the Son'. The reason for this alteration was to remove from the text the offensive implication that the omniscient Son of God did not know when the Day of Judgement would take place.[52]

Discrepancies between different manuscripts may also be accounted for by the scribe adapting the text to the version that was most familiar to him. This seems to have occurred with Luke's version of the Lord's Prayer, which in several manuscripts is reproduced in the longer Matthaean version. The inclusion of 'Our Father in heaven', 'Thy will be done, on earth as in heaven' and 'deliver us from evil' are not present in the earliest manuscripts of Luke. The longer variant reading of Luke's version of the Lord's Prayer is likely to be due to the scribe's having been influenced by the Matthaean version, which was the version commonly used in prayer and worship.

(b) Identifying authentic readings

(1) The criterion of intrinsic probability

This criterion is employed to establish on the basis of the work's language, style and theology which reading is most likely to be authentic. This involves studying the vocabulary of the author and considering whether the vocabulary of the variant reading is compatible with the vocabulary generally favoured by the text(s). This is one of the reasons why the Pastoral Epistles are generally considered not to have been written by Paul, for these letters contain vocabulary which we do not encounter in what are regarded to be the genuinely Pauline letters. The same approach can be applied on a smaller scale to textual variants. If reading A contains words that the author commonly uses, then there are no reasons to deny its originality. If, however, reading B contains words not otherwise encountered in the text of which it forms a part, then it is likely to be inauthentic. Similarly, if a variant reading is written in a style different from that found in the rest of the text, then it is likely to reflect the style of the copyist. If variant readings contain differing theological perspectives, then the authentic reading will be the reading which corresponds more closely to the theology of the text as a whole. A variant which contains a theology that appears to be at odds with the writing as a whole is probably to be attributed to the influence of the copyist's own theological views.

(2) Lectio difficilior lectio potior

That is, the *more difficult* reading is the more probable reading. The more problematic reading is held to be the older and more authentic reading on the grounds that a scribe is more likely to simplify a passage than increase its difficulty through complicated formulations, and is more likely to alter a theologically difficult passage to one that corresponds with orthodox theology. This criterion should be treated with caution, however, since a more difficult reading may have been created by a scribal error. As Bruce Waltke points out, 'a "more difficult reading" does not mean a "meaningless and corrupt reading".'[53] When employing the principle *lectio difficilior lectio potior*, we should thus keep in mind McCarter's warning: 'The more difficult reading is not to be preferred when it is garbage.'[54]

(3) Lectio brevior lectio potior

That is, the *shorter* reading is the more probable reading. Generally, it is more likely that the copyist has added rather than removed material from a text that the copyist regards as sacred. A good example is provided by the Lord's Prayer in Luke (Luke 11.2–4), which in many manuscripts has been expanded to include the doxology present in some versions of Matthew's Gospel (Matt. 6.9–13). It is easier to explain the lengthening of Luke's originally shorter version of the prayer to accommodate it to Matthew's fuller version, which was used in the liturgy, than it is to explain why anyone would shorten the longer version and deliberately exclude the doxology. It is unlikely that the concluding doxology would have been removed if it had been part of the text from the very beginning. The more probable explanation is thus that it was absent from the original text and was added once the longer form with the doxology had established itself as part of the liturgy.

Though useful in certain cases, this rule must be employed with caution. It is possible that a shorter text may be *less original* than a longer text if it can be shown that the brevity of the text stems from a scribal error. This would be the case where the shorter version can be explained by the scribe's eye having skipped a line, as is the case with the reading of the parable of the Good Samaritan given in the Codex Sinaiticus.

(4) The most easily explainable reading is the more probable reading

If it is easier to explain how reading A could have mutated into reading B than vice versa, then we should take reading A as more likely to be authentic than reading B. For example, it is easier to account for the addition of v. 37 to the account of the Ethiopian eunuch's baptism in Acts 8.26–40 than it is to explain its omission. After the eunuch has asked, 'What is there to prevent me being baptized?', several texts belonging to the Byzantine group insert the following verse: 'And Philip said, "If you believe with all your heart, you may." And he replied, "I believe that Jesus Christ is the Son of God."' If this verse had been present in the original text, it is unlikely that a scribe would have removed such a clear affirmation of Jesus' divine Sonship. It is thus more probable that it has been inserted into the text in order to emphasize Jesus' status and also possibly to accommodate the text to the baptismal liturgy in use in the Church. Since this verse is attested in only a few manuscripts and is absent from the earliest manuscripts that have come down to us, it is regarded as a (relatively) late interpolation and is thus omitted from modern translations of the Bible.

(5) Conjectural emendation of the text

Where none of the variant readings seems to make sense, then the text critic has no choice but to propose a reading that is not present in any of the text manuscripts but which seems to be the most likely reading in light of the content, style and theology of the biblical writing in which it appears. Such a conjectural emendation must also be supported by the textual critic's demonstration of how the problematic readings can be derived from scribal error in transcribing the conjectural emendation.

Where there is conflict between these various criteria for deciding which variant reading is authentic, the textual critic must weigh the evidence and decide which criterion should take precedence.

Textual criticism in action
Gen. 2.4b–3.24

There are only minor divergences in the various witnesses to Genesis, a fact which indicates that the text acquired a stable form at a very early date. Here we shall focus on the variant readings which provide us with the clearest illustrations of the work of the textual critic.

2.4b

1. List variants with their manuscript support

Whereas the Masoretic text states that God made 'earth and heaven', the Samaritan Pentateuch, Septuagint, Syriac Peshitta and the Targum Neofiti have 'heaven and earth'.

2. The criterion of transcriptional probability

(a) The criterion of intrinsic probability

This involves studying the vocabulary of a writing and attempting to identify its characteristic style and terminology. Applying the criterion of intrinsic probability enables us to identify those variant readings which may have arisen from a scribe's adaptation of a passage to a style he believes – perhaps unconsciously – to be appropriate to the text he is copying. Since Genesis elsewhere employs the order 'heaven and earth' (e.g. Gen. 1.1; 2.1, 4a), we must ask ourselves whether the reading adopted by the Samaritan Pentateuch, Septuagint, Syriac Peshitta and the Targum Neofiti is likely to be the more original. This question cannot be answered solely on the basis of the criterion of intrinsic probability, however, but must be supplemented by the other criteria of transcriptional probability.

(b) Lectio difficilior lectio potior

Applying the principle of *lectio difficilior lectio potior* would lead us to prefer the Masoretic reading, since the order 'earth and heaven' is unusual and much less common than the order 'heaven and earth'. Indeed, the phrase 'earth and heaven' appears on only one other occasion in the whole of the Hebrew Bible, namely in Ps. 148.13.

(c) The criterion of the most easily explainable reading

As we saw earlier, this criterion is based on the principle that the most easily explainable reading is the more probable reading. Thus if it is easier to explain how reading A could have mutated into reading B than vice versa, then we should take reading A as more likely to be authentic than reading B. Applying this principle to Gen. 2.4b leads us to conclude that the Masoretic text is likely to be the more original reading, since it is easier to explain how 'earth and heaven' could have mutated into 'heaven and earth' than vice versa. It is more likely that the scribes responsible for the reading followed by the Samaritan Pentateuch and other witnesses have assimilated the order of 'earth and heaven' either deliberately or unintentionally and unconsciously to the more familiar phrase of 'heaven and earth'. It is difficult, however, to explain the alteration in the other direction, i.e. that the Masoretes should have changed the more usual 'heaven and earth' to 'earth and heaven', if the former reading was the original wording in the text with which they were working. That the Masoretic text is the more probable reading is corroborated by the fact that an explanation can be given for why the author of Gen. 2.4b should have employed the unusual order 'earth and heaven'. As Wenham points out, the order is due to the author's use of chiasmus, namely: a-heaven, b-earth, c-created, c′-made, b′-earth, a′-heaven.[55] That is, the unusual order is due to the author's wishing to create a poetic effect, which has been overlooked or misunderstood by subsequent copyists.

2.12

1. List variants with their manuscript support

Whereas the Masoretic text reads 'And the gold of that land is good', the Samaritan Pentateuch has 'And the gold of that land is *very* good' (emphasis added).

2. The criterion of transcriptional probability

Since neither reading is difficult we cannot make use here of the criterion of *lectio difficilior lectio potior*, but must rely on the criteria of intrinsic probability and the most easily explainable reading.

(a) The criterion of intrinsic probability

Examination of the text of the Samaritan Pentateuch reveals that the introduction of the superlative is a characteristic feature of its style. The introduction of the term 'very' into Gen. 2.12 would thus seem to reflect the style of the scribe(s) responsible for transmitting the text of Genesis.

(b) The criterion of the most easily explainable reading

It is arguably more probable that the term 'very' has been introduced rather than removed from the text. If the term were in the original version of the text, then it is unlikely that the scribe would have wished to tone down the text's affirmation of the goodness of the gold by removing the superlative. It is more likely that the scribe would have inserted the term in order to emphasize as strongly as possible the utter goodness of the world God had created before the fall of the first human beings.

Employing the criteria of intrinsic probability and the most easily explainable reading thus leads to the conclusion that the Masoretic version of Gen. 2.12 is more likely to be the original reading.

Matt. 15.21–28

There are several variants in the manuscript witness to Matt. 15.21–28, but they are minor and do not fundamentally affect the sense of the text. Several manuscripts insert 'to him' (autō) in 15.22, while one manuscript contains the phrase 'before him' (opisō autou). Another variation that occurs is the use of vocative 'O Son' (huie) instead of the nominative (huios) that appears in several manuscripts, including the Codex Sinaiticus. To illustrate the application of textual criticism, we shall focus on the variant readings of 15.22, 26 and 27.

15.22: 'Just then a Canaanite woman from that region came out and started shouting. "Have mercy on me, Lord, Son of David; my daughter is tormented by a demon"'

1. List variants with their manuscript support

The manuscript evidence gives three different forms of the Greek verb 'to cry', namely: (1) the third person singular imperfect of the verb kradzō, i.e. 'she was crying' (ekradzen); (2) the third person singular aorist indicative of kradzō, meaning 'she cried' (ekraxen), i.e. she cried once (and then stopped); (3) the third person singular aorist indicative of kraugadzo (ekraugasen), a synonym of kradzō.

2. Criterion of best witness

The reading *ekradzen* is supported by a scribal correction to the Codex Sinaiticus, Vaticanus, and D and Θ and minuscules belonging to f[1]. It is this reading that has been incorporated into the text on the basis that it is the version found in the best witnesses.

3. Criterion of reliability

The manuscripts which have *ekradzen* are generally more reliable. This is the dominant reading of the Alexandrian family of manuscripts, which have generally proved themselves to be more reliable than the Western and Byzantine groups.

4. Criterion of transcriptional probability

The next stage is to explain how the variant readings came about. The variant *ekraugasen* is probably due to intentional scribal intervention in the text. It is an alteration by the scribe on the basis of his own sense of style. The reading *ekraxen*, on the other hand, is probably due to scribal error. It is an unintentional modification of the text resulting from a scribal misreading of *ekraxen*, the letters 'z' (ζ) and 'x' (ξ) being very similar in Greek. That it is unlikely that *ekradzen* is a misreading of *ekraxen* is indicated by the fact that the best manuscripts have *ekradzen*. The combination of the criteria of best witness and transcriptional probability thus lead us to prefer *ekradzen* over *ekraxen*.

15.26: 'He answered: "It is not fair to take the children's food and throw it to the dogs"'

1. List variants with their manuscript support

Some authorities have 'it is not lawful' (*ouk exestin*) rather than 'it is not fair' (*ouk estin kalon*).

2. Criterion of best witness

The reading 'it is not fair' (*ouk estin kalon*) is to preferred on the basis of the criterion of best witness. The phrase *ouk estin kalon* is better attested.

3. Criterion of transcriptional probability

The phrase 'it is not fair' (*ouk estin kalon*) is the more difficult reading. Applying the principle of *lectio difficilior lectio potior* leads to the conclusion that it is more likely that *ouk estin kalon* has been changed to *ouk exestin* than vice versa. The phrase *ouk exestin* absolves Jesus from responsibility for his harsh treatment of the woman, whereas *ouk estin kalon* implies that Jesus' own conscience and moral sense prevents him from helping the woman. Since Jesus' harshness is something Christians have had difficulty accepting, it is more probable that a scribe would have replaced the phrase 'it is not fair' with 'it is not lawful' than vice versa, since this attributes Jesus' harsh treatment of the Canaanite woman to the Jewish law rather than to Jesus himself. Applying the criteria of best witness and *lectio difficilior lectio potior* thus leads to the conclusion that 'it is not fair' is more likely to be the authentic reading.

15.27: 'She said, "Yes, Lord, yet even the dogs eat the crumbs that fall from their masters' table"'

1. List variants with their manuscript support

The Codex Vaticanus and the Codex Sinaiticus Syriacus omit 'yet' in Matt.15.27. This omission changes the meaning. If 'yet' is omitted, then the woman's response would seem to mean, 'Yes indeed, Lord, and the little dogs eat the crumbs that fall from their masters' table.' That is, the woman is saying to Jesus: 'You are indeed right. I *am* merely a dog under the table, but if that is so, then can I not have the leftovers from the children's table?' The inclusion of the word 'yet', however, would seem to indicate that the woman's 'Yes, Lord' refers not to Jesus' comment but to her own request. The meaning of her reply would then be: 'Yes, you are right and precisely for that reason, you can help me without detriment to the children.'

2. Criterion of best witness

Which of these two readings is the more likely? On the basis of the criterion of best witness it seems that the reading which includes 'yet' is more likely to be authentic.

3. Criterion of transcriptional probability

How is the omission of 'yet' in certain manuscripts to be explained? Here it is more difficult to establish a clear reason for the omission. It may simply be a scribal error or it may be due to the scribe preferring the meaning of the text that results from the omission of 'yet'.

Evaluation of textual criticism

Clearly both scholars and faith communities need a reliable text for their study and worship. Textual criticism is thus important as a method for deciding between variant readings and establishing as accurately as possible the text of the Bible. There are, however, problems with the method, particularly with regard to the Hebrew Bible, where the distinction between co-authorship and textual corruption is difficult to draw. A further problem with textual criticism is that it is not always possible to see which of its various criteria is appropriate for deciding between competing variant passages. This problem is apparent when certain criteria seem to conflict, such as, for example, the criterion of the more difficult reading and the criterion of the shorter reading. The fact that the application of these criteria may result in different conclusions when applied to the same text indicates that textual criticism can never have the status of a universally valid method, but operates only according to degrees of probability with regard to disputed readings of the text. The development of new computer-based methods, however, may revolutionize the textual criticism of the Bible and open up new ways of establishing the most authentic and original text of the Bible.

CHAPTER FOUR

Source Criticism

Source criticism is based on the presupposition that many biblical writings were constructed from earlier sources.[1] The biblical authors for the most part did not invent their narratives but creatively reworked material handed down in the communities of which they were members. The Bible itself provides evidence to support this view. In the Old Testament there are several references to what appear to be earlier sources. Numbers, for example, quotes a passage from the 'Book of the Wars of the Lord' (Num. 21.14–15), while Joshua and 2 Samuel refer to the 'Book of Jashar' (Josh. 10.12b–13a; 2 Sam. 1.18–27). In the New Testament, Paul refers to the tradition which he has received (1 Cor. 11.23; 15.3), while Luke informs us that 'Many have undertaken to set down an orderly account of the events that have been fulfilled among us, just as they were handed on to us by those who from the beginning were eyewitnesses and servants of the word' (Luke 1.1–2). A further indication that some biblical writings are based on earlier sources is provided by the existence of overlapping narratives. The similarity of Chronicles to Samuel and Kings has led to the view that the author of Chronicles may have used these writings as sources, while the parallels between Matthew, Mark and Luke, and between Jude and 2 Peter, have led scholars to suggest that these writings may have been based on common sources. The close verbal agreement, for example, between such passages as Matt. 21.23–27, Mark 11.27–33 and Luke 20.1–8, or Matt. 8.8–9 and Luke 7.6–7, makes it unlikely that we have here independent witnesses of the same event. The more likely explanation is that there is either a common source for all versions or that one of the Gospels is the source of the others.

The internal evidence of the biblical texts also points to their having been built up from earlier sources. Such evidence is provided by dislocations in the flow of narrative. For example, Jesus' explanation of the parable of the sower would flow more smoothly if Mark 4.11–12 were omitted and the text ran from Mark 4.10 to 4.13. The obvious explanation for this disruption in the flow of narrative is that Mark has inserted 4.11–12 into a text unit which originally consisted of 4.10, 13–20.

Further evidence that the final state of a text is the result of a long period of literary growth is provided by variations in the historical background implicit in the text, such as differences in the cultic, political and theological presuppositions within certain passages in the text. A good example of this is provided by Isaiah. The historical background of chapters 1–39 is the late eighth century BCE, the time of the ministry of Isaiah (Isa. 1.1; 6.1; 7.13, etc.).[2] There is no reference to this period in chapters 40 onwards, where the prophet is clearly living in the period of the Babylonian Exile.[3]

Source criticism is concerned with identifying the sources used in the composition of the biblical texts. It attempts to recover the building blocks from which the final text was constructed. If these building blocks can be shown to be internally consistent when detached from the wider text in which they were embedded, then the source critic can be confident that he or she has identified one of the sources used in the construction of the final text.

Once these sources have been isolated, then the task is to establish the age, author, context and intention of the sources and to trace the process by which biblical writings have been built up from these earlier sources. Source critics have tended to focus primarily on *written* sources. The identification of *oral* sources is the task of form criticism.

In German scholarship, source criticism has been labelled 'literary criticism', a fact which can easily lead to confusion, especially since in the English-speaking world the phrase 'literary criticism' tends to be used as the generic term for the study of literature, irrespective of which methods are employed.[4] In biblical studies, however, the phrase 'literary criticism' has been used in a more specialized and technical sense to describe the method of identifying the earlier layers of text that have (allegedly) been combined to produce the final versions of the biblical texts. Barr provides a useful summary of these two different uses of the phrase 'literary criticism':

> In general literary study we mean by *literary criticism* a study of the structures and the imagery of works, their modes, symbols and myths, their poetic, dramatic and aesthetic effect; but in technical biblical scholarship the same term means the separating out of historically different layers in composite works, the history of the tradition during the period of its development in written form, as distinct from its development in a spoken form before it was written down.[5]

To make matters still more confusing, older commentators described source criticism as 'higher criticism' in contrast to 'lower criticism', which is concerned with the text critical task of establishing the most authentic form of the text. For the sake of clarity we shall restrict ourselves to the use of the term 'source criticism'.

A brief history of source criticism

Source criticism has its origins not in biblical study but in the study of Homer, where it was used to clarify problems concerning the interpretation of the *Iliad* and the *Odyssey*. As we saw in Chapter 2, it was also employed by Niebuhr in his study of the history of Rome. The method was then taken up by biblical scholars who wished to establish the authorship, date, context and intention of biblical texts. It was above all the problems presented by the Pentateuch that prompted the employment of source criticism in Old Testament studies. The repetitions, inconsistencies and tensions in the Pentateuch, such as, for example, the presence of two different creation accounts (Gen. 1.1–2.4a, 2.4b–25), caused scholars to raise questions concerning the integrity and unity of the Pentateuch. One answer to these questions was that the Pentateuch was a conflation of earlier sources. The tensions in the text could be accounted for by the failure of the Pentateuch's editors fully to integrate these sources into the final form of the text.

The pioneer of Old Testament source criticism was the French Roman Catholic physician Jean Astruc (1684–1766). In his *Conjectures on the Reminiscences which Moses Appears to Have Used in Composing the Book of Genesis* (1753) Astruc argued on the basis of the different names used of God in Genesis that Moses had made use of two sources when composing Genesis, which he named the Elohist and Yahwist sources (later known as E and J). Astruc's work was taken up and developed by the German scholar J. G. Eichhorn. In his *Introduction to the Old Testament* Eichhorn used repetitions, style and terminology as criteria for the identification of sources, and applied these criteria to refine Astruc's two-source theory.[6]

An important contribution to understanding the composition of the Pentateuch was made by Alexander Geddes (1737–1802), a Scottish Roman Catholic scholar, who, noting that the law codes of the Pentateuch seemed to be placed alongside each other with little attempt to integrate them into a coherent text, argued that the Pentateuch was the result of the compilation of fragments of varying length.[7] This 'fragmentary hypothesis' was taken up by Johann Severin Vater (1771–1826), who argued that the first stage in the construction of the Pentateuch was the law book (re-)discovered during the reign of Josiah (2 Kings 22.8–9) and which now forms the book of Deuteronomy.[8]

De Wette also made a contribution to the source criticism of the Old Testament. As the rather cumbersome title of his doctoral dissertation indicates, de Wette questioned the Mosaic authorship of the Pentateuch: *A Critical Dissertation by which is Shown that the Fifth Book of Moses is Different from the Remaining Books of the Pentateuch and is the Work of another, younger Author.*[9] In the course of his discussion of Deuteronomy, de Wette argues that Genesis consists of two sources and that Exodus, Leviticus and Numbers are the result of the combining of the work of several different authors.

The weakness of the fragmentary hypothesis was that although it was able to account for the tensions and inconsistencies in the Pentateuch, it was unable to do justice to its overall structural unity. That the editors had attempted to impose some sort of structural coherence on their sources is evident from the fact that the Pentateuch is organized chronologically. The presence of a unifying structure in the Pentateuch raised doubts about the validity of the theory that the Pentateuch had come into existence through the loose juxtaposition of fragmentary sources.

As a result of these criticisms, the fragmentary hypothesis gave way to the 'supplementary hypothesis'. This theory seems to have been first advanced by H. Ewald in his review in the journal *Theologische Studien und Kritiken* [Theological Studies and Critiques] of J. J. Stähelin's *Critical Investigation of Genesis.*[10] Ewald proposed that the Pentateuch began life as an Elohistic text to which other sources subsequently became attached. It is the underlying Elohistic strand that accounts for the Pentateuch's unified structure. By means of this proposal, Ewald was able to account both for the coherence of the Pentateuch and for the diversity of vocabulary, style and theology of certain passages, which he classified as accretions to the original Elohistic text.

It was, however, what has come to be known as the 'documentary hypothesis', which came to dominate Old Testament scholarship. The initiator of this theory was Hermann Hupfeld (1796–1866), who argued in his *The Sources of Genesis and the Nature of their Combination* that the Elohistic source was itself made up of two sources, namely an earlier and a later source.[11] This earlier Elohistic source later came to be known as the Priestly source (P).

A further contribution to the documentary hypothesis was made by de Wette, who argued that the Deuteronomic Code contained in Deuteronomy 12–26 was a distinct source that should be distinguished from the sources identified by his predecessors.[12] De Wette suggested that the Deuteronomic Code was the book discovered in the Temple during the reign of Josiah (2 Kings 22–23). This suggestion allowed de Wette to date the composition of the Deuteronomic Code to the period shortly before its discovery in 621 BCE, a date which provided him with the basis for organizing the chronology of the other sources. The task of establishing the dates of the sources was taken up by Karl Heinrich Graf (1815–1869), who argued in his *The Historical Books of the Old Testament* (1866) that P was the latest of the four sources to be incorporated in the Pentateuch.[13] He based this claim on the argument that the ceremonial and ritual codes contained in the Pentateuch could have emerged only in the post-exilic period. As evidence for this claim, he pointed to the fact that Deuteronomy, Joshua, Judges, 1–2 Samuel and 1–2 Kings contain no allusions to ceremonial and ritual laws. For Graf this indicates that P must have come into existence *after* the composition of the writings from Deuteronomy to 2 Kings.

Graf's argument was supported by Vatke, who argued on Hegelian grounds in his *The Religion of the Old Testament* that ritual and ceremonial laws are the result of a long process of religious development. This insight prompted Vatke to argue that J and E, as well as 1–2 Samuel and 1–2 Kings belong to the earliest stages of Israel's history. This period then gave way to the age of the prophets, who initiated the development of the ethical consciousness that ultimately came to be fixed in the Deuteronomic Code (D). The final source to be incorporated into the Pentateuch was the Priestly source (P), which was the result of the development of ceremonial religion.

Source or 'literary' criticism moved into a new stage with the work of Julius Wellhausen (1844–1918), who was concerned with not only isolating the various sources underlying the Old Testament, but also identifying the context and purpose that had led to the composition of these sources. Taking up the work of Graf and Vatke, Wellhausen developed what has come to be regarded as the classic form of the documentary hypothesis. According to Wellhausen, the Pentateuch came into existence as the result of the conflation of four different sources. The oldest of these sources is the Yahwistic source (J), which Wellhausen held to have been composed around 950 BCE during the reigns of David and Solomon, probably in Judah. According to Wellhausen, J formed the basis for the narrative of Genesis and Exodus, and also supplied some of the material in Numbers. E originated in the northern kingdom around 850 BCE, and begins with the narrative of Abraham in Gen. 15. The Deuteronomic Code (D) forms the basis of Deuteronomy, namely Deut. 12–26. Wellhausen suggests that D originated in the northern kingdom and was brought to Jerusalem by refugees fleeing the Assyrian conquest in 721 BCE. Alternatively, D may have been written by refugees from the north after they had settled in Judah. The last of the sources of the Pentateuch is the Priestly source (P). This source comprises material concerning ritual, ceremony, shrines and genealogies. According to Wellhausen, it was composed in the postexilic period (c. 550 BCE). Leviticus belongs wholly to P, but other elements of P can be found scattered throughout the Pentateuch.

Wellhausen claimed that the Pentateuch was built up in gradual stages. First J was combined with E, probably after the destruction of the northern kingdom. D was then added sometime after its discovery in the Temple in 621 BCE. After the Babylonian exile J, E, and D were combined with P, the authors of which were probably responsible for the editing and organization of the final version of the Pentateuch.

Although Wellhausen's account of the formation of the Pentateuch has been highly influential in Old Testament studies, various criticisms have been levelled against it. Particularly controversial is the validity of E as an independent source. The difficulties of distinguishing E from J have led some scholars to question the existence of E. Even when E has been separated from other Pentateuchal sources, the 'source' that remains is fragmentary and does not constitute a coherent narrative.[14]

Other scholars have accepted the documentary hypothesis and have attempted to refine it still further by identifying modifications and adaptations within the sources. Adherents of this view see the sources not as coherent documents, but as the results of a 'school' that produced multiple documents, which they then adapted to meet new challenges.[15] Other scholars have added to J, E, D and P a series of other sources. Otto Eissfeldt (1887–1973) posited the existence of a Lay source (L), which focused on issues of importance to lay people.[16] Georg Fohrer (1915–2002) suggested the presence in the Pentateuch of a Nomadic source (N), which contained a critique of settled, urban life.[17] Julius Morgenstern (1881–1976) argued for a Kenite source (K), which was concerned with the life of Moses.[18] R. H. Pfeiffer detected a Southern or Seir source (S), which he identified as a source for Genesis.[19] Noth argued for a 'foundational source' or *Grundlage* (G), which he held was the source of J and E.[20]

These new sources have been accepted by only a minority of scholars. The positing of such new sources, however, indicates the complexity of the structure of the Pentateuch and the difficulty in identifying its sources with any degree of precision and certainty. The 'discovery' of such new sources, moreover, raises questions about the coherence of the documentary hypothesis and the notion that the Pentateuch is based on the combination of coherent, continuous documents.

Wellhausen's dating of Pentateuch has also been challenged. Wellhausen's position is based on a Hegelian notion of development from primitive religion to a more 'advanced' ritualistic form of religious belief. If this evolutionary notion of religion is rejected, however, then so too is the dating system that Wellhausen's theory is based upon. The result of discarding Wellhausen's evolutionary framework has been that several scholars have rejected his dating and organization of the Pentateuchal sources and have suggested alternative ways of dating the composition of the Pentateuch.[21]

Until recently the early date of J was generally accepted, but this view too has now been questioned. John Van Seters shifts the composition of

J from the reigns of David and Solomon to the exilic period.[22] He bases this view on the similar vocabulary found in J, the Deuteronomistic History, and Deutero-Isaiah. Hans Heinrich Schmid likewise argues that J was composed in the exilic period on the grounds that J contains evidence of having been influenced by later theological reflection.[23] Schmid bases this claim on the argument that the type of thinking evident in J comes about only when the history of a nation is considered to have come to an end and is thus capable of being understood retrospectively. Erhard Blum is another scholar who argues for an exilic or post-exilic provenance for P and D.[24] Indeed, in late twentieth century biblical studies, there has been a general tendency to date Old Testament writings much later than the periods proposed by Wellhausen and his successors. Thus Otto Kaiser argues for a Hellenistic date for sections of Isa. 1–39,[25] while E. S. Gerstenberger places the composition of the Psalms in the post-exilic period.[26] Another development in the second half of the twentieth century was the attempt to place source criticism on a firmer 'scientific' basis. This was the aim of Wolfgang Richter in his influential *Exegese als Literaturwissenschaft* (1971), in which he applies a rigorous linguistic method to the analysis of the Old Testament.

In the last decades of the twentieth century, source criticism came under increasing pressure. Arguably the most vigorous critique was that of R. N. Whybray in his *The Making of the Pentateuch: A Methodological Study*.[27] Whybray rejects the documentary hypothesis and argues that a single author was responsible for the Pentateuch. The author collected sources, most of which were not ancient, and reworked them according to the historiographical procedures of his day. This author did not eliminate inconsistencies but was intent only on gathering and presenting material concerning the creation of the world and the origins of Israel, possibly, Whybray suggests, as an introduction to the Deuteronomistic History.

Although much scholarly effort has been expended on identifying the sources of the Pentateuch, source criticism has also been applied to other Old Testament works, such as, for example, in the identification of the Succession Narrative (2 Sam. 9–20 and 1 Kings 1–2), which has been integrated into the Deuteronomistic History. Source critical methods have also been employed to show that Isa. 11 has been expanded through the addition of vv. 6–9, 10, 11–16 and that Job 32–37 is an interpolation into an earlier text.

Similar source critical work has taken place in relation to the New Testament. There has long been an awareness of the existence of literary relationships between the four canonical Gospels. Augustine placed the Gospels in the order of composition in which they appear in the New Testament, arguing that the later Gospels were aware of the earlier Gospels and that Mark was an abridged version of Matthew. This view dominated thinking on the composition of the Gospels until the nineteenth century, but the beginnings of its overthrow can be traced to the eighteenth century.

J. D. Michaelis (1717–1791) is significant in being the first to propose the existence of a now lost primal Gospel (*Urevangelium*) from which the four Gospels were derived, and argued for a relationship between the Gospel of John and Gnosticism. Michaelis sees Matthew as a Greek translation of an Aramaic text.[28]

It was not only his publication of a new edition of the Greek New Testament that made Griesbach a significant figure in the development of biblical criticism, but also his publication in 1776 of the first synopsis of the Gospels of Matthew, Mark and Luke.[29] By laying out Matthew, Mark and Luke in parallel columns, Griesbach facilitated the study of the relation between these three Gospels. Since Griesbach the first three Gospels have come to be known collectively as the Synoptic Gospels.

Griesbach's study of the Synoptic Gospels led him to challenge the traditional theory of the relationship between Matthew, Mark and Luke.[30] The traditional view was that Matthew was the most original of the Gospels, which had then been used as a source by Mark. Luke, it was argued, had made use of both Matthew and Mark. Griesbach rejected this theory and argued instead that Mark had made use of both Matthew and Luke and had occasionally supplemented them with material drawn from oral tradition. This question of the relationship between Matthew, Mark and Luke has come to be known as the 'Synoptic Problem' and has been a major area of scholarly debate since the publication of Griesbach's synopsis.

In the course of his argument for Mark's dependence on Matthew and Luke, Griesbach suggested that the original ending of Mark, which he believed had related Jesus' post-resurrection journey to Galilee, had been lost and that the original version of the Gospel now ended at Mark 16.8, Mark 16.9–20 being a later addition. This question of the 'lost ending' of Mark has been an issue in New Testament scholarship ever since.

It was not long before Griesbach's solution to the Synoptic Problem came under fire. The first to propose what was to become the standard theory was Gottlob Christian Storr (1746–1805), who argued that if Mark were indeed dependent upon Matthew and Luke, then it is very difficult to understand why Mark should have omitted from his Gospel so much contained in the other two Gospels. The relationship between the Synoptic Gospels, he argued, is best explained by the argument that Matthew and Luke are dependent upon Mark.[31]

Storr's was not the only rival to Griesbach's theory, however. Lessing sought to explain the relationship between the Synoptic Gospels by arguing for their mutual dependence upon an Aramaic Gospel, explaining the relative brevity of Mark as due to his having had access only to an incomplete version of this primal Gospel.[32] The fact that the evangelists had employed a common source accounts for the similarities between the Gospels, while the different ways in which the evangelists had adapted this source accounts for their differences. Lessing, however, did not develop his theory in detail, a task which Johann Gottfried Eichhorn (1752–1827), a pupil of Michaelis, decided to undertake. In his book *Über die drey ersten Evangelien* [On the First Three Gospels] (1794),[33] Eichhorn argued that the parallels between the Synoptic Gospels cannot be explained by mutual dependence, because none of the three Gospels can be acknowledged in all respects as more original than the other two. That is, in certain passages one Gospel appears to have the more original text, whereas with regard to other texts another Gospel seems to be more authentic. This view led Eichhorn to posit the existence of a common primal Gospel underlying the three Synoptic Gospels. This common basis in a primal Gospel accounts both for the similarities and differences between Matthew, Mark and Luke. The similarities are due to the fact that each of the Gospels has made use of the same source. The differences are accounted for, firstly, by the fact that the evangelists have made use of different forms of the primal Gospel, and secondly, by the fact that they have edited it according to their own interests. Also significant for the development of source criticism was Eichhorn's attempt to explain the common material in Matthew and Luke that was absent from Mark by arguing that Matthew and Luke had drawn on common literary sources unknown to Mark.

Johann Gottfried Herder (1744–1803) followed Lessing and others in arguing for the existence of a primal Gospel. According to Herder, this primal Gospel had been taken up, edited and embellished by each of the evangelists independently of each other. Because of this independence, the interpreter should resist the temptation to harmonize the Gospels, and should instead 'let each retain his special purpose, complexion, time, and locale'.[34] Where Herder differed from his predecessors was in his view that the primal Gospel was not a literary document, but was *oral* in character and 'consisted of individual units, narratives, parables, sayings, pericopes'.[35] In its very earliest form, he claimed, the Gospel was passed on not as a written text but by word of mouth in the form of oral teaching and confession of Jesus as the Messiah.

Evidence for the origins of the canonical Gospels in oral tradition can be observed in the forms the reader encounters in the Gospels, which frequently possess the same stylized structure, a fact which indicates their having been passed down by word of mouth. It was only at a relatively late date, when the original witness of the Apostles was now in the distant past, that the need was felt to fix the oral Gospel in writing. This process, too, can be observed in the Gospels, where there is often an overlap between the individual units but variation in the order, transitions and connections of these units. This variation is due to the editorial interven-tion of the individual evangelist. In his emphasis on the importance of oral tradition and awareness of the different ways oral tradition preserved styl-ized forms, Herder pointed the way forward to the development of what would later come to be known as form criticism.

Of the Gospels Mark is the most ancient, for, Herder asks, 'Is not the briefer, the unadorned, usually the more primitive, to which, then, other occasions later add explanation, embellishment, rounding out?'[36] Herder also holds that Mark has faithfully reproduced the contents of the pri-mal Gospel underlying the Synoptic Gospels. Matthew and Luke have then expanded the more primitive version of the Gospel found in Mark. Matthew, Herder claims, has expanded the primal Gospel in order to show that the longed-for messiah has indeed arrived, whereas Luke, who according to Herder knew Matthew, strove to provide a historical account of Jesus' life according to Hellenistic models. With these insights Herder laid the foundations for the later standard theory of the priority of Mark and the two-document hypothesis, i.e. the theory that Matthew and Luke used as their sources the Gospel of Mark and a now lost source know as Q (named after *Quelle*, the German word for source).

In an article entitled 'The Order of the Narratives in the Synoptic Gospels' (1835),[37] Lachmann advanced several grounds to support Markan priority. Firstly, he pointed out that Matthew and Luke have the same order only when they agree with Mark. When Matthew and Luke diverge from Mark's order, they also diverge from each other. Secondly, the pres-ence of shared non-Markan material in Matthew and Luke suggests the existence of a common source used by the two evangelists. Matthew's divergence from Mark can be explained as due to Matthew's insertion of non-Markan material into the framework provided by Mark. What Lachmann has provided, then, are some powerful arguments for the prior-ity of Mark and the two-document hypothesis.

Christian Gottlob Wilke (1786–1854) arrived at a theory of the priority of Mark independently of Lachmann, whose work he does not seem to have known. In his *The First Evangelist or an Exegetical-Critical Investigation of the Affinity between the First Three Gospels* (1838), Wilke rejects the thesis of a common underlying primal gospel and argues that the agree-ment of the three Synoptic Gospels and the fact that almost all of Mark appears in Matthew and Luke indicate that the latter have made use of Mark in the composition of their Gospels.

In his book *The Synoptic Gospels* Heinrich Julius Holtzmann (1832–1910) took up and consolidated the critical work of his predecessors, sup-porting the theory of Markan priority on the grounds of Mark's more primitive style, and arguing for the existence of an additional source com-mon to Matthew and Luke.[38]

The English scholar B. H. Streeter refined the two-document hypothesis by expanding it into a *four*-document hypothesis. He suggested that Matthew and Luke supplemented Mark and Q with their own special material, which he labelled M and L respectively and which he believed were written documents. In his *Synoptic Studies* (1925–1931), Wilhelm Bussmann even went so far as to argue for the existence of *eight* sources underlying the Synoptic Gospels.[39] Streeter made the further proposal that the Gospel of Luke is the result of the combination of Mark with a document he calls 'Proto-Luke', which consisted of Q and Luke's special material. Matthew is the result of the expansion of Mark with Q and Matthew's own special source of material. The priority of Mark has been challenged, however, by William Farmer, who in his *The Synoptic Problem* (1976) argued for Matthaean priority,[40] but his views have found little support among the majority of scholars.

Although the identification of the sources of the Synoptic Gospels has been a major concern of New Testament scholarship, it is not the only problem to which scholars have applied source criticism. There have been attempts to identify a 'signs source' in John.[41] Similarly, there have been attempts to identify the sources and traditions upon which Paul may have drawn in the composition of his letters.

While source criticism was until the 1960s one of the major activities of the historical criticism of the Bible, since the 1970s it has been relegated to just one of many other methods of biblical interpretation and has slipped down the list of biblical scholars' concerns. The influence of 'New Criticism' in literary studies has led to the emphasis in biblical studies shifting to the treatment of the text as a literary unit and to considering the biblical writings holistically as works of literature rather than as conflations of sources. This has led to the tensions in the biblical texts being treated not so much as evidence of inadequately integrated sources as dramatic literary devices aimed at evoking rhetorical effects in the reader. The shift in biblical studies to treating texts as literary wholes and thus focusing on the final, canonical form of biblical writings has resulted in source criticism losing the prominence it once had.

The method of source criticism

The presuppositions of source criticism

1. Authors have a consistent style. If there are passages which appear to be written in a different style, then this passage is likely to be by another author and therefore to be a source employed by the final author of the text.

2. Authors do not intentionally contradict themselves. If there are contradictions in the text, then these are due to unsuccessful attempts to weave together different sources.

3. Interruptions in the flow of narrative or argument are evidence of the combination of different sources.

The principles of source criticism

1. Identification of sources: How to spot a source

(a) Comparison of parallel texts

The task of identifying sources is easier if two or more versions of a tradition have come down to us. If parallel documents are available, the source critic examines agreement and disagreement between the different versions of the text, and attempts to find an explanation for the similarities and differences that exist between them. This approach is possible in the Old Testament with Kings and Chronicles, and in the New Testament with the Gospels of Matthew, Mark and Luke, and with the letters of Jude and 2 Peter.

A similar order of material in two texts is a strong indicator that one of the texts may be dependent on the other. The fact that Matthew and Luke generally follow the order of Mark's Gospel, but do not follow the same order in their Q material is arguably evidence that Matthew and Luke are dependent on Mark. Mark is unlikely to be dependent on either Matthew or Luke, since it is difficult to envisage why Mark would omit such episodes as the Sermon on the Mount (Matt. 5–7), if he knew Matthew's Gospel or why he would exclude the parable of the Good Samaritan (Luke 10.30–37), if he were aware of Luke. That Matthew and Luke did not use each other's Gospels as a source would seem to be indicated by the fact that they order their common Q material very differently from each other. Luke places it in two large blocks (Luke 6.20–7.35; 9.57–13.34), whereas Matthew scatters the material throughout his Gospel. It is for this reason unlikely that Luke knew Matthew, for it would be difficult to explain why Luke should have extracted the Q material from Matthew and placed it in two blocks. It makes more sense to argue that Luke made use of Mark as his primary source and framework, and decided to slot the Q material into Mark's structure but without confusing his two sources. If Matthew knew the work of Luke or vice versa, then it is likely that the one evangelist would have followed the order of the other, just as they did with their use of the Gospel of Mark.

(b) Contradictions

Where parallel texts are not available, source critics focus on features within the text that may indicate the presence of an earlier source. Source critics identify the possible presence of a source by searching for contradicitons in the text. Lying behind the search for contradictions is the presupposition that authors usually strive for consistency in their writing. Textual tensions and inconsistencies may thus be indications that parts of the text stem not from the author's own pen but are sources which he has taken up and incorporated into his writing. For example, since the presence of John 21 contradicts the conclusion expressed in John 20.30, the final version of the Gospel would seem to be the result of an editor/author combining John 21 with the main part of the Gospel.

(c) Interruptions

Dislocations, disruptions and breaks in the plot, sentence structure or flow of argument may be pointers to the incorporation of a source. Such interruptions may be explained by the writer having slotted material into an existent source. An example is provided by John 14.31, where Jesus says to his disciples, 'Rise, let us be on our way'. The natural understanding of this is that Jesus has finished teaching, as related in chapter 14, and wishes to depart. When we read on from the next verse (John 15.1), however, we find that Jesus continues talking to his disciples for another three chapters. It is only in John 18.1 that he at last concludes his teaching and departs. The text would flow more naturally if John 18.1 ('After Jesus had spoken these words, he went out with his disciples . . .') immediately followed John 14.31 ('Rise, let us be on our way.'). It seems odd for Jesus to command his disciples to depart and then continue to speak for another three chapters. One plausible explanation for this oddity is that John has slotted the teaching material contained in John 15.1–17.26 into the framework provided by an earlier source. On the other hand, it may be that, like all human beings, the biblical writers did not always express themselves with precision. Alleged breaks and interruptions in the text may be due not to the inadequate integration of different sources, but to personal lapses on the part of the author.

(d) Duplications, multiple versions and repetitions

Duplications or 'doublets' are similar, though distinct versions of what appear to be the same story. For example, there are three accounts of Abraham pretending that Sarah is his sister (Gen. 12.10–20; 20.1–18; 26.1–13), two accounts of David sparing Saul's life (1 Sam. 23.19–24.22; 26.1–25), and two accounts of Jesus' miraculous feeding of the multitude (Matt. 14.13–21; 15.32–39). The presence of doublets or multiple versions of what appear to be the same story may indicate that the biblical writer has made use of two or more different sources. This may be the case with Matt. 9.32–34 and 12.22–24, where we have two reports of what appears to be the same episode, namely the Pharisees attributing Jesus' exorcism of a demoniac to 'the ruler of the demons'. One possible explanation of this duplication is that Matthew is using two sources containing different versions of the same tradition, namely Mark and Q (Mark 3.22; Luke 11.15).

We should be wary of placing too much weight on doublets, however. Firstly, there is the difficulty of establishing whether apparent doublets are really two versions of the same story or simply accounts of two similar, but distinct episodes. Secondly, an author may repeat himself for a variety of reasons, such as, for example, to emphasize a point or simply out of forgetfulness. It is not absolutely necessary to attribute doublets to an author's use of two distinct sources.

(e) Variations in style, vocabulary and theology

Source critics assume that the authors of biblical writings possess a consistent style and theology. Consequently, changes in style and vocabulary or a shift in theological position within the text may be evidence of the incorporation of a source. That Job is a conflation of at least two different sources is evident from the fact that the introduction and conclusion are in prose, but the main body of the work is in poetry.

Evidence of the use of an otherwise unknown source may also be provided by testing the coherence of a passage with the remainder of the corpus of an author's writings. This is particularly important in isolating pre-Pauline elements in the letters of Paul. Those passages which do not fully cohere with Paul's theology and style may be due not to Paul himself but to his having taken up and incorporated an earlier source. Thus Bultmann and Käsemann have both argued that Romans 3.25–26 may not have been written by Paul himself but is an earlier source which Paul has taken up and incorporated into his letter.[42] Their reason for making this claim is that Rom. 3.25–26 employs terms that Paul does not otherwise employ, namely, *hilasterion* ('atonement') and *paresis* ('overlooking' or 'passing over' something). Other examples of what may be pre-Pauline elements which Paul has incorporated into his writings are Phil. 2.6–11 and Col. 1.15–20, which may be early Christian hymns. The argument from variation in style has also been cited in support of the view that Luke may have used sources for his birth narratives, which in contrast to the Hellenistic character of the rest of the Gospel are Hebraic in style.

There are, however, difficulties in employing the criterion of variations in style, vocabulary, and theology, for it depends on our being able to ascertain what is typical of an author and then showing that a particular passage is uncharacteristic of him. This will in turn depend on establishing which texts are genuine, which is itself a difficult task. Thus establishing what is characteristic of Paul's style and theology will depend on whether we recognize Colossians and Ephesians as genuinely Pauline. There is the further danger of defining what is characteristic of an author so narrowly that what would otherwise be regarded as legitimate variation in an author's style is taken to be an independent source. We simply do not know enough about the style of ancient authors to be sure that they were not capable of changing their style when they believed it to be appropriate. Furthermore, change in style or vocabulary may be due not to a change of source but to a change of subject matter. It may be, for example, that the difference in the style of the Lucan birth narratives is due not to Luke's having drawn on a Hebraic source but to his varying his style according to what he felt was appropriate to the episode he was relating.

2. Establishment of the relationship between sources

Agreement between different texts implies their dependence upon a common source. Once such agreements have been identified, the task of the source critic is then to establish the nature of the common source that has given rise to them. When we have two versions of the same story, A and B, how do we establish which is dependent upon which? Here the *differences* between two otherwise closely related texts play an important role. The fundamental criterion according to which textual dependence is established is the ease of explaining the divergences between the texts. Are the divergences better explained if A has altered B or B has altered A? That is, can we see reasons why the text may have changed from A to B, rather than vice versa? If the development from A to B is more easily and plausibly explained than the development from B to A, then we can conclude (though never with absolute certainty) that A is the earlier, more primitive version, upon which B is dependent. The difficulty with this criterion is that of establishing whether divergences are due to the use of different sources, the influence of oral tradition, or the editorial input of the author or compiler of the text. The most important differences upon which a conclusion about the direction of textual dependence can be made are as follows.

(a) Stylistic improvements

If text B appears to be written in a more sophisticated style than text A, then it is likely that B is dependent on A. A is unlikely to be dependent on B, since it is more probable that an author would have improved his source than that an author should have deliberately worsened the style. Thus one of the arguments that Mark is the source of both Matthew and Luke is that Mark's style is quite simple, even naïve. This can be seen in the way he links together the various episodes of Jesus' ministry by the use of 'and' and 'immediately'. (This is not apparent in many modern English translations, which have 'improved' Mark's style by eliminating his overuse of 'and'.) In Matthew and Luke, however, we find much less frequent use of 'and' and 'immediately' and a much smoother transition between the various sections of the narrative. It is difficult to see why, if Mark were dependent upon Matthew, he should have replaced Matthew's more sophisticated literary style with a simple, naïve style. The differences between Mark, Matthew and Luke are explicable, however, if we hold that Matthew and Luke have used Mark as a source and have improved his style. This argument is not conclusive, however, for it is possible that Mark may have used Matthew as a source, but paraphrased Matthew in his own language rather than following Matthew slavishly.

(b) Amplifications

If text B has provided detail or explanation that is not present in text A, then it is more likely that text B is dependent on text A than vice versa, for it is more probable that detail and explanation have been added than removed. For example, Matthew often includes Old Testament quotations that are absent from Mark. A good example of this is provided by the parallel passages Mark 1.34/Matt. 8.16-17.

Mark 1.32–34 vs. Matt. 8.16–17

That evening, at sunset, they brought to him all who were sick or possessed with demons. And the whole city was gathered around the door. And he cured many who were sick with various diseases, and cast out many demons; and he would not permit the demons to speak, because they knew him.	That evening they brought to him many who were possessed by demons; and he cast out the spirits with a word, and cured all who were sick. This was to fulfil what had been spoken through the prophet Isaiah, 'He took our infirmities and bore our diseases.'

It is easier to explain this passage on the basis of Matthew's dependence on Mark rather than vice versa. Matthew has added the quotation from Isa. 53.4 to support his theological aim of showing that Christ is the fulfilment of the Old Testament. It is difficult, however, to understand why Mark should have removed such material from his Gospel if he were dependent upon Matthew. Similarly, if Mark had known and used Matthew as a source, then it is puzzling that Mark should have omitted such passages as the Infancy Narrative, the Sermon on the Mount and many of the parables. It is easier to explain such differences between the two texts as due to Matthew's additions to Mark, rather than to attribute them to Mark's omission of material from Matthew.

(c) Clarifications

If text B has clarified a passage that is obscure in text A, then it is likely that text B is dependent on text A. An example of clarification can be seen when we compare Luke 5.29 with Mark 2.15. It is not clear from Mark's version how Jesus came to be in Levi's house. By adding the sentence 'Then Levi gave a great banquet for him in his house', Luke is able to clarify the passage and show why Jesus was eating with tax-collectors and sinners. It is more likely that Luke has added this verse in order to add clarity to Mark's account than it is that Mark has omitted the passage from his copy of Luke.

(d) Omissions

Omissions can also shed light on the relationship between texts. If theologically offensive or stylistically awkward passages that appear in one text are absent from an otherwise parallel text, it may indicate that the theologically difficult text is the source of the less problematic text. It seems likely that the inoffensive text is the result of an author's having 'cleaned up' his source by removing anything that might offend the community for which he was writing. A good example of this can be seen if we compare the accounts of Jesus' return to his home town of Nazareth in Mark 6.5–6 and Matt. 13.58.

Mark 6.5–6	Matt. 13.58
And he could do no deed of power	And he did not do many deeds of
there, except that he laid his	power there,
hands on a few sick people and	
cured them. And he marvelled	
because of their unbelief.[43]	because of their unbelief.

It is easier to explain why Matthew should have altered Mark than vice versa. Mark's version implies that Jesus was *incapable* of performing mighty works. This implication of *incapacity* on Jesus' part is unacceptable to Matthew and he thus adapts Mark to avoid this conclusion. First, he changes 'could' to 'did', and then by linking Jesus' non-performance of miracles to Mark's comment about the unbelief of the people of Nazareth transfers responsibility for the non-occurrence of miracles from Jesus to the Nazarenes. In doing so, the offensive implication that Jesus was *incapable* is removed and a theological point made about the relationship between faith and miracles.

It is, however, far more difficult to defend the hypothesis that Mark is dependent upon and has altered Matthew, for it is hard to explain why Mark should have modified Matthew in the way he supposedly has. On what grounds could Mark have chosen to change Matthew's version so that the *impotence* of Jesus is emphasized? Because it is generally easier in this and many other passages to explain how Matthew might have adapted Mark rather than vice versa, the consensus of opinion in New Testament scholarship is that Matthew is dependent upon Mark.

3. The construction of a hypothesis

The final stage in the work of the source critic is to construct a hypothesis to account for the presence of sources in the text under investigation and to identify their character. A successful hypothesis must be able to explain both points of overlap and divergence, and to take into consideration any relevant external information. Thus, continuing to take the Synoptic Problem as our example, an examination of the parallels between the Synoptic Gospels reveals that Matthew and Luke usually agree with Mark's wording and order, but only very occasionally agree with each other *against* Mark. There are several possible hypotheses to explain this.

- Matthew and Luke used Mark, but not each other.

- Mark has conflated and abbreviated Matthew and Luke.

- Matthew is the source of Mark, and Mark is the source of Luke.

Although these three hypotheses are possible on the basis of the available evidence, the consensus of opinion is that, for the reasons outlined in the previous sections, the theory that fits the evidence best is that of Markan priority. This argument is supplemented by the further argument that Matthew and Luke made use of a common source known as Q. There remains, however, dispute about the character of Q and uncertainty about whether it was a written document, a collection of oral tradition or one document or several.

Source criticism in action
Gen. 2.4b-3.24

1. Identification of sources
(a) Comparison of parallel texts
No parallel texts to Genesis are available, so we are reliant solely on the criteria appropriate for identifying sources *within* texts. What, then, is the internal evidence that may indicate that Genesis is the result of the conflation of earlier sources? To limit our discussion, we shall focus on the claim that Gen. 2.4b–3.24 provides evidence that Genesis is a composite text by considering the arguments that Gen. 2.4b–3.24 can be detached from the surrounding material.

(b) Contradictions
That Gen. 1.1–2.4a and Gen. 2.4b–3.24 are from distinct sources is indicated by the contradictions and inconsistencies that emerge if we assume that the two passages belong to a single, coherent narrative unit. One such inconsistency is the order of God's creation of living creatures, which differs in the two passages. In Gen. 1.1–2.4a, God begins with the creation of animals and concludes with the creation of human beings. In Gen. 2.4b–3.24, however, God first creates man, then animals, before finally creating woman. Another inconsistency between the two passages is that Gen. 1.12–13 tells us that the earth was rich in vegetation, but according to Gen. 2.5, the earth seems to be a barren place devoid of plants until God created the first human being and placed him in a garden 'to till it and keep it' (Gen. 2.15). The conclusion to which these discrepancies force us is that Gen. 1–2 consists of two distinct creation stories that have been placed alongside each other.

(c) Interruptions
Identification of where one source ends and the next begins is provided by the breaks and interruptions present in the text. Thus evidence that a new source begins in Gen. 2.4b is provided by the fact that in this verse God begins to create a second time, which in view of the creation narrative of Gen. 1.1–2.4a would seem to be redundant.[44] The end of the unit can also be

detected by being attentive to interruptions, breaks and shifts in subject matter. Gen. 4.1–26 continues the story of Adam and Eve, and relates the story of the first human family and the first murder. Its narrative is closely related to the preceding narrative of Gen. 2.4b–3.24 and tells of the first tragic consequence of human beings' disobedience of God, namely Cain's murder of his brother Abel. Gen. 4.1–26 is thus likely to belong to the same source as Gen. 2.4b–3.24. In Gen. 5.1, however, there is a clear break in the narrative, when the scene shifts from the story of the children of Adam and Eve, and turns to a genealogy listing the descendants of Adam. The conclusion we can draw from these interruptions, breaks and shifts in the early chapters of Genesis is that chapters 1.1–5.32 consists of the conflation of at least two sources comprising the first creation story of Gen. 1.1–2.4a, the second creation story and expulsion from Eden (Gen. 2.4b–3.24), the story of the first human family (Gen. 4.1–26), and the genealogy of Gen. 5.1–32.

(d) Duplications, multiple versions, and repetitions

Multiple versions of the same story may indicate that the author or editor of a text has combined several distinct sources. The reduplication of creation narratives would seem to indicate that the editors have drawn on (at least) two distinct sources in compiling the book of Genesis. This view would seem to be corroborated by the fact that the brief genealogy integrated into the story of the first human family (Gen. 4.17–22) is repeated though in different style in Gen. 5.1–32.

(e) Variations in style, vocabulary, and theology

The distinctness of Gen. 2.4b–4.26 from the surrounding material can be seen by comparing the style of this passage with that of Gen. 1.1–2.4a and 5.1–32. The style of Gen. 1.1–2.4a is repetitive. The repetition of the phrase 'And God said . . . Let there be . . . And it was so . . . And there was evening and there was morning, the *nth* day' gives Gen. 1.1–2.4a a litany-like character. Another characteristic feature of Gen. 1.1–2.4a is that God creates by divine fiat. The style of Gen. 2.4b–4.26, on the other hand, is noticeably different. The repetition that characterizes Gen. 1.1–2.4a is absent and God creates not by simply commanding things to come into existence, but by actually making human beings out of earth and planting a garden. God is like a craftsman in his workshop or a farmer in his field. The style is thus more anthropomorphic than that of Gen. 1.1–2.4a. A further contrast with Gen. 1.1–2.4a is that Gen. 2.4b–4.26 is a narrative that contains characters, plot, action and dialogue. Whereas Gen. 1.1–2.4a consists of a list of God's acts to bring the world into existence, Gen. 2.4b–3.24 provides a motive for God's creation of human beings, namely his need of a man to till the garden and subsequently the man's need of female companionship. This then lays the basis for the narrative concerning the first human beings' disobedience and expulsion from the garden.

That Gen. 2.4b–3.24 belongs to a unit that also includes Gen. 4.1-26 is indicated by the fact that Gen. 5.1–32 returns to the repetition that characterized Gen. 1.1–2.4a. Gen. 5.1–32 introduces each generation of Adam's descendants with the stereotypical phrase 'When A had lived for X number of years, he became the father of B.' Both Gen. 1.1–2.4a and Gen. 5.1–32 show the same repetitive style, a style that does not appear in Gen. 2.4b–4.26. The conclusion that has been drawn from these stylistic differences is that Gen. 1.1–5.32 comprises two different sources.

There are variations in vocabulary between Gen. 2.4b–3.24 and the material which surrounds it. The most obvious difference is the use of different terms for God. Gen. 1.1–2.4a and Gen. 5.1–32 use the term 'Elohim', whereas in Gen. 2.4b–4.26 God is called 'Yahweh'. Other differences are that while Gen. 1.1–2.4a and Gen. 5.1–32 use the Hebrew word for 'create' to describe God's creation of human beings, the term employed in Gen. 2.4b–4.26 is 'form'. Gen. 2.4b–3.24 also uses a more poetical vocabulary than Gen. 1.1–2.4b. A further difference is that whereas Gen. 1.1–2.4a and Gen. 5.1–32 employ the terms 'male and female', Gen. 2.4b–4.26 prefers the terms 'man and woman'.

Theological differences are also evident in the two creation accounts. Gen. 1.1–2.4a portrays God as transcendent, reigning far above the universe and creating the world by divine decree, but in Gen. 2.4b–4.26 he is portrayed as within the world like a human person, creating human beings like a potter moulds clay to make a pot. God is much closer to the world he has created and breathes his spirit into human beings. Furthermore, whereas God in Gen. 1.1–2.4a is completely in control, in Gen. 2.4b–3.24 he is taken by surprise by events. He even seems to make mistakes such as, for example, creating animals as man's companions before realizing that they cannot fulfil his need for companionship. It is only after discovering the inadequacy of the animals to provide the companionship the man needs that God creates woman. Two different theologies thus appear to be at work in the two creation stories. In Gen. 1.1–2.4a God is majestic, transcendent and distant, while in Gen. 2.4b–3.24 he seems to be a very human God who shares such human emotions as anger and disappointment. These different views of God are matched by different conceptions of humanity in the two accounts. In Gen. 1.1–2.4a, humanity seems to be more exalted than in Gen. 2.4b–3.24. In Gen. 1.26–27 we are told that God made human beings in his own image, whereas in Gen. 2.7 we are told that 'The LORD God formed man from the dust of the ground and breathed into his nostrils the breath of life; and the man became a living creature'.[45] The dependence of human beings is thus much more evident in Gen. 2.4b–3.24. Furthermore, the closeness of human beings to the animal kingdom is more apparent in Gen. 2.4b–3.24, for the text describes both human beings and animals by the same term, namely 'living creature' (Gen. 2.7, 19). This stands in contrast to Gen. 1.1–2.4a, where human beings are created as the climax of God's creative activity to exercise dominion over all that he has created (Gen. 1.26–28).

2. The construction of a hypothesis

The conclusion that scholars have drawn on the basis of the considerations described above is that Gen. 1.1–5.32 consists of two different sources. When these two sources are separated from each other, the problems of inconsistency, difference in style, interruptions and duplications vanish. Gen. 1.1–2.4a; 5.1–32 belongs to what has come to be known as the Priestly source or 'P'. Gen. 2.4b–4.26 belongs to the Yahwist source or 'J', so called because of its use of the term Yahweh (German: *Jahweh*) for God. The source Gen. 2.4b–4.26 has been slotted into the framework provided by Gen. 1.1–2.4a and Gen. 5.1–32.

An important question is whether the sources upon which Gen. 2.4b–3.24 has been constructed were literary or oral in character. Von Rad holds that the irregularities in the text are better explained not as the result of the combination of literary sources but through the growth of tradition. The internal contradictions and inconsistencies within the text are due to the shift in inner motivation that takes place in the transmission of oral tradition.[46] This means that the source critical study of Gen. 2.4b–3.24 must be supplemented by form criticism.

Matt. 15.21-28

1. Identification of sources

Matt. 15.21–28 has a parallel text in Mark 7.24–30, so the first stage in identifying whether Matthew has employed a source is to compare the two texts in order to establish the character of their relationship. An examination of the two passages reveals close verbal agreement between Matt. 15.26–27 and Mark 7.27–28, which would seem to indicate dependence of either Mark upon Matthew or Matthew upon Mark. Furthermore, the episode the text describes occurs in the same order of events in both Matthew and Mark, namely after Jesus' dispute with the Pharisees concerning tradition and before healing miracles and the feeding of the 4000. The evidence would seem to indicate dependence of one of the Gospels on the other or that another source underlies both accounts.

2. Establishment of the relationship between sources

To establish the relationship between the two Gospels, it is necessary to examine how the two versions differ from each other and whether these differences can shed light on the direction of dependence, i.e. whether Matthew is dependent on Mark or vice versa. This means examining the Gospels for evidence of stylistic improvements, amplifications, clarifications and omissions.

(a) Stylistic improvements

In contrast to Mark, Matthew introduces dialogue from almost the beginning of the pericope. Mark does not introduce dialogue until half way through the passage, relying until Mark 7.27 on a third person description of the events. Matthew's structuring of the episode in the form of a dialogue between the Canaanite woman and Jesus has the effect of making the passage more dynamic. The drama of the passage is heightened still further by Matthew's bringing the episode to a climactic conclusion with Jesus' pronouncement: 'Woman, great is your faith! Let it be it done for you as you wish' (Matt. 15.28).

Matthew also introduces terms we know to be typical of him from their use elsewhere in his Gospel. Thus Matthew characteristically introduces the passage with the phrases 'left that place' and 'went away' (Matt. 15.21), which he also employs in Matt. 2.22; 4.12; 12.15; 14.13; 27.5, but which do not appear in Mark and Luke. Furthermore, in contrast to Mark's simple reference to Tyre, Matthew employs the phrase 'Tyre *and Sidon*', a combination which he also employs when he refers to Tyre in Matt. 11.21–22. Whereas Mark tells us that the woman 'fell down at his feet' (Mark 7.25), Matthew employs the theologically more significant term 'she worshipped him' (Matt. 15.25).[47]

(b) Clarifications

Matthew replaces Mark's second reference to 'children' with the term 'masters', which makes clearer the hierarchy between the Jews and Gentiles. The Jews are not 'children' in relation to the Gentiles, but are their superiors. To eliminate the ambiguity caused by Mark's 'children' and to sharpen the point of the woman's comment, Matthew therefore substitutes 'children' with 'masters'. It is difficult to see why, if Mark were dependent on Matthew, he should have changed Matthew's 'masters' to 'children'.

(c) Omissions

Matthew's version omits Mark 7.24b: 'And he entered a house, and would not have any one know it; yet he could not be hid' and Jesus' mitigating comment to the woman 'let the children be fed first' (Mark 7.27) and includes the verse 'I was sent only to the lost sheep of the house of Israel' (Matt. 15.24b).

3. The construction of a hypothesis

The relation between Mark 7.24–30 and Matt. 15.21–28 is a complex one. Although there are clear parallels between the two texts, there are some significant differences. If we leave aside the strong parallels between Matt. 15.26–27 and Mark 7.27–28, there is considerable variation in wording between the two versions. Matthew's version contains 140 words, while Mark's contains 130, but the two Gospels have fewer than forty words in common. If Matthew were dependent on Mark, we would expect a closer correspondence between the vocabulary of the two Gospels. A further difference between the two stories is that there are far more Jewish elements in Matthew's account and it appears to be more hostile to Gentiles than Mark's version. Matthew contains more Semitisms than Mark, notably vv. 23, 24 and 28.

The question is how these differences are to be interpreted. Three theories have been advanced.

1. Matthew has inherited a similar but distinct and independent tradition from Mark.
Perhaps two versions of the pericope were in circulation, one (Mark's) more favourable to the Gentile mission, the other (Matthew's) hostile to the Gentile mission. The original episode underlying both versions was then modified to suit the different purposes of the two evangelists. Mark developed his version into an affirmation of the Gentile mission, though recognizing the pre-eminence of the Jews. Matthew developed his version into a rejection of the Gentile mission. Luke does away with the ambiguity by eliminating the passage altogether.

2. Matthew has conflated his special material with the tradition inherited from Mark.
A possible explanation is that Matthew knew of a different version of the story of the Canaanite/Syro–Phoenician woman, which he has conflated with Mark's account. Alternatively, Matthew may have thoroughly revised Mark in order to adapt Mark's text to suit his theological interests. The question is whether Matthew's expansion of Mark is due to Matthew's access to another source unknown to Mark or whether it is due to Matthew's redactional activity.

3. Matthew has reworked Mark to suit his theological interests and those of the Church.
This theory attributes the differences between Matthew and Mark to Matthew's editorial activity. The differences stem not from an alternative

tradition but from Matthew himself. Supporters of this view cite as evidence the fact that many of the divergent terms in Matthew's version appear in redactional comments elsewhere in the Gospel. The appearance in Matt. 15.21–28 of terms identified as redactional elsewhere in the Gospel of Matthew make it likely that they are due to Matthew rather than to his use of an alternative independent source. Since it is Matthew's practice elsewhere in the Gospel to insert logia into Mark's framework, it may be that he has done so in this passage, and has slotted Matt. 15.24 into the material he has inherited from Mark.

Matthew's omission of Mark 7.24b and 7.27 and addition of Matt. 15.24b can be explained on the basis of what we know of Matthew's theology elsewhere in Gospel. In order to highlight Jesus' status, Matthew has a tendency to remove the passages where Mark has Jesus conceal his messiahship. This may account for why Matthew has omitted Mark 7.24b. He may also have been conscious of the impossibility of Jesus concealing himself in the way described by Mark.

Evaluation of source criticism

Is source criticism necessary? Is it important to identify the sources of a biblical writing? Its proponents certainly think so. The sources we identify and the way we arrange them will determine how we see Israelite and Christian history. Thus if we take Matthew rather than Mark as the earliest Gospel, this will affect the way we view the development of early Christian doctrine. If the Gospel of Mark is a development from rather than the basis of Matthew's Gospel, then our understanding of, for example, the development of the Christology of the early Church will be radically different.

In the nineteenth century, source criticism was of immense importance, for by its careful employment it was believed possible to construct an accurate picture of the life of Jesus. If we are to get back to the historical Jesus, then it is important to identify the earliest sources and to detach them from the later theologizing of the Church. This led, at least initially, to Mark becoming regarded as the primary source for knowledge of the life of Jesus. On the basis of Mark's allegedly historical account of Jesus' life, it was believed that an undogmatic Christology could be constructed that avoided what was regarded as the now untenable Christology inherited from the Church tradition. With the publication of Wilhelm Wrede's book *The Messianic Secret* (1901), however, the confidence that Mark could be employed to enable us to get back to the historical Jesus suffered a severe blow. Wrede showed that Mark had not provided a historically reliable account of Jesus' life, but, like the other Evangelists, had written his

Gospel from a distinct theological perspective that guided his portrayal of Jesus.

Modern source critics have consequently become less ambitious in their employment of source criticism. The aim is no longer to get as close as possible to the historical facts that underlie the writings of the New Testament, but rather to understand the formation of the biblical writings. If we can isolate an author's sources, then we can study how that author has modified and adapted his sources to suit his theological needs and those of the community for which he was writing. This can shed light on the theology of the author and on the character of the community of which he was a member.

There are, however, several criticisms that have been levelled against source criticism. Firstly, source criticism is based on the assumption that the inconsistencies and contradictions in a text mean that that text cannot be considered to be a unity. These tensions indicate that the text has been built up from the conflation of earlier, originally independent sources. This approach thus presupposes that authors strive for consistency in their writing. The problem here is: why did the purported editors of the final text not do a better job at unifying their sources? Why did they not eliminate the tensions and contradictions? Of course, if the editors had eliminated all inconsistencies, then we would not be able to identify the tensions that point to the presence of an earlier source embedded in the text. Source criticism needs to explain, however, why the biblical authors were seemingly unable to eliminate inconsistencies when integrating their sources into their writings.

Secondly, source criticism assumes that modern notions of contradiction and inconsistency were also held by ancient writers. The problem here is that we do not know whether ancient writers were as troubled by contradiction as modern human beings. What if their notion of consistency differed from ours or they were simply not as sensitive to contradictions as modern human beings? Perhaps they were more capable of living with contradictions or simply did not recognize what we call contradictions as contradictions. Presumably the author did not see the alleged textual tensions detected by source criticism as contradictions, otherwise it is difficult to see how he would have included them in the text. And if the author was not conscious of inconsistency, then is the source critic justified in using supposed inconsistences to identify earlier sources the author has supposedly integrated into his writing? Such considerations have led some scholars to argue that the alleged inconsistencies in the text by which source criticism identifies different sources may be due not to the conflation of sources but to oriental modes of thought, which were more tolerant of inconsistency than modern Western thought.[48] Other scholars provide theological and stylistic explanations for the inconsistencies in what they take to be a unified text.[49] The problem here is how to identify *genuine* inconsistencies.

Thirdly, source criticism has been criticized for allegedly ignoring the oral nature of ancient Israelite culture. The view of literary production as the synthesis of earlier *documents* is a modern view, and one which is not appropriate to an oral culture. It has been argued that the variations in style, vocabulary and theology detectable in biblical texts were due not to the conflation of disparate documentary sources, but to the oral transmission of the units that underlie the text. Other critics of source criticism have claimed that source critics presuppose the fragmentary character of the text and read this presupposition into the text. If we worked from the assumption of unity, then the supposedly fragmentary character of the text would not be as apparent as the source critics claim.[50] These views, however, have found only limited acceptance among scholars of the Pentateuch. The variety of style and theology, as well as breaks and inconsistencies in the text are too great, it is argued, to regard the Pentateuch as a unified whole stemming from the pen of a single author.

CHAPTER FIVE

Form Criticism

Form criticism is the identification and analysis of *forms*.[1] Forms are conventional patterns of speech employed in specific contexts. Financial reports, sports reports, letters, wedding announcements, obituaries, invitations, recipes, memos, job applications, prescriptions and so on are recognizable by the fact that they employ standardized formulas and stylized phrases which allow us to identify the type of communication we are reading. For example, if we read a text that begins with the phrase 'Dear Jane' or 'Dear Sir or Madam' and closes with a phrase such as 'best wishes', 'love' or 'yours faithfully', followed by the name of the sender, we know that we are reading a letter. We know this because we recognize the forms used in letter writing, namely that it is customary to begin a letter with 'Dear' and end it with a declaration of faithfulness, sincerity, respect, esteem or love for the addressee. Similarly, if we receive a communication containing such phrases such as 'we request the honour of the company of . . .', 'you are cordially invited . . .', and RSVP, we know we are are dealing with an invitation.

Form criticism is based on the observation that forms are present in the Bible. In the Old Testament the prophets use stereotypical phrases to introduce and authorize their prophecies, such as 'Thus says the Lord.' In Kings and Chronicles, 'regnal reports' are employed to introduce and briefly summarize the life of the kings.[2] In the New Testament, Jesus often employs formulaic 'I-sayings' to speak of himself, his mission and the fate that awaits him (e.g. Mark 10.45; Matt. 5.17; 10.34–36). A formulaic structure is evident in the Beatitudes (Matt. 5.3–10) and in Jesus' pronouncement of woe upon the Pharisees (Matt. 23). Put at its most simple, form criticism is the study of the distinctive literary forms employed in the biblical writings. It is concerned to identify, categorize and catalogue such literary forms as myths, legends, sagas, proverbs, legal sayings, parables and so on.

This concern with the forms in biblical texts has led to several other foci in the work of form critics, namely, concern with the genre, *Sitz im Leben*, the oral prehistory and the history of the transmission of the biblical forms.

(1) Genre

Forms alert us to the *genre* of a text. Because we know that the form 'dear' followed by a name and 'yours faithfully/sincerely', etc. are characteristic of letter writing, we are able to place a document containing these terms in the genre of the letter. We are also able to identify what sort of a letter it is. The forms 'Dear Sir or Madam' and 'yours faithfully' indicate that we are dealing with a formal, official communication rather than, say, a love letter. The knowledge of the conventions of letter writing allows us to recognize that despite the terms of endearment employed in the letter, the letter is not a declaration of love or faithfulness towards to the recipient of the letter, but belongs to the genre of the formal letter.

The relationship between form and genre has been a problematic one in form criticism, however. The problem stems from the difficulty of distinguishing form and genre, the result of which has been their conflation in some form-critical studies of the Bible. Part of the problem is to establish whether it is *form* or *content* that determines genre. As long ago as 1928, B. S. Easton raised this question with regard to Bultmann, asking, 'What *formal* difference is there between the "logion" – Whosoever exalteth himself shall be humbled – the "apocalyptic word" – Whosoever shall be ashamed of me, the Son of Man shall be ashamed of him – and the "church rule" – Whosoever putteth away his wife and marrieth another committeth adultery?'[3] Formally, these three statements seem to be similar, but Bultmann has on the basis of their subject matter classified them as three different types of form. The difficulty of distinguishing between form and genre also accounts for why form criticism has often tended to mutate into genre criticism.[4] Wolfgang Richter, however, argues for the differentiation between form and genre and complains: 'The conflation of form and genre has led to disastrous consequences in form criticism which to this day have still not been eradicated.'[5] Richter argues that 'form' should denote the formal elements of a passage such as its structure and metre, whereas 'genre' should be reserved for the type of literature to which the passage belongs and can be identified on the basis of its sharing formal characteristics with other texts. For the sake of clarity, it is advisable to hold form and genre apart and to conceive of forms as one of the means by which we can identify genres (other means are motive, theme and contents).

(2) Sitz im Leben

As the above examples of the formal letter and the invitation show, we use different forms in different contexts. Forms of language originate and function in particular settings. There is thus a correlation between form, content and the situation in which a form came into existence and the context in which it is used. Thus the context of a sports report will be a society in which sport is played and is of interest not only to those participating in it or watching it, but also to those who are unable to be physically present at the sporting event. Recognition of the form of a writing as a sports report thus tells us something about the society in which that report was produced, namely that it was a society in which sport was so highly valued that it was felt necessary to disseminate the results of sporting events to the general public.

The term used for the setting or situation of a form is the German phrase *Sitz im Leben*, literally 'setting in life'. The term *Sitz im Leben* was coined by Hermann Gunkel and was first employed in his 1906 essay 'Fundamental Problems of Hebrew Literary History'.[6] It has since become a stock phrase in biblical scholarship. Form critics have traditionally been concerned not only to identify forms but also the *Sitz im Leben* in which these forms have come into existence and have been used, preserved and handed down. The identification of the *Sitz im Leben* has provided the basis for the reconstruction of the history of ancient Israel and its institutions and the history of the early Church.

(3) Oral Prehistory

Form critics argue that embedded in the written text are elements whose formulaic character indicates that they are likely to have originated in an oral context. Evidence of oral transmission is that the text is made up of small units which have a stereotyped and easily memorizable form or that the unit can be detached from the context without detriment to its meaning. Brief, formulaic sayings are more easily committed to memory and passed on orally than large blocks of prose, so the existence of pithy formulations in the text may indicate that elements of the text had a pre-literary, oral history.

Evidence that such a text originally existed in oral form is provided if it retains a coherent and independent meaning when detached from its surrounding context. In other words, the surrounding context is not crucial to understanding the unit. Such passages should not be interpreted according to written literary conventions, but according to the conventions appropriate to the social and public occasions in which they would have been used. It is the conviction that forms may have first existed in oral form that opens up the possibility of gaining insights into the pre-literary formation of the biblical text. One of the tasks of the form critic has thus been to identify the oral prototypes of written text.

(4) The history of transmission

Early form criticism was concerned with not only identifying and classifying the forms employed in the Bible but also tracing the development of these forms. Once the forms have been identified, it is allegedly possible to work out the principles according to which they have developed and been handed down. Armed with this knowledge we can then work back to the original pre-literary instance of a particular form. It is this historical dimension of form criticism that accounts for the German term *Formgeschichte*, i.e. 'form *history*', and for the concern with *tradition history*, i.e. with tracing the way units of tradition were handed down orally up to the point of their becoming fixed in their final written state.[7]

Form criticism thus combines two approaches. Firstly, it attempts to identify the forms in a text. The criteria for this are literary and aesthetic. Analysis of the text allows us (1) to identify that it contains forms and (2) to identify what kind of forms the text contains. This leads to genre criticism, which is the attempt to group together forms that resemble each other into families. Secondly, form criticism attempts to identify the setting which gave rise to the forms. This is a historical and sociological exercise which is concerned with identifying (a) the *Sitze im Leben* in which the forms were created and preserved; (b) how forms were modified through their transmission; and (c) how the forms came to be fixed in the final canonical version in the text. Form criticism thus has two purposes, namely the identification of pre-literary stages in the development of a text and the recovery of the social contexts underlying these pre-literary stages.

A brief history of form criticism

It is unclear when and by whom the term 'form criticism' was formulated. The German term employed to denote this method of exegesis is *Formgeschichte*, literally 'form history', although some later German scholars such as Richter have adopted the term *Formkritik*. The term 'form history' seems first to have been employed by the German New Testament scholar Martin Dibelius in the title of his 1919 work *Die Formgeschichte des Evangeliums* [The Form History of the Gospel].[8] This term was taken up by subsequent German scholars. In 1924 Emil Fascher published a study entitled *The Form-Historical Method*,[9] which contains a survey of predecessors of *Formgeschichte* prior to 1919, while in 1927 Ludwig Koehler published his *The Form-Historical Problem of the New Testament*.[10] The earliest English-language use of the term I have been able to identify is that of the American scholar B. S. Easton, who employs the term in his *The Gospel before the Gospel* (1928), where he writes that 'with Dibelius form-history is raised to the rank of a distinct discipline' and that 'in his hands "form-history" becomes "form-criticism" '.[11] The term 'form-criticism' was taken up by subsequent Anglophone scholars and quickly established itself as the standard term for this form of biblical exegesis.

Although the term may first have come into existence with Dibelius, the method of exegesis the term denotes existed much earlier. Easton sees Strauss' analysis of the Gospels in terms of myth as 'only a very special form-history',[12] and holds that many biblical scholars of the late nineteenth and early twentieth centuries he discusses in his first chapter of his book 'used the method more or less unconsciously'.[13] We can, however, arguably trace form criticism back still earlier to de Wette, who, in his commentary on the Psalms (1811),[14] develops a classification of different types of psalms, which he categorizes as hymns praising God, popular psalms alluding to Israelite history and the people's relation to God, Zion and temple psalms, royal psalms and psalms of lament.[15] In his later *On the Explanation of the Edification of the Psalms* (1836), de Wette argues that it is pointless to search for a concrete occasion in which the author, for instance David, composed a particular psalm. Rather, 'I am very inclined to believe that some psalms, especially the psalms of lament and poems of supplication, have as their presupposition and their subject more general than specific circumstances in Israelite life'.[16] Reventlow exclaims, 'That is the foundation of later genre criticism!'[17]

Despite such anticipations of form-critical approaches in the early nineteenth century, the undisputed pioneer of what would later come to be known as form criticism was the German Old Testament scholar Hermann Gunkel (1862–1932). Gunkel himself employed the term 'legend' rather than form, but what he means by 'legend' corresponds closely to what would later be called 'form' by subsequent scholars. Gunkel took up insights from Jakob and Wilhelm Grimm, who had collected and classified German folk tales into fairy tales, myths, sagas and legends, and adapted this classification for use in the study of the Old Testament. Another influence on Gunkel's thinking was his awareness of parallels between the Old Testament and contemporary Near Eastern literature, which was becoming increasingly available during Gunkel's lifetime. Gunkel's insight was that many Old Testament texts had begun life as folk traditions, which were initially passed down not in written form but by word of mouth. It was only later that they came to be fixed in literary forms, many of which had been influenced by the literature of neighbouring cultures.

At the end of the nineteenth century, biblical scholarship was dominated by source criticism. Like the source critics Gunkel was concerned with the history of the literature of the Old Testament, but he came to the conclusion that this history could not be written solely on the basis of establishing the context and aims of the final editors of the texts. It was necessary to trace the way the individual elements of these texts had been handed down before they acquired their final written shape.[18] To achieve this aim, Gunkel attempted to get back to the very earliest forms in the Old Testament, namely the oral traditions which he believed preceded the written text and had been linked together according to theme by later editors and incorporated into the written text. Gunkel focused on identifying the smallest units of tradition, which he believed were the most original forms of oral tradition. Gunkel identified units of tradition according to their brevity and self-sufficiency. This principle of identification was based on his assumption that oral tradition tends initially to transmit brief texts that are easy to commit to memory. These units of oral tradition were then collected into blocks of material organized according to a common theme. Thus material concerning the origin of the world was grouped together into Gen. 1–11, which as a whole is concerned with primeval history. Oral tradition concerning Abraham was grouped together in Gen. 12–25 and the Jacob-Esau material was collected in Gen. 27–35.

In isolating units of tradition from their broader context, Gunkel noted that these brief units frequently shared common features. These common features allowed him to classify units of tradition according to genre. In Genesis, for example, Gunkel identified several distinct genres, namely myths concerning the gods and their involvement in the world (Gen. 6–9); historical sagas (Gen. 14); aetiologies explaining the origins of Israelite customs and practices (Gen. 29–31), ceremonies (Gen. 17), geological features (Gen. 19) and names (Gen. 32). Gunkel went on to apply his approach to other forms of literature in the Bible, notably folk tales, psalms and prophetic literature. He noted that in the Psalms, for example, there is a common pattern and repetition of similar moods, ideas, metaphors and phrases.[19]

The explanation for such similar patterns is that these units of tradition were not composed by a single author, but used repeatedly in similar situations. Identifying stock phrases and formulations will therefore give us an insight into the situations in which they were originally used. It was thus Gunkel's further aim to identify the *Sitz im Leben* in which the legends had developed. He argued that the legends contained in Genesis arose from the attempt to explain some aspect of the life of Israel, and categorized legends according to what it was that the legend attempted to explain. Thus *ethnological* legends explain the relationships between the tribes of Israel. For example, the purpose of the story of Jacob's deception of Esau is to relate how the tribe of Jacob was able to occupy better land than neighbouring tribes. *Etymological* legends, on the other hand, explain the origin and meaning of things important to the ancient Israelites such as the names of tribes, cities, sanctuaries, etc. A good example of an etymological legend is provided by the story that Jacob was born holding on to Esau's heel. This legend was probably prompted by the similarity between the name Jacob and the Hebrew word *'āqēbh*, meaning 'heelholder'. *Ceremonial* legends explain the origin of the ceremonies practised in Israel such as circumcision and resting on the Sabbath. For example, Exod. 4.24–26 explains circumcision as originating from Moses' redemption of his firstborn child. *Geological* legends explain why the landscape of Israel is the way it is. For example, what is the origin of the pillar of salt that resembles a woman? The answer is that it is Lot's wife, turned into a pillar of salt as punishment for looking back at God's destruction of Sodom and Gomorrah (Gen. 19.26).[20]

Tracing the development of a legend is possible by identifying the modifications it has undergone as a result of change of time and environment. Such modifications can be detected in additions to a story that disrupt the flow of narrative. A further indication of the development of a legend is the introduction of explanations that seem to stem from the hand of a later editor, who may be more concerned with placing material together into thematic blocks than preserving the character of the original oral tradition. A good example of this is provided by Genesis 33.18–20; 35.9, which appear to belong together, but have been separated by the insertion of the story of the rape of Dinah (Gen. 34). Another way of tracing the development of oral material is by examining evidence of omissions. Such omissions are probably due to a later editor's removal of material he regarded as objectionable. This can reduce some stories to mere fragments of their original form. Little is left of the legend of Nimrod other than he was 'a mighty hunter before the LORD' (Gen. 10.9). Other stories seem to have lost their original meaning during the process of transmission. For example, the apparent unreasonableness of Judah's commandment that Tamar should remain a widow and not remarry until Shelah grew up prompted the addition of an explanatory note by the editor, who attributes Judah's commandment to his fear that Shelah would die like his brothers (Gen. 38.11).

Gunkel's pupil Sigmund Mowinckel (1884–1965) continued his teacher's approach, devoting particular attention to the context in which units of tradition function and the means by which they were transmitted orally.[21] Mowinckel explored the setting of the Psalms in the worship of the temple cult and employed them to construct a picture of ancient Israelite worship. Whereas Gunkel considered the biblical Psalms to be literary constructions modelled on now lost Psalms used in worship, Mowinckel argued that many of the Psalms were not literary constructions but were themselves the Psalms used in the cult. He further claimed that the Israelites practised a New Year Festival akin to the Babylonian Akitu Festival, which simultaneously celebrated and renewed the kingship of the god and the monarch. Mowinckel argued that many of the Psalms originated and were used in the context of this New Year Festival. Psalms which affirmed Yahweh's sovereignty, praised him for his renewal of creation and celebrated his defeat of Israel's enemies, belonged to this cultic setting. Mowinckel's study of the prophets led him to conclude that the sayings of the prophets were communicated orally by prophetic schools, i.e. groups of disciples who preserved and handed down the sayings of their prophet until they eventually came to be committed to paper in what we now know as the prophetic books.

Another student of Gunkel, Albrecht Alt (1883–1956), was concerned to identify the institutional settings which gave rise to the units of tradition that underlie biblical literature. In his essay 'The Settlement of the Israelites in Palestine' (1925), Alt focused on the formation of ancient Israel, arguing that Israel was created through the amalgamation of tribes moving first into the highlands west of the River Jordan, before eventually clashing with the peoples living on the coastal plain.[22] In his 'The God of the Fathers' (1929), Alt argued that Israelite religion came into existence through the fusion of ancestral cults with religious practices absorbed through the Israelites' encounter with the Canaanites.[23] In his essay 'The Origins of Israelite Law' (1934),[24] Alt distinguished between two types of biblical law, namely 'casuistically formulated laws' and 'apodictically formulated laws'. Casuistic laws are recognized by their use of conditional clauses: 'If action X takes place, then legal action Y is to take place.' An Old Testament example is: 'When someone causes a field or vineyard to be grazed over, or lets livestock loose to graze in someone else's field, restitution shall be made from the best in the owner's field or vineyard' (Exod. 22.5). Apodictic laws are formulated as imperatives or categorical statements: 'Thou shalt not do X,' 'Cursed is whoever does Y.' For example, 'Whoever curses father or mother shall be put to death' (Exod. 21.17). Apodictic laws are unconditional commands and the punishment for their violation is death or a curse. Noting the existence of casuistic laws in contemporary Near Eastern law codes, where they deal primarily with the regulation of an agrarian society, Alt argued that the ancient Israelites had adopted this type of legal ruling from their neighbours and adapted it to their own use. Because he was unable to find parallels in Near Eastern cultures outside Israel, however, Alt claimed that the apodictic laws were unique to the Israelites and had been developed during their nomadic period in the desert before entering Canaan. For Alt, these apodictic laws were closely connected with the tribal cult, which he envisaged as the public recital of God's law to the people to ensure that they adhered to the covenant God had made with Israel. This view has been challenged by some scholars, however, and the argument has been advanced that apodictic laws are not unique to Israel but are a feature of semi-nomadic cultures.[25] Alt also identified hybrid forms which combined elements from casuistic and apodictic laws, such as 'If action X takes place, then thou shalt do Y.' According to Alt, these mixed forms came into existence in the courts which were established after the Israelites had taken possession of Canaan and become a settled society.[26]

The contribution of Gerhard von Rad (1901–1971) to form criticism was to note how smaller units of tradition could function as the foundation for building up bigger collections of material. In his early work on the Hexateuch, von Rad identified brief creeds embedded in the text, such as Deut. 6.20–24; 26.5b–9; and Josh. 24.2b–13, which summarized God's actions on behalf of Israel. He argued that these creedal statements constituted the foundation for collecting and organizing into a coherent narrative the oral traditions which would eventually form the Hexateuch, a process he believed to have been carried out by whoever was responsible for J. The *Sitz im Leben* of this collecting and editing of Israel's national and religious traditions was the newly established Davidic monarchy, for which it had become necessary to provide a theological and historical justification. According to von Rad, the text created by J was recited to the people at the Festival of Sukkot in order to create a sense of communal identity among the Israelite tribes and to weld them together into a single nation with a common history worshipping one and the same God. Von Rad was important for showing how larger bodies of material could be built up from smaller units of tradition.

The contribution of Martin Noth (1902–1968) to form criticism consists in his identification of brief, self-sufficient historical summaries in Joshua-Kings, such as, for example, Josh. 1, 23, and 1 Sam. 12. These summaries recount in a similar style, structure and theological perspective Israel's relationship with God and the responsibility this placed on the Israelites. These observations led Noth to conclude that Joshua-Kings formed a unified Deuteronomistic History. Noth held that a historian, whom he named Dtr, had during the exilic period collated Israel's traditions and organized them into a continuous narrative. The theological motive for this was to provide an explanation for the destruction of the Temple and the exile of Israel from the Promised Land they had received from God. These catastrophic events were interpreted as God's punishment on Israel for the people's failure to observe their covenant with him. In his later work, Noth argued that the Pentateuch came into existence through the amalgamation at a pre-literary stage of five distinct strands of tradition, each of which was organized around a central theme, namely, the exodus, the quest for arable land, the promise to the patriarchs, the wandering in the wilderness and the revelation at Sinai.[27]

The work of von Rad and Noth led to an increasing focus on *tradition history* as the key to understanding the formation of the Pentateuch. This emphasis shifted scholarly attention away from written sources to oral tradition, and provided a new way of understanding the formation of the

Pentateuch. These developments led Rolf Rendtorff (b. 1925) to offer an alternative theory to the documentary hypothesis. Basing his theory on a traditional-historical approach, Rendtorff argued that the Pentateuch came into existence through a gradual process stretching over several centuries in which the combination of smaller units of oral tradition resulted in the creation of ever larger units. These larger units were then combined to form continuous units, which were in turn eventually combined to produce the Pentateuch as we now know it. Rendtorff's approach was taken up by Erhard Blum,[28] who, however, attributes a much greater role to a D redactor, who according to Blum played a leading role in the construction of the Pentateuch through combining D and P.

Claus Westermann's work centred on identifying genres and their life settings. In his early work on the prophets, Westermann identified as characteristics of prophetic speech the messenger form and the prophetic judgement,[29] while in his work on the Psalms he examined cultic laments and hymns of praise.[30]

Emphasis on the oral origins of the Pentateuch has also been prominent among Scandinavian scholars, who argue that conceiving of the Pentateuch in terms of the conflation of *written* sources reflects a modern attitude to the composition of texts and does not do justice to the dominance of oral tradition in the ancient world. Such considerations prompted I. Engnell to reject the notion of parallel documents such as J and E, and their supposed combination into a new document. The inconsistencies and breaks in the text of the Pentateuch are for Engnell due not to the amateurish conflation of different written sources but to the process of oral transmission. It was only when oral communication was threatened by such crises in the life of Israel as the Assyrian destruction of the northern kingdom and the Babylonian Exile that it became necessary to preserve the oral tradition by committing it to writing.

Impulses for the development of New Testament form criticism were provided by Wrede, whose work contributed to a growing awareness that a process of the passing down and moulding of oral stories about Jesus had taken place between Jesus' death and the formation of the Gospels. The task of uncovering this process was taken up during and immediately after the First World War by the pioneers of the application of form criticism to the New Testament: Karl Ludwig Schmidt (1891–1956), Martin Dibelius (1883–1947) and Rudolf Bultmann (1884–1976).

In his *The Framework of the History of Jesus*,[31] Schmidt focused on the framework the evangelists had used to organize their material. Schmidt argued that this framework was not a reflection of the historical outline of Jesus' life, but was a construction the evangelists had imposed upon inherited material according to their theological interests. This includes the Gospel of Mark, whose status as the earliest Gospel does not mean that it was not itself the result of a framework imposed on the Gospel material by its editor. According to Schmidt, the material in Mark originally circulated independently as brief stories or 'pericopes', which were then fitted into a structure of Mark's making. The only likely exception to the circulation of independent units of tradition is the Passion Narrative, which is likely to have been recounted as an entirety. As Schmidt points out, such a lengthy, sustained narrative was necessary if the early Christian community was to answer the question: 'How could Jesus have been brought to the cross by people who were blessed by his signs and wonders.'[32] The fact that the structure of Mark is due to the evangelist means that Mark's Gospel does not relate the genuine chronology of Jesus' life, but reflects the theological concerns of the early Church. The evangelists were not historians attempting to construct an objective historical account of Jesus' life, but were collectors, editors and organizers of folk-tales about Jesus. Schmidt, however, does not develop a method of form criticism as such, but rather lays its foundations by showing how Mark was built up out of originally smaller independent units.

In New Testament scholarship, it was above all Martin Dibelius and Rudolf Bultmann who established form criticism as an important method of interpretation. Their work was quickly followed by a contribution by Martin Albertz (1883–1956), who seems to have developed a type of form criticism independently of Dibelius and Bultmann, and whose book was ready to go to press in 1918. Owing to the crisis caused by Germany's defeat in the First World War, however, his *The Controversy Dialogues of the Synoptic Gospels* was not published until 1921.[33] Another early work in form criticism was by Georg Bertram (1896–1979), who provided a form-critical study of the Passion Narrative in his *The Passion of Jesus and the Christ Cult* (1922).[34]

It was, however, the form criticism developed by Dibelius and Bultmann which was the most influential on subsequent debate in New Testament scholarship and for this reason will be the focus of our discussion here. Dibelius and Bultmann set themselves the task of identifying the processes involved in the transmission of the Gospel tradition and tracking the history of the development of the tradition prior to its being fixed in its final form in the Gospels. As envisaged by Dibelius and Bultmann, form criticism aimed not only at classifying the various forms in the Gospel tradition, but at identifying their role and function in the early Christian community. This entailed attempting to distinguish between forms that went back to Jesus himself and those which were the product of the early Christian community.

In his *Die Formgeschichte des Evangeliums* [Form History of the Gospel] (1919) Dibelius argues that the Gospels are written compilations of material which was originally passed down by word of mouth. The evangelists have simply put together in written form sayings about Jesus and stories about his life and work that had circulated orally in the decades after Jesus' death. This means, Dibelius claims, that the evangelists 'are principally collectors, vehicles of tradition, editors'.[35] Their role 'is concerned with the choice, the limitation, and the final shaping of material, but not with the original moulding'.[36] Form criticism, however, is interested in the stage *before* the writing of the Gospels. It is concerned with identifying individual units of tradition and tracing their development prior to their being incorporated into the Gospels. Dibelius set himself the task of identifying the laws according to which units of oral tradition developed. 'To trace out those laws', he writes, 'to make comprehensible the rise of these little categories, is to write the history of the Form of the Gospel'.[37]

Dibelius posits the existence of two main types of unit of tradition in the Gospels, namely, what he called 'paradigms' and 'tales' or 'novellas'. Both these forms originated in different contexts within the life of the early Church. Dibelius attributes 'paradigms' to early Christian preachers, who were concerned to propagate the good news about Jesus Christ. Paradigms, he argues, belong to a time when the early Christians still lived in expectation of Christ's imminent return. Dibelius believes that the paradigms were intended for use in preaching and had an exemplary function. Hence his description of them as paradigms. They describe events in Jesus' life which are paradigmatic for the life of the Christian believer (see, e.g. Mark 12.13–17).

Dibelius identifies five characteristics of the paradigm: (a) independence of the literary context in which the paradigm appears; (b) brevity and simplicity; (c) a style which is determined not by aesthetic and literary factors but by religious considerations; (d) a didacticism which emphasizes Jesus' words; and (e) a punchline which lends itself to use in preaching and has an exemplary character, e.g. a saying or action of Jesus, or the reaction of the onlookers, which the hearer of the sermon is expected to emulate.

As hopes of an imminent parousia began to fade, however, the Church had to accommodate itself to long-term existence in the world. This led to the development of the second type of form, namely, that which Dibelius describes as the tale or novella. In tales, the emphasis is not on the impending kingdom of God but on Jesus as the miracle worker in whom God can be seen to be acting. Tales are self-enclosed, complete stories which differ from paradigms in that they are longer and contain more detail. Dibelius attributes this elaboration not to the preachers responsible for the paradigms but to storytellers and teachers whose task was to keep the memory of Jesus alive. These storytellers and teachers vividly developed the inherited stories about Jesus. Dibelius suggests that tales may be the result of the elaboration of paradigms and may have in part been prompted by the sheer joy of storytelling. Consequently, tales contain richer descriptions than paradigms, and are distinguished from paradigms by their more elaborate literary style. Another feature which distinguishes tales from paradigms is that they contain a 'lack of devotional motives and the gradual retreat of any words of Jesus of general value'.[38] The purpose of tales is to prove the superiority of the Lord Jesus over all religious competition.

Dibelius suggests three ways in which tales came into existence. Firstly, tales came about when a paradigm became detached from its context in the sermon and was developed by storytellers and teachers, who simply wanted to make the stories more interesting. Secondly, paradigms were extended by incorporating material originally external to the original paradigm. Dibelius believes that this is the case with the story of Jesus walking on the water (Mark 6.45–52), which he suggests may be the result of the conflation of an 'epiphany motif' with an account of a nature miracle. Thirdly, non-Christian stories were sometimes adopted and Christianized by the early Church.

Dibelius places miracle stories in the category of the tale and cites the following miracle stories as examples: Mark 1.40–45; 4.35–41; 5.1–20, 21–43; 6.35–44, 45–52; 7.32–37; 8.22–26; 9.14–29; Luke 7.11–16. Miracle stories of healing are characterized by the following features: (1) a description of the illness; (2) the means Jesus uses to cure the illness; and (3) the success of Jesus' miraculous action. Miracle stories contain more details than paradigms, because it is necessary to emphasize certain actions or events in order to illustrate more fully Jesus' status. Thus miracle stories contain descriptions of Jesus' touching the sick person, speaking a special formula, etc.

Another form Dibelius identifies in the Gospels is the 'legend'. Dibelius describes legends as 'religious narratives of a saintly man in whose works and fate interest is taken'.[39] Legends arose out of the early Christians' interest in Jesus and in the people who knew him. The characteristics of legends are the miraculous birth of a hero figure, recognition of the child as a future hero, threats to the child's life which are thwarted by miraculous means and the early intellectual maturity of the future hero. Such characteristics are common in the descriptions of significant personalities in the ancient world. Dibelius speaks of the 'law of biographical analogy'.

Like paradigms, legends have an upbuilding character, but differ from paradigms in that they focus not on the kerygma, but on the piety and holiness of the hero and how he is protected by God. Legends are mostly unhistorical, though Dibelius does admit the possibility of a historical kernel underlying some legends.[40] According to Dibelius, the birth narratives (Matt. 1.18–2.23; Luke 1.5–2.40) and the stories of Jesus' childhood (Luke 2.41–49) are examples of legend, while Bultmann adds to this list

Jesus' baptism, transfiguration, Jesus' entry into Jerusalem, the Passion Narrative and the empty tomb narrative.

In his *History of the Synoptic Tradition* (1st edn. 1921) Bultmann set out to trace the history of the units of tradition contained in the Synoptic Gospels. Like Dibelius, Bultmann holds that the units of tradition originally circulated separately and not in the context in which they were fixed in the canonical Gospels. By observing how Matthew and Luke have modified material they have borrowed from Mark, Bultmann hoped to identify the laws according to which traditional material had been handed down and modified. These laws could then be applied to Mark and Q in order to identify earlier layers of tradition underlying the written Gospels.

Bultmann questions Dibelius' claim that the preaching of the early Church was the primary context for the development of tradition. There are many other factors that played a role, such as apologetics, polemics, the desire to bolster the position of the Church and the need to enforce Church discipline. Unlike Schmidt and Dibelius, Bultmann holds that the Passion Narrative was not a continuous narrative but, like other material in the Gospels, was built up through a process of the accretion of individual units of tradition. This is evident, he claims, from the fact that the story of the anointing, the prophecy of the betrayal, the Last Supper, Gethsemane and Peter's denial are not dependent on their context in the Passion Narrative.

Bultmann claimed that the first collection of the tradition took place in the primitive Palestinian Church and was motivated by apologetic and polemical concerns. This very early collection consisted of 'apophthegms', i.e. brief, pithy sayings of the Lord Jesus. The need for edification, exhortation of the faithful, the enforcement of Church discipline as well as the existence of Christian prophets in the early Church led to the transmission, production and elaboration of further stories and sayings of the Lord. This led to an undermining of the conciseness of the story. There is also a tendency towards what Bultmann calls 'differentiation and individualization'.[41] Thus whereas Mark (followed by Matthew) does not differentiate between the criminals crucified with Jesus (Mark 15.27; Matt. 27.38), Luke distinguishes between them and describes them conversing with Jesus about their plight (Luke 23.39–43). This differentiation is often accompanied by a tendency to individualize, i.e. to name characters who were anonymous in the original apophthegm. A good example is provided by the Gospel of John. Whereas the Synoptic Gospels identify neither the disciple who drew his sword to defend Jesus in the Garden of Gethsemane, nor the High Priest's servant who was struck, John names them as Peter and Malchus respectively (John 18.10).

While Dibelius regards the miracle story as a subcategory of tales, Bultmann makes a distinction between apophthegms, stories and miracle stories. Miracle stories, however, belong for Bultmann in a different category from that of apophthegms and stories. Bultmann distinguishes between two types of miracle stories, namely miracles of healing and nature miracles. Only stories where the point is the miracle itself are classified by Bultmann as miracle stories. Text units which contain an account of a miracle where the point is not the miracle but a saying of Jesus, such as Mark 3.1–6, belong to the apophthegms, for these passages are told not for the sake of the miracle but to act as a vehicle for the punchline of the apophethegm.

Miracle stories centre on Jesus and are expressions of his status. For this reason, anything which is not directly relevant to Jesus' status as messiah and Son of God is of no interest. Because the emphasis is on Jesus, there is little focus on the recipient of the miracle. Only enough information is provided in order to set the scene for Jesus' miraculous action. Interest ceases in the object of the miraculous cure once the miracle has taken place. Thus there is rarely reference to the gratitude of those healed.

Miracle stories in the Synoptic Gospels, Bultmann points out, have a stereotypical structure, which he describes as follows.

(1) *Exposition*. The exposition is a brief description of the situation, which sets the scene for what is to come. Thus the exposition in the stilling of the storm (Mark 4.35–41) is the description of how Jesus and his disciples take to their boat and a great storm breaks out while Jesus is asleep (Mark 4.35–37). The exposition in the story of the healing of the deaf mute (Mark 7.32–37) consists in the people bringing the deaf mute to Jesus (Mark 7.32a). The purpose of the exposition, Bultmann writes, is to 'depict the gravity of the complaint so as to bring the act of the healer into its proper light'.[42] Bultmann cites the following characteristic features of the exposition: the length of the sickness, the dreadful or dangerous character of the disease, the ineffective treatment of physicians, doubt and contemptuous treatment of the healer.[43]

(2) *Preparation*: The need for Jesus' action is made apparent. Thus in Mark 4.38 the disciples wake Jesus and make him aware of the danger, while in Mark 7.32b the people ask Jesus to lay his hand on the deaf mute.

(3) *Execution*: Jesus carries out the miracle either by means of a word or an action. Thus in Mark 4.39a Jesus commands the wind and sea to be still, while in Mark 7.33–34 Jesus heals by both word and action.

(4) *Demonstration*: The success of the miracle is revealed. Thus in Mark 4.39b calm descends upon the lake, and in Mark 7.35 the deaf mute speaks.

(5) *Reaction*: The onlookers are astounded and/or praise God and/ or Jesus. Mark 4.41 describes the astonishment and awe of the disciples, while Mark 7.37 depicts the astonishment of the onlookers. The reader/ listener is expected to join in with this reaction.

The function of miracle stories is thus to affirm Jesus' authority and the truth of the claims made about him. According to Bultmann, the *Sitz im Leben* of miracle stories was the Church's missionary activity.

Bultmann also examined Jesus' sayings and parables, both of which were in his opinion developed to meet the needs of the early Church. The Church preserved the sayings of Jesus, but as they were transmitted they were according to Bultmann modified to bring out more fully their hortatory character and to make clear the nature of the person who had uttered them. Bultmann identifies four basic types of saying in the Gospels, namely, proverbs, prophetic and apocalyptic sayings, legal sayings and Church rules, and 'I-sayings'.

There are according to Bultmann three basic forms of *proverb* in the Synoptic Gospels, namely principles, exhortations and questions.[44] 'Principles' have 'declaratory form', that is they declare a principle concerning things ('material formulations') or persons ('personal formulations'). As an example of a material formulation, Bultmann cites the statement 'For out of the abundance of the heart the mouth speaks' (Matt. 12.34b). As an example of a personal formulation, Bultmann quotes Jesus' comment that 'the labourer deserves to be paid' (Luke 10.7). Exhortations have 'imperative form'. That is, an exhortatory proverbial saying is expressed in the form of a command. Bultmann cites as examples Luke 4.23 'Doctor, cure yourself', and Matt. 8.22b/Luke 9.60 'let the dead bury their own dead'. Finally, proverbs can take the form of questions, such as 'And can any of you by worrying add a single hour to your span of life?' (Matt. 6.27/Luke 12.25), and 'The wedding-guests cannot fast while the bridegroom is with them, can they?' (Mark 2.19). In such passages, Jesus is portrayed as the teacher of wisdom, and his proverbs are similar to the wisdom literature of the Old Testament and Rabbinic Judaism.

Bultmann suggests three possible origins for the proverbs in the Synoptic tradition: (a) Jesus himself coined some of them; (b) Jesus was simply citing proverbs in common usage; (c) the early Church attributed to Jesus proverbs derived from Jewish wisdom literature. Bultmann's own view is that the proverbs attributed to Jesus are unlikely to go back to Jesus himself.

Bultmann defines *prophetic and apocalyptic sayings* as sayings in which Jesus proclaims the imminent arrival of the kingdom of God. Bultmann distinguishes four types of prophetic and apocalyptic sayings. Firstly, there are sayings which promise salvation to those who respond to Jesus' preaching of the coming kingdom of God (e.g., Luke 10.23–24/Matt. 13.16–17). Bultmann also includes the Beatitudes in this category. The second category consists of 'minatory sayings', which threaten punishment on those who do not accept Jesus and his teaching. Examples of minatory sayings are Luke's woes on the rich (Luke 6.24–26), and the woes pronounced on the scribes and Pharisees in Matthew 23. The third category consists of 'admonitions' and contains exhortations to watchfulness and faithfulness (Luke 12.35–38 and Matt. 24.43–44). Finally, there is the category of 'apocalyptic predictions', which deal with the impending end, the coming of the Son of man, and the dawning of the new age (Mark 9.1; Luke 17.20–21, 23–24). Bultmann claims that the Synoptic Apocalypse (Mark 13.5–27) is Jewish apocalyptic which has been reworked in order to apply it to Jesus. Other apocalyptic passages are early Church constructions which have been ascribed to Jesus, but Bultmann is prepared to concede that some elements may go back to Jesus himself.

Examples of *legal sayings* and *Church rules* are rules concerning the Sabbath (Mark 3.4), the sin against the Holy Spirit (Mark 3.28–29), Jesus' attitude to the law and rules for Church discipline (Matt. 18.15–17, 21–22). Some of the gospel tradition's 'rules of piety' may go back to Jesus himself, such as, Bultmann suggests, 'the brief conflict sayings which express in a parable-like form the attitude of Jesus to Jewish piety, e.g., Mark 7.15; 3.4; Matt. 23.16–19, 23–24, 25–26',[45] but many may have been created by the early Church to deal with issues arising within the community.

Bultmann adds a fourth category of sayings which can appear in each of the three previous categories. These are the *'I'-sayings*, i.e. passages where Jesus speaks of himself, his mission and the fate that awaits him (e.g., Mark 10.45; Matt. 5.17; 10.34–36). Although he admits that it is possible that Jesus spoke in the first person about himself, Bultmann believes that the I-sayings are likely to be early Church constructions. He notes that many of the I-sayings are *vaticinia ex eventu*, i.e. 'prophecies' made *after* the events which they are supposedly prophesying. Other I-sayings seem to presuppose a post-resurrection perspective and are thus likely to have been placed into the mouth of Jesus by the early Church. For these reasons, Bultmann holds that the I-sayings have probably been created by the Church, particularly the Hellenistic church, rather than being authentic words of Jesus himself.

Parables are characterized by conciseness of narrative. Only the persons necessary for the flow of the narrative appear in the story. Thus in the parable of the Prodigal Son there is no mention of the mother, but only the father. Bultmann points out there are usually only two main characters (e.g. Luke 11.5–10; 15.11–24; 17.7–10; 18.1–8, 9–14), at the most three (e.g. Luke 7.41–43; Matt. 18.23–35; 21.28–31) in a parable. A further characteristic of parables is their adherence to what Bultmann calls 'the law of the single perspective'.[46] That is, 'one is not asked to watch two different series of events happening at the same time'. Parables are also notable for their sparseness of characterization.[47] There is a distinct economy of description of events and actions, which leads to the omission of anything that is not essential to the story.[48] Further distinctive characteristics of parables are their use of direct speech and soliloquy,[49] and their calling forth of a judgment from the hearer.[50]

According to Bultmann, the Church has modified the parables and has often placed them in a new context and provided an introduction that was not originally part of the parable. For example, the parable of the Good Samaritan (Luke 10.30–37) uses as its introduction a lawyer's question concerning what he must do to inherit eternal life (Luke 10.25–29). Bultmann also holds that some parables may have been taken from Jewish tradition and put into Jesus' mouth.[51] He thinks that this is likely to have been the case with Luke 16.19–31.

Bultmann's scepticism concerning the historical contents of much of the tradition and his belief that much of the Gospel record did not originate with Jesus but was a creation of the early Church, led to form criticism being viewed with suspicion in some quarters. This was the case in England, where in general form criticism had a limited influence prior to the Second World War. Only Dibelius' book had been published in English prior to the war, and the British reaction was generally hostile to form criticism. In the 1930s, however, form criticism began to make inroads into Anglophone scholarship. In the United States, Frederick C. Grant published in 1934 a form-critical study entitled *Growth of the Gospels*. Grant followed this with his translation of the second, revised edition of Bultmann's *Die Erforschung der Synoptischen Evangelien* (1930),[52] together with a form-critical study by Karl Kundsin.[53] Another American scholar who adopted form criticism was Donald Wayne Riddle, who made use of the method in his *The Gospels: their Origin and Growth* (1939).[54]

In Britain, the pioneers of form criticism were Vincent Taylor (1887–1968), R. H. Lightfoot (1883–1953) and C. H. Dodd (1884–1973).

Vincent Taylor's *Formation of the Gospel Tradition* (1933) played an important role in introducing form criticism to the English-speaking world. In this work, Taylor attempts to avoid some of the excesses of the German form critics. He also attempts to introduce greater terminological precision into the debate, for example, by replacing Dibelius' paradigms and Bultmann's apophthegms with the notion of pronouncement stories.

An important figure in the introduction of form criticism into British biblical scholarship was R. H. Lightfoot. In 1931, Lightfoot visited Germany, where he became acquainted with Bultmann and Dibelius. In his memoir of Lightfoot, Dennis Nineham tells us that this visit marked a turning point in his academic career. For Lightfoot, form criticism confirmed the doubts he was having concerning 'the older, liberal, interpretations of the Gospels' and 'provided him with a more objective and satisfactory basis from which to carry on his search for non-historical principles of interpretation'.[55] The result of his visit to Germany was, Nineham tells us, that he acquired 'a sense of mission to the English theological world'. Nineham continues: 'Form criticism was then little known – or at any rate little appreciated – in England, and, as one who had accidentally stumbled on it and its significance, as he modestly put it, he felt bound to bring it to the notice of English students; for he was convinced that they would not get much further with their interpretation of the Gospels until they took it into account'.[56] This aim of bringing form criticism to the attention of the British theological public prompted Lightfoot to make use of the new method in his Bampton lectures on the Gospel of Mark (1934).[57] He followed his Bampton lectures with the publication of *Locality and Doctrine in the Gospels* (1938),[58] in which he employed form-critical methods to provide a *theological* explanation of the geographical data provided by the Gospels.

C. H. Dodd was another British scholar who played a role in making form criticism acceptable in British theology. Dodd makes use of the notion of *Sitz im Leben* in his attempt to identify the original setting of the parables in Jesus' ministry and to trace the situation in the early Church in which they underwent development to accommodate the needs of the Church.[59] In his *The Parables of the Kingdom* (1935) he states that, 'The most recent school of Gospel criticism, that of *Formgeschichte*, or "Form-criticism", has taught us that in order to understand rightly any passage in the gospels we must enquire into the "setting in life" . . . in which the tradition underlying that passage took form'.[60] Looking back nearly thirty years later, Dodd commented in his *Historical Tradition in the Fourth Gospel* (1963) that, 'while documentary criticism was working itself to a standstill, the application of form-criticism opened up new lines of approach'. He goes on to comment that, 'when all allowance is made for an enthusiasm which has sometimes claimed too much for the method, it is certainly true that the form-critics have done great service in leading us to recognize afresh the importance of oral tradition in the New Testament period'.[61]

Developments were afoot, however, which would lead to the decline of 'classical' form criticism. An early opponent was T. W. Manson (1893–1958), who in Dodd's *Festschrift* commented that form criticism 'is interesting but not epoch-making' and that 'a paragraph of Mark is not a penny the better or the worse as historical evidence for being labelled "apophthegm" or "pronouncement story" or "paradigm"'.[62] Manson questions furthermore the view of the form critics that the Gospels provide knowledge not of the historical Jesus but of the theology of the Church. He argues that 'we are driven back to the business of treating the Gospels – as wholes and in detail – as historical documents'.[63] By the late 1950s, Gerhard Iber had come to the conclusion that form criticism 'is no longer the focus of scholarly discussion. We can with justification speak of a "stagnation of the work of form criticism" '.[64]

This loss of confidence in form criticism can be attributed to three developments: (1) scepticism concerning the possibility of identifying and reconstructing the oral tradition allegedly underlying the biblical writings; (2) uncertainty concerning the methodological coherence of form criticism; and (3) the impact of new approaches to the interpretation of the Bible. We shall now examine each of these three developments in detail.

(1) For much of the twentieth century there existed a consensus among biblical scholars that the texts of the Bible were the culmination of a process of oral tradition. As the twentieth century wore on, however, this consensus was increasingly undermined and questions posed concerning the existence of such an underlying oral prehistory. A representative of this position is Erhardt Güttgemanns, who rejects the focus on oral prehistory and advocates that we focus on what he calls the 'cohesive text' as it has come down to us.[65] Walter Schmithals goes even further and denies the very existence of an oral tradition underlying the biblical writings. Schmithals argues that the influence of oral tradition was minimal and advocates that the Gospels should be treated as the products of the theologians who brought them into existence.[66]

Another significant critic of form-criticism is Gerd Theissen, who writes: 'Classical form criticism has long since become such shopworn dogma in research and teaching that it suggests a false certainty where, instead, we really need new confirmation and assurance.'[67] Theissen advocates a new history of the Synoptic tradition which aims not to isolate oral tradition but to provide 'a historical explanation of the beginning, shaping, and alteration of the most important traditions about Jesus'.[68] Theissen attempts to provide such a history in his *Gospels in Context*, in which he raises doubts concerning the ability of form criticism to reconstruct the oral prehistory of the Gospels and argues for 'a new beginning' based on the study of the cultural context in which the Gospels were written.

(2) Form criticism has suffered from the lack of an agreed methodology. Our survey of the work of Dibelius and Bultmann revealed variations in their terminology and disagreements concerning the defining characteristics and criteria of identification of forms. There has also been a long-running dispute on the relation between forms and their contents. The question centres on whether content is an essential factor for identifying and classifying forms. A close connection between form and content certainly existed in classical form criticism, where Dibelius and Bultmann and others identified such forms as miracle stories on the basis of their subject matter. Richter and his followers have argued, however, for a *distinction* between form and content, and have attempted to classify forms according

to their linguistic structure. Richter's position has been challenged by Steck, however, for whom 'the local content and the thematic direction of the linguistic utterance' are essential for the determination of form. Johannes Floss, however, holds that it is 'methodologically indispensable . . . to distinguish between form and content, on the one hand, and the function of this distinction, on the other'.[69]

This lack of methodological clarity has led since the 1960s to attempts to establish a more viable method of form criticism. Klaus Koch has combined structuralism with form criticism and has attempted a structuralist history of forms of the book of Amos.[70] The first edition of his *Was ist Formgeschichte?* [What is Form History] appeared in 1964, and since then has passed through several editions, the most recent of which is the fifth edition published in 1989 with an afterword on the relation between linguistics and form criticism.[71] The shift from historical reconstruction of the pre-literary oral tradition to consideration of the literary character of forms is evident in Richter's attempt to establish clear methodological criteria for the analysis of forms. He achieves this by distinguishing between an 'ornamental' form, which focuses on phonemes, consonants, vowels and syllables, and a 'structural' form, which consists of the analysis and description of syntax and stylistics and is the basis for investigating the 'deep-structure' of the unit.[72] Floss considers Richter's approach to have brought about a methodological breakthrough in the discipline.[73]

Steck has also attempted to place form criticism on a firmer basis by clarifying its methodological principles. He does this by identifying the following steps in form-critical analysis. Firstly, the form critic must establish the linguistic shape of the text under discussion. This entails delimiting the text, which involves establishing whether the text is an independent, self-enclosed whole, with a clear beginning and end, or whether the text presupposes or is dependent on something preceding or following it. The second step is the identification of the structure of the unit and its structural components such as 'scenic or functional sections, characteristic introductory or concluding formulas, connecting or dividing markings of a linguistic nature (e.g. change of subject), the sequence of the sentences, the types of sentences (e.g. command, nominal sentences), stylistic devices (such as repetition), and the words which bind the sentences to one another (such as "because", "therefore")'.[74] Thirdly, the form critic must endeavour to identify 'linguistic shaping devices' such as style and syntax. This means being attentive to such literary phenomena as alliteration and assonance. Finally, the form critic must identify the author's perspective on the text's subject matter and its addressees. This involves asking questions concerning the purpose of the text and the audience for whom it was written.[75]

(3) In recent years, form criticism has been influenced by the development of new methods of literary criticism such as rhetorical criticism. As is

indicated by the title of James Muilenburg's address in 1968 to the Society of Biblical Literature, 'Form Criticism and Beyond',[76] rhetorical criticism was an attempt to go beyond form criticism by considering not only form and genre but also the rhetorical devices authors employ to win over their readers. Muilenburg argued for the need to extend form criticism beyond its conventional boundaries in order to consider the way the forms and genres of the Bible had been adapted by the biblical writers to serve distinct rhetorical purposes. The way in which the biblical writers have modified conventional forms and genres sheds light on the distinctive message they aim to impart to their listeners or readers. Form criticism should thus be expanded to consider the rhetorical purpose of these modifications, a procedure which Muilenburg named 'rhetorical criticism'. Here form criticism has been supplemented by focus on the rhetorical function of texts and the role of the *audience*. We might say that the *Sitz im Leben* has been expanded to include to a much greater degree the response of the *recipients* intended by the author. This development of form criticism does not constitute the abandonment of form criticism, however, but its modification.

The modification rather than the abandonment of form criticism is evident from the attempts of other scholars to adapt form criticism to meet the criticisms that have been levelled against it. Thus Klaus Berger in his *Einführung in die Formgeschichte* [Introduction to Form History] (1987) holds that the task is not to reconstruct the most original form, but to consider the form in the *present* text. He argues for the development of a 'new form criticism', by which he means not the attempt to isolate units of oral tradition but to trace the genres employed within the biblical texts.[77] The result of this shift in emphasis from oral tradition to the final text has been the detachment of genre analysis as a closely related but distinct method from form criticism. Form criticism focuses on short forms, i.e. aphorisms, parables, pronouncement stories, miracle stories and so on, while genre analysis focuses on 'larger' categories of literature such as letter, apocalyptic, biography, and historical writing.

The consequence of these developments has been that form criticism has increasingly become a synchronic rather than a diachronic exegetical method. Whereas early form criticism was concerned primarily with isolating the oral forms which have been fixed in the final text, later form criticism has been concerned primarily with identifying the conventional forms and structures employed in the written text. This is an independent exercise from the tracing of the history of the forms, and is one of the reasons why more recent scholars have come to see tradition criticism and form criticism as two distinct approaches to the text. Older form critics understand one of the tasks of form criticism to be tracing the history of the development of the forms of the Bible. But more recent form critics see the task of form criticism to be first and foremost the identification and classification of forms. The task of tracing their development is a distinct task and belongs to the discipline of tradition-historical criticism rather than to form criticism proper.

An example of this focus on the literary character of form criticism is provided by George Coats' study of Genesis, which aims 'not to reconstruct the history of the patriarchs or Moses', but 'rather to show that the value of the literary form resides in the form itself rather than in its contribution to a reconstruction of historical process'.[78] Coats' commentary is part of a still ongoing 24-volume series of form-critical commentaries of the Old Testament, published since 1983 by Eerdmans. The latest of these to be published, namely the commentary on Numbers by Rolf Knierim and Coats,[79] claims to be 'the first commentary to be written using the exegetical methods of the recently redesigned form-critical approach to the Old Testament literature'.[80]

The method of form criticism

The presuppositions of form criticism

1. The biblical writings have been constructed out of smaller units.

2. Written texts were preceded by a period of oral tradition. Forms originally circulated *orally* before they were committed to writing.

3. In the process of being passed down orally, the units of tradition acquired a formalized and stereotypical form. Oral transmission necessitates forms that are easy to memorize. Consequently, forms can be recognized by their pithiness.

4. In the pre-literary period some material was grouped together into blocks according to *theme*, not chronology.

5. The biblical writers were not authors in the modern sense. Many biblical texts are not the independent and original compositions of the biblical writers whose names they bear, but have been constructed out of materials they have inherited. The biblical writings are the product of the community rather than of a specific individual, for it was the community which was responsible for preserving and transmitting the materials. The 'authors' of the biblical writings are primarily compilers and editors.

6. It is possible to trace the oral prehistory of forms. It is assumed that the written text bears the marks of the oral transmission of the

materials from which it has been composed. We no longer have access to the oral forms of units of tradition, but they can be reconstructed on the basis of the *written* forms that have come down to us. This involves identifying the smallest intelligible unit in a written unit of tradition, which it is generally assumed is more likely to be the earliest instance of a form. It is a further assumption of form criticism that in the course of transmission a form is more likely to accumulate additional material than to be abbreviated. Form criticism thus attempts to move from the written text back to the oral tradition which allegedly precedes and underlies the written text. Consequently, form criticism is dependent on source criticism. It is necessary to trace the development of the biblical writings to their earlier *written* form before it is possible to begin to identify the pre-literary form of the tradition.

7. Forms originated in a particular cultural, social or religious milieu (*Sitz im Leben*). Every tradition stands in a relationship to the community which preserved and handed it down. Therefore the tradition reflects the social conditions of the community and mirrors its religious, political and philosophical views. This means that the study of forms can shed light on the setting in which they originated.

The principles of form criticism

1. Isolation of the text unit: textual demarcation

The first step in form criticism is to identify what are likely to have originally been independent units of tradition. The task is to get back to the smallest intelligible unit. This involves separating the form from surrounding material, which means distinguishing the unit of tradition from redaction, i.e. from the editorial input of the editor of the final text. Therefore the first task is to establish what is due to the hand of the redactor. The redactor's hand can often be seen in the links that join together different episodes in the text such as 'and', 'now', 'but', 'moreover' and by the use of introductory and concluding formulae. For example, independent prophetic speeches can be identified by their use of the introductory formulae 'The word of the Lord that came to . . .' and 'Hear the word of the Lord . . .' Shifts in tone, style, mood, content, person and tense are further indications of the boundaries of text units. For example, the shift from prose to poetry may indicate the presence of originally independent text units.

2. Identification of oral tradition

Once the unit has been separated from the surrounding material, the form critic searches for evidence that the unit was originally an oral tradition. This involves the examination of the stylistic characteristics of the text. Are these to be attributed to the author or is he taking up forms which he has inherited from oral tradition? The principles the form critic employs to identify the oral origins of a text unit are as follows.

(a) Texts must contain one scene
Text units that contain two scenes, e.g. Mark 5.21–43 or 6.7–31 are literary constructions resulting from the editor interweaving two different stories. It is unlikely that these passages were handed down in this combined state.

(b) Lack of details
Details of time, place, persons and motives are often absent. For example, in the story of the disciples' plucking corn on the Sabbath (Mark 2.23–28), the reader is given no information about why Jesus and the disciples were going for a walk or why they chose a route through a cornfield. Nor are we told why the disciples decided to start plucking ears of corn. The reason that such details are not mentioned is that they are not significant for the main point of the pericope, which is the authority of Jesus. Just enough information is provided to set the scene for the main point to become fully apparent. The narrative is constructed for the sake of the 'punchline' and in order to make it as visible as possible.

(c) (Usually) two main protagonists
There are usually only two main protagonists, e.g., Jesus and the Pharisees. Other persons and groups, if present, appear only as part of the background and play no role in the proceedings.

3. Identification and classification of forms

Identification and classification of forms depend on the criteria we have adopted. This is where some confusion can arise. The problem is that there are considerable variations among form critics concerning the principles of the classification of forms. Dibelius defines the forms on the basis of formal characteristics, while Bultmann defines the forms according to their contents. Richter, on the other hand, defines forms according to their linguistic characteristics. There is also some variation in the way such terms as 'form', 'formula' and 'genre' are employed. This variation accounts for the different terminology employed by form critics. Here we will simplify the notion of forms as much as possible and use it to denote a pithy saying or punchline that can be detached from its context without undermining its basic meaning.

4. Identification of genre

Once the form has been isolated, it must be located in a genre. The form critic notes that particular types of statement are bound to specific literary genres. We can thus group together the forms we have isolated in the biblical writings into their respective genres. This aspect of form criticism is sometimes described as 'genre criticism' (*Gattungskritik*). The criteria for placing a text in a particular genre are structure, content and intention. The identification of genre is important if we are to understand the meaning of the individual text units. Our understanding of the story of the Good Samaritan, for example, will be different if we understand it not as a parable but as a historical narrative. Because we know it to be a parable, we do not raise questions concerning the historical events the story 'reports'. One of the difficulties in interpreting the Bible is that we cannot always identify with certainty the genre of the text in question.

5. Identification of the Sitz im Leben

A further task is to establish the *Sitz im Leben*. The locating of a form in a specific life-setting is closely related to the placing of the form in a particular genre, for both forms and genres, it is held, originate in specific social and cultural contexts. Thus mourning texts belong to the genre of funeral liturgy, while hymns of praise probably stem from communal worship. Consequently, if we encounter a form such as 'We commit this body to the earth', we can be reasonably confident that it stems from the genre of funeral liturgy and has its *Sitz im Leben* in the funerary practices of the community that has produced this form.

We can distinguish three different settings which may have given rise to and preserved forms:

(a) historical setting, i.e. the situation which led to the production of the form.

(b) social setting, i.e. the situation in which the form was preserved.

(c) literary setting, i.e. the role of the form in the literary life of the period.

6. Tradition criticism: tracing the development of forms

The phrase 'tradition criticism' is the English rendering of the German concepts of *Überlieferungsgeschichte* and *Traditionsgeschichte*. Tradition criticism combines the insights of source criticism and form criticism in order to trace the development of biblical texts from the oral to the literary stage.

Classic form critics attempted to trace the way the forms developed between their oral and written phases. New Testament form critics have been particularly concerned to distinguish between Jesus' original words and the creations of the early Church. A number of criteria have been developed to track the development of oral tradition.

(a) The criterion of dissimilarity[81]

If a tradition seems to be at odds with what we know of the early Church and with what we know of Judaism at the time of Jesus, then it is likely that that tradition originated with Jesus himself. It is improbable that the early Church would have invented a tradition at odds with its own theology, and if the tradition is also in conflict with contemporary Judaism, it is unlikely to be inherited from Jesus' Jewish background.

(b) The criterion of multiple attestation

It is reasonable to accept as authentic a tradition that is attested by two or more independent witnesses. The problem here is of establishing whether the witnesses are indeed independent of each other.

(c) The criterion of coherence

The criterion of coherence, as Perrin puts it, or 'consistency' in Fuller's terminology, affirms that material consistent with what has been established as authentic by the criteria of dissimilarity and multiple attestation is also likely to be authentic.

Form criticism in action
Gen. 2.4b–3.24

Form criticism of Gen. 2.4b–3.24 accepts the conclusions of source criticism that this passage belongs to the Yahwist strand, but seeks to go
beyond this insight to the pre-literary traditions that may underlie the
text.

1. Isolation of the text unit: textual demarcation

The first step is to identify the boundaries of the text. From source criticism, the form critic knows that Gen. 2.4b–3.24 belongs to a larger block of
Yahwist material beginning in Gen. 2.4b and continuing to Gen. 4.26. The
form critic examines whether this block of material shows signs of having
been built up from earlier traditions. The first stage in achieving this goal
is to look for seams and breaks that may indicate that elements may have
at one time existed independently of their setting in the final text. Close
examination does indeed indicate that Gen. 2.4b–3.24 has probably been
built up from smaller units. Evidence for this is provided by the presence of
doublets. In Gen. 2.9, God seems to repeat the action of planting a garden,
already described in Gen. 2.8. There seem to be two accounts of how the
earth is watered, namely by a stream rising up from the earth (Gen. 2.6)
and by a network of rivers, which have their source in Eden (Gen. 2.10–14).
There are two accounts of the man's naming of his wife (Gen. 2.24; 3.20)
and two accounts of the clothing of Adam and Eve (Gen. 3.7, 21). There
are *two* magical trees in the narrative, namely the tree of the knowledge of
good and evil and the tree of life. Although two trees are mentioned, however, it is only the tree of knowledge of good and evil that plays a significant
role in the narrative. After its initial mention in Gen. 2.9 the tree of life
disappears from the narrative, playing no role in the dialogue between the
serpent and the woman, and returns only at the conclusion of the narrative
(Gen. 3.24). It may be that the presence of the two trees is the result of the
conflation of two originally independent traditions and that the editor of
these two traditions has been only partially successful in integrating them.
Whether this conflation of traditions is due to the Yahwist or had already
taken place prior to the Yahwist is, however, impossible to establish. There
is also some ambiguity with regard to Eden. On the basis of Gen. 2.8, the
garden seems to form part of a greater geographical unity called 'Eden',

but Gen. 2.10 could be understood to place the garden *outside* Eden. The phrase 'garden of Eden' (Gen. 2.15; 3.23) may be an attempt to combine two distinct narratives, one of which equated Eden with paradise, the other of which understood Eden to be a garden. The presence of such doublets may indicate that the final version of the text is the result of the conflation of similar but distinct traditions.

Further evidence for Gen. 2.4b–3.24 being a composite text is provided by Gen. 2.10–14, which breaks up the narrative describing God's creation of a man to till the garden he has planted. It is thus likely that the discussion of the four rivers issuing from Eden is an interpolation. Another indication that Gen. 2.4b–3.24 has been built up of what were originally independent units is the change from prose to poetry in Gen. 2.23 and 3.14–19. The change from the third to the second person as well as the shift of theme between Gen. 2.25 and 3.1 may indicate that Gen. 3.1–19 once existed independently of its present context.

Gen. 3.23 may well have originally belonged together with Gen. 3.17 and 3.19a, with which it forms a coherent unit.

For these reasons, many scholars hold that Gen. 2.4b–3.24 has been built up from (at least) two originally independent traditions, namely, a tradition about the creation of the first human beings (Gen. 2.4b–7, 18–24) and a tradition about the garden (2.8–17; 3.1–24).

2. Identification of oral tradition

Once the presence of distinct traditions has been established, the next task is to search for evidence that these traditions may have existed in oral form prior to their being committed to writing in the present text. This entails considering whether the markers of the oral origin of texts are present in Gen. 2.4b–3.24, namely, that texts must contain one scene, lack detail concerning time, place, persons and motives, and contain usually only two main protagonists.

An examination of Gen. 2.4b–3.24 reveals that the text contains multiple scenes, which have been integrated into each other in order to create a continuous narrative. This narrative includes details of time, place, persons and motives. The reader is informed that God's creation of the first human being took place when 'no plant of the field was yet in the earth and no herb of the field had yet sprung up – for the LORD God had not caused it to rain upon the earth' (Gen. 2.5). The narrative contains a detailed portrayal of the Garden of Eden and the rivers that water it and provides descriptions of the main characters and their motives. Thus the narrator informs us that 'the serpent was more crafty than any other wild animal that the LORD God had made' (Gen. 3.1). The woman's motive for disobeying God's prohibition and eating the fruit of the tree of the knowledge of good and evil is also made clear: 'So when the woman saw that the tree was good for food, and it that was a delight to the eyes, and that the tree was to be desired to make one wise, she took of its fruit and ate' (Gen. 3.6). The narrative contains multiple protagonists, namely God, the man and the woman, and the serpent, and the narrative is driven forward by the tension and conflict between these protagonists. None of the three criteria for the identification of oral tradition has thus been fulfilled in this passage, prompting the conclusion that the narrative is a literary construction that has been carefully crafted by an unknown author. This does not mean, however, that the text does not contain older elements that may have originated in a pre-literary oral tradition. To identify whether this is the case we must turn to examine the *forms* the text contains.

3. Identification and classification of forms

Although Gen. 2.4b–3.24 as a whole is a literary construct, certain formulaic elements can be detected at various points in the text. Gen. 2.23 is an example of synonymous parallelism: 'This at last is bone of my bones and flesh of my flesh'. A recurrent phrase in the text is 'in the day that', which is a typical formula to denote past events (Gen. 2.4b, 17; 3.5; cf. 5.1, 2). Legal forms are evident in the apodictic prohibition in Gen. 2.17, the cross-examination of the accused in Gen. 3.11–13, and the pronouncement of the sentence in Gen. 3.14–19. In Gen. 3.14–19 we also find examples of the curse form. God's pronouncements of punishment on the serpent, woman and man have the same basic structure, namely, the declaration of the crime ('because you have done this/because you have listened to the voice of your wife'), the pronouncement of the curse ('cursed are you/cursed is the ground') and the passing of the sentence ('upon your belly you shall go'/'in pain you shall bring forth children'/'in toil you shall eat of [the ground]').

A further form that can be identified in Gen. 2.4b–3.24 is the *aetiology*. Gen. 2.24 has the typical introductory formula of the aetiology, namely 'therefore' followed by the explanation. The aetiology in Gen. 2.24 concerns the sex drive. Why is it that men and women are sexually attracted to each other? The answer is that man and woman were originally one flesh and the sex drive is the result of their desire to return to this state of being one flesh.

4. Identification of genre

The identification and classification of the forms of Gen. 2.4b–3.24 allows us to identify the genre or, more accurately, genres of the passage.

The text is first and foremost an aetiology. It explains the sorrow and struggle of life by attributing it to the consequences of human sin. The source of human misery is human beings' relationship with God, a relationship they have damaged through sinful disobedience. As one of the vehicles for this aetiology of human misery, the narrative draws on the language of the court room with its pronouncement of judgement and sentencing of the accused. To this major aetiology are attached other aetiological elements, dealing with such subjects as the origins of men and women's desire for each other (Gen. 2.21–24), why snakes crawl on their bellies (Gen. 3.14), why women suffer in childbirth (Gen. 3.16) and why men must work so hard to produce food (Gen. 3.17–19). These aetiological elements are subordinated to the main narrative.

The narrative also has elements common to Near Eastern myths. Talking animals, trees of life, magical fruit and direct encounters with an anthropomorphic deity are among the characteristics of myth. Another Old Testament allusion to the myth of the fall can be found in Ezek. 28.11–19, which describes how the king of Tyre was cast out of a paradisiacal garden, also called Eden, on the mountain of God as punishment for his disobedience. Underlying Gen. 3 seems thus to be a Near Eastern myth concerning the expulsion of the first human beings from the presence of the gods. The influence of Near Eastern mythology may also be visible in Gen. 3.22, 'The man has become like one of us', where there may be a hint of polytheism. The presence of such elements in Genesis is surprising, since the Old Testament otherwise contains relatively few mythological elements. Israel worshipped only one God. Therefore there was little room for stories about the gods, but we do detect remnants of myths in the Old Testament in such passages as the story of the talking serpent in Gen. 3.1–5 and the marriage between the 'sons of gods' and the daughters of men described in Gen. 6.1–4. It is striking that outside Gen. 3 there are only brief allusions to a 'tree of life' in Proverbs (11.30; 13.12; 15.4). There is no allusion elsewhere in the Old Testament to the tree of the knowledge of good and evil.

These mythical elements are not dominant, however, for the emphasis is very much on the relationship between God and the first human beings and the consequences of human disobedience. What we thus seem to have in Gen. 3 is what Gunkel terms a 'faded myth'. That is, the Genesis story retains vestiges of an older myth, but has abandoned the world view that gave rise to the original myth. Mythical elements have been detached from their original context and placed at the disposal of a very different theology.

Gen. 2.4b–3.24 also has characteristics associated with the *saga*. Sagas have a historical basis, though this basis is often difficult to identify, which is then interwoven with imaginative elements. Sagas are frequently characterized by the remoteness of the places in which the stories take place, the direct presence and intervention of God and the impossibility of the presence of witnesses to the events described. Such features are evident in Gen. 2.4b–3.24 in the setting of the narrative in a mythical garden and God's walking in the garden as if he were a human being. Furthermore, Gen. 2.4b–3.24 describes events that could not possibly have been reported by an eyewitness. At this point in human history there were no other people in existence to witness the events described in the narrative.

What we seem to have in Gen. 2.4b–3.24, then, is a mixed narrative conflating the genres of aetiology, legal terminology, myth and saga. As an entirety, the text can be read as an aetiological saga containing remnants of a faded myth to which other genre elements are subordinated. Aetiological sagas are attempts to explain the present. They refer to-the past only in order to deal with some feature of the present. This is the case with Gen. 2.4b–3.24, which is concerned with explaining the origins of the human plight, which it does by attributing it to human disobedience.

5. Identification of *Sitz im Leben*

What is the *Sitz im Leben* of the entire passage and what is the setting of its individual elements?

The present setting of the entire passage is a literary construction. The Yahwist has drawn together the traditions at his disposal and fused them into the present narrative. Then a post-exilic editor has fixed the Yahwist's contribution with other contributions to make the final text. The likely *Sitz im Leben* for this activity was the need to preserve these traditions and to make them available to the community. Prior to this the constituent elements of the passage would presumably have circulated among the Israelites, and been read aloud if they had already acquired an earlier literary form, or recited from memory if they were still being passed down by word of mouth. Gunkel suggests that sagas may have been circulated by a class of 'story tellers'.[82] If this is the case, then some of the constituent elements of Gen. 2.4b–3.24 may have originated with such a class.

Gen. 2.4b–3.24 retains vestiges of a pre-Yahwist context, namely ideas which fit badly into Yahwist theology and that of Israel in general. This is evident above all in the episode of the serpent. Israelite religion has no place for talking serpents, magical fruit or for a God who is (initially) unaware of the whereabouts of his creatures. The *Sitz im Leben* of this faded myth is now impossible to identify but it would seem to belong to the mythical world view of Israel's neighbours and may have been absorbed by the Israelites through their contacts with other nations.

Of interest is the fact that the story of the expulsion from the garden exists in another form in Ezekiel (Ezek. 28.11–19), where the passage focuses on the king of Tyre's disobedience and his subsequent expulsion from the mountain of God. This prompts Coats to suggest that the *Sitz im Leben* of the original tradition may have been the royal court:

> The Paradise Man is the royal man; his garden, his animals, his wife constitute his court. He exercises dominion over them as he names them (cf. 1:28). The Paradise Man thus wields power in his garden, power to know good and evil, to discriminate between alternatives for the future of his subjects. Yet, the tale is not simply a propaganda piece for the royal man. His knowledge of good and evil was originally denied him. His grasp of it was an act of disobedience, an affront to God. His expulsion from the Garden is a denial of his power. The story thus derives from circles (wisdom?) who stand over against the king to admonish, instruct, and correct him, or finally to impeach him.[83]

6. Tradition criticism: tracing the development of forms

It is difficult to trace the history of the transmission of the passage and its constituent elements. Form criticism is able to tell us something about the types of literature to be found in Gen. 2.4b–3.24, but is not able to state conclusively whether the Yahwist has taken up oral or written sources or a mixture of both. The fact that the passage contains so many genre elements, however, is most likely an indication that the text has undergone a long history of transmission and has accruing to it the remnants of the various stages through which it has passed. Some of the traditions of Gen. 2.4b–3.24 may have already been combined with each other before they were taken up by the Yahwist. A further question is whether these sources that have been taken up into the final text were literary or oral in character. This question is further complicated by the problem of distinguishing between what belongs to earlier sources and what is due to the redactor. On the basis of the presence of 'faded' mythical elements, the fact that sagas have oral origins, and that Gen. 2.4b–3.24 contains poetry and some formulaic expressions, it seems likely that some elements of the text have their origins in oral tradition.

Matt. 15.21–28

1. Isolation of the text unit: textual demarcation

The unit can without difficulty be detached from the surrounding material. As we noted in our discussion in the previous chapter, the introductory formulae 'left that place' and 'went away' are typical of Matthew and therefore are probably redactional interventions made in order to provide a transition from the previous episode to Jesus' encounter with the Canaanite woman. There also appear to be redactional interventions within the pericope itself, which will be the subject of the discussion of redaction criticism in the next chapter.

2. Identification of oral tradition

The simplicity of the basic structure of the episode indicates that it may originally have existed as an independent unit of tradition. Thus it contains a single scene, namely the encounter of Jesus with the Canaanite woman. Only enough detail is provided to enable the reader to grasp the main issues of the story. The narrative serves as a vehicle for Jesus' praise of the Gentile woman's faith. There are only two protagonists, namely, Jesus and the Canaanite woman. The disciples are merely background figures and the Canaanite woman's daughter is significant only in so far as she provides the motive for the woman approaching Jesus. Furthermore, there are, as we shall go on to see, several forms that can be detached from the pericope without detriment to their meaning. On the basis of these considerations, it may be that some elements of this pericope circulated in oral form before Matthew committed it to writing. Alternatively, it may be possible that the story has been created as a framework in which to set what were originally independently circulating forms.

3. Identification and clarification of forms

We can detect the following individual forms in the text:

15.22: 'have mercy on me, Lord, Son of David' appears to be a liturgical form.
15.24: 'I was sent only . . .'. This is both a biographical apophthegm and an 'I-saying'. It is also, like Matt. 15.26 ('It is not fair . . .'), a dominical saying.

15.24, 26: dominical sayings; that is, pronouncements made by Jesus as lord of the Church.

15.25: 'Lord, help me' appears to be a liturgical form.

15.26, 27: exchange of aphorisms.

15.28: '"Let it be done for you as you wish." And her daughter was healed instantly.' This is a form associated with Jesus' healing miracles, as is evident from a similar passage in the healing of the centurion's servant (Matt. 8.5–13), which concludes with a similar punchline: ' "Go; let it be done for you according to your faith." And the servant was healed in that hour' (Matt. 8.13).

4. Identification of genre

The episode belongs at one level to the genre of the *healing miracle*. This is evident not only from the fact that Jesus heals the Canaanite woman's daughter, but also from its similar structure to other healing miracle accounts in the Gospels, the characteristics of which are:

(1) The petitioner's request

(2) An obstacle to the fulfilment of the request

(3) The petitioner's statement of faith in Jesus

(4) Jesus' granting of healing and his dismissal of the petitioner.

In view of the fact that the sick person is not present, but is represented by a third person, we can assign this episode to the subgenre of the healing miracle from a distance.

Although Matt. 15.21–28 at first sight appears to belong to the genre of the healing miracle, it also has some of the characteristics of the *controversy story*. These characteristics arise from the expansion of the second element of the structure of the healing miracle described above, namely the obstacle to the fulfilment of the petitioner's request. Whereas in pure healing miracle stories, the severity of the illness is highlighted in order to emphasize the drama of the healing and to stress Jesus' power and authority, it is the obstacle to Jesus' fulfilment of the Canaanite woman's petition which is the main focus of the pericope and gives it its controversial character. Indeed, the focus is not on the healing but on the Gentile woman's persistence and the strength of her faith in Jesus.

The presence of aphorisms indicates the genre of wisdom literature. Jesus and the Canaanite woman engage in an exchange of proverbs: 'It is not fair to take the children's food and throw it to the dogs'; 'Yet even the dogs eat the crumbs that fall from their masters' table.'

Liturgical forms such as 'Lord, have mercy on me' and 'Lord, help me' indicate that the passage is coloured by the liturgy of the early Church.

The basic genre of Matt. 15.21–28 is thus that of the miracle story, but material has been incorporated which gives it the character of a controversy dialogue. It also has elements of the pronouncement story form. The passage seems to be a hybrid resulting from the conflation of elements from the controversy dialogue and pronouncement story with what was originally a miracle story. What we have in Matt. 15.21–28, then, is a controversy story cast in the form of a healing miracle, which incorporates elements belonging to the genres of wisdom and liturgy.

5. Sitz im Leben

The view of most scholars is that the pericope is the reflection back into the life of Jesus of post-Easter debates concerning the status of Gentiles in the Church. The passage clearly originated in a Palestinian context. In view of its hostility towards the Gentile woman, it is unlikely that such a text could have originated in Gentile Christianity. We would expect a text originating among Gentile Christians to show Jesus to be unequivocally supportive of the Gentile mission rather than the reluctant and ambiguous response described in Matthew.

The question is whether the text originated with Jesus himself or with the Palestinian church. The argument for attributing this passage to Jesus is that there is evidence elsewhere in the Gospel that Jesus initially believed his mission to be directed primarily, if not exclusively, to the Jews (Matt. 10.5–6). There may also be an allusion to this conviction in Rom. 15.8. Perhaps the passage hints at an event in Jesus' life which prompted him to become aware that his ministry was destined to transcend the boundaries of Israel, culminating in his commission to the disciples at the end of the Gospel to make disciples of all nations (Matt. 28.19; cf. 24.14). If the passage originated in the Palestinian church, on the other hand, then it may have served to justify the extension of the Church's mission to Gentiles whose faith warranted their inclusion. The *Sitz im Leben* may thus be controversy in Matthew's church concerning the permissibility of admitting Gentile converts to Christianity and the status of those converts.

6. Tradition criticism: tracing the development of forms

There is a parallel between Matt. 15.21–28 and Matt. 8.5–13. Both concern Gentiles who beg Jesus to heal a sick child. In both cases, each Gentile supplicant addresses Jesus as Lord. Both healings were accomplished at a distance. Furthermore, in both stories, the emphasis is on the faith of the supplicant, not on the healing which Jesus performs.

The heavy redactional interventions into the text, which we will discuss in the next chapter, make it difficult to identify what is tradition and what is redaction. Our view on the tradition history of the passage will depend also on whether we believe Matthew to be dependent on Mark or working with an independent tradition.

The parallel between Matt. 15.21–28 and the healing of the centurion's servant in Matt. 8.5–13 led Bultmann to claim that the two stories are variants of a single tradition. If this is the case, then the history of the tradition may be that the story of a healing from distance circulated originally independently before being modified to address the young Church's needs in its debate on the admissibility of Gentiles. A further possibility is that these two traditions may have existed independently of each, but as a result of their similarity of theme have been assimilated to each other.

Alternatively, if this episode goes back to Jesus, then it may indicate his rejection of the Gentiles and a consciousness that his mission was limited solely to Israel. The tradition was then modified by the early Church in the light of the hostility it encountered from mainstream Judaism, so that it became a statement that although Jesus' mission was initially exclusively to the Jews, because of their rejection of the Gospel his mission has now shifted to the Gentiles.

The difficulty of tracing the tradition history of Matt. 15.21–28 lends weight to the arguments of those scholars who argue for the restriction of form criticism to the identification of forms rather than the identification of oral tradition and its pre-literary development. With respect to the majority of biblical texts, we simply have insufficient information to be able to track their pre-literary development and are forced to resort to speculation.

Evaluation of form criticism

Strengths

1. Form criticism allows us to distinguish between different stages of development in biblical material and to establish what is historically reliable and unreliable. It helps us to distinguish between old traditions and new interpretations. Form criticism thus plays a role in historical reconstruction, allowing the historian to identify the sources closest to the historical events that brought the biblical texts into existence. Through identifying the genres and setting of text units, it becomes possible to reconstruct the

institutions, events and customs of ancient Israel and the early Church. Form criticism also aids interpretation in showing the different meanings a form may have had in its history. Form criticism can furthermore enable the reconstruction of the theologies of earlier sources. It allows us to read the biblical texts as a multitude of witnesses rather than as a single monolithic voice. It thus arguably assists the reader to recover the richness and diversity of meaning present in Scripture.

2. Identifying forms can aid correct interpretation. For example, Klaus Koch has shown that the Beatitudes belong to the form of apocalyptic rather than wisdom literature. This indicates that we should not interpret the Beatitudes as a statement of general Christian ethics, but as a statement of Jesus' eschatology.[84] Furthermore, form criticism has been able to explain puzzling features of the Bible that source criticism was less well able to deal with. A good example of this is provided by the Psalms. Source criticism treats the Psalms as literary creations, but this raises the problem of how to deal with the change of speaker in some Psalms. By seeing the Psalms as having their origin in a specific *Sitz im Leben* form critics are able to deal with this problem. Awareness of the oral origins of the Psalms means that we should read them not as literary but as liturgical texts. A characteristic of liturgy is the use of antiphon, i.e. alternate singing or chanting in which one group of worshippers responds to the chant of another group. Interpreting the Psalms in antiphonic terms allows us to explain the otherwise puzzling shift in speaker that takes place in some Psalms. We would expect such a shift with texts used in public worship, but find it odd in texts supposedly written by a literary author. Form criticism thus enables us to understand features of the Psalms that would be puzzling if we attributed them to a literary author. The form-critical explanation is more satisfactory than the source critical attempt to explain the presence of different speakers in the text as the result of the psychological or spiritual state of the literary author of the Psalms. This identification of the Psalms as originally oral traditions whose *Sitz im Leben* is the liturgy of ancient Israel has an impact on how we evaluate the 'theology' of such texts. Form criticism makes clear that the theological content of the Psalms is not the individual view of a specific author but reflects the religious views of Israelite society.

Weaknesses

1. Form criticism has been criticized as atomistic. It dissolves the unity of biblical texts and reduces them to isolated units and fails to do justice to the final, authoritative, canonical text of the writings as they appear in the Bible.

2. Forms are often classified not according to their form but according to their content. Sometimes there is a correspondence between form and content. For example, miracle stores share the same subject matter and also have a similar structure. But in many other cases, there seems to be no common structure which links texts units classified together by the form critics. They seem here to have resorted to organizing the units according to content, rather than their structure, style and form. This is a particular problem with Bultmann. Focusing purely on 'form' allows Bultmann to identify only two main types in the Gospel material, namely 'I-sayings' and 'Parables'. His identification of other forms is based not on structure but content. Dibelius, too, sometimes resorts to content rather than form to classify the Gospel tradition. Thus his category of myth is based not on form, but on the subject matter of the text unit, namely its description of supernatural events. Thus he classifies the Temptation Narrative as a myth, although its structure would prompt us to see it rather as a controversy dialogue (cf. the similarities with Mark 10.2–9; 11.27–33; 12.18–27). Many text units do not fit easily into the categories identified by form critics, but seem to straddle different categories.

3. The 'laws of tradition' identified by Dibelius and Bultmann are open to question. Their identification of these laws is based on the assumption that the simple develops into the more complex. This principle has yet to be established, and there is dispute among scholars concerning its validity.[85] Sanders has shown that the development can go both ways, i.e., from simple to complex, but also from the complex to the simple.[86]

4. Form criticism can appear to be circular and subjective. Forms are used as a source of knowledge about the *Sitz im Leben* in which they allegedly originated, and yet the *Sitz im Leben* is used to interpret the meaning of forms. Furthermore, there is rarely any external evidence to support claims concerning the *Sitz im Leben*. Thus Bultmann's claim that the controversy stories originated in the conflict over Sabbath observance in the early Church is based on the assumption that they reflect Jewish-Christian tension over this issue. There is, however, little evidence to indicate that this was a contentious issue in early Christian-Jewish debate. The evidence that has come down to us indicates that the conflict in the early Church centred rather on circumcision and the food laws. Thus it may be that passages like Matt. 7.1–23 reflect Jewish-Christian conflict, since there is external evidence to support this claim, but it is by no means certain that texts dealing with Sabbath observance reflect such conflict.

5. H. Riesenfeld and B. Gerhardsson draw on Rabbinic practice for guidance on how early Christian communities may have transmitted oral tradition. The Rabbis were concerned to communicate traditions as

accurately as possible. It may be that the early Christian communities had similar concerns. Consequently, rather than being 'creative communities' reformulating text units to suit its purposes, the early Christian communities may have communicated the tradition with much less revision than that envisaged by the form critics.[87]

6. There are also weaknesses with the individual methods employed by form critics. Thus it is questionable how useful the criterion of dissimilarity is in enabling us to isolate forms that genuinely originated with Jesus. The problem is that our knowledge of first century Christianity and Judaism is far from comprehensive. It may be the case that an apparent dissimilarity is due merely to our possessing insufficient information to show its similarity to either Christianity or first century Judaism. Furthermore, the very fact that the passage was handed down by the Church may indicate that it is not as dissimilar from early Christianity as proponents of the criterion of dissimilarity would have us believe. A further problem with the criterion of dissimilarity is that it rules out any passages where Jesus might be in continuity with early Christianity and Judaism.

The criterion of coherence inherits difficulties associated with the criterion of dissimilarity and adds some of its own. Thus, like the criterion of dissimilarity, it suffers from the problem that it cuts Jesus loose from his context. Because we rule out anything that Jesus might have had in common with contemporary Judaism and first century Christianity, in employing the criterion of coherence we merely exaggerate Jesus' difference still further.

The problem with the criterion of multiple attestation is that the 'multiple witnesses' to a tradition are not independent of each other. The accounts in Matthew and Luke, if we are to believe the two-document hypothesis, are frequently reworkings of Mark. Consequently, they have little value as independent witnesses. The only case where this criterion may be useful is if a tradition is attested by *independent* traditions. This seems to the case, for example, with the parable of the mustard seed, which appears both in Mark (Mark 4.30–32) and Q (Matt. 13.31–32; Luke 13.18–19). The best the criterion of multiple attestation can achieve, however, is to indicate the general themes of Jesus' ministry, namely his teaching concerning the Kingdom of God and the Son of Man, and his association with the outcasts of society. It cannot, however, prove the authenticity of specific events described in the New Testament. The attestation is simply too weak.

As a result of such criticisms, scholars have become less confident in their ability to trace the pre-literary, oral development of the tradition. The view that biblical writers combined originally independent material has also been questioned. It has been suggested that the blocks of tradition present in the final literary text may already have existed as cycles of tradition prior to their being fixed in written form. For this reason the type of form criticism employed by Dibelius and Bultmann has declined. The focus is now on identifying the various literary forms present in the Bible and less on the problematic attempt to trace the development of forms in their pre-literary state. In so far as form criticism enables us to identify the different literary forms in the biblical writings it can still perform a useful task.

CHAPTER SIX

Redaction Criticism

'Redaction' is another word for 'editing' and redaction criticism focuses on how the final authors or compilers of a biblical writing edited their materials so as to create a coherent text. Redaction criticism is thus the study of how the biblical writers have handled the tradition they have inherited.[1] Redaction criticism is consequently dependent on source and form criticism, for it is necessary first to identify the traditions from which the biblical writing has been constructed, before we can identify how the biblical writers have made use of these traditions. Only when the traditions of a biblical writing have been isolated can the redaction critic embark on his or her work.[2] The use of source and form criticism is important in order to identify what belongs to tradition and what belongs to redaction.

Once the traditions employed by a biblical text have been identified by means of source criticism and form criticism, it becomes possible to identify additions and alterations on the part of the editor. Redaction criticism thus examines how the smaller units identified by source and form criticism have been combined into larger blocks of material and how this inherited material has been moulded by later viewpoints. Form criticism, source criticism and redaction criticism thus study different stages in the development of the tradition. Whereas form criticism and source criticism study the building blocks from which a text was constructed, redaction criticism is concerned with the decisions made by the author in the final composition of the text.

To identify the redactor's contribution to the text the redaction critic focuses on the selection of material, the editorial links, summaries and comments, expansions, additions, and clarifications which it is believed the biblical writer has introduced in the composition of his text. It is held that such interventions into the text can reveal insights into the theology of the biblical author and the community of which he was a member.

Redaction criticism thus examines what source criticism and form criticism discard, namely the editorial or redactional work of a biblical writer. As Stein puts it: 'Form criticism "sets aside" the redaction and concentrates its investigation upon the tradition, whereas redaktionsgeschichte "sets aside" the tradition and concentrates its investigation upon the redaction.'[3] In contrast to the source critic and form critic, the redaction critic does not dismiss the editorial elements detectable in a biblical writing as 'secondary' or 'inauthentic', but regards them as important for understanding the final shape of the biblical writing. From this editorial material, we can establish how the biblical writer has handled units of tradition and how the author understood the tradition he has inherited. This emphasis on the *author* is one of the distinctive features of redaction criticism, which marks it off from source criticism and form criticism.

The task of the redaction critic can be complicated by the fact that a text may have gone through several recensions, in which case there may be several layers of redaction in the text, where a redactor has edited a unit of tradition and a subsequent redactor has edited the redacted text when taking it up and incorporating it into a later text. The situation is complicated still further by the fact that there can be redaction of individual passages and also redaction of the entire writing. That is, there can be different stages of redaction and different redactors involved at these different stages. Identification of the character and purpose of redactional insertions, however, may shed light on these stages. This involves asking the questions: is a redactional element aimed at elucidating the immediate passage or is it employed in order to integrate the passage into the overall structure of the entire writing?

The work of the redaction critic is made easier if there are parallel texts which he or she can employ as points of comparison. This is the case with the investigation of Samuel-Kings and Chronicles in the Old Testament and Matthew, Mark and Luke in the New Testament. Where parallel texts are unavailable, the redaction critic must search for internal indications that redactional activity has taken place in the text.

There are several levels of redactional intervention:

(a) Codification of the final oral stage of the text.

Here redactional activity consists in the redactor's fixing in written form what was previously in oral circulation. The questions raised by this form of redactional intervention centre on the character of this final codification. Has the redactor simply listed the units of tradition as they have come down to him or has he attempted to incorporate them into a framework of some kind? If the latter is the case, then what is the organizing principle of this framework? These questions lead to the search for evidence of further levels of redactional intervention.

(b) The first fixing of a written version of an orally transmitted text may be accompanied by a reworking of the text by a redactor. Redactional reworking of the text can be recognized by examining the linguistic characteristics of the text and establishing to what degree they cohere with the literary context. This involves establishing the profile of the redactor in order to separate redactional material from the original orally transmitted text. It is here that the question of 'tradition or redaction' arises, i.e. separating out older elements from the later reworking of the text by the redactor.

(c) The redactor may create new material in order to create the narrative framework appropriate to his theological interests in reworking the tradition. For example, the redactor may create summaries at certain points in the narrative or create sayings that express the key points of his theological position. This new material can be of two kinds. Firstly, it can consist of the insertion of brief links between units of tradition. Secondly, it can consist of larger blocks of text which sum up the redactor's understanding of the meaning of the tradition he has inherited. Larger redactional insertions are important for shedding light on the aims of the redactor. They are also important for restructuring the entire writing.

(d) Not all redactional elements need be created by the redactor. Some redactional interventions may consist of the insertion of traditional elements in order to expatiate on or explain a point in the original text. These elements have been detached from their original context in order to fill out the text into which they have been incorporated.

(e) Redactional revision can be achieved through the *ordering* of the tradition. The imposition of a new macrostructure can influence the meaning of the received material. This may result in a realignment of the writing. For example, the redactor can group units together according to genre such as psalms, proverbs, legal sayings, ancestral narratives, oracles of woe and pronouncements of salvation. The way the redactor organizes this material can affect its meaning. For example, how are the individual wisdom sayings in Proverbs affected by their being incorporated into a work introduced by the personification of wisdom in Prov. 1–9? Another example is the effect of placing cultic psalms such as Pss. 46 and 47 in a larger collection of psalms. This compilation of related material is the work of the redactor and is the subject of study for the redactional critic.

(f) By examining how the final editor or editors of a biblical text have taken up and used their sources we can gain an insight into the theology and social background of the community within which the final text was produced. For example, discerning the way the evangelists have edited, modified and adapted their sources reveals much about their own theology and the nature of the community for which they were writing. Thus Matthew's modification of Mark's account of Peter's confession of Jesus as the Messiah at Caesarea Philippi sheds light on Matthew's own theological interests and concerns. Matthew's addition of the phrase 'the Son of the living God' (Matt. 16.16) to Mark's 'You are the Christ'

(Mark 8.29) strengthens the Christological significance of the passage and makes clear Jesus' divine status. Furthermore, the *order* in which the evangelists have placed their sources also tells us something about their theology. Thus the fact that Matthew has apparently placed Jesus' teaching in the Sermon on the Mount (Matt. 5–7) into five sections that parallel the five books of the Torah is arguably an expression of Matthew's theology of Jesus as the new law-giver, and has been taken by some scholars to indicate that Matthew was writing his Gospel for a Jewish-Christian community.

Redaction criticism thus has consequences for the debate concerning the historicity of the events related by the Bible. Because redaction criticism assumes that biblical texts reflect the community in which they were written, they can be used to construct a picture of that community. Since, however, the texts have been moulded according to the needs of that community, they may be unreliable as sources of information on the events they describe. To take the Gospels as an example, redaction critics such as Norman Perrin hold that they reflect more about the communities in which the Gospels were produced than about the historical Jesus. Taking Mark 8.27–9 as his example, Perrin comments that earlier interpretations of this passage have understood it to be a historical account of 'the turning point of Jesus' ministry and as the moment of the revelation of the totally different conceptions of messiahship held by Jesus, on the one hand, and his disciples, on the other'.[4] In contrast to such interpretations, however, redaction criticism sees the text not as a historical account of an episode in the life of Jesus, but as a text which Mark has constructed for his own theological purposes. Perrin concludes from this that redaction criticism has important consequences for Life of Jesus research and Life of Jesus theology.[5] Since much of the Gospel material is due to the theologically motivated intervention of the evangelist or redactor of earlier layers of the tradition, 'we must take as our starting point the assumption that the Gospels offer us directly information about the theology of the early Church and not about the teaching of the historical Jesus, and that any information we may derive from them about Jesus can only come as a result of the stringent application of very carefully contrived criteria for authenticity'.[6] For Perrin, redaction criticism 'reveals how very much of the material ascribed to the Jesus who spoke in Galilee or Judea must in fact be ascribed to the Jesus who spoke through a prophet or evangelist in the early church'.[7] Consequently, redaction criticism 'forc[es] us to recognize that a Gospel does not portray the history of the ministry of Jesus from A.D. 27–30, or whatever the dates may actually have been, but the history of Christian experience in any and every age'.[8] This places considerable obstacles in the way of the identification of the historical Jesus and the construction of a Life of Jesus.

In summary, the aim of redaction criticism is to identify the editorial input into the construction of biblical texts. This involves attempting to ascertain the reasons for the editor's modification of inherited material, isolating the leitmotifs in the redactional material, and identifying the theological interests of the editor or compiler of a biblical writing.

A brief history of redaction criticism

The term 'redaction criticism' is the Anglicized version of the German term *Redaktionsgeschichte* [redaction history]. The German term seems to have been coined by Willi Marxsen,[9] who employed the adjective *redaktionsge-schichtlich* [redaction-historical] in an article published in 1955,[10] while in his *Mark the Evangelist* he employs the noun *Redaktionsgeschichte*.[11] This term has been rendered in English as 'redaction criticism', a term which has itself a German counterpart in *Redaktionskritik*, which is employed by Richter.[12]

The difference in terminology in German-speaking and English-speaking scholarship may be due to a different conception of redaction criticism. John Donahue comments:

> In Germany [redaction criticism] was primarily a *historical* discipline where the focus was on the origin and settings of traditions, on the conditions of their development, and on the historical circumstances that best explained their final editing. Using terminology that became current only later, we can say that in Germany, redaction criticism concentrated on 'the world behind the text'. In the United States, redaction criticism developed primarily as an exercise in *literary* criticism, where the emphasis was on the final product as a unitary composition with concern for the overarching themes and motifs, and for the structure of the whole and of the individual parts.[13]

On these grounds, it is arguably advisable to employ the term 'redaction criticism' for the study of the redactional intervention evident from the final form of the text, whereas *Redaktionsgeschichte* or 'redaction history' might be reserved for attempts to track the *history* of these interventions.

Although the term *Redaktionsgeschichte* did not come into existence until the 1950s, the method the term describes existed much earlier. Marxsen points out: 'Theoretically, it would have been possible for redaction-historical research to have begun immediately after literary criticism [i.e. *source* criticism].'[14] That is, redaction criticism is not as such dependent on form criticism, for it could have been applied to the redaction of the *sources* identified by source criticism. Thus it could have been applied to examine how Matthew and Luke have redacted their two sources of Mark and Q. Indeed, Marxsen finds it astonishing that redaction criticism did not follow the general acceptance of the two-source solution to the Synoptic Problem, 'for soon after Wernle's fixing of the two-source theory, beginnings were made which should have led automatically in that direction'.[15] As examples of such beginnings Marxsen cites Wrede and Wellhausen.[16] Marxsen suggests, however, that the results of their work 'robbed scholars of the courage to pursue their *methods* in thoroughgoing fashion'. Instead of building on the work of Wrede and Wellhausen by searching for further motifs originating in Mark's point of view, 'the evangelists were examined almost exclusively from literary standpoints'.[17]

Barton, however, suggests that the earliest hints of what would later be called redaction criticism are to be found in Origen, who attributes the absence in the Gospel of John of the accounts of Jesus' temptation by Satan and his agony in the Garden of Gethsemane to John's intention to portray a 'divine' Christ. Since the temptation and Gethsemane narratives fitted badly with the notion of a divine Christ, John simply removed these passages from his account. That is, Origen attributes the differences between the Gospel of John and the Synoptic Gospels to the redaction of his sources by the author of John's Gospel. As Barton points out, however, 'such explanations are rare in the Fathers. There is very little sense of what we might call the integrity of each Gospel as a complete story in its own right. The Gospels are seen as providing raw materials for the harmonizer to work with, not as literary works'.[18]

To find the next hints of redaction criticism, we must leap over 1500 years to Reimarus, whom Perrin claims can be regarded as a forerunner of redaction criticism. Perrin makes this claim on the grounds that Reimarus aimed to show that the Gospels do not recount history, but are the result of the disciples' reworking of the story of Jesus in light of their own interests. As we saw in Chapter 2, Reimarus held Jesus to be a political leader who aimed to seize power from the Romans and attracted disciples precisely because they hoped to occupy positions of power and influence once Jesus had achieved his political goals. After Jesus' political mission had failed, the disciples' political ambitions and desire for status were thwarted and they were confronted with the unpalatable prospect of returning to work and the humiliation of conceding that they had followed a failed messiah. To avoid this fate, they created stories of Jesus performing miracles, predicting his own execution, and fulfilling Old Testament prophecy, all of which according to Reimarus reflect not the realities of Jesus' life but the period after his death. The purpose of these inventions was to enable the disciples to remain at the head of the movement started by Jesus, whom they now transformed from a political messiah to a spiritual, suffering redeemer who laid down his life for the sins of humankind. For Reimarus, then, the disciples have edited the tradition in order to adapt it to their own purposes. He is thus advancing an early form of redaction criticism and, Perrin claims, can be described as the 'father of our discipline'.[19]

According to Perrin, 'the mantle of Reimarus descended upon David Friedrich Strauss', the effect of whose interpretation of the life of Jesus in terms of 'myth' was 'to call attention to "a creative element" in the Gospel narratives'.[20] Hints of redaction criticism can also be seen in the work of F. C. Baur, who in his *The Gospel of Mark According to Its Origin and Character* (1851) argued that Mark had conflated Matthew and Luke in order to reconcile the differences between the Jews and Gentiles that these two supposedly earlier Gospels reflected.[21] Baur's work can be regarded as an early attempt in redaction criticism, because he is concerned with examining how Mark edited his sources in order to further his own theological interests.

Another work that has been regarded as a forerunner of redaction criticism is Wrede's book on the messianic secret. In contrast to his predecessors, Wrede rejected the so-called 'Markan hypothesis', i.e. the widely held view that Mark provided a historically reliable portrayal of the life of the historical Jesus,[22] and argued that Mark had organized his Gospel according to theological motives, namely the need to explain why Jesus had not been recognized as the messiah during his lifetime. According to Wrede, Mark's account of Jesus keeping his identity secret does not reflect historical reality, but is Mark's own theological construct, which he has imposed on the material he has inherited. As Wrede puts it, 'I would go further and assert that a historical motive is really out of the question; or, to put it positively, that the idea of the messianic secret is a theological idea'.[23] This emphasis on Mark's organization of his Gospel according to theological motives has led to Wrede being regarded as a forerunner of redaction criticism. Indeed, for Johannes Schreiber, it is Wrede who is the father of redaction criticism,[24] while Perrin goes so far as to claim that 'Wrede's work on the Messianic Secret is in many ways the first product of this discipline'.[25]

In the latter part of his *History of the Synoptic Tradition*, Bultmann too considers the redactional input of the Synoptists in a chapter entitled 'the editing of the traditional material'.[26] Other scholars who can be regarded as forerunners of redaction criticism are Karl Kundsin,[27] Adolf Schlatter[28] and Ernst Lohmeyer,[29] all of whom devote some attention to the redactional activity of the evangelists.

In English-speaking scholarship, hints of redaction criticism can be found in R. H. Lightfoot's Bampton lectures entitled *History and Interpretation in the Gospels*. In his third Bampton lecture, Lightfoot employs what can be regarded as a form of redaction criticism, although he does not use this term. He states his intention to draw on *form* criticism in order 'to examine the doctrine set forth in this gospel (Mark)'.[30] For Perrin, 'To all intents and purposes, this lecture is an exercise in redaction criticism',[31] which prompts him to describe Lightfoot 'actually the first redaction critic'.[32] Anticipations of a redactional-critical approach can also be found in the work of B. W. Bacon, N. B. Stonehouse, Philip Carrington and A. M. Farrer.[33]

It was only after the Second World War, however, that redaction criticism became a significant approach. Two factors seem to have come together to create the conditions in which redaction criticism could flourish.

(1) Decline of the quest of the historical Jesus

One of the factors that may have contributed to the rise of redaction criticism is the disintegration of the old quest of the historical Jesus. The quest of the historical Jesus was dependent on the so-called 'Markan hypothesis', i.e. the view that Mark was the nearest in time to the life of Jesus and provided a historically trustworthy source for the knowledge of Jesus. As we have seen, this hypothesis was undermined by Wrede. Redaction criticism was able to sidestep the problem caused by Wrede by making its focus not the *historicity* of the Gospels but the *theology* of the Gospels. As Marxsen puts it, 'With this [redaction-critical] approach, the question as to what really happened is excluded from the outset . . . [That question] is of interest only to the degree it relates the situation of the primitive community in which the Gospels arose'.[34] The key to understanding the Gospels is not to identify their historical kernel but to establish their function as kerygma. As Rohde puts it, 'the gospels must be understood as *kerygma*, and not as biographies of Jesus of Nazareth'.[35] Clifton Black points out that liberal theologians regarded redaction criticism's turning away from the historical Jesus as something positive, for, 'It seemed to bridge the enormous temporal and hermeneutical gap between Mark as interpreter of the Jesus-traditions and the twentieth-century theologian as interpreter of the Second Gospel by functionally locating both in the same position: that of elucidator, not of Jesus of Nazareth, but of the early Christian *kerygma* about Jesus'.[36] Redaction criticism seemed to some to provide the basis for allowing the Bible to speak to us today, since the Gospel writers were engaged in creatively mediating the kerygma to their age, just as it is the task of the theologian and preacher to do so today.

(2) The assimilation of the results of form criticism

Although redaction criticism was theoretically possible on the basis of source criticism, it was in reality only when form criticism had identified the units of tradition of the biblical texts that it became possible to distinguish between tradition and redaction. This is a point made by Stein, who comments that, 'it was not until form criticism separated the pericopes from the redaction that redaktionsgeschichte was really possible'.[37] The reason that it was not until after the Second World War that redaction criticism became established was that time had been needed for form criticism to establish itself and for the results of its investigations to be absorbed into biblical scholarship. Only when form-critical insights had become generally accepted was it possible for redaction criticism to build on the work of the form critics.

Although the term 'redaction criticism' has been employed less frequently in Old Testament studies than in the study of the New Testament, it is nevertheless a method that has been exploited by some Old Testament scholars in order to trace the way the Old Testament writings acquired their structure. Key figures in the development of Old Testament redaction criticism were Gerhard von Rad and Martin Noth, whose studies of Genesis and Joshua-Kings provide classic examples of its application to Old Testament texts. Richter and Steck have contributed to the development of Old Testament redaction criticism by endeavouring to clarify its methodology in relation to the Hebrew Bible.[38]

The pioneers of redaction criticism in the post-war period, however, were the New Testament scholars Bornkamm, Conzelmann and Willi Marxsen (1919–1993).

Bornkamm's first venture in redaction criticism was a brief article on Matthew's account of the Stilling of the Storm (Matt. 8.23–7), published in 1948 in the journal of the theological seminary at Bethel and subsequently in English translation in *Tradition and Interpretation in Matthew* (1963).[39] Bornkamm identifies Matthew's redactional input by comparing the pericope with Mark's version. This enables him to show that by modifying Mark's order and introducing the phrase 'men of little faith', Matthew has shifted the focus of the passage from the disciples' lack of faith to the challenges of Christian discipleship as such, thereby transforming the passage into 'a symbol of the distresses involved in discipleship as a whole'.[40] Matthew has reworked his source, Mark 4.35–41, to create 'a kerygmatic paradigm of the danger and glory of discipleship'.[41] Bornkamm followed up his study of Matt. 8.23–7 with redaction-critical analysis of other passages from Matthew's Gospel. In 1954 he gave a lecture entitled

'Matthew as Interpreter of the Words of the Lord', which formed the basis of his contribution to C. H. Dodd's *Festschrift* and which Perrin claims is 'the first thoroughgoing redaction critical investigation of the theological peculiarities and theme of Matthew's Gospel'.[42] In this essay, entitled 'End-Expectation and Church in Matthew', Bornkamm examines how Matthew has modified Jesus' discourses to reflect his understanding of the Church, the end-time, the law and Christ. Bornkamm concludes that Matthew was an 'interpreter of the tradition which he collected and arranged'.[43] According to Perrin, 'The Bornkamm article proved to be a real opening of the door to the future'.[44]

Although Bornkamm may have been the first of the genuine redaction critics, for Perrin 'Hans Conzelmann is certainly the most important'.[45] Conzelmann's publication of his *Die Mitte der Zeit* in 1954 (ET: *The Theology of Luke* (1960)) firmly placed redaction criticism on the agenda of biblical scholarship. Writing in 1966, Perrin described Conzelmann as 'the greatest practitioner of this methodology to date',[46] while in 1977 Stephen Smalley held that Conzelmann's book 'marks a watershed in Gospel studies and an important advance in the method of redaction criticism itself'.[47]

The German title of Conzelmann's book refers to his view that Luke portrays Jesus' life as the centre of time, an allusion that is lost in the title of the English translation. In contrast to previous studies of Luke, which had tended to see him primarily as a historian, Conzelmann argues that Luke was first and foremost a theologian who organized his Gospel and the Acts of the Apostles according to theological principles. A good example of Luke's theological intervention is his placing of Jesus' resurrection appearances exclusively in Jerusalem and his making no mention of the Galilean appearances described in Mark 16.7 and Matt. 28.16.

Conzelmann argues that a notion of salvation history provides the theological motivation of Luke's Gospel and finds this expressed above all in Luke 16.16 and 13.31–5. According to Conzelmann, Luke understands salvation history to consist of three stages. The first stage is the history of Israel, which reached its climax in the person of John the Baptist. The second stage is Jesus' ministry, which is the 'centre of time' that gave Conzelmann's book its German title. This second stage came to a conclusion with Jesus' ascension. The third stage is the age of the Church, which is still ongoing. In this third age, believers look back to the salvation wrought by and in Christ and look forward to his coming again in the parousia. Conzelmann holds that this three-fold structure underlying the Gospel is the result of Luke's reflection on the crisis caused by the delay of Christ's return and the need of the Church to adjust to long-term existence in the world.

Of the three pioneers of redaction criticism, it was Marxsen who provided the new approach with a methodological grounding. In his *Mark
the Evangelist*, Marxsen provided four redaction-critical studies of Mark,
namely on Mark's portrayal of John the Baptist, the geographical references in the Synoptic Gospels, the concept of Gospel and the Markan
apocalypse. Of particular importance is Marxsen's differentiation between
three *Sitze im Leben*, a distinction which is considered by some scholars to
be one of Marxsen's most important contributions to redaction criticism.[48]
Marxsen adds to Joachim Jeremias' two *Sitze im Leben*, namely the setting in the life of Jesus and the setting in the early Church, a third *Sitz im
Leben*, which is the setting of the evangelist who was responsible for bringing the Gospel material into a coherent whole.[49] Concern with this third
Sitz im Leben focuses on 'the situation of the community in which the
Gospels arose'.[50] Consequently, 'a sociological element is present throughout', but, Marxsen emphasizes, 'over against form history this element is
joined to an "individualistic" trait oriented to the particular interest and
point of view of the evangelist concerned'.[51] The problem, however, Perrin
notes, 'is that of finding an appropriate terminology' for this threefold *Sitz
im Leben*. To address this problem, Perrin proposes the following three
terms: '(1) Setting in the life of Jesus; (2) setting in the life and work of the
early church; (3) setting in the work and purpose of the evangelist'.[52]

The result of the works of Bornkamm, Conzelmann and Marxsen and
their followers was that redaction criticism became a major focus of New
Testament scholarship from the 1950s until the 1970s. As Perrin put it in his
1966 article, 'The Wredestrasse has become the Hauptstrasse, and it is leading
us to new and exciting country'.[53] Bornkamm's approach was taken up by his
pupils Gerhard Barth and Heinz Joachim Held, who followed Bornkamm's
lead in their studies of Matthew.[54] Another pupil of Bornkamm's, Heinz
Eduard Tödt, applied Bornkamm's approach to the Son of man tradition
in the Synoptic Gospels,[55] while Ferdinand Hahn applied the method to
Christology.[56] In 1969 Stein commented that the numerous works that had
appeared since the publication of the works of Conzelmann and Marxsen
'indicates that redaktionsgeschichte has today become the most important
area of gospel studies'.[57]

In the English-speaking world, Norman Perrin played an important role
in enabling redaction criticism to establish itself. Welton Seal goes so far as to
speak of a Perrin *school*,[58] among whom he cites several scholars who have
written significant works in redaction criticism such as Richard Edwards,
John Donahue and Werner Kelber.[59]

R. H. Stein's contribution to redaction criticism was to attempt to place
it on a firmer methodological basis. His doctoral dissertation was devoted
to this issue with reference to the Gospel of Mark.[60] This led in 1971 to the
publication of an article summarizing the argument of his dissertation.[61] In

this article, Stein identifies four questions with which the redaction critic approaches the Gospels:

(1) 'What unique theological views does the evangelist present which are foreign to his sources?'

(2) 'What unusual theological emphasis or emphases does the evangelist place upon the sources he received?'

(3) 'What theological purpose or purposes does the evangelist have in writing his gospel?'

(4) 'What is the *Sitz im Leben* out of which the evangelist writes his gospel?'[62]

As well as attempting to introduce methodological clarity into redaction criticism, Stein points to the difficulties of applying redaction criticism to Mark. These stem in part from the fact that Mark's sources are unavailable to us and therefore provide us with no basis for comparison. This is in contrast to the redaction criticism of Matthew and Luke, where we can conduct such a comparison because we have available one of their major sources, namely Mark. Stein further points out that Mark has 'made our task more complicated . . . because he has "marcanized" the traditions, both oral and written, which were available to him'.[63] This makes it difficult to ascertain where Mark departs from the traditions he has inherited. Nevertheless, despite these difficulties, Stein holds that light can be thrown on Mark's redaction by attending to the seams, insertions, summaries, modifications, selection, omission, arrangement, introduction, conclusion, vocabulary and Christological titles evident in the Gospel.

Computers have been enlisted in the attempt to distinguish redaction from tradition. Such an attempt was made in 1973 by Lloyd Gaston, who used computer analysis to investigate the vocabulary of the Synoptic Gospels.[64] Gaston's study, as Black has pointed out, suffers from the fact that Gaston has taken as his starting point for his discussion of Markan redaction 'the "common agreement" among investigators that certain passages are redactional'.[65] The problem with this assumption, Black argues, is that 'there is reason to wonder whether, as Gaston implies, such a consensus of opinion or "common agreement" on Markan redactional passages actually exists'.[66] Subsequent attempts to identify Mark's redactional input have been made by E. J. Pryke and David Barrett Peabody.[67]

Since the 1970s, there have been increasingly vigorous criticisms of redaction criticism. Firstly, the method has been criticized for allegedly failing to do justice to the literary character of the biblical writings. R. M. Frye, for example, has argued on literary grounds against the method.

Drawing on secular literary criticism, he has criticized redaction criticism for 'disintegrating' the Gospels and hindering their study as literary wholes.[68] Secondly, its application to the Gospel of Mark has been argued to be untenable. Despite his pioneering work on redactional criticism, by 1976, Perrin had come to recognize its inadequacies as a method for interpreting the Gospel of Mark. The weakness of redaction criticism is that 'it defines the literary activity of the author too narrowly', the consequence of which is that it overlooks the richness of the text and in doing so fails to do justice 'to the text of the Gospel as a coherent text with its own internal dynamics'.[69] Black thinks that the problems with identifying Markan redaction are so great that they are not capable of resolution.[70] Indeed, for Black, 'given the enormous theoretical and practical problems entailed by the practice of Markan redaction criticism, especially when predicated on the assumption of Markan priority, one wonders why this exegetical approach for so long has held so many interpreters in thrall'.[71] The problem is that there is simply insufficient knowledge concerning the development of the tradition before Mark. All attempts to reconstruct this development contain a large element of speculation based on unfounded presuppositions on how the tradition developed. Reconstruction of the development of the pre-Markan tradition has tended to be based on projecting the way Matthew and Luke have handled Mark back onto the period preceding Mark.

Because of the difficulties of studying the redaction of texts where we do not have parallel or related texts, Joachim Rohde holds that redaction criticism can be applied only to the Synoptic Gospels and Acts, and possibly to James, but not to the remainder of the New Testament.[72] The method has, however, been employed beyond these writings, notably by J. D. Crossan, who has applied the method to non-canonical works.[73] It has also been employed in feminist criticism of the Bible by Elisabeth Schüssler Fiorenza.[74]

Because of the impossibility of identifying with certainty the redactional activity of the author, there has taken place a shift to the *themes* of Mark's Gospel. Black points out, however, that, 'Although the identification of the Gospel's themes could be incorporated into a larger redaction-critical paradigm, *such a determination is not an intrinsically redaction-critical criterion but a literary-critical assessment*'.[75]

As a result of these problems, redaction criticism has tended to mutate into new literary approaches to the study of the Bible. Indeed, because of its concern with the text as a unity, redaction criticism constitutes a bridge to later literary approaches and may have prepared the ground for the advent of the literary theories that have come to dominate biblical scholarship at the end of the twentieth and beginning of the twenty-first centuries. Black comments, 'Indeed, without the redaction-critical emphasis on authors and literary products, the current movement toward newer literary-critical approaches might not have been as expeditious'.[76] This transition from redaction criticism to literary methods of interpretation can be tracked in the thought of one of the leading redaction critics, namely Norman Perrin, who later in life turned away from redaction criticism to literary criticism and hermeneutics.[77]

Redaction and composition

In the early phase of redaction criticism, there was little differentiation between redaction and *composition*. The problems faced by redaction criticism, however, have led to attempts to supplement it with what has come to be known as *composition criticism*. This stems from a distinction between the meanings of redaction and composition, where 'redaction' denotes a loose ordering of units of tradition, while 'composition' is used of a tighter, more sustained and unified fusion of the material.[78]

Composition criticism restricts itself to the final form of the text and focuses on how the author has arranged the material and imposed a coherent narrative on the text. In contrast to redaction criticism, it is not concerned with distinguishing between tradition and redaction, but with tracing the arrangement and emphases in the text considered as a unified, coherent whole. We might say that the difference between redaction and composition lies in the degree to which the sources and forms have been integrated into a coherent, flowing narrative. The greater the coherence, the more the text as a whole should be considered a composition. The less the coherence, the more the text should be considered a redaction. The way the author has welded together the tradition and created a coherent narrative can be regarded as composition, whereas the term 'redaction' can be reserved for the specific instances where there is a demonstrable editorial adaptation of units of tradition. Thus for Richter, a principle of composition is scarcely evident in Proverbs. In works such as Kings and Chronicles, on the other hand, the authors have composed their texts and integrated their material according to an overarching organizational principle and have thereby imposed a coherent structure on the text. It is thus more precise to speak of *redaction* in the case of Proverbs, but more accurate in the case of Kings and Chronicles to speak of *composition*. The boundary between composition and redaction is an imprecise one, however. There is a sliding scale between complete integration into a seamless composition, which would make redaction criticism impossible, to minimal integration where the redactor's work consists merely in listing units of tradition. Even here, however, the order in which the redactor lists the units sheds some light on the redactional process.

Another way of distinguishing between redaction criticism and composition criticism is to say that redaction criticism is *diachronic*, while composition criticism is *synchronic*. That is, redaction criticism is concerned with tracing the development of texts through time and identifying the different layers from which they have been built up, whereas composition criticism is concerned with the structure of the final text rather than with its preceding history of development.

An early form of composition criticism was proposed by Ernst Haenchen, who considered redaction criticism to be the second stage of form criticism and suggested naming this second stage *Kompositionsgeschichte*, i.e. composition history.[79] Haenchen, then, simply identifies composition with redaction and makes no attempt to differentiate between the two terms. By the time Perrin came to publish his *What is Redaction Criticism?* (1970), however, awareness had developed of the possibility of distinguishing between redaction and composition, and of the possibility of developing the new discipline of composition criticism. While on the opening page of his book Perrin comments that 'although the discipline is called redaction criticism, it could equally be called "composition criticism"', towards the end of the book he comments: 'It is becoming evident that one problem connected with redaction criticism is and will increasingly become the problem of the relationship between redaction and composition.'[80] For Perrin, however, the time for the development of composition criticism as a distinct discipline had not yet arrived: 'It may well be that one day the discipline will have developed to the point where composition criticism has to be distinguished from redaction criticism as redaction criticism now has to be distinguished from form criticism, but that day is not yet and we are concerned with the discipline as it is currently being practised'.[81] Similarly, writing in 1977 Smalley suggested that redaction criticism and composition criticism might become distinct disciplines but did not hold this to be the case at the time of writing.[82] Over two decades later, however, Randall K. J. Tan believed that the time had indeed arrived when 'redaction criticism proper and composition criticism should be recognized as distinct disciplines'.[83] For Tan, redaction criticism or 'strict editorial criticism', as he puts it, 'looks for the evangelist's theology in the redactional text after separating out redaction from tradition by means of source and form criticism'.[84] Composition criticism, on the other hand, 'locates the patterns and emphases of the evangelists without systematically identifying or separating out redaction from tradition'.[85] Tan welcomes composition criticism's supersession of redaction criticism, commenting that, 'Composition analysis becomes, in practice, a welcome return to a grammatical-historical interpretation that seeks to ascertain authorial intent from the meaning expressed through the written language of the evangelists in the Gospel texts'.[86]

The development of composition criticism is arguably a parallel development to form criticism's move away from concern with the pre-literary history of the text, which many believe to be impossible to carry out with any degree of confidence, to a concern with the text as it now is. Just as 'new' form criticism focuses on identifying forms and genres in the text as a literary unit, so too does composition criticism focus on the evidence in the text for the compositional patterns imposed on the texts by the biblical writers.

The method of redaction criticism

Presuppositions

1. Redaction criticism shares the presuppositions of source criticism and form criticism that text units originally circulated independently of their context in the Gospels. Whereas source criticism and form criticism attempt to identify and classify these sources, however, redaction criticism focuses on what the biblical authors have done with them.

2. Redaction criticism shares with form criticism the assumption that it is possible to reconstruct the tradition of the oral period. It is the isolation of this oral tradition that allows the redaction critic to identify redactional interventions into the text.

3. Like source criticism and form criticism, redaction criticism assumes that it is possible to show literary dependence and to identify the motives underlying the modification of sources. If the ability of source criticism and form criticism to identify earlier sources is placed in doubt, then redaction criticism is also undermined.

4. Redaction criticism emphasizes the biblical writers as *authors*. In contrast to form criticism's tendency to see the biblical authors as merely compilers or editors of inherited material, redaction criticism sees them as religious thinkers with distinct theological perspectives.

5. The organization of the units of tradition identified by form criticism and source criticism are reflections not of historical reality but are due to the creative input of the redactor. It is the biblical writers who have provided the context for individual passages and provided the narrative framework.

The Principles of Redaction Criticism

1. Isolation of the unit of tradition

Like source criticism and form criticism, redaction criticism is concerned with isolating the individual units of text from the context in which they have been placed in the final version of the biblical writing. Whereas source and form criticism do this in order to identify the sources upon which a biblical text is based, the redaction critic does so in order to identify the contribution made by those responsible for composing the biblical writings. Thus whereas source criticism and form criticism identify redactional interventions in order to discard them so as to allow earlier layers of tradition to become apparent, the redaction critic makes such interventions the focus of his/her study. This is done by paying attention to the introductory and concluding formulae of a passage, and considering to what degree they are distinct from the passage to which they are attached. If they can be shown to be distinct, then it is likely that they are not part of an original source but are due to the editorial activity of the biblical writer.

Editorial interventions may also be ascertained by examining the *seams* in the text, which may indicate that two independent units have been joined together. *How* these units have been joined together sheds light on the redaction of the work. The identification of seams is particularly important with texts where no parallels exist, as is the case with Mark, for which unlike Matthew and Luke we have no points of comparison.

2. Identification and examination of editorial interventions in the text (comments, summaries, explanations, and omissions)

Redaction criticism is more straightforward when parallel texts exist that allow comparisons to be made between similar passages. Thus redactional analysis is easier to conduct with Matthew and Luke than it is with Mark, since – if we accept the theory of the priority of Mark – we can compare Matthew and Luke with Mark, but we have no earlier source with which to compare Mark. In cases of parallel texts, it is not only insertions but also omissions that can shed light on how the redactor has handled his sources. Redactional criticism is more difficult with texts where no such parallels are available. Where this is the case, the redaction critic focuses on passages where the editor seems to have intervened directly in the text to clear up misunderstanding or to stress points he apparently regards as worthy of emphasis. This requires the redaction critic to be attentive to the transitional phrases, summaries, modifications, insertions and omissions in the text. Such passages shed light on the redactor's understanding of the inherited tradition and reveal his own theological perspective.

3. Identification of distinctive terminology

What are the key terms employed in the text? Are they employed elsewhere in the Gospel or unique to the passage under investigation? Are they due to a source or to the biblical writer's editorial activity? The answers to these questions can give us clues to the author's own position. Resolving such issues involves closely examining the vocabulary of the text in order to establish whether it contains distinctive terms that reflect the biblical writer's theology and are thus more likely to be editorial interventions than to belong to an inherited unit of tradition. This procedure is easiest in the Synoptic Gospels, where we can compare three parallel texts and establish the terminology favoured by the individual evangelist. But it is also possible in other writings if we can identify a distinctive authorial style.

4. Examination of the arrangement and ordering of the material

The order and framework in which a biblical author has placed his material can provide information about his understanding of the material and shed light on his theological interests.

5. Identification of the *Sitz im Leben*

Examination of the editorial interventions can give us an insight into the community of which the redactor was a member and in which the final version of the text was produced.

Redaction criticism in action

Gen. 2.4b-3.24

1. Isolation of the unit of tradition

Redaction criticism is dependent on the isolation of sources and units of tradition achieved by source criticism and form criticism. Whereas the source critic and form critic then focus on the unit they have detached from its overall context in the biblical writing, the redaction critic focuses on the means by which the unit has been integrated into this overall context. The redaction-critical examination of Gen. 2.4b–3.24 thus focuses on those elements of the text which serve to link together the units of tradition into a coherent narrative.

2. Identification and examination of editorial interventions in the text (comments, summaries, explanations and omissions)

The redactional interventions of the editor seem to be restricted to providing links to weld the tradition he has inherited into a coherent whole. It is difficult to detect summaries or explanations that reflect a distinctive perspective on the part of the redactor. There are, however, several examples of what appear to be editorial attempts to link units of tradition into a coherent whole.

The mention of 'tree of the knowledge of good and evil' in Gen. 2.9 looks very much like a redactional addition. The tree of life had already been mentioned as being situated 'in the midst of the garden', and it is in Hebrew syntactically and stylistically strained to tack the reference to the 'tree of the knowledge of good and evil' on to what appears to be an independent and fully formulated sentence. It is likely that the phrase had been added by an editor in order to create a link with the prohibition in Gen. 2.17 and the following drama.

A further example of redactional intervention is provided by Gen. 2.10–14, which seems to be an editorial insertion aimed at providing more information about Eden. That this is probably an insertion is indicated by the fact that it interrupts the story of God's creating the man to till the garden. The narrative flows more naturally if we understand it to have initially consisted of Gen. 2.4b–9, 16–17. Gen. 2.15 ('The LORD God took the man and put him in the garden of Eden to till it and keep it') is thus likely to be a redactional formulation which the editor has inserted in order to return the text to the narrative of God's creation of the first human being, which had been interrupted by the description of the topography of the Garden of Eden. That Gen. 2.15 is probably redactional is further indicated by the fact that it repeats what had already been said in Gen. 2.8. Since God had already placed the man in the garden in Gen. 2.8, it is superfluous for God to do it again in Gen. 2.15. The incorporation of Gen. 2.15 makes sense, however, if it is a redactional intervention aimed at reminding the reader of the main theme of the narrative after the digression of the description of the river system and geological features of the area in which Eden was situated.

Gen. 2.25 may be redactional. It may have been inserted into the text in order to create a link with Gen. 3.7, thereby combining two originally distinct traditions into a coherent whole. Similarly, the reference in Gen. 3.1 to the serpent, which 'the LORD God had made', may be a redactional insertion linking the narrative of Gen. 3.1–19 to the preceding account of God's creation of the animals in Gen. 2.18. The emphasis that the serpent is one of God's creatures may also be motivated by the redactor's concern to avoid creating the impression that the serpent was a rival power to God. By emphasizing that God had created the serpent, the redactor makes clear that the serpent was not himself a god, but belongs to the created order. If this passage is a 'faded myth' reflecting a polytheistic belief in a serpent god, then the redactor may have recast the episode to make it compatible with Israel's monotheism. In doing so, he has shifted the emphasis of the myth from being a struggle between rival gods to a theological reflection on the origins of sin and the need of human beings for grace.

3. Identification of distinctive terminology

Evidence of redactional intervention may be provided by the phrase Yahweh-Elohim. This is a syntactically odd formulation, and it appears (with one exception in the Pentateuch, namely Exod. 9.30) only in the story of the Garden of Eden and the fall of the first human beings. It is difficult to see how such an odd phrase could have arisen within the tradition, but it is possible to find an explanation on the basis of redactional intervention. The term may a construct on the part of the final editor of Genesis to make clear the connection between the two creation stories. That is, the redactor has added 'Elohim' to 'Yahweh' in order make clear that both creation stories are narratives about one and the same God.

4. Examination of the arrangement and ordering of the material

Examination of the redactional interventions into Gen. 2.4b–3.24 seems to indicate that they consist primarily of links aimed at fusing a diverse collection of traditions into a coherent whole and imposing upon them a consistent narrative. This raises the question of the framework that these editorial links have created and whether this can tell us anything about the theological motives of the redactor. Examination of the framework reveals that the redactor has grouped together sayings concerning the first human beings as well as passages about mythical trees. The theological purpose appears to be to set up the situation of disobedience that drives the subsequent narrative. The first sin described in Gen. 2.4b–3.24 is compounded by the sin of the first children of the first human beings described in Gen. 4.1–16. It is striking that God does not follow through with his threat that the first human beings would die if they ate of the fruit of the tree of the knowledge of good and evil (Gen. 2.17; 3.3). The first human beings do not die, but receive God's curse and are expelled from the garden. Despite the curse he pronounces, however, God does not give up on human beings. He does not follow through with his threat that to eat of the fruit of the tree spells death and he prepares human beings for their life outside the garden by making clothes for them (Gen. 3.21). The Yahwist has taken up the aetiology expressed in the curses and has fused it with a theology of grace.

What redaction-critical analysis of the framework of Gen. 2.4b–3.24 reveals, then, is that the Yahwist has collated a series of what were probably originally independent traditions and has welded them together into a theological narrative of creation, sin and grace. In the manner in which the Yahwist has imposed this theology upon his materials we can see that he was much more than a mere anthologist, but a creative theologian who reworked the traditions he had inherited to convey a profound theological insight.

5. Identification of the *Sitz im Leben*

As we saw in our form-critical analysis of Gen. 2.4b–3.24, underlying the story of the first human beings' expulsion from the Garden of Eden may be a Near Eastern myth of the expulsion of a king from the mountain of the gods. In its present form, however, the text is a reflection on human beings' thirst for knowledge, their disobedience of God, and the terrible consequences of this disobedience. The myth of the disobedient king has thus been reworked by the redactor into an insight into the human condition. Such insight into the human condition is reminiscent of the wisdom literature of the Old Testament such as Proverbs, Job and Ecclesiastes, works which explore the human condition and reflect on the consequences of human choices. Similar sentiments to those expressed in Gen. 2.4b–3.24 can, for example, be found in Prov. 10.8–9: 'The wise of heart will heed commandments, but a babbling fool will come to ruin. Whoever walks in integrity walks securely, but whoever follows perverse ways will be found out.' Whereas Proverbs expresses this insight in the form of a pithy saying, however, Gen. 2.4b–3.24 expresses it in the form of a dramatic narrative. The parallels with wisdom literature may indicate that the *Sitz im Leben* of the redactor of Gen. 2.4b–3.24 was a school of wisdom in ancient Israel.[87]

If this suggestion is correct, it also sheds light on the redactional history of Gen. 2.4b–3.24. It becomes clear that this passage has probably undergone multiple recensions. Firstly, myths concerning the expulsion of a royal figure from the presence of the gods and a struggle between a serpent god and his rival(s) may have been in circulation. These were then taken up and reworked in the light of the monotheism of ancient Israel. It is impossible to say whether the Yahwist was responsible for this reworking or whether it already existed in the traditions he inherited as a result of the redactional activity of earlier collectors of these traditions. These traditions were then taken up and made the vehicle of a theology of creation and fall by the Yahwist. Finally, the Yahwist's material was taken up and brought together with the material now known as P and E into what is now the Book of Genesis. It has been suggested that this final stage took place during the Babylonian Exile, when Israel's scribes and priests may have been concerned to preserve the identity and culture of their people by collecting the nation's traditions.

Matt. 15.21–28

Our identification of the redactional elements in Matthew will depend on our view of Matthew's sources. We will come to different decisions depending on whether we believe Matthew to have used Mark only, to have conflated Mark with his own special material or to be using an independent source which he favours in this instance over Mark's version.

1. Isolation of the unit of tradition

From source and form criticism, we can be confident that this tradition was originally independent of its current position in Mark's Gospel and can be equally easily uncoupled from its present location in Matthew's Gospel. The unit is capable of being detached without loss of meaning from the surrounding material.

2. Identification and examination of editorial interventions in the text (comments, summaries, explanations and omissions)

The examination of editorial interventions is aided by the fact that there exists a parallel version of this text unit in Mark 7.24–30. If we believe that Matthew has used Mark as one of his sources, then we can identify Matthew's redaction by examining the changes he has made to Mark. There are several changes that Matthew seems to have made to Mark's original version of the story.

15.21

Matthew has inherited from Mark the tradition of Jesus' going to the region of Tyre, but he has modified Mark's reference from 'the region of Tyre' to 'the district of Tyre and Sidon'. The explanation for this alteration may be that Matthew wishes to reproduce Old Testament usage, where the two towns were usually linked as symbols of wealth and warned of coming judgement.[88]

Matthew has omitted from Matt. 15.21 Mark's comment that Jesus 'entered a house and did not want anyone to know he was there. Yet he could not escape notice' (Mark 7.24). Matthew's omission of Mark's reference to Jesus entering the house is presumably because this contributes little to the episode, but also perhaps because it creates the impression that the Canaanite/ Syro–Phoenician woman's encounter with Jesus took place indoors. The fact that Mark states in the next verse (Mark 7.25) that the woman came to him with her request implies that Jesus had entered a Gentile house. An encounter between a Jewish man and a Gentile woman under the same roof may have offended Matthew's sense of propriety and would have been offensive to the religious sensibilities of Matthew's Jewish Christian readers. By removing Mark 7.24 Matthew makes clear that the episode took place in the open countryside. Alternatively, Matthew's omission of Mark 7.24 may be due to Matthew's reluctance to concede that there were occasions when Jesus was not able to carry out his wishes. Another example where Matthew omits a Markan reference to Jesus' incapacity is Matt. 13.58, where Matthew replaces Mark's comment that Jesus '*could* do no deed of power there. . . And he was amazed at their unbelief' (Mark 6.5–6) with 'he *did* not do many deeds of power there, because of their unbelief' (Matt. 13.58). Matthew's alteration of these two passages so as to remove any hint of incapacity on Jesus' part is consistent with his emphasis on Jesus' majesty and lordship, and his tendency to diminish or remove references to Jesus' apparent weakness.

Finally, Matthew has removed Mark's description of the daughter's affliction (Mark 7.25) and has incorporated a modified version of the illness into the woman's petition.

15.22

If Matthew is dependent upon Mark, then Matt. 15.22–4 would appear to be a Matthaean interpolation into the Markan framework. The question here is whether this is Matthew's own creation or whether he is drawing on his own special material. In Matt. 15.22 there are three possible redactional interventions on Matthew's part.

(a) 'a Canaanite woman'

Whereas Mark describes the woman as Syro–Phoenician, Matthew changes this to 'Canaanite'. Various theories have been advanced to explain this alteration.

(i) Matthew is following a different tradition from Mark.

(ii) The term 'Canaanite' was a synonym for 'Syro–Phoenician'. Thus Ulrich Luz suggests that 'Canaanite' may have been 'the self-designation of the Phoenicians at the time of Matthew'.[89]

(iii) The term 'Canaanite' has Old Testament resonances. Like his modification of 'Tyre' to 'Tyre and Sidon', the insertion of 'Canaanite' may be due to Matthew's desire to accommodate his source more closely to the language of the Old Testament. The reason for this may be in order to heighten the contrast between the Old Testament notion of the people of God and the Gentile, Canaanite woman, who as a Canaanite belongs to a people who were the traditional enemies of Israel. Jesus' mercy to her shows that his mission extends even to the Canaanites.

(b) 'Have mercy on me, Lord.' This is the language of prayer. Matthew often inserts such liturgical elements in order to bring out Jesus' significance. Another good example is provided by the Stilling of the Storm (Matt. 8.23–7). Whereas Mark describes the disciples as complaining 'Teacher, do you not care that we are perishing?' (Mark 4.38), Matthew has them cry out 'Lord, save us! We are perishing!' (Matt. 8.25). As we saw in our form-critical discussion of this verse, the phrase 'Have mercy on me, Lord' is a form that has its *Sitz im Leben* in the liturgy. Although the form itself is not Matthew's formulation, it is likely that its appearance in the text at this point is due to his redactional intervention.

(c) 'Son of David'. Like the phrase 'Have mercy on me, Lord', this is not Matthew's formulation, but its presence in Matt. 15.21 is most likely due to Matthew's editing of his Markan source. Christological titles such as Lord and Son of David appear on the lips of a Gentile, who acknowledges Jesus' lordship. The effect of these two interventions is to heighten the Christological character of the passage. By addressing Jesus as Lord and Son of David the Gentile woman acknowledges him as the messiah and on that basis makes her appeal to him – indeed, she *prays* to him in the words of the liturgy: 'Lord, have mercy'. There is an implicit contrast with the failure of the Pharisees in the previous pericope (Matt. 15.1–20) to recognize Jesus' true status.

15.23: 'But he did not answer her at all. And his disciples came and urged him, saying, "Send her away, for she keeps shouting after us." '

Matthew has created this verse in order to create the context for Jesus' statement in Matt. 15.24 concerning the limits of his mission. Matthew sharpens the encounter by having Jesus demonstrably ignore the woman. This is not the case in Mark, where Jesus simply points out that Israel has precedence (Mark 7.27).

15.23–5

Matthew adds two extra appeals to those narrated by Mark, each of which is introduced by some form of 'he answered'. On the woman's first appeal

Jesus 'did not answer her at all' (Matt. 15.23). To his disciples' appeal to send the woman away, 'He answered, "I was sent only to the lost sheep of the house of Israel"' (Matt. 15.24). When the woman makes her second appeal, 'he answered' by comparing Gentiles to dogs (Matt. 15.26). The woman's final appeal 'he answered' by praising her and granting her wish (Matt. 15.28). This structuring of the story around appeal and answer, and Matthew's replacement of Mark's indirect speech with direct speech arguably creates a more lively encounter between Jesus and the woman than is present in Mark's version. Matthew seems to have introduced stylistic improvements to his source in order to heighten the tension of the story.

15.24: 'I was sent only to the lost sheep of the house of Israel.'

This is an odd answer to the disciples. The verse would make more sense if it followed 15.22. Why does Jesus respond with silence, but then give the disciples an answer to a question they have not asked? The reason is probably that this verse continues the sharpening of the encounter by having Jesus state baldly that he is not sent to Gentiles. Mark does not state this, but merely has Jesus give precedence to Israel (Mark 7.27), which does not imply that Gentiles are excluded from Jesus' ministry, but merely that they are secondary in importance. The question is whether this is a redactional composition or a traditional utterance that Matthew has incorporated into the Markan framework. The argument for the verse being a redactional creation is its similarity to Matt. 10.6 and that Matt. 15.24 contains terms that often appear in clearly redactional passages in the Gospel, notably 'sheep' and 'Israel'. Furthermore, there is a similar reference to 'towns of Israel' in Matt. 10.23, which does not appear in Mark or Luke and may thus be a Matthaean formulation. The fact that neither Matt. 10.6 nor 10.23 have parallels in Mark or Luke may indicate that Matt. 15.24 is a Matthaean redactional construction. An alternative view is that Matt. 15.24 may be a genuine utterance of Jesus that originally circulated independently of its current context. An argument for this is the fact that the passage contains Semitisms, namely the phrases used to express 'only', 'sent to' and 'house of Israel'. A possible explanation of the appearance of this utterance in Matt. 15.24 is that Matthew inherited it from the tradition and inserted it at two points in the Gospel where it seemed particularly appropriate, namely here and in Matt. 10.6. Whether it is a redactional composition or a traditional utterance, the effect of its insertion at this point is to intensify the rejection of the woman. Its presence means that the reader identifies the children with the Israelites and therefore associates the 'dogs' with the Gentiles.

15.26: 'He answered: "It is not fair to take the children's food and throw it to the dogs."'

This verse is a difficult one for most Christians, who find it hard to believe that Jesus could have been so lacking in sympathy and so harsh in his treatment of the Canaanite woman. Matthew has sharpened Jesus' reply by removing Mark's statement 'let the children first be fed'. In Mark's version, the reference to dogs is made to support a point about Jewish priority. Food should be given *first* to the children (i.e. Jews) and *then* to the dogs (i.e. the Gentiles). Matthew's version, however, shifts the emphasis of the passage by omitting Mark 7.24a, thereby excluding the term 'first', which removes the hierarchical sense implicit in Mark's version. This omission transforms Jesus' reply from being a statement of Israel's priority into an outright refusal to assist a Gentile. This omission is puzzling, since the view that Jesus gave priority to the Jews, but did not exclude the Gentiles, would fit in better with Matthew's theology of mission. To resolve this puzzle, some commentators have suggested that Mark's 'let the children first be fed' was a later interpolation introduced to soften Jesus' comment, and that it was not present in Matthew's copy of Mark.[90] There is, however, no textual evidence to support this suggestion. Davies and Allison, on the other hand, suggest: 'Mark's πρωτον [*prōton*, first] may have been omitted because it could imply that the pre-Easter Jesus himself would some day turn to the Gentiles, or that once the Gentiles have begun to be fed, the Jews should henceforth be excluded – two thoughts the evangelist could not have countenanced.'[91] Other commentators have attempted to weaken the offensiveness of Jesus' reply to the woman by emphasizing the diminutive form of the term dog (*kunarion*) used in the text. It is claimed that the use of the diminutive, which could be translated into English as 'doggies', means that Jesus sees the Gentiles as like household pets. That is, they too are members of God's family, but are subordinate to their 'masters', God's chosen people of Israel. Another suggestion is that Jesus was quoting a widespread proverb that meant the equivalent of 'charity begins at home'.

Whatever the explanation, Matthew's alterations result in a change in meaning of the text. Whereas for Mark the question is whether the time has arrived for Jesus' ministry to be extended to the Gentiles, Matthew's version seems to raise the question of whether there should be any kind of Gentile mission at all.

15.27: 'She said, "Yes, Lord, yet even the dogs eat the crumbs that fall from their masters' table."'

The woman's response acknowledges in a witty way the priority of Israel by taking up Jesus' metaphor and showing that it does not of itself necessitate

the exclusion of the Gentiles. It is possible both to acknowledge the priority of
Israel – something which she does not wish in any way to challenge – and for
Jesus to extend his help to a Gentile. There is no reason, she points out, why
the dogs should not be fed at the same time as the children.

In this verse, the woman addresses Jesus as Lord for the third time. The
repetition of the word 'Lord' makes clear that her request and debate with
Jesus take place within the context of her acknowledgement of Jesus' lordship.
The woman points out that it is not necessary to give the dogs the children's
bread, for the dogs will receive the leftovers. Matthew adds the adjective
piptontōn ('fall') to make explicit what is only implied by Mark.

Matthew replaces Mark's reference to children with the phrase 'from the
table of the masters'. There are several possible reasons for why Matthew has
made this alteration. The phrase 'masters' (*kuriōn*) may have been introduced
in order to pick up on the woman's use of 'Lord' (*kurie*) to address Jesus. The
woman's point would then be to acknowledge Jesus as Lord and to point out
that the dogs can live off the crumbs that fall from the table of their lords.
Another possible explanation is that Matthew has introduced the phrase
'table of the masters' in order to heighten the emphasis on the inferiority of the
Gentiles. Davies and Allison make a third suggestion, namely: 'While most
commentators, from Chrysostom on down, have held the κυριων [*kuriōn*,
masters] to be the Jews, one could argue that the word stands in effect only for
Jesus, explaining the plural as required by the logic of the preceding parable.
The one plural, "dogs", demands the other plural, "masters".'[92]

15.28: 'Then Jesus answered her, "Woman, great is your faith! Let it be done for you as you wish." And her daughter was healed instantly'.

Jesus has not been convinced by the woman to rethink his mission. There is
no indication of his revoking his view that his mission is to Israel and not to
the Gentiles. But the woman's wit and her acknowledgement of Jewish superiority and Gentile inferiority have convinced him of the magnitude of her
faith, and it is this faith that he chooses to reward. Matthew thus introduces
a reference to the woman's *faith*, which is lacking in Mark. Whereas Mark's
version implies that Jesus rewards the woman for her wit, Matthew turns the
episode into a story about faith. It is the strength of her faith that prompts
Jesus to respond to the woman's request, not because he feels he has been
bested in debate.

Matthew has replaced Mark's description of the woman's return home, where
she finds her daughter exorcised of the demon, with an immediate healing of the
daughter. Matthew's lack of concern with the girl's ailment is indicated by the fact
that he makes no mention of demon possession in this final verse, but speaks only

of healing. In reworking Mark's version into an instantaneous healing, Matthew has enhanced the miracle and in doing so presents a more impressive account of Jesus' power than does Mark. Yet although at one level Matt. 15.21–8 can be viewed as a healing miracle, the purpose of the passage is not to show Jesus' great works, but to focus on the debate between Jesus and the woman and on the greatness of her faith. It is the woman's faith rather than Jesus' healing miracle that is the focus of the passage.

3. Identification of distinctive terminology

As we have seen, Matthew has modified his Markan source in order to accommodate the episode more closely to the language of the Old Testament and to emphasize typically Matthaean themes: Jesus is Lord, the Son of David, the messiah, and is recognized as such by a Gentile woman. He is the merciful Lord who answers the prayers even of Gentiles.

4. Examination of the arrangement and ordering of the material into the final work

Matthew follows Mark's order. The pericope appears in the same place as in Mark, i.e. after the debate with the Pharisees and scribes about following Jewish tradition concerning hand washing and before a summary of healing miracles and the feeding of the 4000. Although Matthew follows Mark's order, he has imposed a clearer thematic structure on the material. Matthew's version of the story of the Canaanite woman complements the previous pericope more closely than is the case in Mark's version, and sets up a clearer contrast between the Pharisees and the Canaanite woman. The Pharisees neglect familial obligations on the basis of their self-centred interpretation of the law and their reliance on man-made tradition. The Canaanite woman, however, fulfils her familial obligations by seeking help for her daughter. The woman stands outside the Jewish tradition, but has faith. The Pharisees stand within the Jewish tradition, but have no faith. By bringing to the fore the faith of the woman, Matthew integrates the text into his theological concerns.

Matthew has modified the text stylistically and theologically. Stylistically, he has replaced Mark's indirect speech with direct speech in order to create a more lively encounter between Jesus and the woman. Theologically, Matthew has removed Mark's notion of the messianic secret. For Matthew, Jesus is openly identified as the Christ, even by a Gentile woman. Another theme that Matthew has made more prominent than Mark is that of perseverance in prayer. Despite Jesus' initial rebuff of the woman's entreaties, she does not give up but continues to plead with Jesus. The message is that even when Christ appears not to answer we should not give up praying to him.

A further issue is the status of the Gentiles. Matthew seems to have reworked this passage to make clear that Jesus' mission during his earthly ministry was first and foremost to the Jews, but that Gentiles would ultimately be accepted into Christianity by merit of their faith. The emphasis of Matthew's Jesus on the priority of Israel may be in order to make clear that Jesus took seriously Israel's covenant with God and the Israelites' status as God's chosen people. Jesus was thus indeed the messiah spoken of and expected in the Old Testament, and fulfilled Israel's messianic expectations, despite Israel's rejection of him. Furthermore, Matthew may have been wishing to continue to affirm the centrality of Israel in God's plans, despite their rejection of Christ. Despite Israel's hostility, as expressed, for example, in the immediately preceding passage (Matt 15.1–20), Jesus did not give up on Israel. The reason for Matthew's reworking of his Markan source may thus be in order to affirm Israel's centrality despite the fact that elsewhere he speaks of the kingdom passing from Israel and being given to others (Matt. 8.11–12; 21.43). Israel still has priority as God's chosen people and an important place in the divine plan despite its rejection of Jesus. Nevertheless, despite Israel's centrality Jesus' mission will ultimately be extended after his resurrection beyond Israel to all peoples (Matt. 24.14; 28.16–20). The story can thus be read as an anticipation and justification of the post-Easter Church of Jews *and* Gentiles. Matthew's inclusion of this passage may thus be to indicate that Jesus' ministry, though initially only to the Jews, who remain God's people, would ultimately be extended to the Gentiles.

Matthew thus seems to occupy a position midway between the Jewish Christians who wished Christianity to remain exclusively Jewish and Luke. It is easy to see why Luke has omitted the passage. It simply does not fit in with his theology of the universality of Jesus' ministry, as expressed in Luke 4.16–30, which implies that God *prefers* Gentiles (Luke 4.25–7). Luke omits Matt. 15.21–8/Mark 7.24–30 precisely because he rejects the exclusion of the Gentiles from Jesus' mission. Matthew, however, is not prepared to go as far as Luke. He is prepared to acknowledge that the Gospel includes the Gentiles, but only in a subordinate and inferior position to Israel. But Matthew also makes clear that Gentiles are accepted by Jesus on the basis of their faith. So Matthew states that God's message extends even to the Gentiles, not by birth but by faith. It is faith not ancestry that is crucial.

5. Identification of the *Sitz im Leben*

The *Sitz im Leben* may be resistance to the Gentile mission in Matthew's community. Matthew has sharpened Mark's story of the Syro–Phoenician woman to create a narrative in which this clash is seen at its starkest, and to show that Jesus himself rejects the exclusion of Gentiles from his mission when he is confronted by the woman's faith. The *Sitz im Leben* of Matt. 15.21–8 is thus probably the struggle within the early Church between those who wished Christianity to remain a Jewish sect and those who wished to extend it to the Gentiles.

Alternatively, the ambiguous portrayal of Judaism may be because Matthew was writing for a Jewish-Christian community whose relations with mainstream Judaism had become strained because of the community's alleged antinomianism. This would explain the ambiguities towards the Law and the Gentiles in Matthew's Gospel, and the fact that Matthew brings out more fully than the other evangelists the Jewish character of Jesus' ministry, while at the same time allowing the exclusivity of this Jewishness to be subverted in passages like Matt. 15.21–8, 24.14, and 28.16–20. This Jewish emphasis of the Gospel, while simultaneously extending the good news to the Gentiles may indicate that the *Sitz im Leben* of the passage is the struggle of a Jewish-Christian community both to retain its links with mainstream Judaism and to affirm Christ as Lord of Jews and Gentiles alike.

Evaluation of redaction criticism

Strengths

Some of its supporters have made dramatic claims for redaction criticism. Perrin, for example, states that, 'there can be no doubt that the insights being gained through redaction criticism are of such importance that all previous presentations of the theology of the evangelists are now simply outdated'.[93] He is also confident of the validity of its methodology, claiming that, 'the way that redaction criticism is able to make sense of the phenomena demonstrably present in the text is itself a validation of the methodology'.[94]

Proponents of redaction criticism have claimed that the method has the following advantages.

1. Redaction criticism obviates the need to harmonize parallel but distinct biblical writings to protect the 'historicity' of the biblical accounts. Thus it is not necessary to search for ways of reconciling the variant accounts of the same events described in Samuel-Kings and Chronicles or in the four Gospels. Redaction criticism attributes the differences between such works not to inconsistency in the biblical accounts but to the editorial activity of the biblical writers. Variations between parallel biblical accounts do not undermine

their veracity, but simply reflect the biblical writers' theological interests and those of the communities for which they were writing. Redaction criticism thus helps us to appreciate the four Gospels, for example, as four witnesses to Christ, each with its own distinctive theological insights, rather than as inconsistent, incompatible descriptions.

2. Redaction criticism treats biblical texts as coherent literary wholes. It thus counteracts and corrects the fragmentary tendencies of source criticism and form criticism.

3. Redaction criticism enables us to identify the contribution of the biblical writers to the texts of the Bible and can give us some insight into why the biblical writers wrote their texts.

Weaknesses

1. Redaction criticism's focus on the biblical writer's *modification* of the tradition creates a lopsided understanding of the biblical writer's relation to the tradition, for it leaves out of account the fact that the author may sometimes have simply accepted a tradition without alteration. Leaving a unit of tradition unaltered is also an expression of the redactional purpose of a biblical writer, but this preservation rather than alteration and modification of the tradition has not been the focus of redaction criticism.

2. From the perspective of recent literary theory redaction criticism appears to be built on the intentional fallacy, i.e. the mistaken view that the meaning of a text is determined by its author's intention. Redaction criticism thus privileges the author's voice over all other voices in the text. Postmodernist approaches challenge the identification of a text's meaning with its authorial intention. Focusing on the identification of the author's meaning distracts us from the many other levels of meaning that can be elicited from the text and blinds us to the role of the reader in creating textual meaning.[95]

3. Redaction criticism does not do justice to biblical texts as *literary* creations. It treats them as sources for historical knowledge and fails to take sufficiently into account their character as works of *literature* rather than history.

4. There is the problem of what Barton, following a suggestion of
    N. T. Wright's, has called 'the disappearing redactor', a phrase
    which succinctly draws attention to an underlying contradiction
    in the method of redaction criticism. The problem, as Barton puts
    it, is: 'The more impressive the critic makes the redactor's work
    appear, the more he succeeds in showing that the redactor has, by
    subtle and delicate artistry, produced a simple and coherent text out
    of the diverse materials before him; the more also he reduces the
    evidence on which the existence of those sources was established
    in the first place.'[96] That is, the more skilful the redactor is shown
    to be in uniting his sources into a coherent whole, the weaker the
    evidence becomes that the redactor has indeed unified what were
    once independent sources. If the redactor was so competent that he
    was able to integrate his sources into a smooth, seamless unity, then
    the evidence that he had used sources is undermined. The result is
    that the redactor disappears, since there is no longer evidence that
    the work into a conflation of sources, and the redactor is replaced
    simply by the author of the text in its entirety.

5. The widely divergent results of redaction criticism raise questions
    concerning its methodological status. After all, if it were a genuine
    method we would expect it to produce similar and consistent results.
    The diversity of reconstructions of the tradition advanced by redaction
    critics, however, arguably indicates the impossibility of establishing
    with any confidence the contours of the development of the tradition
    edited by the redactor. There is simply not enough information upon
    which an understanding of the tradition can be established which
    has the support of the majority of the scholarly community. Stephen
    Smalley attributes this problem, on the one hand, to redaction critics
    being over subtle and, on the other hand, to redaction criticism being
    a young discipline. He writes: 'Redaction critics are at times too
    subtle and subjective in their approach to the Gospels, and in their
    assessment of the evangelists' motives and methods. This is the reason
    for the wide variation in their results; although this need not surprise
    us with a discipline still in its infancy.'[97] Since Smalley wrote these
    words, over thirty years have passed. There is, however, little evidence
    that redaction criticism has emerged from its infancy and become a
    coherent, rigorous method that can produce assured results. Writing
    in 2001 Tan argued that one of the reasons why redaction criticism is
    bankrupt is the lack of consensus among redaction critics on which
    techniques should be used to separate redaction from tradition.[98] The
    lack of agreement among redaction critics concerning the criteria that
    should be employed to identify redactional interventions in biblical

texts raises questions about whether redaction criticism constitutes a genuinely coherent method of biblical interpretation.

6. The methodological problems faced by redaction criticism are compounded by the difficulty of verifying the results of redaction-critical interpretation of the Bible. Black holds that, 'redaction criticism of Mark (on the assumption of Markan priority) has sought answers to exegetical question that are, by definition, unverifiable'.[99] This unverifiability stems from the individual redaction critic's speculative assumptions concerning the pre-literary history of biblical writers. As Black puts it, 'in order to discern the earliest Evangelist's redactional (= authorial) activity, every investigator is compelled to engage in often highly speculative conjectures about the history of traditions *behind* the Evangelist, assumptions unamenable to empirical analysis yet invariably determinative of that research's exegetical or methodological results'.[100] Frye also considers redaction criticism to be speculative, commenting that, 'claims to reconstruct the stages of such growth and change will usually be speculative guesses', unless there is clear evidence of changes within a text and objective internal and external evidence to support the argument that developments and alterations have taken place.[101] Redaction criticism may be useful where such evidence is available. With regard to texts where no such evidence is forthcoming, however, the results of redaction criticism are speculative and depend on a series of questionable assumptions on the part of the redaction critic. This raises questions about the validity of the results of redaction criticism. Thus, as Black puts it in relation to the redaction criticism study of Mark, the conclusions 'scatter in all directions and are impossible to validate, for they are primarily a function of their proponents' divergent perspectival starting points, and only minimally the result of a controlled method of interpretation'.[102]

7. The view that redaction criticism restores the wholeness of the text after its fragmentation by form criticism has also been challenged by some scholars. Stein comments, 'Even though redaction criticism treats the Gospels holistically, rather than atomistically as in form criticism, it does not seek the whole theology of the Evangelists but rather that which is unique to them.'[103] Adherents of 'New Criticism' and advocates of literary approaches also claim that redaction criticism continues the processes of fragmentation initiated by source and form criticism.[104] Dan O. Via provides a good example of this criticism with reference to Mark:

Literary criticism seeks to apprehend a text as a whole or as a totality . . . From Marxsen up to the most recent times, however, redaction critics . . . have split Mark into tradition (sources) and redaction and have sought to establish chronological-genetic-causal relations between these two strata . . . As provocative and interesting as these studies often are for historical purposes, the text as a whole, as a narrative, in the form in which it confronts the reader and needs explication, is lost sight of.[105]

Similarly, despite his being one of the pioneers of English-language redaction criticism Perrin eventually came to recognize that 'it defines the literary activity of the Evangelist too narrowly. It does not do justice to the full range of the literary activity of the Evangelist as author; hence it cannot do justice to the full range of the text he has created'.[106]

8. Other critics have questioned specific features of the redaction-critical method. R. M. Frye is critical of the notion of 'additions' which underlies much redaction-critical work. One of the criteria upon which redaction-critical identification of additions is based is *repetition*. Thus the claim that the redactor has often added what were originally independent aphorisms to Jesus' parables is based on the fact that these aphorisms sometimes appear in two closely related variant forms in different places in the Gospel record. An example is provided by Jesus' pronouncement: 'every one who exalts himself will be humbled, but he who humbles himself will be exalted'. Luke places his first version of this aphorism at the end of the parable of the guest at a wedding banquet (Luke 14.11). A second version of the aphorism appears, however, after the parable of the Pharisees and tax collector (Luke 18.14b), which closely parallels Matt. 23.12, where the aphorism appears among Jesus' woes on the Pharisees. Because of the repetition of this aphorism in three different contexts, some New Testament scholars regard it as having originally been an independent saying of Jesus which has subsequently been added by Matthew and Luke to units of tradition where they thought it would be most appropriate. They thus conclude that Jesus' use of the aphorism on the occasions related in the Gospels was not a historical event but is a redactional composition by the two evangelists. Frye, however, points out that there is no reason to suppose that Jesus may not have used the aphorism on many different occasions. Teachers often have favourite expressions, which they may draw on in a variety of different contexts when it seems appropriate. Furthermore, a teacher many repeat a point for emphasis. For Frye there is thus no reason to assume that the

appearance of the aphorism at the end of the parable of the Pharisee and tax collector is due to redaction, just as there is no reason to assume that there was only one form of the parable that Jesus always used. For Frye, 'The variations and embellishments or adaptations of the parable form that we find in the Gospels are entirely within the range of a single individual, even of an individual considerably less gifted than Jesus seems to have been.'[107]

CHAPTER SEVEN

The End of the Historical–Critical Method?

Since the 1970s historical criticism has come under sustained attack from several quarters. Indeed, some scholars have gone so far as to claim that the historical–critical method has run its course and has now entered a period of terminal decline. In 1973 Walter Wink opened his book *The Bible in Human Transformation* with the claim that 'Historical biblical criticism is bankrupt'.[1] In 1974 there appeared in Germany a critique of historical criticism by Gerhard Maier significantly entitled *The End of the Historical–Critical Method*. In 1984 Eugen Drewermann published the first volume of his *Tiefenpsychologie und Exegese* [Depth Psychology and Exegesis], in which he described the historical–critical method's concern with identifying the historical reality behind the units of tradition and redactional additions as 'the most shallow and superficial of all questions which can be asked of a religious text, but it is the only question which is permitted methodologically'.[2] Elisabeth Schüssler Fiorenza challenged both the hegemony and antiquarian mindset of historical criticism in her 1987 presidential address to the Society of Biblical Literature and again in her later paper given at the 1999 international meeting of the society at Helsinki.[3] By 2000 Fernando Segovia claimed that 'the historical–critical model may even be described as defunct from a theoretical point of view'. Indeed, for Segovia, 'From a theoretical perspective, the method is so defunct that it has been unable to mount a serious and informed defense of its own methodological principles or reading strategy and underlying theoretical orientation'.[4] He is nevertheless prepared to concede that 'from a practical perspective, the [historical–critical] method is alive, though at various stages of health'.

In this concluding chapter, I wish to sketch the reasons for the claim that the historical–critical method is defunct or in terminal decline and to consider to what extent they are justified.

1. The fragmentation of the Bible

Critics of the historical–critical method claim that its concern to separate out the earliest forms of biblical tradition results in the 'atomization' of the text, i.e. its fragmentation into ever smaller sources. An example of such atomization is provided by the historical–critical treatment of the Pentateuch, which has been concerned with isolating the sources from which the final form of the Pentateuch was constructed. Such an approach, it is claimed, leads to the dissolution of the Bible into a series of fragments and undermines the integrity of Scripture. This was a point made by Helen Gardner in her 1956 Riddell Memorial Lectures *The Limits of Literary Criticism*, in which she comments that form criticism 'disintegrates the separate Gospels, and is open to the literary objection that it is not dealing with the work itself, but with the materials out of which it was made; and these materials, the oral preaching of the Apostles, do not exist'.[5] More recently, Segovia has claimed that in historical criticism 'there was little conception of the text as a literary, strategic, and ideological whole'.[6] The main point underlying these criticisms is that historical criticism has led to such fragmentation of the Bible that it is in danger of losing its function as Scripture.

This atomization of the Bible has been accompanied by the imposition of a hierarchy of authenticity on the textual layers identified by the historical–critical method. Historical criticism privileges the supposedly earlier layers over alleged later layers in the text, treating the former as superior to the latter. This leads to a questionable gradation of value imposed on the Bible, which, as Brevard Childs has argued, does not do justice to the canonical shape of the biblical texts and the role they play in their entirety in the life of the community of faith.

It has also been argued that the historical–critical method is guilty of circular reasoning. Because it presupposes that biblical texts are generally not literary wholes, but constructed from earlier sources, the historical–critical method reads the texts in such a way that it will inevitably find evidence of such sources. This is a point made by Segovia, who holds that historical criticism's identification of aporias in the text led to the attempt to read the text in terms of a juxtaposition of literary layers. According to Segovia, however, 'In fact, it was the juxtaposition of such layers that created the *aporias*, which served in turn as guideposts for the process of composition and analysis.'[7] Furthermore, the identification of layers on the basis of a text's supposed aporias assumes that ancient writers shared the same notions of coherence and consistency as modern human beings. They may, however, have been able to live with a higher level of cognitive dissonance than is the case today. In short, the discovery of textual layers and sources in biblical texts may arise not from the texts themselves but be due to the imposition of a modern, Western mindset on the Bible.

When the attempt has been made to combine the sources identified by historical criticism into a unified whole, this has been done on the basis of criteria which do not do justice to the character of the biblical texts. This is a point made by Wink, who claims: 'The new analytical approach . . . broke down every total construction in order to arrive at smaller units which might then be recombined through the category of causality.'[8] The question is whether the category of causality upon which the historical–critical reconstruction of the biblical texts is based does justice to the principles upon which the biblical authors constructed their texts.

The historical–critical analysis of the Bible into ever smaller units resulted in the detachment of the biblical texts from the theology of history in which they had been embedded and on the basis of which they had previously been understood. This analysis of the Bible and the challenge it posed to the conservative handling of the text performed a useful service, Wink concedes, in so far as 'it was seeking breathing room for the spirit and the right of the intellect to free inquiry', for 'it sought to destroy an existent state of reality for the sake of one which it conceived to be better'.[9] The destruction of the old understanding of the Bible, however, has not been accompanied a new, more adequate way of engaging with the Bible. For Wink, 'It is as if, at the moment of its victory, it had forgotten why it had fought, and settled down on the field of battle to inventory its weapons in hope of discovering some clue as to their further usefulness. Here, as in other revolutions, those who were fit to overthrow were not fit to govern.'[10] The historical–critical method, then, fragments the Bible but has not found adequate ways of reconstructing the Bible in a way that enables it to speak to communities of faith and individual believers.

2. The loss of the theological meaning of the Bible

Closely connected with the charge of fragmentation is the accusation of its critics that the historical–critical method *brackets* out theology. Some scholars make a virtue of this. Philip Davies, for example, argues that theological and non-theological approaches to the Bible are 'so fundamentally divergent as to require and to imply *separate disciplines*'.[11] He thus calls for two disciplines of the study of the Bible, namely 'biblical studies', which is non-confessional, humanistic, etic and treats the Bible as a purely human book, and 'scripture', 'which is that subdiscipline of theology that deals with "the Bible" '.[12] Others, however, regard bracketing out theology from the study of the Bible as undermining an essential feature of the Bible, namely, its role in mediating the Word of God. Carl Braaten and Robert W. Jenson in *Reclaiming the Bible for the Church* complain that, 'Questions of every conceivable kind have been put to the biblical texts, but for many in the church – pastors, teachers, and laity – the Bible seems to have lost its voice. Can the Bible still speak to the church in an age of critical historical awareness? Or better, does God continue to speak his Word through the Bible as a whole?'[13] Childs makes a similar point, claiming that, 'in spite of a plethora of new information, the true theological witness of the text is rendered mute. The critic presumes to stand above the text, outside the circle of tradition, and from this detached vantage point adjudicate the truth and error of the New Testament's time-conditionality'.[14] Drewermann attributes the loss of theological meaning to the historical–critical method's ignoring of *feeling*: 'In its detachment from feeling, in its isolation from the subject, in its incapacity to take inner, psychical reality as infinitely more real than the plane of outward "facts", this form of "exegesis" is in principle godless, regardless of how often it may utter the name "God" '.[15] The historical–critical method's focus on non-theological issues results in the loss of the theological meaning of the Bible and its replacement with a secular understanding.[16]

Alternatively, theological meaning can be subordinated to historical reconstruction. Here the work of the historical critic is conceived of as the *precondition* of theology. That is, it is only when we have reconstructed the events that lie behind and gave rise to the texts of the Bible that we can begin the task of formulating what these texts now mean theologically. This involves subordinating the biblical texts to modern conceptions of history and privileging the present over the past. Only what is reconcilable with our modern understanding can be accepted as historical and only on the basis of the identification of the historically valid events underlying the Bible can a viable understanding of the Bible be constructed for the present. This creates two problems.

Firstly, it has been argued that this approach is anachronistic. Underlying the historical–critical method is the implicit assumption of the superiority of the modern world view over earlier ages. This is frequently expressed as belief in progress. Human beings are on an upward journey from the primitive, mythological thought-forms of the ancients to the enlightened, rational and scientific thinking of the modern world. This upward journey culminates in what the historical critic unreflectively assumes is the superiority of the present over the past. The historical–critical method is uncritically employed in the service of this ideology of the superiority of the present.[17]

Secondly, making theological meaning dependent on the work of the historical critic creates the problem of bridging the gap between the biblical past identified by the historical–critical method and the use of the Bible today by communities of faith and individual believers. In his *Introduction to the Old Testament*, Childs argues that the focus of investigation of historical criticism on tracing the history of the development of Hebrew literature and its lack of concern with Scripture's role as the canonical literature of the synagogue and the church means that 'there always remains an enormous hiatus between the description of the critically recovered literature and the actual canonical text which has been received and used as authoritative Scripture by the community'.[18]

A further criticism is made by Paul Minear, who points out that by focusing on the historical character of the biblical texts the historical–critical method is concerning itself with what was of little significance to those responsible for composing, collating and preserving the biblical texts. Historical criticism does not in fact capture the genuine history of the early Christians because by concentrating on the historical it ignores what was to them of significance in the historical events the Bible records, namely their belief that God had acted in these events. As Minear puts it: 'The net used fails to catch the data that to early Christians constituted the significance of the events in which they shared, while the data that the historians do recapture would have been to them of only secondary importance.'[19] Wink makes a similar point, noting that: 'The writers of the New Testament bore witness to events which had led them to faith. They wrote "from faith to faith," to evoke or augment faith in their readers.'[20] The biblical writings have been collated, edited and preserved precisely because these texts were significant for the religious life and identity of the believing community. To focus on history is thus to focus on what is peripheral in the Bible at the expense of its central message.

In short, historical criticism's over-privileging of the *historical* meaning of the Bible at the expense of its theological meaning creates the problem of bridging the gap between the past and the present. If the Bible is treated primarily as a historical work, then it can no longer speak meaningfully to the present about the subject with which it is most concerned: humankind's relationship with God.

3. The undermining of *praxis*

The historical–critical method has been criticized for undermining Christian *praxis*. This critique has been made from a variety of different perspectives. An early example is provided by the Danish thinker Søren Kierkegaard (1813–1855), whose pseudonym Johannes Climacus states in *Concluding Unscientific Postscript* (1846) that the historical approach to the Bible results in a never-ending approximation process.[21] Faith is made dependent on first establishing the truth of the Bible, which must be secured by means of historical investigation. The problem is that historical certainty is never attained, for it is always possible that new discoveries might be made or new methods developed which undermine the supposedly certain results achieved by earlier historical studies. All that can at best be achieved by historical study is an *approximation* to the truth, never the truth itself. This raises the question of when the investigator will ever reach the point when he or she can act on the results of historical investigation. Kierkegaard makes this point in *Concluding Unscientific Postscript* when he cites an anecdote by Plutarch concerning the philosopher Eudamidas: 'When Eudamidas in the academy saw the senescent Xenocrates seeking the truth together with his followers, he asked: Who is this old man? And when the reply was given that he was a wise man, one of those seeking after virtue, he exclaimed, "When, then, will he use it?" '[22] The result of historical investigation of the Bible is that the decision of faith is postponed indefinitely. It is not possible ever to secure an adequate historical foundation for faith, because there always exists the possibility of discovering new historical data which might throw previous conclusions concerning the reliability of Christianity's historical foundations into doubt. Kierkegaard holds, however, that even if it were possible to establish certainty with regard to the historical events upon which Christianity is based, it would be of no avail, for there is no direct transition from history to faith. Merely showing the historical validity of the Bible does not of itself bring about faith, because faith belongs to an entirely different sphere from historical knowledge and is dependent on a non-rational personal leap of faith on the part of the individual. Indeed, for Kierkegaard, historical investigation of the Bible is a distraction from the challenge the Bible presents to the individual, since the investigator gets enmeshed in minor details that distract from the core message of the Bible. Historical criticism is in any case unnecessary, since the core message of the Bible is evident without its assistance. The Bible is God's love letter to humankind and although there may be problematic material in the Bible, the Bible as a whole is sufficiently intelligible to allow the honest reader to discern God's will. As Kierkegaard puts it in *For Self-Examination* (1851), 'It is only all too easy to understand the requirement contained in God's Word.' As evidence for the intelligibility of the Bible Kierkegaard cites such biblical passages as giving one's property to the poor and turning the other cheek. Such New Testament passages, Kierkegaard comments, are 'all just as easy to understand as the remark "The weather is fine today." '[23] Far from facilitating our understanding of the Bible, Kierkegaard complains, 'All this interpreting and interpreting and scholarly research and new scholarly research that is produced on the solemn and serious principle that it is in order to understand God's Word properly – look more closely and you will see that it is in order to defend oneself against God's Word.'[24]

The notion of the biblical critic as the detached, neutral observer allowing the text to speak for itself has also come under fire on the grounds that such a method is simply inappropriate to the type of literature which the Bible is, for the question of the Bible's truth, as Wink puts it, 'can only be answered participatively, in terms of a lived response'.[25] The historical–critical method, however, adopts the procedures of modern science and historical enquiry, namely, 'the suspension of evaluative judgements and participational involvement in the "object" of research'. For Wink, 'such detached neutrality in matters of faith is not neutrality at all, but already a decision against responding'.[26] Far from being objective, then, biblical scholars have in their employment of the historical–critical method taken an a priori decision *against* responding with faith in their encounter with the Bible. Consequently, the objective neutrality it claims to employ 'requires a sacrifice of the very questions the Bible seeks to answer'.[27]

Other commentators have attacked the historical–critical method for its alleged irrelevance to communities of faith. Maier argues that historical criticism has had little practical effect on preaching and the results of historical criticism cannot be made the basis of practical life in the Church, not least because these results are subject to revision. For Maier historical criticism results in the alienation of theological scholarship from the life of the Church.[28] Wink makes a similar point, stating that as a result of the historical investigation of the Bible, 'biblical criticism became cut off from any community for whose life its results might be significant'.[29] The outcome of this 'is a trained incapacity to deal with the real problems of actual living persons in their daily lives'.[30]

Liberation theologians have criticized historical criticism for undermining the biblical call to *act*. This is dramatically expressed by the Statement of the Ecumenical Dialogue of Third World Theologians: 'We reject as irrelevant an academic type of theology that is divorced from action. We are prepared for a radical break in epistemology which makes commitment the first act of theology and engages in critical reflection on the praxis of the Third World.'[31] The problem with the historical–critical method is that it reduces the reader of the Bible to an 'armchair theologian', who is merely an onlooker rather than an actor in the Bible's call to oppose oppression and show solidarity with the poor.[32] Leonardo and Clodovis Boff put this point vividly in their comment with reference to the beast of the Revelation of St John that 'the "doctors of theology" . . . can count every hair in the beast's coat but never look it in the face'.[33] Carlos Mesters draws on a different metaphor to make a similar point: 'In many cases the exegete is like the person who had studied salt and knew all its chemical properties but didn't know how to cook with it. The common people don't know the properties of salt well, but they do know how to season a meal.'[34] In his parable of the house, Mesters employs a still more vivid analogy to convey the destructiveness of the historical–critical method to ordinary people's encounter with the living word of the Bible. The parable can be paraphrased as follows:

> Long ago there was a 'house of the people'. This house was a house in which the people felt at home, in which they lived together, laughed, and danced. One day two scholars arrived who took it upon themselves to provide an academic analysis of the house. The result of their labours was the transformation of the house of the people into a museum, which one could enter only through a side entrance. After a long time had passed a beggar stumbled across the main entrance, and, entering, discovered the lost rooms of the house. Before long the people once again began to live in those rooms as in days of old. They were even joined by a scholar, who lived and worked with them.[35]

In short, the problem with historical criticism is that it results in the readers of the Bible becoming enmeshed in historical questions which prevent them from arriving at the point where they can *act*.

4. The ideological bias of historical criticism

The ideal of 'scientific' biblical scholarship is for the interpreter to be detached, dispassionate, rational, free of ideology, including theology, in order to achieve objective, value-neutral interpretation of the biblical texts. The historical–critical method aims to allow the text to speak for itself without interference from the interpreter's own personal position.[36] As Jowett puts it: 'The true use of interpretation is to get rid of interpretation, and leave us alone in company with the author.'[37] The interpreter should purge him/herself of prejudices and take a step back from the text in order to observe it from a detached neutral standpoint. To its critics, however, this 'scientific' ethos of biblical scholarship draws a veil over the political and ideological assumptions of its practitioners.

Far from being an objective, value-free analysis of the biblical texts, historical criticism is in reality in thrall to a particular world view, namely that of the so-called 'Enlightenment project', which is characterized by rationalism, positivism, historicism, objectivity and commitment to the stability of textual meaning. These are not neutral, unprejudiced principles, but expressions of a secular world view which rules out certain positions and possibilities of interpretation in advance. Furthermore, historical criticism is ideologically motivated. It is not a 'scientific' method of reading the Bible, but is an 'advocacy' reading, albeit a covert one, which has been developed in order to serve the needs of a particular group in society and to defend its interests. Critics of historical criticism have identified the following 'ideological' elements in the historical–critical method.

(a) Rationalism and positivism

Historical criticism is rationalistic and positivistic in the sense that it accepts a scientific world view which rules out a priori such events as divine intervention and miracles. A classic example of this approach is provided by Strauss, who claims that: 'Our modern world . . . after many centuries of tedious research, has attained a conviction that all things are linked together by a chain of causes and effects, which suffers no interruption.'[38] For Strauss, 'the totality of finite things forms a vast circle, which, except that it owes its existence and laws to a superior power, suffers no intrusion from without'.[39] These 'known and universal laws' are corroborated by 'all just philosophical conceptions and all credible experience'. Strauss concludes that, 'From this point of view, at which nature and history appear as a compact tissue of finite causes and effects, it was impossible to regard the narratives of the Bible, in which this tissue is broken by innumerable instances of divine interference, as historical'.[40] As we saw in chapter two, on the basis of this scientific world view Strauss develops a set of criteria for distinguishing what is unhistorical in the Gospel narrative, one of which is the negative criterion that an account is unhistorical: 'when the narration is irreconcileable with the known and universal laws which govern the course of events'.[41] Human reason is thus made the judge of the Bible, which results in the rejection of those elements that cannot be justified by rational criteria. For Strauss, the 'discordancy' of biblical history 'with our idea of the world' furnishes a test of its unhistorical nature.[42]

The subordination of the question of the historicity of the Bible to what is compatible with reason is not, however, an objective perspective, as its proponents claim, but is based on the presuppositions of the omnipotence of human reason and the primacy of reason over faith. Such presuppositions mean that historical criticism of the Bible is not objective and neutral, but is an ideology that imposes its view of what can and cannot happen, what is valid and invalid on the biblical texts. It brackets out those elements of the Bible that do not fit in with its rationalist ideology and claims that what remains is an objective, scientific evaluation of the biblical texts. Several commentators have sought to expose this ideological bias and challenge the claim of historical criticism's methodological neutrality. Drewermann draws attention to the logocentrism of historical criticism, which holds 'words to be more important than images, actions as more important than feelings, and the literary form of the tradition as more important than the experiences from which the individual forms have grown'.[43] For Wink, historical criticism 'pretends to be unbiased when in fact the methodology carries with it a heavy rationalistic weight which by inner necessity tends toward the reduction of irrational, subjective, or emotional data to insignificance or invisibility. It pretends to search for "assured results," "objective knowledge," when in fact the method presumes radical epistemological doubt, which by definition devours each new spawn of "assured results" as a guppy swallows her children. It pretends to suspend evaluations, which is simply impossible, since research proceeds on the basis of questions asked and a ranked priority in their asking. But such judgments presuppose a system of values and an ontology of meanings which not only give weight to the questions but make it possible to ask them at all'.[44]

(b) Historicism

Related to the charge of rationalism and positivism is the claim that historical criticism is guilty of 'historicism', i.e. the attempt, as the *Oxford English Dictionary* puts it, 'to view all social and cultural phenomena, all categories, truths, and values, as relative and historically determined, and in consequence to be understood only by examining their historical context, in complete detachment from present-day attitudes'. The historicism of the historical–critical method manifests itself in its identification of a text's meaning with its historical origins and in the view that the meaning of the text is not to be found in the text itself, but in the historical facts underlying the text. If these historical facts can be identified, then we have isolated the building blocks upon which an understanding of the text can be constructed. Another presupposition is the view that the 'original' or earliest version of a text is more 'authentic' and carries greater significance than later versions. Accompanying this view and closely related to it is the unarticulated assumption that the authority of a biblical text stems from the author responsible for the first, 'original' version. Subsequent additions and modifications or 'accretions', as historical critics sometimes describe them, have less authority than the original version allegedly penned by the author. This is not an objective, neutral way of treating the Bible, however, for it is based on a set of problematic assumptions.

The first of these problematic assumptions is the presupposition that the meaning of texts depends on their referential function. The 'truth' of the Bible depends on its ability to refer to historical events and describe them accurately. Historical criticism thus implicitly accepts a correspondence theory of the truth in which the assertions of the Bible can be mapped on to historical reality. Those that cannot be shown to refer to historical events are to be downgraded as 'mythical' and considered as merely reflections of an outmoded world view. This imposition of a correspondence theory of truth onto the Bible, however, fails to do justice to the richness of the Bible. This is a point made by Childs, who complains that, 'the critical method reflected in most introductions rests on the assumption of a uniformly historical–referential reading of the biblical text. At least from a theological perspective the serious objection must be raised that the Bible bears witness to a multi-dimensional theological reality which cannot be measured solely on the basis of such a correspondence theory of truth'.[45]

The second problematic assumption of the historical–critical method is that meaning lies *behind* the text in some way and can be extracted by application of the correct, 'scientific' methods, so that, as Jowett puts it: 'The universal truth easily breaks through the accidents of time and place in which it is involved.'[46] This means, however, bypassing the text of the Bible itself and seeking for its meaning in historical facts that lie outside the text. This is a criticism which Barth makes: 'The idea against which we have to safeguard ourselves at this point is one which has tacitly developed in connexion with modern theological historicism. It is to the effect that in the reading and understanding and expounding of the Bible the main concern can and must be to penetrate past the biblical texts to the facts which lie behind the texts. Revelation is then found in these facts as such (which in their factuality are independent of the texts).'[47] For Barth, this was the wrong road 'because at bottom it means succumbing to the temptation to read the Canon differently from what it is intended to be and can be read'.[48] For Barth, there is an inextricable link between form and content which means that the historical 'facts' cannot be separated from the biblical text in the way attempted by the historical–critical method. For Barth, then, 'Theology at least, even and especially historical theology, which applies itself particularly to the biblical texts, ought to have (let us say it at once) the tact and taste, in face of the linking of form and content in those texts of which it must still be aware, to resist this temptation, to leave the curious question of what is perhaps behind the texts, and to turn with all more attentiveness, accuracy and love to the texts as such.'[49]

(c) The fallacy of stable, objective textual meaning

Another problematic presupposition of the historical critical method is its view that texts have a single, definitive, objective, stable, universal meaning, which is usually identified with the meaning supposedly intended by the original author. An example of this assumption is provided by Jowett, who states that: 'Scripture has one meaning – the meaning which it had to the mind of the prophet or evangelist who first uttered or wrote, to the hearers or readers who first received it.'[50] It is the task of the historical critic to identify this single, 'correct' meaning and to distinguish it from the false readings that may have occurred in the history of the interpretation of the text.

The notion of univocal, objective meaning has been challenged on a number of fronts. Firstly, focusing on a single, authoritative meaning in the text creates a blindness to levels or possibilities of meaning not envisaged by the historical–critical method. If there is supposedly only one meaning in the text, then once we have located it, there is no need to look further. As Wink puts it: 'We ask only those questions which the method can answer. We internalize the method's questions and permit a self-censorship of the questions intrinsic to our lives. Puffy with pretensions to "pure scholarship," this blinkered approach fails to be scholarly enough, precisely because it refuses to examine so much that is essential to understanding the intention of the text and our interest in reading it.'[51]

Secondly, Schüssler Fiorenza argues that the social location of the interpreters of texts and of the texts themselves indicates that texts should not be treated as windows to historical reality. Historical sources should not be understood as 'data and evidence' but rather should be seen 'as perspectival discourses constructing their worlds and symbolic universes'.[52] This means that there is not one single authoritative, objective meaning of a text. As Schüssler Fiorenza puts it: 'Since alternative symbolic universes engender competing definitions of the world, they cannot be reduced to one meaning. Therefore, competing interpretations of texts are not simply either right or wrong, but they constitute different ways of reading and constructing historical meaning.'[53] These competing interpretations of the text arise from the multiple perspectives from which it is possible to read the text. These multiple perspectives stem from the different social locations of the text's readers. Readers in the modern Western world will inevitably read texts from a different location from readers from the poorest classes of the developing world. This dependence of the construction of meaning on the interaction of text and the social location of the reader undermines the claim to objectivity and neutrality made by the historical–critical method. This means that the biblical interpreter should not pretend to objectivity, but rather articulate the rhetorical and political underpinnings of the social location from which he or she is reading the text. For Schüssler Fiorenza, 'Not detached value-neutrality but an explicit articulation of one's rhetorical strategies, interested perspectives, ethical criteria, theoretical frameworks, religious presuppositions, and socio-political locations for critical public discussion are appropriate in such a rhetorical paradigm of biblical scholarship.'[54] A similar approach is advocated by Segovia, who argues: 'I would eschew any type of formulation that would imply or suggest, no matter how lightly or unintentionally, the presence of a pre-existing, independent, and stable meaning in the text, the mind of the author, or the world of the text – formulations along the lines of the meaning "back then," being true to the past, or achieving a fuller meaning of the text.'[55]

Historical criticism's assumption of the univocity of meaning has also been challenged on the basis of recent developments in literary theory. Poststructuralism accepts the structuralist claim that there is no necessary relation between signs and the concepts signs designate but takes it a stage further by arguing that not only is there no relation, but the sign is constantly breaking free from its concept. The sign cannot be pinned down to a single, unequivocal meaning corresponding to an unproblematic concept, but is constantly detaching itself from its concepts. Poststructuralists describe this in terms of fluidity and describe the mismatch between sign and concept as 'spillage' or 'slippage'. As the Postmodern Bible puts it: 'Whatever a text is, it is not a stable, self-identical, enduring object but a place of intersection in a network of signification.'[56] Approaches such as deconstruction draw attention to the fact that texts contain breaks, inconsistencies and fissures, and make these the basis of its reading of texts. Furthermore, texts are incomplete, prompting the reader to fill in the gaps left in the text in the act of reading. Texts are not stable but fluid. Consequently, textual meaning cannot simply be read from the text, but is the result of a creative interaction between the reader and the text. Historical criticism's assumption of a stable meaning located in the historical sense of the Bible is thus a failure to grasp the multiple layers of meaning present in texts and constitutes an attempt to silence the Bible's multiple voices.

(d) Historical criticism as 'advocacy interpretation'

Historical critics of the Bible have failed to recognize that not only is the perspective of the biblical authors culturally and historically conditioned, but so too is their own perspective. Consequently, we need to be attentive not only to the *Sitz im Leben* of the biblical texts and their authors but also of the interpreter engaged in interpreting the texts. The problem with historical critics is that they have ignored this fact and have naively assumed that they are employing an objective and ideologically neutral method. Thus Wink complains that the historical–critical method 'pretends detachment when in fact the scholar is attached to an institution with a high stake in the socialization of students and the preservation of society, and when he himself has a high stake in advancement in that institution by publication of his researches'.[57] Schüssler Fiorenza makes a similar point, complaining that, 'Biblical studies appears to have progressed in a political vacuum, and scholars seem to have understood themselves as accountable solely – as Robert Funk puts it – to the vested interests of the "fraternity of scientifically trained scholars with the soul of a church" '.[58] Or as she puts it in her 1989 essay 'Biblical Interpretation and Commitment', 'As an institutional and intellectual discursive practice biblical scholarship is "positioned" within a historical web of power relationships. Intellectual neutrality is not possible in a world of exploitation and oppression. *Bildungswissen* – knowledge for its own sake – functions either as *Herrschaftswissen* – as knowledge for the sake of domination, or as *Befreiungswissen* – as knowledge for the sake of liberation.'[59]

The failure of historical critics to reflect on their social location and their own unacknowledged prejudices has led to the historical–critical method becoming the tool of Western, middle class, male interests, and its employment as a means of oppressing women and minorities. It is the biblical interpretation practised by what Schüssler Fiorenza calls 'the malestream'.[60]

Marxist commentators on the other hand have criticized historical criticism for failing to recognize the class bias of its methods. Füssel comments that historical criticism places the Bible in the hands of an intellectual elite who determine the legitimate interpretation of the Bible and thereby support authoritarian structures: 'Scholarly exegetical interest and the hermeneutic which guides it have been directed unilaterally to the acquisition of authoritarian knowledge in the service of an elitist claim to dominance on the part of a few "reading experts" in the church. Exegesis has thus become a legitimating science, and authentic exegesis has turned into ideology.'[61]

The result of historical criticism's blindness to its own ideological agenda has been the creation of a new slavery. Although the historical–critical method originally came into existence as a liberating force which enabled human beings to break free from the control of the Church and ecclesial dogma, it has now metamorphosed into a new form of oppression. This is a point made by R. S. Sugirtharajah, who claims that: 'Though historical criticism was liberative particularly to the Western, white and middle class, it had a shackling and enslaving impact on women, blacks and people of other cultures.'[62]

Historical criticism is thus not exegesis, but eisegesis. White male scholars read their own interests into the text, and in doing so justify the oppression of women and the poor. We might say that despite its pretensions the historical–critical method is not a universal method but is merely a local method appropriate to Western males. Historical criticism, then, is not a neutral and objective 'scientific' method, but is a way of reading the

Bible in support of the interests of a particular group. Historical criticism is thus just as much an 'advocacy' interpretation as liberation and feminist readings of the Bible, only the historical critic refuses or is unable to acknowledge it. It is an advocacy reading of the Bible which justifies and reinforces the interests of white male scholars.

Responses to the critique of the historical–critical method

Is the historical–critical method defunct? Do the criticisms outlined above indicate that the historical–critical method is no longer a viable way of reading the Bible? Defenders of historical criticism have advanced a series of arguments in the attempt to rebut such criticisms of the historical–critical method.

1. The response to the charge of fragmentation

It is indeed true that the various methods employed in historical criticism break down the text into smaller units. This need not of itself lead to fragmentation and atomization of the text for several reasons, however. Firstly, the identification of the textual elements that are believed to underlie the final text is not undertaken out of a perverse pleasure in dismantling the text, but is carried out in order to *protect* the unity and coherence of the text. Thus von Rad in his commentary on Genesis emphasizes that historical criticism is necessary in order that we do *not* see biblical texts such as the Pentateuch as chaotic and garbled. The study of sources allows us to see *how* the Pentateuch is a coherent whole, despite the tensions and inconsistencies we encounter in the text. It is precisely because this unity and coherence does not appear to be present on the surface level of the text that historical critics have examined the possibility of the final canonical form of the text being the result of the conflation of earlier sources. Similarly, Barton points out that, 'it is only because the critics approached the text with an expectation it would be such a whole that they were struck by the features that often mean it cannot be so. They did not set out to find "aporias"; they noticed them just because they were trying to read the text as coherent'.[63] As our discussion in Chapter 2 of the Church Fathers' concern with such inconsistencies shows, this identification of tensions in the text is not a new phenomenon, nor is it merely the product of a sceptical age.

Secondly, the atomizing, fragmenting tendency of historical criticism is accompanied by the attempt to recombine the textual elements into a coherent whole. The historical–critical method is an analytical approach which consists in analysing the text so as to reveal its component elements. This analysis is usually followed by a process of synthesis by which the textual elements are brought together in a new and supposedly more adequate unity. Barton points out that, 'in essence the critical approach begins with the very opposite of an atomizing tendency', for 'biblical criticism has regard to the whole gestalt of the text in question, and asks how the story in its entirety hangs together. Once this is done, it becomes apparent that many noncritical solutions will not work, that the discrepancies are real ones'.[64] The key question is not so much the identification of individual sources as the way some historical critics have combined them into a new understanding of the text. That is, it is not the *analysis* of the Bible into its component elements which is problematic, since the identification of such component elements is demanded by the character of the text. It is rather the *synthesis* of these component elements which is problematic, since the way some historical critics have synthesized them has resulted in an understanding of the Bible that diverges from believers' traditional understanding. Critics of historical criticism might thus be better advised to concentrate their fire not on the *analysis* but on the *synthesis* practised by some historical critics.

Thirdly, some critics argue that historical criticism ignores the fact that ancient writers had a different notion of coherence and that it is therefore mistaken to impose modern notions of coherence on the biblical texts. Barton points out that, 'this itself is a critical argument, which tries to identify how texts held together in the ancient mind, and in effect is an accusation of anachronism against the critical scholar: it is not in any way a defense of precritical reading but a plea for biblical criticism to be more sensitive to ancient literary genres than it is'.[65] That is, if we are to identify what understanding of coherence existed in the cultures in which the biblical writings were composed, we must engage in historical–critical study of those cultures. Only then will we be able to establish if there is a mismatch between the modern understanding and the biblical notion of coherence and whether it is inappropriate to expect modern standards of coherence from the Bible. Barton makes the further important point, 'All literary study must assume that even quite remote cultures have *some* affinities with our own.'[66] If this is not the case, then it becomes impossible to read texts from other cultures with understanding. If the texts of the Bible are written from an outlook that is utterly alien to that of twenty-first century human beings, then there would seem to be no point in reading them at all. It is one of the tasks of the historical critic to identify the affinities between the ancient cultures that produced the Bible and our own culture, and thereby play a role in allowing these ancient texts to speak to us today.

2. Response to the charge of
loss of theological meaning

There are two possible responses to the criticism that the historical–critical method results in the loss of theological meaning. The first response is to welcome this. Some scholars have distinguished between confessional and non-confessional approaches to the Bible, the former being appropriate within the context of the faith community, the latter being appropriate within the academy. Those who do not wish to follow this path, however, have attempted to address the loss of theological meaning allegedly brought about by the historical–critical method by integrating the method into a theological hermeneutic. What is needed is for the historical–critical method to be grounded in a hermeneutic that is appropriate to its subject matter.

Francis Watson provides an example of such an attempt to integrate historical criticism into a theological hermeneutic. Watson distinguishes theological interpretation from the secular interpretation of the Bible by stating that the former is attentive to the 'communicative actions' of the biblical texts by means of which God aims to evoke a particular type of response. This means focusing both on the literal sense of the biblical texts, which for Watson means focusing on their verbal meaning, illocutionary and perlocutionary force, and relation to the centre, and the way the biblical texts seek as communicative actions 'to convey a meaning in order to evoke a particular response'. Consequently, 'to concern oneself with the literal sense is therefore to reflect on "application" as well as on verbal meaning, for without this dimension the texts are no longer understood as communicative actions. The criteria by which scriptural communicative actions are assessed derive from God's definitive communicative action in the incarnation of the Word'.[67] Because the biblical texts are concerned with communicating God's Word to human beings, we fail to do them justice if we do not incorporate this concern into our interpretation of the literal sense of the texts.

The question is whether such attempts to integrate historical criticism into a theological hermeneutic undermine the methodological neutrality that the historical–critical method has striven for. Our answer to this question will depend on to what extent we believe that neutrality is possible. As we saw above, many recent commentators believe such neutrality is impossible and that all methods of biblical interpretation are influenced by the social location of the interpreter. It seems to me, however, that the historical–critical method can be an important tool in the development of a theological hermeneutic, so long as it is detached from the historicist, objectivist ideology to which it has sometimes been subordinated. That is, it is not the method as such that is at fault, but the ideologies which it has sometimes served. Historical criticism, as Barth and others have argued, has not been critical enough. It needs to critique the ideologies held by its users and consider whether these ideologies are appropriate to the kinds of text that make up the Bible. This need not result in the loss of theological meaning, but rather opens up the space in which the texts can encounter the reader as far as is possible *in their own right*. The historical–critical method must be accompanied by ideology critique, so that even if the social location of the interpreter cannot and should not be excluded from the act of interpretation, we can at least be aware of how it influences our application of the tools of the historical–critical method and the way we read the text. This means that there will be a dialectical tension between the historical–critical method, the biblical text, and the ideology of the interpreter. Ideally, the way this tension is resolved and its three elements are synthesized will allow theological meanings to emerge that are both fair to the text and yet speak to the present, although they will always and inevitably be conditioned by the social location of the individual who constructs these theological meanings.

An example of how such a creative relationship can be sustained between historical criticism and the quest for a theological meaning is indicated by the call to read the Bible kerygmatically. The question is: what is the biblical kerygma? The historical–critical method can here play a role in cultivating clarity concerning the character of the kerygma. It can make clear what it is to which the individual is called upon to respond when encountering the kerygma embedded in the biblical texts. The kerygma identified by the use of the historical–critical method will not be set in stone and we should recognize that the way we identify and respond to it will be influenced by our social location. Nevertheless, the historical–critical method can assist us in becoming aware of the character of the kerygma and the choice with which it confronts us.

A further role the historical–critical method can play with regard to the theological meaning of the Bible is to help protect us from idolatry in our encounter with the biblical texts. Without some control on our reading, we can all too easily read our own interests into the Bible, so that we make the Bible in our own image rather than allow ourselves to be questioned, challenged and transformed by our encounter with it. Historical criticism can help us to identify inadequate readings that fail to do justice to the reality of the text. The concern, as Moberly puts it, 'is not so much the history of ideas and religious practices (though this remains an important critical control) as the necessities of hermeneutics and theology proper, that is, the question of what is necessary to enable succeeding generations of faithful, or would-be faithful, readers to penetrate and grasp the meaning and significance of the biblical text; that is, to say "God is here" in such a way that the words can be rightly understood without lapse into idolatry, literalism, bad history, manipulation, or the numerous other pitfalls into which faith may stumble.'[68]

3. The response to the charge that historical criticism undermines praxis

Connected with the criticism that the historical–critical method results in the loss of theological meaning is the accusation that it undermines praxis. The charge is that the historical critic becomes so absorbed in historical questions raised by the Bible that he or she forgets that the Bible is a call to action that is personally addressed to the reader, including the historical critic. It is the alleged failure of the historical critic to move from interpretation of the text to acting on the basis of the text that has led to accusations that the historical–critical method is a way of evading the challenge of the Bible. It seems to me that this is perhaps the most significant critique that has been made of the historical–critical method. Certainly it is possible, as Kierkegaard pointed out, that the historical critic can become enmeshed in a never-ending 'approximation process' in which his/her response to the message of the Bible is constantly postponed to the time when the absolute truth of the Bible has been established.

Barton attempts to deal with this problem by drawing on Schleiermacher's elaboration of Ernesti's distinction between three steps in the process of interpretation: (1) the *subtilitas intelligendi*; (2) the *subtilitas explicandi*; (3) the *subtilitas applicandi*, i.e. understanding, explanation and application. The problem is that the term 'interpretation' is sometimes used of all three stages, which easily leads to confusion. Barton point out that as a result of this confusing use of the term 'interpretation', the phrase 'theological interpretation' of the Bible may mean three different things: 'A "theological interpretation" of the Bible may mean (a) that the exegesis of the text attends to the fact that the content is theological: very little biblical criticism has ignored this fact. It may, however, mean (b) that once the exegesis is complete, the interpreter then goes on to ask about the text's theological truth or falsehood, or to show how the text can be theologically productive. This has happened patchily, but still to a significant extent, in biblical studies. But, thirdly, it may mean (c) that the exegesis itself is controlled by a theological or religious vision, so that the meaning found in the text in the course of exegesis is determined by prior theological commitments. It is the third sense that is usually present in the current calls for theological (postcritical, committed) interpretation.'[69] Barton believes that this third sense of theological interpretation 'is a confusion of the *subtilitas explicandi* with the *subtilitas applicandi*'. He further points out that theological interpretation in the third sense of the term 'does not at all rule out the other two possible senses of theological interpretation. Proponents of theological interpretation in the third sense seem often to overlook the other two possibilities, with the result that they portray traditional biblical criticism as much more positivistic and theologically unconcerned than in fact it is'.[70]

If we take Barton as our guide then historical criticism need not undermine praxis. What is needed is greater clarity on the position of the historical-critical method in the threefold structure of the process of interpretation. Historical criticism is a danger to praxis only if it is identified with the third of Schleiermacher's threefold distinction, namely with the *subtilitas applicandi*. Historical criticism, however, arguably belongs to the first two stages, namely *subtilitas intelligendi* and *subtilitas explicandi*. It is the means by which we ensure that it is indeed the biblical text itself that we are applying and not merely a conception of what we would like the text to say.

4. The response to the charge that historical criticism is ideologically biased

As Barton points out, there is one sense in which the historical-critical method is indeed positivistic, namely in the sense that 'textual study . . . has its own proper kind of positivism – either a given word occurs in a text or it does not'.[71] Historical criticism is positivistic in the sense that it deals with a given text, but this does not mean that the historical-critical method is positivistic in the negative sense intended by its critics. The historical-critical method is positivistic only in the sense that it insists that we should treat the text on its own terms and not impose upon it meanings which are not true to the phenomena of the text. We should not confuse rigour with positivism. Attempting to use linguistic and semantic tools to identify as precisely as possible how a term was used and understood in its original context is not positivistic in the negative sense, but is the attempt to do justice to the reality of the text.

Although there may be cases where the historical-critical method has been employed in the service of scientism, positivism and historicism, this need not be the case. Historical criticism is a method, not an ideology, although it can be placed in the service of ideologies. We need to separate the method from the motives of those who apply it. Employing the historical-critical method means above all being attentive to the character of the texts. That this attentiveness may be influenced by the critic's own presuppositions and ideology is something to which the critic should be attentive and to which he or she should also apply the critical tools associated with historical criticism. In short, it is possible for the historical critic by careful attention to the way s/he engages with the text to avoid simply imposing his/her interests upon the text and to allow the voice of the text itself to be heard.

The argument that texts comprise multiple meanings does not of itself undermine historical criticism, but shows only that it should be complemented by other methods capable of doing justice to the layers of meaning that lie outside the competence of the historical–critical method. Furthermore, recognition of the different layers in the text does not mean that anything goes and that *all* meanings are possible and legitimate. The fact that a text is multilayered does not mean that it has *no* stable meaning. Multiple layers of meaning should not be confused with instability. Barton also makes the important point with regard to Segovia that denial of a stable meaning in the text 'deeply undermines exactly the kind of postcolonial criticism of traditional biblical study that Segovia is engaged in, since it makes it quite impossible ever to *appeal* to the text against its interpreters. The idea of a stable meaning – a meaning which colonial interpreters have signally failed to grasp – ought to be Segovia's best friend'.[72]

In short, the accusation that the historical–critical method is ideologically driven undermines not the method itself, but draws attention to the need to supplement historical criticism with a critique of the ideology of the practitioners of the method.

The abiding significance of the historical–critical method

Is the historical–critical method defunct? It should be noted that even some of the critics of historical criticism have emphasized its importance, while at the same time drawing attention to its shortcomings. Even Wink makes clear that the bankruptcy of the historical–critical method does not mean that it is without value, just as 'a business which goes bankrupt is not valueless, nor incapable of producing useful products'.[73] For Wink, 'Biblical criticism is not bankrupt because it has run out of things to say or new ground to explore. It is bankrupt solely because it is incapable of achieving what most of its practitioners considered its purpose to be: so to interpret the Scriptures that the past becomes alive and illumines our present with new possibilities for personal and social transformation'.[74] Other critics of the historical–critical method such as David Steinmetz and Schüssler Fiorenza make similar points. Despite holding that pre-critical exegesis is in some senses superior to historical criticism, Steinmetz still considers that it has value, but needs correction: 'When biblical scholarship shifted from the hermeneutical position of Origen to the hermeneutical position of Jowett, it gained something important, and valuable. But it lost something as well, and it is the painful duty of critical scholarship to assess its losses as well as its gains'.[75] Schüssler Fiorenza holds that the critical-rhetorical paradigm shift she believes to be taking place in biblical studies 'requires that biblical studies continue its descriptive analytic work utilizing all the critical methods available for illuminating our understanding of ancient texts and their historical location'.[76] Even some of its most vigorous critics, then, do not write historical criticism off, but call for its integration into a more adequate hermeneutic.

What, then, should be the role of the historical–critical method in biblical scholarship? My own view is that its claims to *hegemony* must be renounced. Historical criticism should not be regarded as the sole correct, 'objective' method that can bring about assured results. It should not, however, for that reason be thrown overboard, since it can play an important role in *limiting* the range of interpretations possible when reading a text. If there is no limitation on the meanings that can be constructed in the reader's engagement with the text, then the text ceases to mean anything or simply become the vehicle for the prejudices and self-interest of the interpreter. The historical–critical method can help to protect the rights of the text. This means not that the historical–critical method stands in judgement over other ways of reading the Bible, but that historical criticism is one of the voices to which we must listen if we are truly to hear God's Word in this ancient collection of texts.

APPENDIX

Gen. 2.4b–3.24

In the day that the LORD God made the earth and the heavens (v. 4b), when no plant of the field was yet in the earth and no herb of the field had yet sprung up – for the LORD God had not caused it to rain upon the earth, and there was no one to till the ground (v. 5); but a stream would rise from the earth, and water the whole face of the ground – (v. 6); then the LORD God formed man from the dust of the ground, and breathed into his nostrils the breath of life; and the man became a living being (v. 7). And the LORD God planted a garden in Eden, in the east; and there he put the man whom he had formed (v. 8). Out of the ground the LORD God made to grow every tree that is pleasant to the sight and good for food, the tree of life also in the midst of the garden, and the tree of the knowledge of good and evil (v. 9).

A river flows out of Eden to water the garden, and from there it divides and becomes four branches (v. 10). The name of the first is Pishon; it is the one that flows around the whole land of Havilah, where there is gold (v. 11); and the gold of that land is good; bdellium and onyx stone are there (v. 12). The name of the second river is Gihon; it is the one that flows around the whole land of Cush (v. 13). The name of the third river is Tigris, which flows east of Assyria. And the fourth river is the Euphrates (v. 14).

The LORD God took the man and put him in the garden of Eden to till it and keep it (v. 15). And the LORD God commanded the man, 'You may freely eat of every tree of the garden (v. 16); but of the tree of the knowledge of good and evil you shall not eat, for in the day that you eat of it you shall die (v. 17).'

Then the LORD God said, 'It is not good that the man should be alone; I will make him a helper as his partner' (v. 18). So out of the ground the LORD God formed every animal of the field and every bird of the air, and brought them to the man to see what he would call them; and whatever the man called each living creature, that was its name (v. 19). The man gave names to all cattle, and to the birds of the air, and to every animal of the field; but for the man there was not found a helper as his partner (v. 20). So the LORD God caused a deep sleep to fall upon the man, and he slept; then he took one of his ribs and closed up its place with flesh (v. 21). And the rib that the LORD God had taken from the man he made into a woman and brought her to the man (v. 22). Then the man said,

'This at last is bone of my bones
and flesh of my flesh;
this one shall be called Woman,
for out of Man this one was taken.' (v. 23)

Therefore a man leaves his father and his mother and clings to his wife, and they become one flesh (v. 24). And the man and his wife were both naked, and were not ashamed (v. 25).

3   Now the serpent was more crafty than any other wild animal that the LORD God had made. He said to the woman, 'Did God say, "You shall not eat from any tree in the garden"?'(v. 1). The woman said to the serpent, 'We may eat of the fruit of the trees in the garden (v. 2); but God said, "You shall not eat of the fruit of the tree that is in the middle of the garden, nor shall you touch it, or you shall die"' (v. 3). But the serpent said to the woman, 'You will not die (v. 4); for God knows that when you eat of it your eyes will be opened, and you will be like God, knowing good and evil' (v. 5). So when the woman saw that the tree was good for food, and that it was a delight to the eyes, and that the tree was to be desired to make one wise, she took of its fruit and ate; and she also gave some to her husband, who was with her, and he ate (v. 6). Then the eyes of both were opened, and they knew that they were naked; and they sewed fig leaves together and made loincloths for themselves (v. 7).

They heard the sound of the LORD God walking in the garden at the time of the evening breeze, and the man and his wife hid themselves from the presence of the LORD God among the trees of the garden (v. 8). But the LORD God called to the man, and said to him, 'Where are you?' (v. 9). He said, 'I heard the sound of you in the garden, and I was afraid, because I was naked; and I hid myself' (v. 10). He said, 'Who told you that you were naked? Have you eaten from the tree of which I commanded you not to eat?' (v. 11). The man said, 'The woman whom you gave to be with me, she gave me fruit from the tree, and I ate' (v. 12). Then the LORD God said to the woman, 'What is this that you have done?' The woman said, 'The serpent tricked me, and I ate' (v. 13). The LORD God said to the serpent,

'Because you have done this,
cursed are you among all animals
and among all wild creatures;

upon your belly you shall go,

and dust you shall eat

all the days of your life (v. 14).

I will put enmity between you and the woman,

and between your offspring and hers;

he will strike your head,

and you will strike his heel.' (v. 15)

To the woman he said,

'I will greatly increase your pangs in childbearing;

in pain you shall bring forth children,

yet your desire shall be for your husband,

and he shall rule over you.' (v. 16)

And to the man he said,

'Because you have listened to the voice of your wife,

and have eaten of the tree about which I commanded you,

"You shall not eat of it",

cursed is the ground because of you;

in toil you shall eat of it all the days of your life (v. 17);

thorns and thistles it shall bring forth for you;

and you shall eat the plants of the field (v. 18).

By the sweat of your face you shall eat bread

until you return to the ground, for out of it you were taken;

you are dust, and to dust you shall return.' (v. 19)

The man named his wife Eve, because she was the mother of all who live (v. 20). And the LORD God made garments of skins for the man and for his wife, and clothed them (v. 21).

Then the LORD God said, 'See, the man has become like one of us, knowing good and evil; and now, he might reach out his hand and take also from the tree of life, and eat, and live for ever' – (v. 22) therefore the LORD God sent him forth from the garden of Eden, to till the ground from which he was taken (v. 23). He drove out the man; and at the east of the garden of Eden he placed the cherubim, and a sword flaming and turning to guard the way to the tree of life (v. 24).

Matt. 15.21–8

Jesus left that place and went away to the district of Tyre and Sidon (v. 21). Just then a Canaanite woman from that region came out and started shouting, 'Have mercy on me, Lord, Son of David; my daughter is tormented by a demon' (v. 22). But he did not answer her at all. And his disciples came and urged him, saying, 'Send her away, for she keeps shouting after us' (v. 23). He answered, 'I was sent only to the lost sheep of the house of Israel' (v. 24). But she came and knelt before him,* saying, 'Lord, help me' (v. 25). He answered, 'It is not fair to take the children's food and throw it to the dogs' (v. 26). She said, 'Yes, Lord, yet even the dogs eat the crumbs that fall from their masters' table' (v. 27). Then Jesus answered her, 'Woman, great is your faith! Let it be done for you as you wish.' And her daughter was healed instantly (v. 28).

---

*Greek: prosekunei, i.e. 'worshipped'.

NOTES

Chapter One

1 The historical–critical method is also sometimes called the *historico*-critical method, particularly in nineteenth-century works.

2 Josephus, *Antiquities*, 17.135; 18.1–2.

3 James Barr, *Holy Scripture: Canon, Authority, Criticism* (Oxford: Clarendon Press, 1983), 105.

4 John Barton, *The Nature of Biblical Criticism* (Louisville: Westminster John Knox, 2007), 33; original emphasis.

5 Ibid., 34–35.

6 Ibid., 53.

7 Ibid., 5.

8 Ibid., 1.

9 Ibid., 33, n.4.

10 Ibid., 123–30.

11 Ibid., 123.

12 Ibid., 123, original emphasis.

13 Ibid., 124.

14 Ibid., 1, 53.

15 Reinhart Kosellek, *Critique and Crisis: Enlightenment and the Pathogenesis of Modern Society* (Oxford, New York and Hamburg: Berg, 1988), 105.

16 Barr, *Holy Scripture*, 34.

17 Gerhard Maier, *Das Ende der historisch-kritischen Methode* (Wuppertal: Theologischer Verlag Rolf Brockhaus), 1974. ET: *The End of the Historical–Critical Method*, trans. by Edwin W. Leverenz and Rudolph F. Norden (Eugene, Oregon: Wipf and Stock, 1977), 11.

18 Ibid., 11.

19 Christopher R. Seitz, *Word without End: The Old Testament as Abiding Theological Witness* (Grand Rapids: Eerdmans, 1998), 11.

20 Maier, *The End of the Historical–Critical Method*, 23.

21 Barton, *Nature of Biblical Criticism*, 49.

22 Ibid.

23 Ibid., 3.

24 Andrew Louth, *Discerning the Mystery: An Essay on the Nature of Theology*
    (Oxford: Clarendon, 1983), 9, citing George Steiner, 'The Retreat from the
    Word', in *Language and Silence* (Harmondsworth, 1969), 31–56.

25 Ibid.,10.

26 Ibid., 13.

27 Ibid., 27.

28 Ibid., 30.

29 Ibid., 30.

30 Barton, *Nature of Biblical Criticism*, 62.

31 Ibid., 62–3.

32 John Barton, *Reading the Old Testament: Method in Biblical Study* (London:
    Darton, Longman and Todd, 1984), 26.

33 Barton, *Nature of Biblical Criticism*, 64.

34 Ibid., 65.

35 Ibid., 66, emphasis added.

36 Ibid., 58.

37 Paul Feyerabend goes so far as to argue for the abandonment of attempts
    to formulate a universally valid scientific method and denies that science
    has a privileged status over other forms of knowledge. The only method
    of scientific research is an anarchistic 'method' in which 'anything goes'.
    Paul Feyerabend, *Against Method: Outline of an Anarchistic Theory of
    Knowledge* (London: Verso, 1988).

38 Thomas S. Kuhn, *The Structure of Scientific Revolutions*, 3rd edn (Chicago:
    University of Chicago Press, 1996 [1st edn 1968]).

39 Karl Popper, *The Logic of Scientific Discovery* (London: Routledge, 1997), 33.

40 Barton, *Nature of Biblical Criticism*, 66–7.

41 Ibid.

42 Robert Alter, *The Art of Biblical Narrative* (New York: Basic Books, 1981), 13.

43 Barton, *Nature of Biblical Criticism*, 73.

44 Ibid., 78–9.

45 For fuller discussion see Barton, *Reading the Old Testament*, 147–51.

46 See Stefan Collini (ed.), *Interpretation and Overinterpretation: Umberto Eco
    with Richard Rorty, Jonathan Culler, Christine Brooke-Rose* (Cambridge:
    Cambridge University Press, 1992), 68. Barton provides another good
    example of how lack of knowledge of how terms were used in the past can
    lead to a questionable interpretation in the present: 'Words are not constant
    in their meaning across time. To take a simple example, in the novels of
    Trollope we often find a female character saying that a male friend "made
    love to her the whole evening." It is crucial in understanding Trollope to
    realize that in his day this expression meant showing a romantic or sexual
    interest in someone, not having sexual intercourse with them. Otherwise we

shall get a very distorted idea of what happened in Victorian drawing rooms.'
Barton, *Nature of Biblical Criticism*, 80.

47 Brevard S. Childs, 'The Sensus Literalis of Scripture: An Ancient and Modern Problem', in H. Donner, R. Hanhart, and R. Smend (eds), *Beiträge zur alttestamentlichen Theologie: Festschrift für Walther Zimmerli zum 70. Geburtstag* (Göttingen: Vandenhoeck & Ruprecht, 1977), 80–95.

48 Barton, *Nature of Biblical Criticism*, 101.

49 Ibid.

50 Ernst Troeltsch, 'Über historische und dogmatische Methode in der Theologie', in *Gesammelte Schriften*, 4 vols. (Tübingen: J. C. B. Mohr, 1913, 1922), 2: 729–53; reprinted in Gerhard Sauter, *Theologie als Wissenschaft* (Munich: C. Kaiser, 1971), 105–27; ET: 'Historical and Dogmatic Method in Theology (1898)', in Ernst Troeltsch, *Religion in History*, translated by James Luther Adams and Walter F. Bense with an introduction by James Luther Adams (Edinburgh: T & T Clark, 1991), 11–32; 13; cf. 'Historiography', in James Hastings (ed.), *Encyclopaedia of Religion and Ethics* (New York: Charles Scribner's Sons, 1914), 6:716–23.

51 Troeltsch, 'Historiography', 718; cf. 'Historical and Dogmatic Method in Theology', 13–14.

52 Troeltsch, 'Historical and Dogmatic Method in Theology', 13.

53 Van A. Harvey, *The Historian and the Believer: the Morality of Historical Knowledge and Christian Belief*, with a New Introduction by the Author (Urbana and Chicago: University of Illinois Press, 1966, 1996), 14–15.

54 Adams and Bense translate this term as 'mutual interrelation': Troeltsch, 'Historical and Dogmatic Method in Theology', 13.

55 Troeltsch, 'Historical and Dogmatic Method in Theology', 14.

56 Ibid.

57 Van Harvey, *The Historian and the Believer*, 15.

Chapter Two

1 This view is held by: Gerhard Ebeling, 'Bedeutung der historisch-kritischen Methode für die protestantische Theologie und Kirche', *Zeitschrift für Theologie und Kirche* 47 (1950): 1–46; ET: 'The Significance of the Critical Historical Method for Church and Theology in Protestantism', in *Word and Faith*, translated by James W. Leitch (London: SCM, 1963), 17–61; 46–48; William Baird, 'New Testament Criticism', in David Noel Freedman (ed.), *Anchor Bible Dictionary* (New York and London: Doubleday, 1992), 1:730–36; see esp. 730; *History of New Testament Research, vol. 1: From Deism to Tübingen* (Minneapolis: Fortress Press, 1992); Edgar Krentz, *The Historical–Critical Method* (Philadelphia: Fortress Press, 1975), 16–22.

2 Some scholars have gone so far as to identify a specific individual who initiated the historical approach to the interpretation of the Bible, although there is divergence among scholars on who should receive the title of founder of historical criticism. See Klaus Scholder, *The Birth of Modern Critical Theology: Origins and Problems of Biblical Criticism in the Seventeenth Century*, translated by John Bowden (London: SCM, 1990), 9–14. Candidates are: (1) Spinoza. According to Georg Bohrmann, 'Spinoza is the first to practise immanent and thus historical criticism; he is founder of historical–critical research into the Bible'. Georg Bohrmann, *Spinozas Stellung zur Religion. Eine Untersuchung auf der Grundlage des theologisch-politischen Traktats* (Giessen: Alfred Töpelmann, 1914), 24. See also Leo Strauss, *Die Religionskritik Spinozas als Grundlage seiner Bibelwissenschaft: Untersuchungen zu Spinozas theologisch-politischem Traktat* (Berlin: Akademie-Verlag, 1930); ET: Leo Strauss, *Spinoza's Critique of Religion* (Chicago: Chicago University Press, 1997). (2) J. S. Semler. For Emanuel Hirsch, Semler 'is the first German Protestant theologian who was able to see the Bible with the eyes of the historian of religion and critical historical researcher'. Emanuel Hirsch, *Geschichte der neuern evangelischen Theologie im Zusammenhang mit den allgemeinen Bewegungen des europäischen Denkens*, 5 vols. (Gütersloh: C. Bertelsmann, 1949–1954), IV:59. See also Gottfried Hornig, *Die Anfänge der historisch-kritischen Theologie: J. S. Semlers Schriftverständnis und seine Stellung zu Luther* (Göttingen: Vandenhoeck & Ruprecht, 1961). (3) Richard Simon. See Hans-Joachim Kraus, *Geschichte der historisch-kritischen Erforschung des Alten Testaments von der Reformation bis zur Gegenwart* (Neukirchen-Vluyn: Neukirchener Verlag, ³1982), 65–70. (4) F. C. Baur. According to Heinz Liebing, 'historical–critical theology in the full sense only came into existence after Baur'. Heinz Liebing, 'Historisch-kritische Theologie. Zum 100. Todestag Ferdinand Christian Baurs am 2. Dezember 1960', *Zeitschrift für Theologie und Kirche* 57 (1960), 302–317, 303; quoted in Scholder, *Birth of Modern Critical Theology*, 1. Although a significant exponent of the historical–critical method, as Barton points out, 'surely Baur is far too late for this accolade'. Barton, *Nature of Biblical Criticism*, 119.

3 Ebeling, 'The Significance of the Critical Historical Method for Church and Theology in Protestantism', in *Word and Faith*, 55.

4 Wolfhart Pannenberg, 'The Crisis of the Scripture Principle', in *Basic Questions in Theology*, trans. by George H. Kehm, 3 vols. (London: SCM, 1970–1973), 1:1–14; 5–6.

5 Rudolf Bultmann, *Jesus Christ and Mythology* (London: SCM, 1958). Ebeling, 'The Significance of the Critical Historical Method for Church and Theology in Protestantism', in *Word and Faith*, 55–60. Ernst Käsemann, 'Vom theologischen Recht historisch-kritischer Exegese', *Zeitschrift für Theologie und Kirche* 64 (1967), 259–281.

6 Troeltsch, 'Historiography', 716.

7 Ibid.

8 Barton, *Nature of Biblical Criticism*, 124. A similar view is advanced by
J. C. O'Neill, who writes: 'The foundations of modern biblical criticism
were laid in the Renaissance with the recovery of knowledge of Greek and
the editing and printing of ancient sources.' J. C. O'Neill, 'Biblical Criticism:
History of Biblical Criticism', in David Noel Freedman (ed.), *Anchor Bible
Dictionary* (New York and London: Doubleday, 1992), 1: 725–730; 726–727.

9 Edgar Krentz, *The Historical–Critical Method* (Philadelphia: Fortress Press,
1975), 7.

10 For surveys of the history of biblical interpretation see Frederic W. Farrar,
History of Interpretation (London: Macmillan, 1886). Krentz, *The
Historical Critical Method*, 6–32. Ronald E. Clements, *One Hundred
Years of Old Testament Interpretation* (Philadelphia: Westminster, 1976).
F. F. Bruce, 'The History of New Testament Study', in I. Howard Marshall,
New Testament Interpretation: Essays in Principles and Methods (Exeter:
Paternoster, 1977), 21–59. Werner Georg Kümmel, *The New Testament: the
History of the Investigation of its Problems*, translated by S. McLean and
Howard C. Kee (London: SCM, 1978). Kraus, *Geschichte der historisch-
kritischen Erforschung*. Robert M. Grant with David Tracy, *A Short History
of the Interpretation of the Bible*, 2nd revised and enlarged edition (London:
SCM, 1984). John Haralson Hayes and Frederick C. Prussner, *Old Testament
Theology: its History and Development* (London: SCM, 1985). E. J. Epp
and G. W. McRae (eds), *The New Testament and its Modern Interpreters*
(Philadelphia: Fortress, 1989). John K. Riches, *A Century of New Testament
Study* (Cambridge: Lutterworth, 1993). Henning Graf Reventlow, *Epochen
der Bibelauslegung*, 4 vols. (München: C. H. Beck, 1990–2001). Anthony C.
Thiselton, 'New Testament Interpretation in Historical Perspective', in Joel
B. Green (ed.), *Hearing the New Testament: Strategies for Interpretation*
(Grand Rapids, Mich.: William B. Eerdmans, 1995), 10–36. John H.
Hayes, *Dictionary of Biblical Interpretation*, 2 vols. (Nashville: Abingdon,
1999). Magne Sæbø (ed.), *Hebrew Bible/Old Testament: the History of
its Interpretation*, 2 vols., vol. 1: *From the Beginnings to the Middle Ages
(until 1300)*; vol. 2: *From the Renaissance to the Enlightenment* (Göttingen:
Vandenhoeck & Ruprecht, 1996, 2008). William Baird, *History of New
Testament Research*, 2 vols. (Minneapolis: Fortress Press, 1992, 2003);
James Barr, 'The Old Testament', in Ernest Nicholson (ed.), *A Century
of Theological and Religious Studies in Britain* (Oxford: Published for
the British Academy by Oxford University Press, 2003), 29–50. William
Horbury, 'The New Testament', in Nicholson, *A Century of Theological
and Religious Studies in Britain*, 51–134. Alan J. Hauser and Duane F.
Watson (eds), *A History of Biblical Interpretation*, 2 vols., vol. 1: *The
Ancient Period*; vol. 2: *The Medieval through the Reformation Periods*
(Grand Rapids, Mich.: William B. Eerdmans, 2003, 2009). Scot McKnight
and Grant R. Osborne (eds), *The Face of New Testament Studies: A Survey
of Recent Research* (Grand Rapids, Mich.: Baker Academic, 2004). John
Sandys-Wunsch, *What Have They Done to the Bible? A History of Modern
Biblical Interpretation* (Collegeville, Minn.: Liturgical Press, 2005). Donald
K. McKim (ed.), *Dictionary of Major Biblical Interpreters* (Downers Grove,

Illinois: IVP Academic, ¹1998, ²2007). Rudolf Smend, *From Astruc to Zimmerli*, translated by Margaret Kohl (Tübingen: Mohr Siebeck, 2007). Henry Wandsbrough OSB, *The Use and Abuse of the Bible: A Brief History of Biblical Interpretation* (London: T & T Clark, 2010). For an anthology of key works in the history of biblical interpretation see William Yarchin, *History of Biblical Interpretation: A Reader* (Peabody, Mass.: Henrickson, 2004).

11 Pseudo-Heraclitus, *Quaestiones homericae*, 6; quoted in Grant and Tracy, *A Short History of the Interpretation of the Bible*, 19.

12 For discussions of allegorical interpretation see R. P. C. Hanson, *Allegory and Event: A Study of the Sources and Significance of Origen's Interpretation of Scripture* (London: SCM, 1959); 'Biblical Exegesis in the Early Church', in P. R. Ackroyd and C. F. Evans (eds), *The Cambridge History of the Bible*, vol. 1: *From the Beginnings to Jerome*, 307–77 (Cambridge: Cambridge University Press, 1970), 412–453. M. F. Wiles, 'Origen as Biblical Scholar', *Cambridge History of the Bible*, 1:489–509. Philip Rollinson, *Classical Theories of Allegory and Christian Culture* (Pittsburgh: Duquesne University Press, 1980). Joseph Wilson Trigg, *Origen: The Bible and Philosophy in the Third-Century Church* (London: SCM 1984). Karen Jo Torjesen, *Hermeneutical Procedure and Theological Structure in Origen's Exegesis* (Berlin: de Gruyter, 1986). Gerald L. Bruns, *Hermeneutics Ancient and Modern* (New Haven: Yale University Press, 1992). David Dawson, *Allegorical Readers and Cultural Revision in Ancient Alexandria* (Berkeley, Calif.: University of California Press, 1992). J. F. Procopé, 'Greek Philosophy, Hermeneutics and Alexandrian Understanding of the Old Testament', in Sæbø, *Hebrew Bible/Old Testament*, I/1:451–477. J. N. B. Carleton Paget, 'The Christian Exegesis of the Old Testament in the Alexandrian Tradition', in Sæbø, *Hebrew Bible/Old Testament*, I/1:478–542. Frances M. Young, *Biblical Exegesis and the Formation of Christian Culture* (Peabody, MA: Hendrickson, 2002); 'Alexandrian and Antiochene Exegesis', in Hauser and Watson, *A History of Biblical Interpretation*, 1: 334–354. Craig A. Evans, *The Interpretation of Scripture in Early Judaism and Christianity: Studies in Language and Tradition* (London: T&T Clark, 2004).

13 Jerome, *Ep.* 53, § 7; cf. *Ep.* 48, § 15.

14 Jerome, *Prol. in Es.* v.10.

15 Jerome, *Comm. in Gal.* iii.3; i.6; *Comm. in Jer.* 27; cf. *Ep. ad Pammach.* 84, § 9.

16 Jerome, *Praef. in lib. v. Comm. in Esaiam.*

17 Jerome, *Comm. in Ezech.* c. 16, init.

18 Eusebius, *Hist. Eccl.* 6.31; Jer. *Catal.* 63. An English translation of the correspondence between Africanus and Origen can be found in volume IV of the Ante-Nicene Fathers Library: Alexander Roberts and James Donaldson (eds), *The Ante-Nicene Fathers: Translations of the Writings of the Fathers down to A.D. 325*, vol. IV (Grand Rapids: Eerdmans, 1971).

19 For a list of these points see Barton, *Nature of Biblical Criticism*, 131.

20 Eusebius, *Hist. Eccl.* 6.25.

21 Eusebius, *Hist. Eccl.* 7.25.

22 Jerome, *De Viris Illus.* 1.

23 For a study of Jerome's exegesis see H. F. D. Sparks, 'Jerome as Biblical Scholar', *Cambridge History of the Bible*, 1:510–540. René Kieffer, 'Jerome: His Exegesis and Hermeneutics', in Sæbø, *Hebrew Bible/Old Testament*, I/1:663–681.

24 Jerome, *Comm. in Ezech.* xi; *in Jer.* xxi.2; *Ep.* 21, § 13.

25 Jerome, *Ep.* 121, *ad Algas.* 7–11; *Comm. in Acts*, xxvi.6; *Gal.* iii.1; iv.24; vi.2; *Eph.* iii.3, 8; *Ep.* 120, *ad Hedib.* qu. 11; *Ep. ad Algas.* qu. 10.

26 Jerome, *Comm. in Gal.* iii.15.

27 For discussions of Augustine's interpretation of the Bible see Gerald Bonner, 'Augustine as Biblical Scholar', *Cambridge History of the Bible*, 1:541–562. David F. Wright, 'Augustine: His Exegesis and Hermeneutics', in Sæbø, *Hebrew Bible/Old Testament*, I/1:701–730. Richard A. Norris, Jr., 'Augustine and the Close of the Ancient Period of Interpretation', in Hauser and Watson, *A History of Biblical Interpretation*, 1:380–408.

28 Augustine, *De Civ. Dei*, xv.

29 Augustine, *C. Adimant.* xiv. § 2.

30 Augustine, *De Cons. Evang.* ii.12, 24, 28, 66.

31 Augustine, *in Joann. tract.* 1, § 1.

32 Augustine, *Conf.* vii.21; *De Gen. Ad Litt.* v.8.

33 Barton, *Nature of Biblical Criticism*, 132.

34 Ibid.

35 For studies of the Antiochenes see: Rowan A. Greer, *Theodore of Mopsuestia: Exegete and Theologian* (London: Faith, 1961). Dimitri Z. Zaharopoulos, *Theodore of Mopsuestia on the Bible: A Study of His Old Testament Exegesis* (New York: Paulist Press, 1989); Rudolf Bultmann, *Die Exegese des Theodor von Mopsuestia* (Stuttgart: Kohlhammer, 1984). Young, *Biblical Exegesis and the Formation of Christian Culture*; 'Alexandrian and Antiochene Exegesis;' Sten Hidal, 'Exegesis of the Old Testament in the Antiochene School with its Prevalent Literal and Historical Method', in Sæbø, *Hebrew Bible/Old Testament*, I/1:543–568. Robert C. Hill, *Reading the Old Testament in Antioch* (Leiden: Brill, 2005).

36 Hidal points out: 'In contrast to the catechetical school in Alexandria, there never existed a school in the strict sense of the word at Antioch. Rather, we can observe a marked tendency in the theological work, a development and strengthening of certain characteristics.' Hidal, 'Exegesis of the Old Testament in the Anthiochene School', 544.

37 Theodore of Mopsuestia, *Commentary on Galatians* 4.24, in Maurice Wiles and Mark Santer (eds), *Documents in Early Christian Thought* (Cambridge: Cambridge University Press, 1975), 151.

38 Farrar, *History of Interpretation*, 210.

39 Ibid.

40 Ibid., 211.

41 Grant and Tracy, *A Short History of the Interpretation of the Bible*, 66. For a more positive assessment of Origen, see Hanson, *Allegory and Event*, esp. 359–374.

42 Young, *Biblical Exegesis and the Formation of Christian Culture*, 166.

43 Ibid., 167.

44 For the West's knowledge of Antiochene exegesis see M. L. W. Laistner, 'Antiochene Exegesis in Western Europe', *Harvard Theological Review*, xl (1947), 19–32.

45 Beryl Smalley, *The Study of the Bible in the Middle Ages* (Oxford: Basil Blackwell, ²1952), 15–16.

46 Ibid., 18.

47 Laistner, 'Antiochene Exegesis in Western Europe', 31.

48 Smalley, *Study of the Bible in the Middle Ages*, 19.

49 Ibid., 357.

50 For a summary of these developments see Ulrich Köpf, 'The Institutional Framework of Theological Studies in the Late Middle Ages', in Sæbø, *Hebrew Bible/Old Testament*, II:123–153.

51 For a discussion of Medieval Jewish interpretation see Robert A. Harris, 'Medieval Jewish Biblical Exegesis', in Hauser and Watson, *A History of Biblical Interpretation*, 2:141–171. For the influence of Jewish exegesis on Christian thought see G. R. Evans, 'Masters and Disciples: Aspects of Christian Interpretation of the Old Testament in the Eleventh and Twelfth Centuries', in Sæbø, *Hebrew Bible/Old Testament*, I/2:237–260; 254–257.

52 For a survey of Medieval Christian exegesis see Christopher Ocker, 'Scholastic Interpretation of the Bible', in Hauser and Watson, *A History of Biblical Interpretation*, 2: 254–279.

53 See Rainer Berndt, 'The School of St. Victor in Paris', in Sæbø, *Hebrew Bible/Old Testament*, I/2:467–495; 486–489.

54 Smalley, *Study of the Bible in the Middle Ages*, 83–106, esp. 93–97.

55 For discussions of the biblical interpretation of Albertus Magnus and Thomas Aquinas see Karlfried Froehlich, 'Christian Interpretation of the Old Testament in the High Middle Ages', in Sæbø, *Hebrew Bible/Old Testament*, I/2:496–558.

56 Quoted in Smalley, *Study of the Bible in the Middle Ages*, 300.

57 Erika Rummel, 'The Renaissance Humanists', in Hauser and Watson, *A History of Biblical Interpretation*, 2:280–298; 280.

58 Lorenzo Valla, *De falso credita et ementita Constantinii donatione declamatio*. For the English translation see Christopher B. Coleman, *The Treatise of Lorenzo Valla on the Donation of Constantine: Text and Translation into English* (New Haven: Yale University Press, 1922). For

discussions of Valla see Jerry H. Bentley, *Humanist and Holy Writ: New Testament Scholarship in the Renaissance* (Princeton, NJ: Princeton University Press, 1983), 32–69. Henning Graf Reventlow, *Epochen der Bibelauslegung*, vol. III: *Renaissance, Reformation, Humanismus* (Munich: C. H. Beck, 1997), 15–26.

59 For studies of Erasmus see Bentley, *Humanist and Holy Writ*, 112–193. Reventlow, *Epochen der Bibelauslegung*, III:55–67. Erika Rummel, 'The Textual and Hermeneutic Work of Desiderius Erasmus of Rotterdam', in Sæbø, *Hebrew Bible/Old Testament*, II:215–230.

60 See Jared Wicks, 'Catholic Old Testament Interpretation in the Reformation and Early Confessional Eras', in Sæbø, *Hebrew Bible/Old Testament*, II:617–648; 617–623.

61 Bentley, however, has challenged the view of Colet as a forerunner of the historical–critical method: 'Though routinely hailed as a harbinger of Reformation exegesis, Colet's real achievement was simply to provide a running literary commentary in the patristic fashion, abandoning the late medival style of exegesis, which often subordinated the scriptures to the needs of scholastic theology.' Bentley, *Humanist and Holy Writ*, 9–10. For a discussion of Colet see Reventlow, *Epochen der Bibelauslegung*, III:50–55.

62 See Reventlow, *Epochen der Bibelauslegung*, III:33–39. Sophie Kessler Mesguich, 'Early Christian Hebraists', in Sæbø, *Hebrew Bible/Old Testament*, II:254–275.

63 Richard Griffiths (ed.), *The Bible in the Renaissance: Essays on Biblical Commentary and Translation in the Fifteenth and Sixteenth Centuries* (Aldershot: Ashgate, 2001).

64 For a discussion of the various English translations of the Bible see S. L. Greenslade, 'English Versions of the Bible, 1525–1611', in S. L. Greenslade (ed.), *The Cambridge History of the Bible*, vol 3: *The West from the Reformation to the Present Day* (Cambridge: Cambridge University Press, 1963), 141–174. David Daniell, *The Bible in English: its History and Influence* (New Haven: Yale University Press, 2003). Henry Wansbrough, 'History and Impact of English Bible Translations', in Sæbø, *Hebrew Bible/Old Testament*, II:536–552.

65 See Roland H. Bainton, 'The Bible in the Reformation', in Greenslade (ed.), *Cambridge History of the Bible*, 3:1–37.

66 For studies of Luther's interpretation of the Bible see Reventlow, *Epochen der Bibelauslegung*, III:68–90. Siegfried Raeder, 'The Exegetical and Hermeneutical Work of Martin Luther', in Sæbø, *Hebrew Bible/Old Testament*, II:363–406. Mark D. Thompson, 'Biblical Interpretation in the Works of Martin Luther', in Hauser and Watson, *A History of Biblical Interpretation*, 2: 299–318.

67 *Luther's Works: American Edition*, 55 vols., vol. 54: *Table Talk*, edited and translated by Theodore G. Tappert (Philadelphia: Fortress, 1967), 406.

68 For discussions of Calvin's interpretation of the Bible see See Reventlow, *Epochen der Bibelauslegung*, III:118–140. Peter Opitz, 'The Exegetical and Hermeneutical Work of John Oecolampadius, Huldrych Zwingli and

John Calvin', in Sæbø, *Hebrew Bible/Old Testament*, II:407–451; 428–451. Barbara Pitkin, 'John Calvin and the Interpretation of the Bible', in Hauser and Watson, *A History of Biblical Interpretation*, 2:341–371.

69 For a summary of Flacius' interpretation of the Bible see Bernt T. Oftesad, 'Further Development of Reformation Hermeneutics', in Sæbø, *Hebrew Bible/Old Testament*, II:602–616; 604–611.

70 Matthias Flacius Illyricus, *Clavis Scripturae seu de sermone sacrarum literarum, plurimas generales regulas continentis, altera pars* [Key to the Scripture, or concerning the language of Holy Scripture, wherein numerous general rules are contained, Part 2] (Leipzig, 1965) col. 2, no. 5; col. 72; col. 25, par. 1. Cited in Kümmel, *New Testament*, 28.

71 Ibid. cols. 82–83; cited in Kümmel, *The New Testament*, 29.

72 Ibid.

73 Ibid.

74 Ibid.

75 Ibid. col. 2, no. 5; col. 72; col. 25, par. 1; cited in Kümmel, *The New Testament*, 28.

76 Joachim Camerarius, *Commentarius in Novum Foedus: In quo et figurae sermonis, et verborum significatio, et orationis sententia, ad illius Foederis intelligentiam certiorem, tractantur* [Commentary on the New Coventant: in which are treated figures of speech, the meaning of words . . .] (Cambridge, 1642). See Kümmel, *The New Testament*, 31–33.

77 Spinoza, *Tractatus Theologico-Politicus (Gebhardt Edition, 1925)*, translated by Samuel Shirley with an Introduction by Brad S. Gregory (Leiden: Brill, 1989), 141. For literature on Spinoza see note 2 and Steven Nadler, 'The Bible Hermeneutics of Baruch de Spinoza', in Sæbø, *Hebrew Bible/Old Testament*, II:827–836.

78 Ibid.

79 Ibid., 142.

80 Ibid., 143.

81 Ibid., 144.

82 Ibid., 145.

83 See Reventlow, *Epochen der Bibelauslegung*, IV:31–78; 'English Rationalism, Deism and Early Biblical Criticism', in Sæbø, *Hebrew Bible/Old Testament*, II:851–874.

84 See Johannes Wallmann, 'Scriptural Understanding and Interpretation in Pietism', in Sæbø, *Hebrew Bible/Old Testament*, II:902–925.

85 Cited in Henning Graf Reventlow, *Epochen der Bibelauslegung*, vol. IV: *Von der Aufklärung bis zum 20. Jahrhundert* (Munich: C. H. Beck, 2001), 131.

86 See Martin Brecht, 'Johann Albrecht Bengels Theologie der Schrift', *Zeitschrift für Theologie und Kirche* 64 (1967): 106.

87 Reventlow, *Epochen der Bibelauslegung*, IV:141–142.

88 Ibid., IV:146.

89 *De Sacrae Scripturae interpretandae Methodo tractatus bipartitus, in quo Falsae Multorum Interpretum Hypotheses Refelluntur, veraque interpretandae Sacrae Scripturae Methodus adstruitur, Auctore Joanne Alphonso Turretino* [A Bipartite Tractate concerning the Method by which the Sacred Scriptures are to be interpreted, in which the false Hypotheses of Interpretation used by many are refuted, and the true Method by which the Sacred Scriptures are to be interpreted is presented by Jean Alphonse Turretini] (Trajecti Thuviorum, 1728), quoted in Kümmel, *The New Testament*, 58–60; 59.

90 For discussions see John Sandys-Wunsch, 'Early Old Testament Critics on the Continent', in Sæbø, *Hebrew Bible/Old Testament*, II:971–984; 976–980.

91 See Reventlow, *Epochen der Bibelauslegung*, IV:189, for a discussion of the appropriateness of this title. For a discussion of Michaelis see Sandys-Wunsch, 'Early Old Testament Critics on the Continent', 980–984.

92 J. S. Semler, 'Historische Einleitung in die dogmatische Gottesgelersamkeit', in S. J. Baumgarten (ed.), *Evangelische Glaubenslehre*, 3 vols. (Halle, 1759–60), vol. 2.

93 See Reventlow, *Epochen der Bibelauslegung*, IV:179.

94 J. S. Semler, *Abhandlung von freyer Untersuchung des Canon*, 4 vols. (Halle: C. H. Hemmerde, 1771-1775); reprinted as *Abhandlung von freier Untersuchung des Canon*, ed. by Heinz Scheible (Gütersloh: Mohn, 1967). See John Hayes, 'Historical Criticism of the Old Testament Canon', in Sæbø, *Hebrew Bible/Old Testament*, II:985–1005; 995–1005.

95 Quoted in Reventlow, *Epochen der Bibelauslegung*, IV:182.

96 Quoted in Reventlow, *Epochen der Bibelauslegung*, IV:184.

97 Ibid.

98 See Henning Graf Reventlow, 'Towards the End of the "Century of Enlightenment": Established Shift from *Sacra Scriptura* to Literary Documents and Religion of the People of Israel', in Sæbø, *Hebrew Bible/Old Testament*, II:1024–1063; 1051–1057.

99 An English translation is available in *Reimarus, Fragments*, edited by Charles H. Talbert, translated by Ralph S. Fraser (London: SCM, 1971). For a discussion of Reimarus' importance for biblical criticism see Christoph Bultmann, 'Early Rationalism and Biblical Criticism on the Continent', in Sæbø, *Hebrew Bible/Old Testament*, II:875–901; 878–884.

100 Albert Schweitzer, *The Quest of the Historical Jesus* (London: SCM, 2000), 14.

101 Bultmann, 'Early Rationalism and Biblical Criticism on the Continent', 893–901.

102 Lessing, 'On the Proof of the Spirit and of Power', *Lessing's Theological Writings*, selections in translation with an Introductory Essay by Henry Chadwick (London: Adam & Charles Black, 1956), 51–56.

103 *G. W. Leibniz's Monadology: An Edition for Students*, by Nicholas Rescher (London: Routledge, 1991), §33, p. 120.

104 G. W. Leibniz, *New Essays on Human Understanding*, translated and edited by Peter Remnant and Jonathan Bennett (Cambridge: Cambridge University Press, 1996), I.i.80.

105 G. W. Leibniz's *Monadology*, §33, p. 120.

106 Lessing, 'On the Proof of the Spirit and of Power', 52.

107 Ibid.

108 Ibid., 53.

109 Ibid.

110 Ibid.

111 Ibid. 54.

112 Ibid. 55.

113 Ibid. 55.

114 Lessing, 'The Education of the Human Race', § 4, in *Lessing's Theological Writings*, 82–98.

115 Ibid., §§ 52–58.

116 Ibid., § 85, original emphasis.

117 Reventlow, *Epochen der Bibelauslegung*, IV:210.

118 Ibid., IV:211.

119 Gabler, in Johann Gottfried Eichhorns *Urgeschichte*, edited with introduction and notes by Johann Philipp Gabler, 2 vols. (Altdorf and Nuremberg: Monath and Kussler, 1790–1792), I, Einleitung, 72; quoted in Reventlow, *Epochen der Bibelauslegung*, IV:212.

120 Reventlow, *Epochen der Bibelauslegung*, IV:219.

121 Ibid..

122 For discussion of Gabler see Reventlow, 'Towards the End of the "Century of Enlightenment"', 1057–1063.

123 Gabler, in Eichhorn, *Urgeschichte*, II, 482–490; quoted in Reventlow, *Epochen der Bibelauslegung*, IV:217–218.

124 Gabler, in Eichhorn, *Urgeschichte*, I, XV.

125 Georg Lorenz Bauer, *Hebräische Mythologie des Alten und Neuen Testaments, mit Parallelen aus der Mythologie anderer Völker, vornehmlich der Griechen und Römer*, 2 vols. (Leipzig: Weygand, 1802).

126 Quoted in Reventlow, *Epochen der Bibelauslegung*, IV:297.

127 For a study of de Wette see John W. Rogerson, *W. M. L. de Wette, Founder of Modern Biblical Criticism* (Sheffield: Sheffield Academic Press, 1992).

128 De Wette, *Beiträge* II, 1; quoted in Reventlow, *Epochen der Bibelauslegung*, IV:231.

129 De Wette, *Beiträge* II, 398; quoted in Reventlow, *Epochen der Bibelauslegung*, IV:232.

130   See Reventlow, *Epochen der Bibelauslegung*, IV:232–233.

131   Quoted in Reventlow, *Epochen der Bibelauslegung*, IV:232–233.

132   Wilhelm Martin Leberecht de Wette, *Lehrbuch der historisch-kritischen Einleitung in die kanonischen Bücher des Neuen Testaments* (Berlin: G. Reimer, 1826); ET: *An Historico-Critical Introduction to the Canonical Books of the New Testament*, translated from the fifth, improved and enlarged edition by Frederick Frothingham (Boston: Crosby, Nichols, and Company, 1858). *Kurzgefasstes exegetisches Handbuch zum Neuen Testament*, 3 vols. (Leipzig: S. Hirzel, 1836–48).

133   Heinrich Eberhard Gottlob Paulus, *Philologisch-kritischer und historischer Kommentar über die drey ersten Evangelien, in welchem der griechische Text, nach einer Recognition der Varianten, Interpunctionen und Abschnitte, durch Einleitungen, Inhaltsanzeigen und ununterbrochene Scholien als Grundlage der Geschichte des Urchristentums synoptisch und chronologisch bearbeitet ist*, 3 vols. (Lübeck: Johann Friedrich Bohn, 1800–1802); quoted in Kümmel, *The New Testament*, 91–93; 91.

134   Ibid.

135   Ibid.

136   Heinrich Eberhard Gottlob Paulus,, *Das Leben Jesu, als Grundlage einer reinen Geschichte des Urchristentums*, 4 vols. (Heidelberg: C. F. Winter, 1828).

137   Heinrich Eberhard Gottlob Paulus, *Exegetisches Handbuch über die drei ersten Evangelien* (Heidelberg: C. F. Winter, 1830–1833).

138   Karl Hase, *Das Leben Jesu: Ein Lehrbuch zunächst für akademische Vorlesungen* (Leipzig: Johann Friedrich Leich, 1829).

139   See Kümmel, *The New Testament*, 95–97.

140   Karl August Gottlieb Keil, *Lehrbuch der Hermeneutik des neuen Testaments nach Grundsätzen der grammatisch-historischen Interpretation* (Leipzig: Friedrich Christian Wilhelm Vogel, 1810).

141   Keil, *Lehrbuch der Hermeneutik*, 7.

142   L. I. Rückert, *Commentar über den Brief Pauli an die Römer* (Leipzig: Hartmannsche Buchhandlung, 1831).

143   Heinrich August Wilhelm Meyer, *Kritisch-exegetischer Kommentar über das Neue Testament*, 16 volumes (Göttingen: Vandenhoeck und Ruprecht, 1832–1859). ET: *Meyer's Commentary on the New Testament*, 20 vols. (Edinburgh: T. & T. Clark, 1873–1882).

144   Friedrich Düsterdieck, *Kritisch Exegetisches Handbuch über die Offenbarung Johannis* (Göttingen: Vandenhoeck und Ruprecht, 1859).

145   T & T Clark published all the volumes up to Jude. The final volume, namely Düsterdieck's commentary on the Johannine Apocalypse was published by the New York publisher Funk and Wagnalls. Friedrich Düsterdieck, *Critical and Exegetical Handbook to the Revelation of John*, trans. from the 3rd edn. of the German by Henry E. Jacobs (New York: Funk & Wagnalls, 1887).

146 Meyer's biblical commentaries continue to be published by Vandenhoeck & Ruprecht under the editorship of Dietrich-Alex Koch.

147 See Kümmel, *The New Testament*, 113–116.

148 F. D. E. Schleiermacher, *Hermeneutics: The Handwritten Manuscripts*, edited by Heinz Kimmerle, translated by James Duke and Jack Forstman (Atlanta, GA: Scholars Press, 1977), 112.

149 See, e.g., Werner G. Jeanrond, *Theological Hermeneutics: Development and Significance* (London: SCM, 1994), 44.

150 Theobald Ziegler, *David Friedrich Strauss*, 2 vols. (Strasbourg: Karl J. Trübner, 1908), I:197.

151 Wilhelm Vatke, *Die Religion des Alten Testaments nach den kanonischen Büchern entwickelt* (Berlin: G. Bethge, 1835). This work was intended to form the first part of the first volume of a larger work entitled *Die biblische Theologie wissenschaftlich dargestellt* [A Scientific Portrayal of Biblical Theology]. Due to the negative reaction provoked by *Die Religion des Alten Testaments* and in order to secure an academic position, however, Vatke decided not to publish any further parts of the work.

152 David Friedrich Strauss, *Das Leben Jesu, kritisch bearbeitet* (Tübingen: C. Osiander, 1835–36). ET: *The Life of Jesus, Critically Examined*, translated by Marian Evans (George Eliot) (London: Chapman Brothers, 1846).

153 Ziegler, *David Friedrich Strauss*, I:197.

154 Ibid., I:196–197.

155 Strauss, *Leben Jesu*, I: 71, emphasis added. I have been unable to locate this passage in the fourth edition. It seems to be one of the omissions Strauss made in the hope of making the work less provocative. Since George Eliot made her translation from the fourth edition, the passage is also absent from the English translation.

156 John Macquarrie, *Jesus Christ in Modern Thought* (London: SCM, 1990), 226.

157 Strauss, *Life of Jesus*, 86–87.

158 Ibid., 742.

159 Ibid., 87.

160 Ibid., 88.

161 Ibid.

162 Ibid., 89.

163 Ibid., 777–778.

164 David Friedrich Strauss, *Das Leben Jesu für das deutsche Volk bearbeitet* (Brockhaus: Leipzig, 1864); translated as *A New Life of Jesus* (London: Williams and Norgate, 1865).

165 F. C. Baur, 'Die Christuspartei in der korinthischen Gemeinde, der Gegensatz des petrinischen und paulinischen Christenthums in der ältesten Kirche, der

Apostel Petrus in Rom', *Tübinger Zeitschrift für Theologie* (1831, no. 4), 61–206.

166 Ferdinand Christian Baur, *Die sogenannten Pastoralbriefe des Apostels Paulus aufs neue kritisch untersucht* (Stuttgart and Tübingen: J. G. Cotta, 1835).

167 Ferdinand Christian Baur, *Das Christenthum und die Kirche der drei ersten Jahrhunderte* (Tübingen: L. Fr. Fues, 1853).

168 Karl Lachmann, 'De ordine narrationum in evangeliis synopticis', in *Theologische Studien und Kritiken* 8 (1835), 570–590. An abbreviated translation of Lachmann's essay can be found in N. H. Palmer, 'Lachmann's Argument', *New Testament Studies* 13/4 (1967), 368–378.

169 Christian Gottlob Wilke, *Der Urevangelist: Oder Exegetisch Kritische Untersuchung über das Verwandtschaftsverhältnis der ersten drei Evangelien* (Dresden and Leipzig: Gerhard Fleischer, 1838).

170 Christian Hermann Weisse, *Die evangelische Geschichte kritisch und philosophisch bearbeitet*, 2 vols. (Leipzig: Breitkopf and Härtel, 1838).

171 Frederick Temple et al., *Essays and Reviews* (London: John W. Parker and Son, 1860). For discussions of the reaction to *Essays and Reviews* see Vernon F. Storr, *The Development of English Theology in the Nineteenth Century: 1800–1860* (London: Longmans, Green and Co., 1913), 429–454; L. E. Elliott-Binns, *Religion in the Victorian Era* (London and Redhill: Lutterworth Press, 1946), 146–149; Owen Chadwick, *The Victorian Church*, 2 parts (London: SCM, 1970–1972), 2: 75–97.

172 Benjamin Jowett, 'On the Interpretation of Scripture', in *Essays and Reviews*, 330–433; 339.

173 See John W. Rogerson, *The Bible and Criticism in Victorian Britain: Profiles of F. D. Maurice and William Robertson Smith* (Sheffield: Sheffield Academic Press, 1997). Gillian M. Bediako, *Primal Religion and the Bible: William Robertson Smith and His Heritage* (Sheffield: Sheffield Academic Press, 1997). Bernhard Maier, *William Robertson Smith* (Tübingen: Mohr Siebeck, 2009).

174 Charles Gore (ed.), *Lux Mundi* (London: John Murray, 1889).

175 Albrecht Ritschl, *Die christliche Lehre von der Rechtfertigung und Versöhnung*, 3 vols. (Bonn: Adolph Marcus, 1870–1874); ET: *The Christian Doctrine of Justification and Reconciliation: the Positive Development of the Doctrine*, translated by H. R. Mackintosh and A. B. Macaulay (Edinburgh: T. & T. Clark, 1900). Willibald Herrmann, *Der Verkehr des Christen mit Gott: Im Anschluss an Luther dargestellt* (Stuttgart: Cotta, 1886); ET: *The Communion of the Christian with God: A Discussion in Agreement with the View of Luther*, translated from the second thoroughly revised edition, with special annotations by the author, by J. Sandys Stanyon (London: Williams and Norgate, 1895). Adolf von Harnack, *Das Wesen des Christentums. Sechzehn Vorlesungen vor Studierenden aller Facultäten im Wintersemester 1899/1900 an der Universität Berlin gehalten* (Leipzig: J. C. Hinrichs'sche Buchhandlung, 1900); ET: *What is Christianity? Sixteen Lectures Delivered in the University of Berlin during the Winter-Term 1899–1900*, translated by Thomas Bailey Saunders (London: Williams and Norgate, 1901).

176 Ernest Renan, *Vie de Jésus* (Paris: Michel Levy Frère, 1863); ET: *The Life of Jesus* (London: Trubner & Co., 1863). F. W. Farrar, *The Life of Christ* (London: Cassell Petter and Galpin, 1872).

177 Franz Overbeck, *Ueber die Christlichkeit unserer heutigen Theologie. Streit- und Friedensschrift* (Leipzig: Fritzsch, 1873). In the second edition of 1903 (Leipzig: Naumann), Overbeck removed the subtitle. English translations: *On the Christianity of Theology*, trans. and ed. by John Elbert Wilson (San Jose, California: Pickwick 2002) and *How Christian is our Present-Day Theology?*, translated and edited by Martin Henry, with a foreword by David Tracy (London: T & T Clark/Continuum 2005.) Franz Overbeck, *Christentum und Kultur. Gedanken und Anmerkungen zur modernen Theologie* (Basel: Schwabe 1919).

178 Overbeck, *Christentum und Kultur*, 8.

179 Johannes Weiss, *Die Predigt Jesu vom Reiche Gottes* (Göttingen: Vandenhoeck & Ruprecht, 1892; 2nd revised edition, 1900); ET: *Jesus' Proclamation of the Kingdom of God*, translated, edited and with an introduction by Richard Hyde Hiers and David Larrimore Holland (Philadelphia: Fortress Press, 1971).

180 Weiss, *Jesus' Proclamation of the Kingdom of God*, 131.

181 Albert Schweitzer, *The Mystery of the Kingdom of God: the Secret of Jesus' Messiahship and Passion*, translated with an introduction by Walter Lowrie (New York: Dodd, Mead and Company, 1914). First published under the title of *Das Messianitäts- und Leidensgeheimnis: Eine Skizze des Lebens Jesu* as the second part of *Das Abendmahl im Zusammenhang mit dem Leben Jesu und der Geschichte des Urchristentums* (Tübingen and Leipzig: J. C. B. Mohr (Paul Siebeck), 1901).

182 Albert Schweitzer, *Von Reimarus zu Wrede: Eine Geschichte der Leben-Jesu-Forschung* (Tübingen: J. C. B. Mohr (Paul Siebeck), 1906); ET: *The Quest of the Historical Jesus*, 1st complete edition, edited by John Bowden (London: SCM, 2000), 479–480.

183 Schweitzer, *Quest of the Historical Jesus*, 480.

184 Ibid.

185 Martin Kähler, *Der sogenannte historische Jesus und der geschichtliche biblische Christus* (Leipzig: A. Deichert, 1892), 22; quoted in Kümmel, *The New Testament*, 224. ET: Martin Kähler, *The So-Called Historical Jesus and the Historic, Biblical Christ*, translated by Carl E. Braaten (Philadelphia: Fortress Press, 1964).

186 Kähler, *Der sogenannte historische Jesus*, 4; quoted in Kümmel, *The New Testament*, 223.

187 Quoted in Kümmel, *The New Testament*, 223.

188 Quoted in Grant with Tracy, *Interpretation of the Bible*, 123.

189 Wilhelm Wrede, *Das Messiasgeheimnis in den Evangelien: zugleich ein Beitrag zum Verständnis des Markusevangeliums* (Göttingen: Vandenhoeck & Ruprecht, 1901); ET: *The Messianic Secret*, trans. by J. C. G. Greig (Cambridge: James Clarke, 1971) .

190 Adolf Hausrath, *Neutestamentliche Zeitgeschichte*, I, ix; quoted in Kümmel, *The New Testament*, 206.

191 Otto Pfleiderer, *Die Entstehung des Christentums*, 1; quoted in Riches, *Century of New Testament Study*, 7. ET: Otto Pfleiderer, *Christian Origins* (London: Fisher Unwin, 1906).

192 Pfleiderer, *Die Entstehung des Christentums*, 16; quoted in Riches, *Century of New Testament Study*, 8.

193 H. Gunkel, Review of M. Reischle's 'Theologie und Religionsgeschichte', in *Deutsche Literaturzeitung*, 25 (1904), 1109; quoted in Kümmel, *The New Testament*, 307.

194 Hermann Gunkel, *Zum religionsgeschichtlichen Verständnis des Neuen Testaments* (Göttingen: Vandenhoeck & Ruprecht, 1903); selections quoted in Kümmel, *The New Testament*, 258–259.

195 R. Reitzenstein *Die hellenistischen Mysterienreligionen* (Leipzig and Berlin: B. G. Teubner, 1910; 2nd revised edn. 1920); ET: Richard Reitzenstein, *The Hellenistic Mystery-Religions: Their Basic Ideas and Significance*, trans. by John E. Steely (Pittsburgh: Pickwick Publications, 1979); R. Reitzenstein, *Das iranische Erlösungsmysterium: religionsgeschichtliche Untersuchungen* (Bonn: Marcus & Weber, 1921).

196 Wilhelm Bousset, *Kyrios Christos: Geschichte des Christusglaubens von den Anfängen des Christentums bis Irenaeus* (Göttingen: Vandenhoeck & Ruprecht, 1913); ET: *Kyrios Christos: A History of the Belief in Christ from the Beginnings of Christianity to Irenaeus*, trans. by John E. Steely, intro. by Rudolf Bultmann (Nashville: Abingdon Press, 1970).

197 Martin Dibelius, *Die Geisterwelt im Glauben des Paulus* (Göttingen: Vandenhoeck & Ruprecht, 1909); *Die urchristliche Überlieferung von Johannes dem Täufer* (Göttingen: Vandenhoeck & Ruprecht, 1911). Rudolf Bultmann, *Der Stil der paulinischen Predigt und die kynischstoische Diatribe* (Göttingen: Vandenhoeck & Ruprecht, 1910); 'Das religiöse Moment in der ethischen Unterweisung des Epiktet und das Neue Testament', *Zeitschrift für die neutestamentliche Wissenschaft und die Kunde der älteren Kirche*, 13 (1912), 177–191.

198 Krister Stendahl, 'Biblical Theology, Contemporary', first published in *The Interpreter's Dictionary of the Bible*, 4 vols. (Nashville: Abingdon Press, 1962), 1:418–32; reprinted in Heikki Räisänen, Elisabeth Schüssler Fiorenza, R. S. Sugirtharajah, Krister Stendahl, James Barr, *Reading the Bible in the Global Village: Helsinki* (Atlanta: Society of Biblical Literature, 2000), 67–106. References are to the latter edition.

199 Stendahl, 'Biblical Theology, Contemporary', 69.

200 Ibid. 70.

201 Ibid.

202 Ibid.

203 Ibid.

204 Ibid.

205 Ibid.

206 Paul Billerbeck, *Kommentar zum Neuen Testament aus Talmud und Midrasch*, 4 vols. (Munich: Beck, 1922–1928).

207 Gerhard Kittel, *Die Probleme des palästinischen Spätjudentums und das Urchristentum* (Stuttgart: Kohlhammer, 1926).

208 Julius Schniewind, *Euangelion. Ursprung und erste Gestalt des Begriffs Evangelium*, 2 parts (Gütersloh: 1927, 1931).

209 Bultmann, 'Der religionsgeschichtliche Hintergrund des Prologs zum Johannes-Evangelium', in Hans Schmidt (ed.), *Eucharisterion: Studien zur Religion und Literatur des Alten und Neuen Testaments: Hermann Gunkel zum 60. Geburtstage*, 2 parts (Göttingen: Vandenhoeck & Ruprecht, 1923), 2:1–26; 'Die Bedeutung der neu erschlossenen mandäischen und manichäischen Quellen für das Verständnis des Johannesevangeliums', *Zeitschrift für die neutestamentliche Wissenschaft und die Kunde der älteren Kirche* 24 (1925). Both essays reprinted in Bultmann, *Exegetica: Aufsätze zur Erforschung des Neuen Testaments* (J. C. B. Mohr (Paul Siebeck), 1967).

210 Walter Bauer, *Das Johannesevangelium erklärt* [The Gospel of John Explained] (Tübingen: J. C. B. Mohr (Paul Siebeck), ²1925).

211 Ernst Lohmeyer, *Die Offenbarung des Johannes* [The Revelation of John] (Tübingen: J. C. B. Mohr (Paul Siebeck), 1926).

212 Hans Windisch, *Der Hebräerbrief erklärt* [The Letter to the Hebrews explained] (Tübingen: J. C. B. Mohr (Paul Siebeck), ²1931).

213 Karl Holl, *Urchristentum und Religionsgeschichte* (Gütersloh: C. Bertelsmann, 1925); ET: *The Distinctive Elements in Christianity*, translated by N. V. Hope (Edinburgh: T & T Clark, 1937).

214 Gerhard Kittel (ed.), *Theologisches Wörterbuch zum Neuen Testament*, 10 vols. (Stuttgart: W. Kohlhammer, 1933–1979). ET: *Theological Dictionary of the New Testament*, trans. by Geoffrey W. Bromiley 10 vols. (Grand Rapids, Mich.: Eerdmans, 1964–1976.

215 Karl Barth, *Der Römerbrief* (Munich: C. Kaiser, ¹1919, ²1922). ET: *The Epistle to the Romans*, trans. from the sixth edn. by Edwyn C. Hoskyns (London: Oxford University Press, 1933).

216 Karl Girgensohn, 'Geschichtliche und übergeschichtliche Schriftauslegung' [Historical and Suprahistorical Interpretation of Scripture], in *Allgemeine Evangelisch-lutherische Kirchenzeitung*, 55 (1922), for selections see Kümmel, *The New Testament*, 371–372; Girgensohn, 'Die Grenzgebiete der systematischen Theologie', *Greifswalder Reformgedanken zum theologischen Studium* (Munich, 1922), 90–91. See also Albrecht Oepke, *Geschichtliche und übergeschichtliche Schriftauslegung* (Gütersloh: Bertelsmann, 1931).

217 Bultmann, *Jesus and the Word* (New York: Charles Scribner's Sons, 1934); selections quoted in Kümmel, 373–376.

218 Ernst Fuchs, *Zur Frage nach dem historischen Jesus* (Tübingen: J. C. B. Mohr (Paul Siebeck), 1960); ET: *Studies of the Historical Jesus* (London: SCM, 1964).

219 Gerhard Ebeling, *Das Wesen des christlichen Glaubens* (Tübingen: J. C. B. Mohr (Paul Siebeck), 1959); ET: *The Nature of Faith*, trans. by Ronald Gregor Smith (London: Collins, 1961). See also his *Introduction to a Theological Theory of Language*, trans. by R. A. Wilson (London: Collins, 1973).

220 See also Cornelius van Til, *The New Hermeneutic* (Nutley, NJ: Presbyterian and Reformed Publishing Co., 1974), esp. 1–18.

221 James M. Robinson and John B. Cobb (eds), *The New Hermeneutic*, 2 vols. (New York: Harper & Row, 1964).

222 Ernst Käsemann, 'Das Problem des historischen Jesus', in Ernst Käsemann, *Exegetische Versuche und Besinnungen*, vol.I (Göttingen: Vandenhoeck und Ruprecht, 1960), 187–214. ET: 'The Problem of the Historical Jesus', in Ernst Käsemann, *Essays on New Testament Themes*, translated by W. J. Montague (London: SCM, 1964).

223 Günther Bornkamm, *Jesus of Nazareth* (London: Hodder & Stoughton, 1960). See also Ferdinand Hahn, Wenzel Lohff, Günther Bornkamm, *What can we know about Jesus? Essays on the New Quest*, translated by Grover Foley (Philadelphia: Fortress, 1969).

224 Ernst Fuchs, *Studies of the Historical Jesus* (London: SCM, 1964).

225 Gerhard Ebeling, 'The Question of the Historical Jesus and the Problem of Christology', in *Word and Faith*, 288–304.

226 Hans Conzelmann, *Jesus* (Philadelphia: Fortress, 1973); first published as an essay in 1958.

227 James M. Robinson, *A New Quest of the Historical Jesus* (London: SCM, 1959).

228 'The General Council of Trent, Fourth Session (8 April 1546)', in J. Neuner S.J. and J. Dupuis S. J., *The Christian Faith in the Doctrinal Documents of the Catholic Church*, ed. by Jacques Dupuis, sixth revised and enlarged edition (New York: Alba House, 1996), pp. 97–98.

229 'The First Vatican General Council, Third Session: Dogmatic Constitution *Dei Filius* on the Catholic Faith (1870)', in Neuner and Dupuis, *The Christian Faith in the Doctrinal Documents of the Catholic Church*, p. 99.

230 For discussions of Simon see J. Steinmann, *Biblical Criticism* (London: Burns & Oates, 1959), 46–48. Kraus, *Geschichte der historisch-kritischen Erforschung des Alten Testaments*, 59–64. David Weiss Halivni, *Revelation Restored: Divine Writ and Critical Responses* (London: SCM, 2001). John W. Rogerson, 'Early Old Testament Critics in the Roman Catholic Church – Focussing on the Pentateuch', in Sæbø, *Hebrew Bible/Old Testament*, II:837–850; 838–843.

231 Pius X, 'Decree *Lamentabili* of the Holy Office (1907): Articles of Modernism Condemned', in Neuner and Dupuis, *The Christian Faith in the Doctrinal Documents of the Catholic Church*, pp. 102–103.

232 Encyclical Letter ('Pascendi Gregis') of Our Most Holy Lord Pius X: On the Doctrine of the Modernists (London: Burns & Oates, 1907).

233 'Encyclical Letter *Divino Afflante Spiritu* (1943)', in Neuner and Dupuis, *The Christian Faith in the Doctrinal Documents of the Catholic Church*, pp. 106–109.

234 'Instruction of the Biblical Commission *Sancta Mater Ecclesia* (1964) on the Historical Truth of the Gospels', in Neuner and Dupuis, *The Christian Faith in the Doctrinal Documents of the Catholic Church*, pp. 111–113.

For an assessment of the Instruction see Joseph A. Fitzmyer, S. J., 'The Biblical Commission's Instruction on the Historical Truth of the Gospels', *Theological Studies* 25 (1964), 386–408.

235 'Dogmatic Constitution on Divine Revelation', *The Documents of Vatican II*, ed. Walter M. Abbott, S. J. (New York: Herder and Herder, 1966), para III, 12: 120–121.

236 Pontifical Biblical Institute, *The Interpretation of the Bible in the Church* (Rome: Libreria editrice vaticana, 1993). Excerpts in Neuner and Dupuis, *The Christian Faith in the Doctrinal Documents of the Catholic Church*, pp. 130–134.

237 For a Roman Catholic defence of historical criticism see Joseph A. Fitzmyer, S.J., *The Interpretation of Scripture: In Defense of the Historical–Critical Method* (New York/Mahweh, NJ: Paulist Press, 2008). See also Joseph G. Prior, *The Historical Critical Method in Catholic Exegesis* (Rome: Gregorian University Press, 2001).

238 Fernando F. Segovia, *Decolonizing Biblical Studies: A View from the Margins* (Maryknoll, NY: Orbis Books, 2000), 3.

239 Segovia, *Decolonizing Biblical Studies*, 9 n. 8.

240 Peter Stuhlmacher, *Historical Criticism and Theological Interpretation of Scripture: Towards a Hermeneutic of Consent*, translated by Roy A. Harrisville (London: SPCK, 1979), 19.

241 Ibid., 20–21.

242 Ibid., 21.

243 N. R. Petersen, *Literary Criticism for New Testament Critics* (Philadelphia: Fortress Press, 1978), 9–10.

244 Segovia, *Decolonizing Biblical Studies*, 8.

245 Elisabeth Schüssler Fiorenza, 'Biblical Interpretation and Critical Commitment', *Studia Theologica* 43 (1989), 5-18, reprinted in Yarchin, *History of Biblical Interpretation*, 385–397; 386.

246 Schüssler Fiorenza, 'Biblical Interpretation and Critical Commitment', 389.

247 Schüssler Fiorenza, 'The Ethics of Biblical Interpretation: Decentering Biblical Scholarship', first published in *Journal of Biblical Literature* 107 (1988), 3–17; reprinted in Räisänen et al., *Reading the Bible in the Global Village: Helsinki*, 107–123; 119, original emphasis. Cf. 'Biblical Interpretation and Critical Commitment', 391–392; 'Defending the Center, Trivializing the Margins', in Räisänen et al., *Reading the Bible in the Global Village: Helsinki*, 29–48; 43–48; *Rhetoric and Ethic: The Politics of Biblical Studies* (Minneapolis: Fortress, 1999).

248 Schüssler Fiorenza, 'Ethics of Biblical Interpretation', 120, original emphasis.

249 Segovia, *Decolonizing Biblical Studies*, 5.

250 Ibid., 7.

251 Ibid.

252 Ibid., 6.

253 Edgar V. McKnight, *The Bible and the Reader: An Introduction to Literary Criticism* (Minneapolis, MN: Fortress, 1985), a section of which is reprinted in Yarchin, *History of Biblical Interpretation*, 377–382; 377.

254 McKnight, *The Bible and the Reader*, 377.

255 Ibid.

256 Odil Hannes Steck, *Old Testament Exegesis: A Guide to the Methodology*, translated by James D. Nogalski (Atlanta, Ga.: Scholars Press, 1995), 24.

257 Heikki Räisänen, 'Biblical Critics in the Global Village', in Räisänen et al., *Reading the Bible in the Global Village: Helsinki*, 9–28; 20, 22.

258 Schüssler Fiorenza, 'Defending the Center, Trivializing the Margins', in Räisänen et al., *Reading the Bible in the Global Village: Helsinki*, 29–48; 29.

259 Ibid., 35.

260 For surveys of recent scholarship in Biblical Studies see J. W. Rogerson, 'History of the Discipline in the Last Seventy Years: Old Testament', in J. W. Rogerson and Judith M. Lieu, *The Oxford Handbook of Biblical Studies* (Oxford: 2010), 5–26, and Robert Morgan, 'New Testament', in Rogerson and Lieu, *Oxford Handbook of Biblical Studies*, 27–49.

261 For a discussion of the relationship between historical criticism and the social sciences see Stephen C. Barton, 'Historical Criticism and Social-Scientific Perspectives in New Testament Study', in Green, *Hearing the New Testament*, 61–89.

262 Rogerson, 'History of the Discipline in the Last Seventy Years: Old Testament', 16.

263 See, for example, Hans G. Kippenberg, *Religion und Klassenbildung im antiken Judäa. Eine religionssoziologische Studie zum Verhältnis von Tradition und gesellschaftlicher Entwicklung* (Göttingen: Vandenhoeck & Ruprecht, ¹1978, ²1982).

264 Gerd Theissen, *The First Followers of Jesus: Sociological Study of the Earliest Christianity*, translated by John Bowden (London: SCM, 1978); *The Social Setting of Pauline Christianity: Essays on Corinth*, edited and translated with an introduction by John H. Schütz (Edinburgh: T & T Clark, 1982); *Social Reality and the Early Christians: Theology, Ethics, and the World of the New Testament* (Minneapolis: Fortress Press, 1992); *The Gospels in Context: Social and Political History in the Synoptic Tradition*, translated by Linda M. Maloney (Edinburgh: T & T Clark, 1992).

265 Wayne Meeks, *The Social World of the First Christians* (New Haven: Yale University Press, 1983); *The Origins of Christian Morality* (New Haven: Yale University Press, 1993); *In Search of the Early Christians: Selected Essays* (New Haven: Yale University Press, 2002).

266 Bruce Malina, *The New Testament World: Insights from Cultural Anthropology* (Atlanta: John Knox, ¹1981, ²1993, ³2001).

267 E. P. Sanders, *Paul and Palestinian Judaism: A Comparison of Patterns of Religion* (London: SCM, 1977); *Paul, the Law and the Jewish People* (Philadelphia: Fortress Press, 1983).

268 Heikki Räisänen, *Paul and the Law* (Tübingen: J. C. B. Mohr, 11983, 21987).

269 Francis Watson, *Paul, Judaism and the Gentiles: A Sociological Approach* (Cambridge: Cambridge University Press, 1986); revised ed.: *Paul, Judaism and the Gentiles: Beyond the New Perspective* (Grand Rapids, Mich.: William B. Eerdmans, 2007).

270 E. P. Sanders, *Jesus and Judaism* (London: SCM, 1985); *The Historical Figure of Jesus* (Harmondsworth, Middlesex: Penguin, 1993).

271 Geza Vermes, *Jesus the Jew: A Historian's Reading of the Gospels* (London: Collins, 1973); *Jesus and the World of Judaism* (London: SCM, 1983); *The Religion of Jesus the Jew* (London: SCM, 1993); *The Passion* (London: Penguin, 2005); *The Nativity: History and Legend* (London: Penguin, 2006); *The Resurrection* (London: Penguin, 2008).

272 Gerd Theissen, *The Shadow of the Galilean* (London: SCM, 1987); Gerd Theissen and Annette Merz, *The Historical Jesus: A Comprehensive Guide*, translated by John Bowden (London: SCM, 1998); Gerd Theissen and Dagmar Winter, *The Quest for the Plausible Jesus: The Essential Problem of the Criterion*, translated by M. Eugen Boring (Louisville, KA: Westminster/ John Knox Press, 2002).

273 Among his many works see esp. John Dominic Crossan, *The Historical Jesus: the Life of a Mediterranean Jewish Peasant* (Edinburgh: T & T Clark, 1991); *Who Killed Jesus? Exposing the Roots of Anti-Semitism in the Gospel Story of the Death of Jesus* (San Francisco: HarperSanFrancisco, 1995); *The Birth of Christianity: Discovering What Happened in the Years Immediately After the Execution of Jesus* (San Francisco: Harper SanFrancisco, 1998); *Jesus: A Revolutionary Biography* (London: Harper Collins, 2009).

274 Raymond Brown, *The Death of the Messiah* (London: G. Chapman, 1994).

275 N. T. Wright, *Jesus and the Victory of God* (London: SPCK, 1996). See also Marcus Borg and N. T. Wright, *The Meaning of Jesus: Two Visions* (San Francisco: Harper, 11999, 22007).

276 John P. Meier, *A Marginal Jew: Rethinking the Historical Jesus*, 4 vols. (New Haven: Yale University Press, 1991–2009).

277 James D. G. Dunn, *The Evidence for Jesus: the Impact of Scholarship on our Understanding of how Christianity Began* (London: SCM, 1985); *Jesus Remembered* (Grand Rapids, MI: Eerdmans, 2003). See also James D. G. Dunn and Scot McKnight (eds), *The Historical Jesus in Recent Research* (Winona Lake, IN.: Eisenbrauns, 2005).

278 Richard Bauckham, *Jesus and the Eyewitnesses: The Gospels as Eyewitness Testimony* (Grand Rapids, MI: Eerdmans, 2006).

279 Dale C. Allison, Jr., *The Historical Jesus and the Theological Jesus* (Grand Rapids, MI: Eerdmans, 2009); *Constructing Jesus: Memory, Imagination, and History* (Grand Rapids, MI: Baker Academic, 2010).

280 James A. Sanders, *Torah and Canon* (Philadelphia: Fortress Press, 1972); *From Sacred Story to Sacred Text: Canon as Paradigm* (Philadelphia: Fortress Press, 1987). Brevard S. Childs, *Introduction to the Old Testament as Scripture* (London: SCM, 1979); *The New Testament as Canon: An Introduction* (London: SCM, 1984).

Chapter Three

1 For literature on textual criticism see G. D. Kilpatrick, 'Western Text and Original Text in the Gospels and Acts', *Journal of Theological Studies*, xliv (1943), 24–36. 'Western Text and Original Text in the Epistles', *Journal of Theological Studies*, xlv (1944), 60–5. Bleddyn J. Roberts, *The Old Testament Text and Versions* (Cardiff: University of Wales Press, 1951). Heinz Zimmermann, *Neutestamentliche Methodenlehre: Darstellung der Historisch-Kritischen Methode* (Stuttgart: Kath. Bibelwerk, 1966), 32–82. Shemaryahu Talmon, 'The Old Testament Text', in Ackroyd and Evans, *Cambridge History of the Bible*, 1:155–99. J. N. Birdsall, 'The New Testament Text', in *Cambridge History of the Bible*, 1:308–76. Jack Finegan, *Encountering New Testament Manuscripts: A Working Introduction to Textual Criticism* (Grand Rapids, MI: Eerdmans, 1974). Bruce M. Metzger, *The Early Versions of the New Testament: Their Origin, Transmission, and Limitations* (Oxford: Oxford University Press, 1977). B. J. Roberts, 'The Textual Transmission of the Old Testament', in G. W. Anderson (ed.), *Tradition and Interpretation* (Oxford: Oxford University Press, 1979), 1–30. E. J. Epp and G. D. Fee (eds), *New Testament Textual Criticism – Its Significance for Exegesis: Essays in Honour of Bruce M. Metzger* (Oxford: Clarendon Press, 1981). J. Weingreen, *Introduction to the Critical Study of the Text of the Hebrew Bible* (Oxford: Clarendon, 1982). Kurt and Barbara Aland, *The Text of the New Testament: An Introduction to the Critical Editions and to the Theory and Practice of Modern Textual Criticism*, translated by Erroll F. Rhodes (Grand Rapids: Eerdmans/Leiden: Brill, 1987). Emanuel Tov, *Textual Criticism of the Hebrew Bible* (Minneapolis: Fortress Press, 1992). Ellis R. Brotzman, *Old Testament Textual Criticism: A Practical Introduction* (Grand Rapids, Michigan: Baker Books, 1994). Ernst Würthwein, *The Text of the Old Testament: An Introduction to the Biblia Hebraica*, trans. by Erroll F. Rhodes (Grand Rapids, Michigan: William B. Eerdmans, ²1995). Bart D. Ehrman, 'Textual Criticism of the New Testament', in Green, *Hearing the New Testament*, 127–45. P. Kyle McCarter Jr., *Textual Criticism: Recovering the Text of the Hebrew Bible* (Philadelphia: Fortress, 1986). Christopher Tuckett, *Reading the New Testament* (London: SPCK, 1987), 21–40. G. D. Kilpatrick, *The Principles and Practice of New Testament Textual Criticism: Collected*

Essays, ed. by J. K. Elliott (Leuven: Leuven University Press/Peeters, 1990). J. K. Elliott, *Essays and Studies in New Testament Textual Criticism*, 3 vols. (Cordoba: Ediciones el Almendro, 1992). E. J. Epp and G. D. Fee, *Studies in the Theory and Method of New Testament Textual Criticism* (Grand Rapids: Eerdmans, 1993). Bruce M. Metzger, *A Textual Commentary on the Greek New Testament* (London, New York: United Bible Societies, ²1994). Steck, *Old Testament Exegesis*, 39–47. J. K. Elliott and I. Moir, *Manuscripts and the Text of the New Testament: An Introduction for English Readers* (Edinburgh: T & T Clark, 1995). Bart D. Ehrman and Michael W. Holmes, *The Text of the New Testament in Contemporary Research: Essays on the Status Quaestionis* (Grand Rapids, Mich.: Eerdmans, 1995). Eldon Jay Epp, 'Textual Criticism in the Exegesis of the New Testament, with an Excursus on Canon', in Stanley J. Porter (ed.), *Handbook to Exegesis of the New Testament* (Leiden: Brill, 1997), 45–97. Bruce M. Metzger and Bart D. Ehrman, *The Text of the New Testament: its Transmission, Corruption, and Restoration* (Oxford: Oxford University Press, ⁴2005). Paul D. Wegner, *A Student's Guide to Textual Criticism of the Bible: its History, Methods & Results* (Downers Grove, IL: InterVarsity Press, 2006). Russell Fuller, 'The Text of the Tanak', in Hauser and Watson, *A History of Biblical Interpretation*, 2:201–26. J. K. Elliott, 'The Text of the New Testament', in Hauser and Watson, *A History of Biblical Interpretation*, 2: 227–53. Arie van der Kooij, 'Textual Criticism', *Oxford Handbook of Biblical Studies*, 579–90.

2 See Solomon Grayzel, *A History of the Jews from the Babylonian Exile to the Present 5728–1968* (New York and Toronto: The New American Library, 1968), 240.

3 Ibid., 241–42.

4 For discussions of the Tiberian Masoretes see Moshe H. Goshen-Gottstein, 'The Rise of the Tiberian Bible Text', in Sid Z. Leiman (ed.), *The Canon and Masorah of the Hebrew Bible* (New York: Ktav, 1974). Israel Yeivin, *Introduction to the Tiberian Masorah*, translated and edited by E. J. Revell (Atlanta: Society of Biblical Literature, 1980).

5 See Paul Kahle, *The Cairo Geniza* (Oxford: Blackwell, 2nd revised edn. 1959). An inventory and digitization of all Cairo Genizah manuscripts is currently being undertaken by the Friedberg Genizah Project: http://www.genizah.org/

6 See Frank M. Cross, *The Ancient Library of Qumran and Modern Biblical Studies* (Grand Rapids, MI: Baker, 1980).

7 Brotzman, *Old Testament Textual Criticism*, 94. Tov, *Textual Criticism of the Hebrew Bible*, 115.

8 See Cross, *The Ancient Library of Qumran and Modern Biblical Studies*, 181–6; also Frank M. Cross, 'The Contribution of the Qumran Discoveries to the Study of the Biblical Text', in Frank M. Cross and Shemaryahu Talmon (eds), *Qumran and the History of the Biblical Text* (Cambridge: Harvard University Press, 1975), 278–92; 279–80. Bruce K. Waltke, 'The Samaritan Pentateuch and the Text of the Old Testament', in J. B. Payne (ed.), *New*

Perspectives on the Old Testament (Waco: Word, 1979), 212–39. Tov, *Textual Criticism of the Hebrew Bible*, 19, 81–2.

9 Tov, *Textual Criticism of the Hebrew Bible*, 116–17.

10 Ronald S. Hendel, 'Assessing the Text-Critical Theories of the Hebrew Bible after Qumran', in Timothy H. Lim and John J. Collins (eds), *Oxford Handbook of the Dead Sea Scrolls* (Oxford: Oxford University Press, 2010), 281–302; 293.

11 The discovery of the Dead Dea Scrolls has also helped to resolve some of the textual difficulties of the Masoretic text. For example, the awkwardness of the transition from 1 Sam. 10.27 to 11.1 has been removed through the discovery of a continuation of 1 Sam. 10.27 in 4QSamᵃ. The truncated and puzzling version of 1 Sam. 10.27 in the Masoretic text seems to have come about as a result of a scribal error, which the textual witness of the Dead Sea Scrolls has been able to rectify. An English translation of the restored verse has now been incorporated into the NRSV.

12 Eugene Ulrich, *The Dead Sea Scrolls and the Origins of the Bible* (Grand Rapids: William B. Eerdmans, 1999), 11.

13 Ibid., 24.

14 Ibid., 51.

15 Ibid., 12.

16 George Brooke, 'The Qumran Scrolls and the Demise of the Distinction between Higher and Lower Criticism', in Jonathan G. Campbell, William John Lyons and Lloyd K. Pietersen (eds), *New Directions in Qumran Studies* (London, New York: T & T Clark International, 2005), 26–42; 31. For other recent discussions of the significance of the Dead Sea Scrolls for textual criticism see Tov, *Textual Criticism of the Hebrew Bible*, 313–50; Ulrich, *The Dead Sea Scrolls and the Origins of the Bible*.

17 There is some disagreement about the exact number of agreements. Würthwein cites 1900, while Klein identifies only 1600. Würthwein, *Text of the Old Testament*, 46. Ralph W. Klein, *Textual Criticism of the Old Testament* (Philadelphia: Fortress, 1974), 17.

18 Paul Kahle, 'Untersuchungen zur Geschichte des Pentateuchtextes', *Theologische Studien und Kritiken* 88 (1915), 399–439; reprinted in *Opera Minor: Festgabe zum 21. Januar 1956* (Leiden: Brill, 1956), 3–37.

19 Würthwein, *Text of the Old Testament*, 39 n. 86.

20 Yeivin, *Introduction to the Tiberian Masorah*, 31.

21 Würthwein, *Text of the Old Testament*, 39.

22 See Ronald Hendel, 'The Oxford Hebrew Bible: Prologue to a New Critical Edition', *Vetus Testamentum* 58 (2008), 324–51. http://ohb.berkeley.edu/

23 For discussions of Erasmus' contribution to textual criticism see Rummel, 'The Textual and Hermeneutic Work of Desiderius Erasmus of Rotterdam', 215–30. Elliott, 'The Text of the New Testament', 232–37.

24 For a discussion of Erasmus and Beza see Jans Krans, *Beyond What is Written: Erasmus and Beza as Conjectural Critics of the New Testament* (Leiden: Brill, 2006).

25 Spinoza, *Tractatus Theologico-Politicus*, 145.

26 Richard Simon, *Histoire critique du Vieux Testament* (Rotterdam: Reinier Leers, ¹1678, ²1685).

27 John Mill, *Novum Testamentum Graecum cum lectionibus variantibus* (Amsterdam, 1710).

28 Kümmel, *The New Testament*, 47–8.

29 J. A. Bengel, *Novum Testamentum Graecum ita adornatum ut Textus probatarum editionum medullam. Margo variantium lectionum in suas classes distributarum locorumque parallelorum delectum. Apparatus subjunctus criseos sacrae Millianae praesertim compendium, limam, supplementum ac fructum inserviente* [Greek New Testament . . . with variant readings in the margin . . . and apparatus attached. . .] (Tübingen: Georg Cotta, 1734).

30 Quoted in Kümmel, *The New Testament*, 48.

31 Johann Jacob Wettstein, *Novum Testamentum Graecum editionis receptae cum lectionibus variantibus*, 2 vols. (Amsterdam: Officina Dommeriana, 1751–52).

32 Karl Lachmann, *Novum Testamentum Graece* (Berlin: G. Reimer, 1831).

33 Karl Lachmann, *Novum Testamentum Graece et Latine. Carolus Lachmannus recensuit, Philippus Buttmanus Graece lectionis autoritates apposuit* [New Testament in Greek and Latin, ed. Karl Lachmann; authorities for the readings of the Greek appended by Philip Buttmann], 2 vols. (Berlin: G. Reimer, 1842–50).

34 Constantinus de Tischendorf, *Novum Testamentum Graece* (Leipzig: J. C. Hinrich, 1869–1872).

35 Metzger, *A Textual Commentary on the Greek New Testament*, 10*.

36 B. H. Streeter, *The Four Gospels. A Study of Origins, Treating of the Manuscript Tradition, Sources, Authorship, and Dates* (London: Macmillan, 1924).

37 Nestle-Aland, 'Introduction', *Novum Testamentum* (Stuttgart: Deutsche Bibelgesellschaft, ²⁶1979), p. 43*. Kurt and Barbara Aland, *The Text of the New Testament*, 34.

38 D. C. Parker, *An Introduction to the New Testament Manuscripts and Their Texts* (Cambridge: Cambridge University Press, 2008), 1.

39 James Barr, *Comparative Philology and the Text of the Old Testament* (Oxford: Clarendon Press, 1968), 3.

40 Ibid., 4.

41 Ibid., 4–5.

42 Ibid., 5.

43 Ibid., 5.

44 Ibid., 2.

45 Cross, 'The Contribution of the Qumran Discoveries to the Study of the Biblical Text', 282. Cross is following Albright's distinction between Babylonian, Egyptian, and Palestinian recensions, but argues that these are better described as local textual families than recensions. William F. Albright, 'New Light on Early Recensions of the Hebrew Bible', in Cross and Talmon, *Qumran and the History of the Biblical Text*, 140–46.

46 Shemaryahu Talmon, 'The Textual Study of the Bible – A New Outlook', in Frank M. Cross and Shemaryahu Talmon (eds), *Qumran and the History of the Biblical Text* (Cambridge: Harvard University Press, 1975), 324–5. Emanuel Tov, 'A Modern Textual Outlook Based on the Qumran Scrolls', *Hebrew Union College Annual* 53 (1982), 11–27; 11.

47 Cross, 'The Contribution of the Qumran Discoveries', 290–2.

48 For discussions of scribal error and alterations see Friedrich Delitzsch, *Die Lese- und Schreibfehler im Alten Testament nebst den dem Schrifttexte einverleibten Randnoten klassifiziert: ein Hilfsbuch für Lexikon und Grammatik, Exegese und Lektüre* (Berlin and Leipzig: Walter de Gruyter & Co., 1920). Artur Weiser, *The Old Testament: Its Formation and Development*, trans. by Dorothea M. Barton (New York: Association Press, 1961), 355–7. Aage Bentzen, *Introduction to the Old Testament* (Copenhagen: Gad, 1948), 1:98–9. Würthwein, *Text of the Old Testament*, 107–12. McCarter, *Textual Criticism*, 26–61. Tov, *Textual Criticism*, 6–13, 232–85.

49 For this and other instances of the confusion of similar letters see Würthwein, *Text of the Old Testament*, 108.

50 Whereas older English translations such as the AV, RV, and RSV followed the Masoretic text's *Dodanim*, more recent translations have adopted *Rodanim* (NRSV, REB, NIV).

51 For a discussion of the *scriptio continua* and the Hebrew Bible, see Alan R. Millard, '"Scriptio Continua" in Early Hebrew: Ancient Practice or Modern Surmise?' *Journal of Semitic Studies* 15 (1970), 2–15.

52 For Old Testament examples, see Delitzsch, *Lese- und Schreibfehler*; Würthwein, *The Text of the Old Testament*, 107–112; Tov, *Textual Criticism*, 6–13, 232–85; McCarter, *Textual Criticism*, 26–61.

53 Bruce K. Waltke, 'The Textual Criticism of the Old Testament', in Frank E. Gaebelein (ed.), *The Expositor's Bible Commentary* (Grand Rapids: Zondervan, 1979), vol. 1, pp. 211–28; 226.

54 McCarter, *Textual Criticism*, 73.

55 Gordon J. Wenham, *Word Bible Commentary, Vol 1: Genesis 1–15* (Nashville: Thomas Newslon Publishers, 1987), 46.

Chapter Four

1 For summaries of the methods employed by source criticism see Zimmermann, *Neutestamentliche Methodenlehre*, 83–127. Wolfgang Richter, *Exegese als Literaturwissenschaft: Entwurf einer alttestamentlichen Literaturtheorie und Methodologie* (Göttingen: Vandenhoeck & Ruprecht, 1971), 50–72. David Wenham, 'Source Criticism', in Marshall, *New Testament Interpretation*, 139–52. Barton, *Reading the Old Testament*, 20–9. Tuckett, *Reading the New Testament*, 78–94. Wilhelm Egger, *Methodenlehre zum Neuen Testament: Einführung in linguistische und historisch-kritische Methoden* (Freiburg im Breisgau: Herder, ³1987), 162–70. Steck, *Old Testament Exegesis*, 49–63. Pauline A. Viviano, 'Source Criticism', in Steven L. McKenzie and Stephen R. Haynes (eds), *To Each Its Own Meaning: Biblical Criticisms and Their Application*, revised and expanded edition (Louisville, Ky.: Westminster John Knox, 1999), 35–57. R. N. and R. K. Soulen, 'Source Criticism', *Handbook of Biblical Criticism* (Louisville, Ky.: Westminster/John Knox Press, 2001). Suzanne Boorer, 'Source and Redaction Criticism', in Thomas B. Dozeman (ed.), *Methods for Exodus* (Cambridge: Cambridge University Press, 2010), 95–130.

2 Isa. 1–39 is itself not a unified text, as is evident from such passages as Isa. 11.11–16; 21.1–10.

3 See Isa. 45.1 and the references to Cyrus (d. 530 BCE) in Isa. 47; 52.7–12, and elsewhere.

4 The term 'literary criticism' has sometimes been used in English in the sense of source criticism. See, for example, Norman Habel, *Literary Criticism of the Old Testament* (Philadelphia: Fortress, 1971).

5 James Barr, 'Reading the Bible as Literature', *Bulletin of the John Rylands Library 56* (1973), 10–33; 21.

6 J. G. Eichhorn, *Einleitung in das Alte Testament* (Leipzig: Weidmanns, 1780–1783).

7 A. Geddes, *The Holy Bible*, vol. 1 (London: J. David, 1792); *Critical Remarks on the Hebrew Scriptures*, vol. 1 (London: Davis, Wilks, and Taylor, 1800). See William McKane, 'Early Old Testament Critics in Great Britain', in Sæbø, *Hebrew Bible/Old Testament*, II:953–70; 964–970.

8 J. S. Vater, *Commentar über den Pentateuch* (Halle: Waisenhaus, 1802–1805).

9 Reventlow, *Epochen der Bibelauslegung*, IV:228.

10 Ewald's review of Stähelin's *Kritische Untersuchungen über die Genesis* (Basel: J. G. Neukirch, 1830) can be found in *Theologische Studien und Kritiken* 4 (1831), 595–606.

11 Hermann Hupfeld, *Die Quellen der Genesis und die Art ihrer Zusammensetzung* (Berlin: Wiegandt und Grieben, 1853).

12 W. M. L. de Wette, *Dissertatio critico-exegetica, qua Deuteronium a prioribus Pentateuchi libris diversum, alius suiusdam recentoris auctoris opus esse monstratur* (1805).

13 Karl Heinrich Graf, *Die geschichtlichen Bücher des Alten Testaments* (Leipzig: T. O Weigel, 1866).

14 This point was made by Johannes Pedersen, *Israel: Sjæleliv og Samfundliv* (Copenhagen: Pios, 1920); ET: *Israel: Its Life and Culture* London: Oxford University Press, 1926).

15 See, for example, Rudolf Smend, *Die Erzählung des Hexateuch auf ihre Quellen untersucht* (Berlin: G. Reimer, 1912); Gerhard von Rad, *Die Priesterschrift im Hexateuch* (Stuttgart and Berlin: W. Kohlhammer, 1934).

16 Otto Eissfeldt, *Hexateuch-Synopse* (Leipzig: J. C. Hinrich, 1922).

17 Georg Fohrer, *Introduction to the Old Testament*, trans. by David E. Green (Nashville: Abingdon, 1968).

18 Julian Morgenstern, 'The Oldest Document of the Hexateuch', *Hebrew Union College Annual* 4 (1927), 1–138.

19 R. H. Pfeiffer, 'A Non-Israelite Source of the Book of Genesis', *Zeitschrift für die alttestamentliche Wissenschaft* 48 (1930), 66–73; *Introduction to the Old Testament* (New York: Harper & Brothers, 1941).

20 Martin Noth, *A History of Pentateuchal Traditions*, trans. by B. W. Anderson (Englewood Cliffs, NJ: Prentice-Hall, 1972); first published in German in 1948.

21 See, for example, Adam C. Welch, *The Code of Deuteronomy: A New Theory of Its Origin* (London: J. Clarke, 1924); 'On the Present Position of Old Testament Criticism', *Expositor* 25 (1923), 344–370; 364–5. Ernst Sellin, *Einleitung in das Alte Testament* (Leipzig: Quelle & Meyer, ⁵1929). J. Kaufmann, 'Probleme der israelitisch-jüdischen Religionsgeschichte', *Zeitschrift für die alttestamentliche Wissenschaft* 48 (1930), 23–32; 51 (1933): 35–47. Gustav Hölscher, 'Komposition und Ursprung des Deuteronomiums', *Zeitschrift für die alttestamentliche Wissenschaft* 40 (1922): 161–255.

22 John Van Seters, *Abraham in History and Tradition* (New Haven, CT: Yale University Press, 1975); *Prologue to History: the Yahwist as Historian in Genesis* (Louisville, KY: Westminster/John Knox Press, 1992).

23 H. H. Schmid, *Der sogenannte Jahwist* (Zürich: Theologischer Verlag, 1976).

24 Erhard Blum, *Studien zur Komposition des Pentateuch* (Berlin: de Gruyter, 1990).

25 Otto Kaiser, *Der Prophet Jesaja Kapitel 13–39* (Göttingen: Vandenhoeck & Ruprecht, 1973).

26 E. S. Gerstenberger, *Psalms Part 1, with an Introduction to Cultic Poetry* (Grand Rapids, MI: Eerdmans, 1988).

27 R. N. Whybray, *The Making of the Pentateuch: A Methodological Study* (Sheffield: JSOT, 1987).

28 See Kümmel, *The New Testament*, 69–73.

29 *Synopsis Evangeliorum Matthäi Marci et Lucae una cum iis Joannis pericopis quae omnino cum caeterorum Evangelistarum narrationibus conferendae sunt. Textum recensuit . . .* J. J. Griesbach [Synopsis of the Gospels of Matthew, Mark, and Luke, together with those pericopes in which all the evangelists can be compared as to their narratives. The text edited by J. J. Griesbach] (Halle: Curtiana, 1776).

30 J. J. Griesbach, *Commentatio qua Marci Evangelium totum e Matthaei et Lucae commentariis decerptum esse monstratur* [Demonstration in which the entire Gospel of Mark is shown to be excerpted from the narratives of Matthew and Luke], 1789–90; reprinted in extended form in *Commentationes Theologicae*, ed. J. C. Velthusen, C. Th. Kuinoel, and G. A. Ruperti, Vol. I (1794), pp. 360ff.

31 Gottlob Christian Storr, *Über den Zweck der evangelischen Geschichte und der Briefe Johannis* (Tübingen: Jakob Friedrich Heerbrandt, [1]1786, [2]1810), 274–8, 287–95.

32 G. E. Lessing, ' 'New Hypothesis Concerning the Evangelists Considered as merely Human Historians', in Chadwick, *Lessing's Theological Writings*, 65–81.

33 Johann Gottfried Eichhorn, 'Über die drey ersten Evangelien: Einige Beyträge zu ihrer künftigen kritischen Behandlung', in Eichhorn, *Allgemeine Bibliothek der biblischen Litteratur* vol. 5 (Leipzig: Weidmann, 1793), 759–996.

34 J. G. Herder, *Christliche Schriften*. Second Collection: *Vom Erlöser der Menschen. Nach unsern drei ersten Evangelien* (Riga: Johann Friedrich Hartknoch, 1796). Third Collection: *Von Gottes Sohn, der Welt Heiland. Nach Johannes Evangelium. Nebst einer Regel der Zusammenstimmung unserer Evangelien aus ihrer Entstehung und Ordnung*. Also in Herder's *Sämmtliche Werke*, ed. B. Suphan, 32 vols. (Berlin: Weidmann, 1877–1913), vol. XIX; quoted in Kümmel, *The New Testament*, 79.

35 Ibid, quoted in Kümmel, *The New Testament*, 82.

36 Ibid.

37 C. Lachmann, 'De ordine narrationum in evangeliis synopticis,' *Theologische Studien und Kritiken*, 8 (Hamburg, 1835), 570–90.

38 Heinrich Julius Holtzmann, *Die Synoptischen Evangelien: ihr Ursprung und geschichtlicher Charakter* (Leipzig: Wilhelm Engelmann, 1863).

39 Wilhelm Bussmann, *Synoptische Studien*, 3 vols. (Halle: Buchhandlung des Waisenhauses, 1925–1931).

40 William R. Farmer, *The Synoptic Problem: A Critical Analysis* (Dillsboro, NC: Western North Carolina Press, 1976).

41 See Robert Tomson Fortna, *The Gospel of Signs: A Reconstruction of the Narrative Source Underlying the Fourth Gospel* (Cambridge: Cambridge University Press, 1970). John Ashton, *Understanding the Fourth Gospel* (Oxford: Clarendon, 1993).

42 Rudolf Bultmann, *Theology of the New Testament*, translated by Kendrick Grobel, 2 vols. (London: SCM, 1952), 1:46. Ernst Käsemann, *Commentary on Romans* (London: SCM, 1980), 95–8.

43 Translation modified.

44 There is some dispute whether Gen. 2.4b is the end of the first creation story or beginning of the second.

45 Translation modified. NRSV: 'living being'.

46 Gerhard von Rad, *Genesis: A Commentary*, trans. by John H. Marks (Philadelphia: Westminster, rev. edn 1972), 74.

47 The significance of this change of vocabulary is lost in many modern translations, which render the Greek *prosekunei* as 'knelt before him'.

48 See, for example, Benno Jacob, *Das erste Buch der Tora: Genesis übersetzt und erklärt* (Berlin: Schocke, 1934); ET: Benno Jacob, *The First Book of the Torah, Genesis: translated with commentary by B. Jacob* (New York: Ktav Publishing House, 1974).

49 See Umberto Cassuto, *La Questione della Genesi* (Florence: F. Le Monnier, 1934); *The Documentary Hypothesis and the Composition of the Pentateuch*, translated by Israel Abrahams (Jerusalem: Magnes, 1961). Yehezkel Kaufmann, *The Religion of Israel from its Beginnings to the Babylonian Exile*, trans. by M. Greenberg (London: Allen & Unwin, 1960).

50 Arguments of this type have been advanced by R. K. Harrison and J. W. Wenham. R. K. Harrison, *Introduction to the Old Testament with a Comprehensive Review of Old Testament Studies and a Special Supplement on the Apocrypha* (Grand Rapids: Eerdmans, 1969), 505–41. J. W. Wenham, 'Moses and the Pentateuch', in D. Guthrie and J. A. Motyer (eds), *New Bible Commentary Revised* (London: Inter-Varsity Press, 1970), 41–3. See Barr's response to this type of argument in his *Fundamentalism.* (London: SCM, 1981), 145–9.

Chapter Five

1 For studies of form criticism see E. T. Ryder, 'Form Criticism of the Old Testament', in Matthew Black and H. H. Rowley (eds), *Peake's Commentary on the Bible* (Sunbury-on-Thames, Middlesex: Thomas Nelson and Sons, 1962), 91–5. E. Dinkler, 'Form Criticism of the New Testament', *Peake's Commentary on the Bible*, 683–5. Zimmermann, *Neutestamentliche Methodenlehre*, 128–213. Donald Guthrie, *New Testament Introduction* (London: Tyndale, 1970), 188–219. Richter, *Exegese als Literaturwissenschaft*, 72–125. Gene

M. Tucker, *Form Criticism of the Old Testament* (Philadelphia: Fortress Press, 1971). John H. Hayes (ed.), *Old Testament Form Criticism* (San Antonio: Trinity University Press, 1974). Stephen H. Travis, 'Form Criticism', in Marshall, *New Testament Interpretation*, 153–64. Erhardt Güttgemanns, *Candid Questions Concerning Gospel Form Criticism: A Methodological Sketch of Form and Redaction Criticism*, translated by William G. Doty (Pittsburgh, PA.: Pickwick, 1979). Gerhard Lohfink, *The Bible: Now I Get It! A Form-Criticism Handbook* (New York: Doubleday, 1979). Barton, *Reading the Old Testament*, 30–44. Tuckett, *Reading the New Testament*, 95–115. Steck, *Old Testament Exegesis*, 99–125. Marvin A. Sweeney, 'Form Criticism', in McKenzie and Haynes, *To Each Its Own Meaning*, 59–89. M. J. Buss, *Biblical Form Criticism in Its Context* (Sheffield: Sheffield Academic Press, 1999).

2 See Marvin Alan Sweeney, *I & II Kings: A Commentary* (Louisville, KY: Westminster John Knox Press, 2007), 7–11.

3 Burton Scott Easton, *The Gospel before the Gospels* (London: George Allen & Unwin, 1928), 74.

4 For discussions of genre criticism see Richter, *Exegese als Literaturwissenschaft*, 125–52. James L. Bailey, 'Genre Analysis', in Green, *Hearing the New Testament: Strategies for Interpretation*, 197–221. Kenton L. Sparks, 'Genre Criticism', in Dozeman, *Methods for Exodus*, 55–94.

5 Richter, *Exegese als Literaturwissenschaft*, 46.

6 Hermann Gunkel, 'Die Grundprobleme der israelitischen Literaturgeschichte', in *Reden und Aufsätze* (Göttingen: Vandenhoeck & Ruprecht, 1913), 29–38. ET: Hermann Gunkel, 'Fundamental Problems of Hebrew Literary History', in Hermann Gunkel, *What Remains of the Old Testament and Other Essays*, translated by A. K. Dallas (London: George Allen & Unwin, 1928), 57–68.

7 There is some dispute concerning the meaning of 'tradition history' and its relation to form criticism. See Douglas A. Knight, *Rediscovering the Traditions of Israel*, revised edn (Missoula, Montana: Society of Biblical Literature and Scholars Press, 1975), 21–9. The view taken by the present author is that tradition criticism is dependent on form criticism. It is only when forms have been identified that the question concerning the way they have been handed down can be raised. Tradition criticism can thus be regarded as a branch of form criticism. We shall thus treat tradition criticism as a possible stage in the work of form criticism rather than as a distinct and independent method of interpretation. For studies of tradition criticism see Richter, *Exegese als Literaturwissenschaft*, 152–65. Egger, *Methodenlehre zum Neuen Testament*, 170–83. Bruce Chilton, 'Traditio-Historical Criticism and Study of Jesus', in Green, *Hearing the New Testament*, 37–60. David R. Catchpole, 'Tradition Criticism', in Marshall, *New Testament Interpretation*, 165–80. Steck, *Old Testament Exegesis*, 65–77 (transmission historical approach), 127–49 (tradition historical approach). Robert A. Di Vito, 'Tradition-Historical Criticism', in McKenzie and Haynes, *To Each Its Own Meaning*, 90–104.

8 Martin Dibelius, *Die Formgeschichte des Evangeliums* (Tübingen: J. C. B. Mohr (Paul Siebeck), 1919). ET: Martin Dibelius, *From Tradition to Gospel*), translated from the second revised edition by Bertram Lee Woolf (London: Ivor Nicholson and Watson, 1934).

9 Emil Fascher, *Die formgeschichtliche Methode* (Giessen: Alfred Töpelmann, 1924).

10 Ludwig Koehler, *Das formgeschichtliche Problem des Neuen Testaments* (J. C. B. Mohr (Paul Siebeck), 1927).

11 Easton, *Gospel before the Gospels*, 32.

12 Ibid.

13 Ibid.

14 Wilhelm Martin Leberecht de Wette, *Commentar über die Psalmen* (Heidelberg: J. C. B. Mohr, [1]1811, [5]1856).

15 Reventlow, *Epochen der Bibelauslegung*, IV:235.

16 W. M. L. de Wette, *Ueber die erbauliche Erklärung der Psalmen* (Heidelberg: J. C. B. Mohr, 1836), 36, quoted in Reventlow, *Epochen der Bibelauslegung*, IV:236.

17 Reventlow, *Epochen der Bibelauslegung*, IV:236.

18 Hermann Gunkel, *The Folktale in the Old Testament*, trans. by Michael D. Rutter (Sheffield: Almond Press, 1987). German edition published in 1917.

19 Gunkel discussed these issues in two important works: 'Die israelitische Literatur', in *Die Kultur der Gegenwart*, 32 vols. (Leipzig: Teubner, 1905–26), I.7:51–102, and 'Fundamental Problems of Hebrew Literary History', in *What Remains of the Old Testament*, 57–68.

20 Gunkel, *Legends of Genesis*, 29.

21 Sigmund Mowinckel, *Psalmenstudien I-VI* (Kristiana: J. Dybwad, 1921–24); *The Psalms in Israel's Worship*, 2 vols., trans. by D. W. Ap-Thomas (Nashville: Abingdon, 1961). *Prophecy and Tradition: The Prophetic Books in Light of the Study of the Growth and History of the Tradition* (Oslo: J. Dybwad, 1946).

22 Albrecht Alt, 'The Settlement of the Israelites in Palestine', *Essays on Old Testament History and Religion*, trans. by R. A. Wilson (Garden City, NY: Doubleday, 1967), 173–221; German edition published in 1925.

23 Alt, 'The God of the Fathers', *Essays on Old Testament History and Religion*, 1–100; German edition published in 1929.

24 Alt, 'The Origins of Israelite Law', *Essays on Old Testament History and Religion*, 101–71; German edition published in 1934.

25 See Erhard S. Gerstenberger, *Wesen und Herkunft des 'Apodiktischen Rechts'* (Neukirchen: Neukirchener, 1965). See also his 'Covenant and Commandment', *Journal of Biblical Literature* 84 (1965), 38–51.

26 Other attempts to employ form criticism to recover the workings of the Israelite law courts have been made by B. Gemser, 'The Rîb- or Controversy Pattern in Hebrew Mentality', in M. Noth and D. Winton

Thomas (eds), *Wisdom in Israel and the Ancient Near East* (Leiden: Brill, 1955). Ludwig Koehler, 'Justice in the Gate', in his *Hebrew Man*, translated by Peter R. Ackroyd (London: SCM, 1956), 127–50. Hans Joachim Boecker, *Redeformen des Rechtslebens im Alten Testament* (Neukirchen-Vluyn: Neukirchener Verlag, ¹1964, ²1970). Kirsten Nielsen, *Yahweh as Prosecutor and Judge: An Investigation of the Prophetic Law Suit (rîb-pattern)* (Sheffield: Journal for the Study of the Old Testament, 1978).

27 Noth, *A History of Pentateuchal Traditions*.

28 Rolf Rendtorff, *The Problem of the Process of Transmission in the Pentateuch*, translated by John J. Scullion (Sheffield: Sheffield Academic Press, 1990). First published in German in 1977. Blum, *Studien zur Komposition des Pentateuch*.

29 Claus Westermann, *Basic Forms of Prophetic Speech*, trans. by H. C. White (Cambridge: Lutterworth, 1991). First German edition published in 1960.

30 Claus Westermann, *The Praise of God in the Psalms*, trans. by Keith R. Crim (Richmond: John Knox, 1965). First German edition published in 1961.

31 Karl Ludwig Schmidt, *Der Rahmen der Geschichte Jesu: literarkritische Untersuchungen zur ältesten Jesusüberlieferung* (Berlin: Trowitsch, 1919).

32 Schmidt, *Der Rahmen der Geschichte Jesu*, 305.

33 Martin Albertz, *Die synoptischen Streitgespräche: ein Beitrag zur Formgeschichte des Urchristentums* (Berlin: Trowitzsch, 1921). See Vincent Taylor, *Formation of the Gospel Tradition* (London: Macmillan, 1933), 15.

34 Georg Bertram, *Die Leidensgeschichte Jesu und der Christuskult: eine formgeschichtliche Untersuchung* (Göttingen: Vandenhoeck & Ruprecht, 1922).

35 Martin Dibelius, *Die Formgeschichte des Evangeliums* (Tübingen: J. C. B. Mohr (Paul Siebeck), ¹1919, ²1933); ET: *From Tradition to Gospel*, translated by Bertram Lee Woolf (Cambridge: James Clarke, 1971), 3. References are to the English edition. See Kümmel, *The New Testament*, 331–4, for excerpts.

36 Dibelius, *From Tradition to Gospel*, 3.

37 Ibid., 4.

38 Ibid., 79.

39 Ibid., 104.

40 Ibid., 109.

41 Bultmann, *History of the Synoptic Tradition*, 309.

42 Ibid., 221.

43 Ibid.

44 Ibid., 70.

45 Ibid., 147.

46 Ibid., 188.

47 Ibid., 189.

48 Ibid., 190.

49 Ibid., 191.

50 Ibid., 192.

51 Ibid., 203.

52 First published in 1925. Rudolf Bultmann, *Die Erforschung der Synoptischen Evangelien* (Giessen: Alfred Töpelmann, ¹1925, ²1930).

53 Rudolf Bultmann and Karl Kundsin, *Form Criticism: Two Essays on New Testament Research*, translated by Frederick C. Grant (New York: Harper & Row, 1934).

54 Donald Wayne Riddle, *The Gospels: their Origin and Growth* (Chicago: Chicago University Press, 1939).

55 D. E. Nineham, 'Robert Henry Lightfoot', in D. E. Nineham (ed.), *Studies in the Gospels: Essays in Memory of R. H. Lightfoot* (Oxford: Basil Blackwell, 1955), vi–xvi; x.

56 Nineham, 'Robert Henry Lightfoot', x.

57 Published as R. H. Lightfoot, *History and Interpretation in the Gospels* (London: Hodder and Stoughton, 1935).

58 R. H. Lightfoot, *Locality and Doctrine in the Gospels* (London: Hodder and Stoughton, 1938).

59 C. H. Dodd, *The Parables of the Kingdom* (London: Nisbet & Co., 1935), see ch. IV 'The "Setting in Life"'.

60 C. H. Dodd, *Parables of the Kingdom*, 111.

61 C. H. Dodd, *Historical Tradition in the Fourth Gospel* (Cambridge: Cambridge University Press, 1963), 6.

62 T. W. Manson, 'The Life of Jesus: Some Tendencies in Present-Day Research', in W. D. Davies and D. Daube (eds), *The Background of the New Testament and its Eschatology* (Cambridge: Cambridge University Press, 1954, 1964), 211–21; 212.

63 Ibid., 219.

64 Gerhard Iber, 'Zur Formgeschichte der Evangelien', *Theologische Rundschau* 24 (1957/58), 337; quoted in Robert H. Stein, 'What is Redaktionsgeschichte?', *Journal of Biblical Literature* 88 (1969), 45–56; 46 n. 7. Reprinted in Robert H. Stein, *Gospels and Tradition: Studies on Redaction Criticism of the Synoptic Gospels* (Grand Rapids, Mich.: Baker Book House, 1991).

65 E. Güttgemanns, *Offene Fragen zur Formgeschichte des Evangeliums. Eine methodologische Skizze der Grundlagenproblematik der Form- und Redaktionsgeschichte* (Munich: C. Kaiser, 1970, 2nd edn., 1971). Translated by W. J. Doty as *Candid Questions Concerning Gospel Form Criticism. A Methodological Sketch of the Fundamental Problematics of Form and Redaction Criticism* (Pittsburgh, Pennsylvania: Pickwick Press, 1979).

66 Walter Schmithals, 'Kritik der Formkritik', *Zeitschrift für Theologie und Kirche* 77 (1980), 149–85; *Einleitung in die ersten drei Evangelien* (Berlin: de Gruyter, 1985).

67 Gerd Theissen, *The Gospels in Context. Social and Political History in the Synoptic Tradition*, translated by Linda M. Maloney (Edinburgh: T & T Clark, 1992), 1.

68 Theissen, *Gospels in Context*, 1.

69 Johannes P. Floss, 'Form, Source, and Redaction Criticism', in J. W. Rogerson and Judith M. Lieu, *The Oxford Handbook of Biblical Studies* (Oxford: Oxford University Press, 2010), 591–614; 595.

70 K. Koch et al., *Amos: Untersucht mit den Methoden einer strukturalen Formgeschichte*, 3 vols. (Neukirchen-Vluyn: Neukirchener Verlag; Butzon & Bercker, 1976).

71 Klaus Koch, *Was ist Formgeschichte? Methoden der Bibelexegese*, (Neukirchen-Vluyn: Neukirchener Verlag, ¹1974, ⁵1989). ET: *The Growth of the Biblical Tradition: The Form-Critical Method*, translated by S. M. Cupitt (London: Adam & Charles Black, 1969).

72 Richter, *Exegese als Literaturwissenschaft*, 79–103.

73 Floss, 'Form, Source, and Redaction Criticism', 596–98.

74 Steck, *Old Testament Exegesis*, 108.

75 Ibid. 109–110.

76 James Muilenburg, 'Form Criticism and Beyond', *Journal of Biblical Literature* 88 (1969), 1–18.

77 Klaus Berger, *Formgeschichte des Neuen Testaments* (Heidelberg: Quell and Meyer, 1984); *Einführung in die Formgeschichte* (Tübingen: Francke, 1987).

78 George W. Coats, *Genesis, with an Introduction to Narrative Literature* (Grand Rapids, MI: Eerdmans, 1983), 3.

79 Rolf P. Knierim and George W. Coats, *Numbers* (Grand Rapids, Mich.: Eerdmans, 2005).

80 Eerdmans website: http://www.eerdmans.com/shop/product.asp?p_key =9780802822314

81 Norman Perrin, *Rediscovering the Teaching of Jesus* (London: SCM, 1967), 39–47. Perrin claims that he and Fuller developed these criteria independently of each other. Norman Perrin, *What Is Redaction Criticism?* (Philadelphia: Fortress Press, 1969), 71. R. H. Fuller, *A Critical Introduction to the New Testament* (London: Duckworth, 1966), 96–8.

82 Hermann Gunkel, *Die Sagen der Genesis* (Göttingen: Vandenhoeck & Ruprecht, 1901); ET: *The Legends of Genesis: The Biblical Saga and History*, translated by W. H. Carruth, introduction by William F. Albright (New York: Schocken, 1964).

83 Coats, *Genesis*, 59.

84 Koch, *The Growth of the Biblical Tradition*, 6–8; cf. 17–18, 28–9.

85 J. A. Baird, *Audience Criticism and the Historical Jesus* (Philadelphia: Westminster Press, 1969); Güttgemanns, *Candid Questions concerning Gospel Form Criticism.*

86 E. P. Sanders, *The Tendencies of the Synoptic Tradition* (Cambridge: Cambridge University Press, 1969).

87 Harald Riesenfeld, *The Gospel Tradition and its Beginnings: A Study in the Limits of 'Formgeschichte'* (London: Mowbray, 1957); Birger Gerhardsson, *Memory and Manuscript: Oral Tradition and Written Transmission in Rabbinic Judaism and Early Christianity* (Lund: C. W. K. Gleerup, 1961).

Chapter Six

1 For discussions of redaction criticism see Joachim Rohde, *Rediscovering the Teaching of the Evangelists* (London: SCM, 1968). Zimmermann, *Neutestamentliche Methodenlehre*, 214–57. Richter, *Exegese als Literaturwissenschaft*, 165–73. Stephen S. Smalley, 'Redaction Criticism', in Marshall, *New Testament Interpretation*, 181–95. Georg Strecker, 'Redaktionsgeschichte als Aufgabe der Synoptikerexegese', in Georg Strecker, *Eschaton und Historie: Aufsätze* (Göttingen: Vandenhoeck & Ruprecht, 1979), 9–32. Barton, *Reading the Old Testament*, 45–60. Tuckett, *Reading the New Testament*, 116–35. Egger, *Methodenlehre zum Neuen Testament*, 183–94. Robert H. Stein, *Gospels and Redaction: Studies on Redaction Criticism of the Synoptic Gospels* (Grand Rapids, MI: Baker Book House, 1991). Steck, *Old Testament Exegesis*, 79–98. Gail P. C. Streete, 'Redaction Criticism', in McKenzie and Haynes, *To Each Its Own Meaning*, 105–21. Suzanne Boorer, 'Source and Redaction Criticism', in Dozeman, *Methods for Exodus*, 95–130.

2 The dependence of redaction criticism on form criticism has led some scholars to subsume redaction criticism under form criticism and treat redaction criticism as merely a movement within or a subcategory of form criticism. For a list of those who argue this see Stein, 'What is *Redaktionsgeschichte*?', 50 n. Stein follows Kurt Frör in arguing that, 'It would be an error to make redaktionsgeschichte part of form criticism', since whereas form criticism is 'primarily concerned with the investigation of the individual pericopes and the oral period', 'Redaktionsgeschichte is concerned with the theological conception of each gospel as an individual entity' (Stein, 'What is *Redaktionsgeschichte*?', 52, referring to Kurt Frör, *Wege zur Schriftauslegung* (Dusseldorf: Patmos, 1963), 254). Stein thus recommends that, 'We should limit by definition form criticism to the investigation of the oral forms of the tradition and not include in form criticism the investigation of the particular use and interpretation of these traditions by the evangelist' (Stein, 'What is *Redaktionsgeschichte*?', 52–3).

3 Stein, 'What is *Redaktionsgeschichte?*', 56.

4 As an example of a scholar who treats Mark 8.27–9 in this way Perrin cites T. W. Manson's, *The Servant-Messiah* (Cambridge: Cambridge University Press, 1953), 71ff. Norman Perrin, 'The Wredestrasse becomes the Hauptstrasse: Reflections on the Reprinting of the Dodd Festschrift', *Journal of Religion*, vol. 46, no. 2 (April 1966), 296–300; 298.

5 Perrin, *What is Redaction Criticism?*, 68.

6 Ibid., 69.

7 Ibid., 73.

8 Ibid., 75.

9 Several commentators have cited Marxsen as the originator of the term. See, for example, Richter, *Exegese als Literaturwissenschaft*, 172 n. 28. Stein on the other hand claims that: 'Although this term was used before Marxsen (cf. Marxsen, p. 11, n. 1), it has become a *terminus technicus* through his use of it.' Stein, 'What is *Redaktionsgeschichte?*', 48 n. 15. Stein fails to provide examples of the use of the term prior to Marxsen, however.

10 Willi Marxsen, 'Redaktionsgeschichtliche Erklärung der sogenannten Parabeltheorie des Markus', *Zeitschrift für Theologie und Kirche* 52 (1955), 255–71.

11 W. Marxsen, *Der Evangelist Markus* (Göttingen: Vandenhoeck & Ruprecht, ²1959), 11; ET: *Mark the Evangelist* (Nashville: Abingdon, 1969), 21.

12 Richter, *Exegese als Literaturwissenschaft*, 167–72.

13 John R. Donahue S. J., 'Redaction Criticism: Has the *Hauptstrasse* Become a *Sackgasse?*', in Elizabeth Struthers Malbon and Edgar V. McKnight (eds), *The New Literary Criticism and the New Testament* (Sheffield: Sheffield Academic Press, 1994), 27–57; 34.

14 Marxsen, *Mark the Evangelist*, 21.

15 Ibid., 22. Marxsen is referring to Paul Wernle, *Die synoptische Frage* (Freiburg im Breisgau: J. C. B. Mohr, 1899).

16 Wilhelm Wrede, *Das Messiasgeheimnis in den Evangelien.* Julius Wellhausen, *Das Evangelium Marci*, (Berlin: Georg Reimer, ²1909); *Einleitung in die drei ersten Evangelien*, (Berlin: Georg Reimer, ²1911).

17 Marxsen, *Mark the Evangelist*, 22.

18 Barton, *Nature of Biblical Criticism*, 19.

19 Perrin, *What is Redaction Criticism?*, 4.

20 Ibid., 12.

21 F. C. Baur, *Das Markusevangelium nach seinem Ursprung und Charakter* (Tübingen: Ludw. Friedr. Fues, 1851).

22 The Markan hypothesis was advanced by C. G. Wilke and C. H. Weisse. C. G. Wilke, *Der Urevangelist: oder, exegetische kritische Untersuchung*

über das Verwandschaftsverhältnis der drei ersten Evangelien (Dresden & Leipzig: G. Fleischer, 1838). C. H. Weisse, *Die Evangelienfrage in ihrem gegenwärtigen Stadium* (Leipzig: Breitkopf & Härtel, 1856).

23 Wrede, *Messianic Secret*, 67.

24 Johannes Schreiber, *Theologische Erkenntnis und unterrichtlicher Vollzug. Dargestellt am Beispiel des Markusevangeliums* (Hamburg: Furche, 1968), 9.

25 Perrin, *What is Redaction Criticism?*, 12.

26 Rudolf Bultmann, *Die Geschichte der synoptischen Tradition* (Göttingen: Vandenhoeck und Ruprecht, 1921); ET: *History of the Synoptic Tradition*, translated by John Marsh (Oxford: Blackwell, 1963), 319–74.

27 Karl Kundsin, *Topologische Überlieferungsstoffe im Johannes-Evangelium* (Göttingen: Vandenhoeck & Ruprecht, 1925).

28 Adolf Schlatter, *Der Evangelist Matthäus* (Stuttgart: Calwer, 1929).

29 Ernst Lohmeyer, *Galiläa und Jerusalem* (Göttingen: Vandenhoeck & Ruprecht, 1936).

30 Lightfoot, *History and Interpretation*, 57.

31 Perrin, *What is Redaction Criticism?*, 23.

32 Ibid., 22.

33 Benjamin W. Bacon, *Studies in Matthew* (London: Constable, 1931). N. B. Stonehouse, *The Witness of Luke to Christ* (London: Tyndale, 1951). Philip Carrington, *According to Mark: A Running Commentary on the Oldest Gospel* (Cambridge: Cambridge University Press, 1960). A. M. Farrer, *St. Matthew and St. Mark* (Westminster: Dacre, 1954). See also J. Rohde, 'Precursors of Redaction Criticism', in *Rediscovering the Teaching of the Evangelists*, 31–46.

34 Marxsen, *Mark the Evangelist*, 23–4.

35 Rohde, *Rediscovering the Teaching of the Evangelists*, 11.

36 C. Clifton Black, 'The Quest of Mark the Redactor: Why has it been pursued, and what has it taught us?' *Journal for the Study of the New Testament* 33 (1988), 19–39; 25.

37 Stein, 'What is *Redaktionsgeschichte*?', 47–8.

38 Richter, *Exegese als Literaturwissenschaft*, 165–73; Steck, *Old Testament Exegesis*, 79–98.

39 Günther Bornkamm, 'The Stilling of the Storm in Matthew', in Günther Bornkamm, Gerhard Barth, Heinz Joachim Held, *Tradition and Interpretation in Matthew*, translated by Percy Scott (Philadelphia: Westminster, 1963). First published in *Wort und Dienst: Jahrbuch der theologischen Schule Bethel* (1948), 49–54.

40 Bornkamm, 'Stilling of the Storm', 56.

41 Ibid., 57.

42 Günther Bornkamm, 'Enderwartung und Kirche im Matthäusevangelium', in Davies and Daube (eds), *The Background of the New Testament and its Eschatology*, 222–60. ET: Bornkamm, 'End-Expectation and Church in Matthew', 15–51, in Bornkamm et al., *Tradition and Interpretation in Matthew*. Perrin, *What is Redaction Criticism?*, 27.

43 Bornkamm, 'End-Expectation and Church in Matthew', 49.

44 Perrin, 'The Wredestrasse becomes the Hauptstrasse', 297.

45 Perrin, *What is Redaction Criticism?*, 28.

46 Perrin, 'The Wredestrasse becomes the Hauptstrasse', 297.

47 Smalley, 'Redaction Criticism', 183.

48 Perrin, *What is Redaction Criticism?*, 34; Smalley, 'Redaction Criticism', 184.

49 Marxsen, *Mark the Evangelist*, 23.

50 Ibid., 24.

51 Ibid., 24.

52 Perrin, *What is Redaction Criticism?*, 34–5.

53 Perrin, 'The Wredestrasse becomes the Hauptstrasse', 297–98.

54 Gerhard Barth, 'Matthew's Understanding of the Law', in Bornkamm et al., *Tradition and Interpretation in Matthew*, 58–164. Heinz Joachim Held, 'Matthew as Interpreter of the Miracle Stories', in Bornkamm et al., *Tradition and Interpretation in Matthew*, 165–299.

55 H. E. Tödt, *The Son of Man in the Synoptic Tradition* (Philadelphia: Westminster Press, 1965).

56 Ferdinand Hahn, *Christologische Hoheitstitel: Ihre Geschichte im frühen Christentum* (Göttingen: Vandenhoeck & Ruprecht, ¹1963, ²1964); ET: *The Titles of Jesus in Christology*, translated by Harold Knight and George Ogg (London: Lutterworth, 1969).

57 Stein, 'What is *Redaktionsgeschichte*?', 46.

58 Welton O. Seal, Jr, 'Norman Perrin and his "School": Retracing a Pilgrimage', *Journal for the Study of the New Testament*, 20 (1984), 87–107.

59 Seal, 'Norman Perrin and his "School"', 88, 95–6, 97, 98, 99.

60 R. H. Stein, 'The Proper Methodology for Ascertaining a Markan *Redaktionsgeschichte*', ThD Dissertation, Princeton Theological Seminary, 1968.

61 R. H. Stein, 'The Proper Methodology for Ascertaining a Markan Redaction History', *Novum Testamentum* 13 (1971): 181–198; reprinted as 'Ascertaining a Marcan Redaction History', in *Gospels and Traditions: Studies on Redaction Criticism of the Synoptic Gospels* (Grand Rapids: Baker, 1991), 49–67.

62 Stein, 'What is *Redaktionsgeschichte*?', 54.

63 Stein, 'Ascertaining a Marcan Redaction History', 51.

64 Lloyd Gaston, *Horae Synopticae Electronicae: Word Statistics of the Synoptic Gospels* (Missoula, MT: Society of Biblical Literature, 1973).

65 C. Clifton Black, *The Disciples according to Mark: Markan Redaction in Current Debate* (Sheffield: Sheffield Academic Press, 1989), 191.

66 Ibid.

67 E. J. Pryke, *Redactional Style in the Marcan Gospel* (Cambridge: Cambridge University Press, 1978). David Barrett Peabody, *Mark as Composer* (Macon, GA: Mercer University Press, 1987). See Black's discussion of these two works in his *The Disciples according to Mark*, 205–18.

68 R. M. Frye, 'Literary Criticism and Gospel Criticism', *Today* 36 (1979): 207–219.

69 Norman Perrin, 'The Interpretation of the Gospel of Mark', *Interpretation* 30 (1976), 115–24; 120.

70 See his discussion in *The Disciples according to Mark*.

71 Black, 'The Quest of Mark the Redactor', 19.

72 Rohde, *Rediscovering the Teaching of the Evangelists*, 9.

73 John Dominic Crossan, *Four of The Gospels: Shadows on the Contours of the Canon* (Minneapolis: Winston-Seabury, 1985); *The Cross That Spoke* (San Francisco: Harper & Row, 1988).

74 Elisabeth, Schüssler Fiorenza, *In Memory of Her: A Feminist Theological Reconstruction of Christian Origins* (New York: Crossroad, 1983).

75 Black, 'The Quest of Mark the Redactor', 31.

76 Ibid., 28.

77 Norman Perrin, *A Modern Pilgrimage in New Testament Christology* (Philadelphia: Fortress Press, 1974), 1.

78 See, for example, Richter, *Exegese als Literaturwissenschaft*, 166 n. 4.

79 Ernst Haenchen, *Der Weg Jesu* (Berlin: Alfred Töpelmann, 1966), 24.

80 Perrin, *What is Redaction Criticism?*, 65.

81 Ibid., 66–7.

82 Smalley, 'Redaction Criticism', 181.

83 Randall K. J. Tan, 'Recent Developments in Redaction Criticism: From Investigation of Textual Prehistory back to Historical-Grammatical Exegesis?' *Journal of the Evangelical Theological Society* 44/4 (December 2001), 599–614; 600.

84 Ibid., 600.

85 Ibid.

86 Ibid., 614.

87 For a discussion of wisdom schools in ancient Israel see G. I. Davies, 'Were there schools in ancient Israel?', in John Day, Robert P. Gordon, H. G. M. Williamson (eds), *Wisdom in Ancient Israel* (Cambridge: Cambridge University Press, 1995), 199–211.

88 See, for example, Ezek. 28; Jer. 25.22; 27.3; 47.4; Joel 3.4; Zech. 9.1–4; 1
    Macc. 5.15; Jdt. 2.28; cf. Matt.11.21/Luke 10.13.

89 Ulrich Luz, *Matthew 8–20: A Commentary*, trans. by James E. Crouch
    (Minneapolis: Fortress Press, 2001), 338.

90 This view is advanced by Bultmann, *History of the Synoptic Tradition*, 38.

91 W. D. Davies and Dale C. Allison, *The Gospel according to Saint Matthew*,
    3 vols. (Edinburgh: T & T Clark, 1988–1997), II: 553.

92 Davies and Allison, *Gospel of* Matthew, II:555–6.

93 Perrin, *What is Redaction Criticism?*, 67.

94 Ibid., 40.

95 In response to such criticisms Black comments: 'it is one thing to suggest, as do
    William Wimsatt and Monroe Beardsley, "that the design or intention of the
    author is neither available nor desirable as a standard for judging the *success*
    of a work of literary art"; it is quite another thing, and rather doctrinaire,
    to argue that the meaning intended by an author like Mark evaporated once
    the ink was dry, or that such meaning is unworthy of critical pursuit, or
    that a text is only some free-floating sequence of words whose meaning has
    nothing whatever to do with the author who wrote them.' Black, *The Quest
    of Mark the Redactor*, 29.

96 Barton, *Reading the Old Testament*, 57.

97 Smalley, 'Redaction Criticism', 191.

98 Tan, 'Recent Developments in Redaction Criticism', 600.

99 Black, 'The Quest of Mark the Redactor', 30.

100 Ibid.

101 Frye, 'Literary Criticism and Gospel Criticism', 213.

102 Black, 'The Quest of Mark the Redactor', 30.

103 Stein, *Gospels and Tradition*, 18.

104 See Frye, 'Literary Criticism and Gospel Criticism', 207–19.

105 Dan O. Via, Jr., *Kerygma and Comedy in the New Testament: A Structuralist
    Approach to Hermeneutic* (Philadelphia: Fortress Press, 1975), 72–3.

106 Norman Perrin, 'The Interpretation of the Gospel of Mark', *Interpretation* 30
    (1976), 115–24; 120.

107 Frye, 'Literary Criticism and Gospel Criticism', 211.

Chapter Seven

1 Walter Wink, *The Bible in Human Transformation: Toward a New Paradigm
   for Biblical Study* (Philadelphia: Fortress Press, 1973; reprinted with new
   preface, 2010), 1.

2 Eugen Drewermann, *Tiefenpsychologie und Exegese* (Zürich and Düsseldorf: Walter Verlag, ¹1984–1985, ⁵1997–1998), 25.

3 Elisabeth Schüssler Fiorenza, 'The Ethics of Biblical Interpretation: Decentering Biblical Scholarship', first published in *The Journal of Biblical Literature* 197 (1988), 3–17; reprinted in Heikki Räisänen et al., *Reading the Bible in the Global Village: Helsinki* (Atlanta: Society of Biblical Literature, 2000), 107–23. Cf. 'Defending the Center, Trivializing the Margins', in ibid., 29–48.

4 Segovia, *Decolonizing Biblical Studies*, 9 n. 8.

5 Helen Gardner, *The Business of Criticism* (London: Oxford University Press, 1959), 107.

6 Segovia, *Decolonizing Biblical Studies*, 13.

7 Ibid.

8 Wink, *The Bible in Human Transformation*, 10.

9 Ibid.

10 Ibid.

11 Philip R. Davies, *Whose Bible is it Anyway?* (Sheffield: Sheffield Academic Press, 1995), 13, emphasis added.

12 Ibid., 24.

13 Carl E. Braaten and Robert W. Jenson, 'Introduction: Gospel, Church, and Scripture', in Carl E. Braaten and Robert W. Jenson (eds), *Reclaiming the Bible for the Church* (Edinburgh: T. & T. Clark, 1996), ix–xii; ix–x.

14 Childs, *The New Testament as Canon: An Introduction*, 52.

15 Drewermann, *Tiefenpsychologie und Exegese*, 1:12.

16 See Karl P. Donfried, 'Alien Hermeneutics and the Misappropriation of Scripture', in Braaten and Jenson, *Reclaiming the Bible for the Church*, 19–45; 20.

17 See Wink, *The Bible in Human Transformation*, 3.

18 Brevard S. Childs, *Introduction to the Old Testament as Scripture*, quoted in Yarchin, *History of Biblical Interpretation*, 309.

19 Paul S. Minear, *The Bible and the Historian: Breaking the Silence about God in Biblical Studies* (Nashville: Abingdon, 2002), 48.

20 Wink, *The Bible in Human Transformation*, 2.

21 Søren Kierkegaard, *Concluding Unscientific Postscript to Philosophical Fragments*, translated and edited by Howard V. Hong and Edna H. Hong with Introduction and Notes, 2 vols. (Princeton: Princeton University Press, 1992), esp. I:23–34. See also his discussion of the epistemological problems of historical knowledge in *Philosophical Fragments* (1844). Søren Kierkegaard, *Philosophical Fragments/Johannes Climacus*, translated and edited by Howard V. Hong and Edna H. Hong with

Introduction and Notes (Princeton: Princeton University Press, 1985), esp. 74–88.

22 Kierkegaard, *Concluding Unscientific Postscript*, 1:33 note.

23 Søren Kierkegaard, *For Self-Examination and Judge for Yourself!*, translated and edited by Howard V. Hong and Edna H. Hong with Introduction and Notes (Princeton: Princeton University Press, 1990), 34.

24 Ibid.

25 Wink, *The Bible in Human Transformation*, 2.

26 Ibid.

27 Ibid.

28 Maier, *The End of the Historical Critical Method*, 22.

29 Wink, *The Bible in Human Transformation*, 8.

30 Ibid., 5.

31 'Statement of the Ecumenical Dialogue of Third World Theologians', in Sergio Torres and Virginia Fabella (eds), *The Emergent Gospel* (Maryknoll, NY: Orbis, 1978), 269–70.

32 See Georges Casalis's discussion of the 'death of the armchair theologian' in his *Correct Ideas Don't Fall From the Skies* (Maryknoll, NY: Orbis, 1984), 78–83.

33 Leonardo Boff and Clodovis Boff, *Introducing Liberation Theology* (London: Burns & Oates, 1988), 17.

34 Carlos Mesters, 'The Use of the Bible in Basic Christian Communities', in Sergio Torres and John Eagleson (eds), *The Challenge of Basic Christian Communities*, translated by John Drury (Maryknoll, NY: Orbis, 1981), 197–210; 210.

35 Carlos Mesters, *Por Tras das Palavras* (Petrópolis: Vozes, 1984). Cited in Horst Klaus Berg, *Ein Wort wie Feuer: Wege lebendiger Bibelauslegung* (Kösel: Calwer, 1991), 277–8.

36 See Bernhard W. Anderson, 'The Problem and Promise of Commentary', *Interpretation* 36.4 (1982), 341–55.

37 Jowett, 'On the Interpretation of Scripture', 384.

38 Strauss, *Life of Jesus*, 71.

39 Ibid.

40 Ibid., 71–2.

41 Ibid., 87.

42 Ibid., 70.

43 Drewermann, *Tiefenpsychologie und Exegese*, 1: 16.

44 Wink, *The Bible in Human Transformation*, 5–6.

45 Childs, *The New Testament as Canon: An Introduction*, 36.

46 Jowett, 'On the Interpretation of Scripture', 412.

47 Barth, *Church Dogmatics* (Edinburgh: T. & T. Clark, 1956), I/2:492.

48 Ibid., 493.

49 Ibid., 493–4.

50 Jowett, 'On the Interpretation of Scripture', 378.

51 Wink, *The Bible in Human Transformation*, 7–8.

52 Schüssler Fiorenza, 'Ethics of Biblical Interpretation', 119.

53 Ibid.

54 Ibid.

55 Segovia, *Decolonizing Biblical Studies*, 91.

56 George Aichele et al. (The Bible and Culture Collective), *The Postmodern Bible* (New Haven, Conn.: Yale University Press, 1995), 130.

57 Wink, *The Bible in Human Transformation*, 5.

58 Schüssler Fiorenza, 'The Ethics of Biblical Interpretation', 114, citing Robert W. Funk, 'The Watershed of the American Biblical Tradition: the Chicago School, First Phase, 1892–1920', *Journal of Biblical Literature* 95 (1976), 7.

59 Schüssler Fiorenza, 'Biblical Interpretation and Critical Commitment', 389.

60 Elisabeth Schüssler Fiorenza, *Jesus: Miriam's Child, Sophia's Prophet. Critical Issues in Feminist Christology* (London: Continuum, 1994), 3.

61 Kurt Füssel, 'The Materialist Reading of the Bible: Report on an Alternative Approach to Biblical Texts', in Norman K. Gottwald and Richard A. Horsley (eds), *The Bible and Liberation. Political and Social Hermeneutics* (Maryknoll, NY: Orbis, 1993; revised edn.), 116–27; 119.

62 R. S. Sugirtharajah, 'Critics, Tools and the Global Arena', in *Reading the Bible in the Global Village: Helsinki*, 49–60; 52.

63 Barton, *Nature of Biblical Criticism*, 20 n.20.

64 Ibid., 24.

65 Ibid., 24–5. On this subject see also John Barton, 'What is a Book? Modern Exegesis and the Literary Conventions of Ancient Israel', in J. C. de Moor (ed.), *Intertextuality in Ugarit and Israel* (Leiden: Brill, 1998), 1–14.

66 Barton, *Reading the Bible*, 28–9.

67 Francis Watson, *Text and Truth: Redefining Biblical Theology* (Edinburgh: T. & T. Clark, 1997), 123.

68 R. W. L. Moberly, *The Bible, Theology, and Faith: A Study of Abraham and Jesus* (Cambridge: Cambridge University Press, 2000), 43.

69 Barton, *Nature of Biblical Criticism*, 177.

70 Ibid., 177.

71 Ibid., 50.

72 Ibid., 103 n. 73.

73 Wink, *The Bible in Human Transformation*, 1.

74 Ibid., 1–2.

75 David C. Steinmetz, 'The Superiority of Pre-Critical Exegesis', originally published in *Theology Today* 37 (1980); reprinted in Yarchin, *History of Biblical Interpretation*, 322–32; 323.

76 Schüssler Fiorenza, 'Ethics of Biblical Interpretation', 122.

BIBLIOGRAPHY

Abbott, S. J. Walter M. (ed.), *The Documents of Vatican II* (New York: Herder and Herder, 1966).

Aichele, George et al. (The Bible and Culture Collective), *The Postmodern Bible* (New Haven, CT: Yale University Press, 1995).

Aland, Kurt and Barbara, *The Text of the New Testament: An Introduction to the Critical Editions and to the Theory and Practice of Modern Textual Criticism*, translated by Erroll F. Rhodes (Grand Rapids: Eerdmans/Leiden: Brill, 1987).

Albertz, Martin, *Die synoptischen Streitgespräche: ein Beitrag zur Formgeschichte des Urchristentums* (Berlin: Trowitzsch, 1921).

Albright, William F., 'New Light on Early Recensions of the Hebrew Bible', in Cross and Talmon, *Qumran and the History of the Biblical Text*, 140–146.

Allison, Jr., Dale C., *The Historical Jesus and the Theological Jesus* (Grand Rapids, MI: Eerdmans, 2009).

—, *Constructing Jesus: Memory, Imagination, and History* (Grand Rapids, MI: Baker Academic, 2010).

Alt, Albrecht, 'The Settlement of the Israelites in Palestine', *Essays on Old Testament History and Religion*, trans. by R. A. Wilson (Garden City, N. Y.: Doubleday, 1967), 173–221.

—, 'The God of the Fathers', *Essays on Old Testament History and Religion*, 1–100.

—, 'The Origins of Israelite Law', *Essays on Old Testament History and Religion*, 101–171.

Alter, Robert, *The Art of Biblical Narrative* (New York: Basic Books, 1981).

Anderson, Bernhard W., 'The Problem and Promise of Commentary', *Interpretation* 36 (1982), 341–355.

Ashton, John, *Understanding the Fourth Gospel* (Oxford: Clarendon, 1993).

Bacon, Benjamin W., *Studies in Matthew* (London: Constable, 1931).

Bailey, James L., 'Genre Analysis', in Green, *Hearing the New Testament: Strategies for Interpretation*, 197–221.

Bainton, Roland H., 'The Bible in the Reformation', in Greenslade (ed.), *Cambridge History of the Bible*, 3:1–37.

Baird, J. Arthur, *Audience Criticism and the Historical Jesus* (Philadelphia: Westminster Press, 1969).

Baird, William, 'New Testament Criticism', in David Noel Freedman (ed.), *Anchor Bible Dictionary* (New York and London: Doubleday, 1992), 1:730–736.

—, *History of New Testament Research*, 2 vols. (Minneapolis: Fortress Press, 1992, 2003).

Barr, James, *Comparative Philology and the Text of the Old Testament* (Oxford: Clarendon Press, 1968).

—, 'Reading the Bible as Literature', *Bulletin of the John Rylands Library* 56 (1973), 10–33.

—, *Fundamentalism* (London: SCM, ²1981).

—, *Holy Scripture: Canon, Authority, Criticism* (Oxford: Clarendon Press, 1983).

—, 'The Old Testament', in Ernest Nicholson (ed.), *A Century of Theological and Religious Studies in Britain* (Oxford: Published for the British Academy by Oxford University Press, 2003), 29–50.

Barth, Gerhard, 'Matthew's Understanding of the Law', in Bornkamm et al, *Tradition and Interpretation in Matthew*, 58–164.

Barth, Karl, *Der Römerbrief* (Munich: C. Kaiser, ¹1919, ²1922). ET: *The Epistle to the Romans*, trans. from the sixth edn. by Edwyn C. Hoskyns (London: Oxford University Press, 1933).

—, *Church Dogmatics* (Edinburgh: T. & T. Clark, 1956), I/2.

Barton, John, *Reading the Old Testament: Method in Biblical Study* (London: Darton, Longman and Todd, 1984).

—, 'What is a Book? Modern Exegesis and the Literary Conventions of Ancient Israel', in J. C. de Moor (ed.), *Intertextuality in Ugarit and Israel* (Leiden: Brill, 1998), 1–14.

—, *The Nature of Biblical Criticism* (Louisville: Westminster John Knox, 2007).

Barton, Stephen C., 'Historical Criticism and Social-Scientific Perspectives in New Testament Study', in Green, *Hearing the New Testament*, 61–89.

Bauckham, Richard, *Jesus and the Eyewitnesses: The Gospels as Eyewitness Testimony* (Grand Rapids, Mich. Eerdmans, 2006).

Bauer, Georg Lorenz, *Entwurf einer Hermeneutik des Alten und Neuen Testaments* (Leipzig: Weygand, 1799).

—, *Hebräische Mythologie des Alten und Neuen Testaments, mit Parallelen aus der Mythologie anderer Völker, vornehmlich der Griechen und Römer*, 2 vols. (Leipzig: Weygand, 1802).

Bauer, Walter, *Das Johannesevangelium erklärt* (Tübingen: J. C. B. Mohr (Paul Siebeck), ²1925).

Baur, Ferdinand Christian, 'Die Christuspartei in der korinthischen Gemeinde, der Gegensatz des petrinischen und paulinischen Christenthums in der ältesten Kirche, der Apostel Petrus in Rom', *Tübinger Zeitschrift für Theologie*, 4 (1831), 61–206.

—, *Die sogenannten Pastoralbriefe des Apostels Paulus aufs neue kritisch untersucht* (Stuttgart and Tübingen: J. G. Cotta, 1835).

—, *Das Markusevangelium nach seinem Ursprung und Charakter* (Tübingen: Ludw. Friedr. Fues, 1851).

—, *Das Christenthum und die Kirche der drei ersten Jahrhunderte* (Tübingen: L. Fr. Fues, 1853).

Bediako, Gillian M., *Primal Religion and the Bible: Willam Robertson Smith and His Heritage* (Sheffield: Sheffield Academic Press, 1997).

Bengel, J. A., *Novum Testamentum Graecum ita adornatum ut Textus probatarum editionum medullam. Margo variantium lectionum in suas classes distributarum locorumque parallelorum delectum. Apparatus subjunctus criseos sacrae Millianae praesertim compendium, limam, supplementum ac fructum inserviente* (Tübingen: Georg Cotta, 1734).

Bentley, Jerry H., *Humanist and Holy Writ: New Testament Scholarship in the Renaissance* (Princeton, NJ: Princeton University Press, 1983).

Bentzen, Aage, *Introduction to the Old Testament* (Copenhagen: Gad, 1948).

Berg, Horst Klaus, *Ein Wort wie Feuer: Wege lebendiger Bibelauslegung* (Kösel: Calwer, 1991).

Berger, Klaus, *Formgeschichte des Neuen Testaments* (Heidelberg: Quell and Meyer, 1984).

—, *Einführung in die Formgeschichte* (Tübingen: Francke, 1987).

Berndt, Rainer, 'The School of St. Victor in Paris', in Sæbø, *Hebrew Bible/Old Testament*, I/2:467–495.

Bertram, Georg, *Die Leidensgeschichte Jesu und der Christuskult: eine formgeschichtliche Untersuchung* (Göttingen: Vandenhoeck & Ruprecht, 1922).

Billerbeck, Paul, *Kommentar zum Neuen Testament aus Talmud und Midrasch*, 4 vols. (Munich: Beck, 1922–1928).

Birdsall, J. N., 'The New Testament Text', in *Cambridge History of the Bible*, 1:308–376.

Black, C. Clifton, 'The Quest of Mark the Redactor: Why has it been pursued, and what has it taught us?' *Journal for the Study of the New Testament* 33 (1988), 19–39.

—, *The Disciples according to Mark: Markan Redaction in Current Debate* (Sheffield: Sheffield Academic Press, 1989).

Blum, Erhard, *Studien zur Komposition des Pentateuch* (Berlin: de Gruyter, 1990).

Boecker, Hans Joachim, *Redeformen des Rechtslebens im Alten Testament* (Neukirchen-Vluyn: Neukirchener Verlag, [1]1964, [2]1970).

Boff, Leonardo and Boff, Clodovis, *Introducing Liberation Theology* (London: Burns & Oates, 1988).

Bohrmann, Georg, *Spinozas Stellung zur Religion. Eine Untersuchung auf der Grundlage des theologisch-politischen Traktats* (Giessen: Alfred Töpelmann, 1914).

Bonner, Gerald, 'Augustine as Biblical Scholar', *Cambridge History of the Bible*, 1:541–562.

Boorer, Suzanne, 'Source and Redaction Criticism', in Dozeman, *Methods for Exodus*, 95–130.

Borg, Marcus and Wright, N. T., *The Meaning of Jesus: Two Visions* (San Francisco: Harper, [1]1999, [2]2007).

Bornkamm, Günther, 'The Stilling of the Storm in Matthew', in Günther Bornkamm, Gerhard Barth, Heinz Joachim Held, *Tradition and Interpretation in Matthew*, translated by Percy Scott (Philadelphia: Westminster, 1963). First published in *Wort und Dienst: Jahrbuch der theologischen Schule Bethel* (1948), 49–54.

—, 'Enderwartung und Kirche im Matthäusevangelium', in W. D. Davies and D. Daube (eds), *The Background of the New Testament and its Eschatology* (Cambridge: Cambridge University Press, 1956), 222–260. ET: Bornkamm, 'End-Expectation and Church in Matthew', in Bornkamm et al., *Tradition and Interpretation in Matthew*, 15–51.

—, *Jesus of Nazareth* (London: Hodder & Stoughton, 1960).

Bornkamm, Günther; Barth, Gerhard; Held, Heinz Joachim, *Tradition and Interpretation in Matthew*, translated by Percy Scott (Philadelphia: Westminster, 1963)

Bousset, Wilhelm, *Kyrios Christos: Geschichte des Christusglaubens von den Anfängen des Christentums bis Irenaeus* (Göttingen: Vandenhoeck & Ruprecht, 1913); ET: *Kyrios Christos: A History of the Belief in Christ from the Beginnings of Christianity to Irenaeus*, trans. by John E. Steely, intro. by Rudolf Bultmann (Nashville: Abingdon Press, 1970).

Braaten, Carl E. and Jenson, Robert W., 'Introduction: Gospel, Church, and Scripture', in Carl E. Braaten and Robert W. Jenson (eds), *Reclaiming the Bible for the Church* (Edinburgh: T. & T. Clark, 1996), ix–xii.

Brecht, Martin, 'Johann Albrecht Bengels Theologie der Schrift', *Zeitschrift für Theologie und Kirche* 64 (1967), 99–120.

Brooke, George, 'The Qumran Scrolls and the Demise of the Distinction between Higher and Lower Criticism', in Jonathan G. Campbell, William John Lyons and Lloyd K. Pietersen (eds), *New Directions in Qumran Studies* (London, New York: T & T Clark International, 2005), 26–42.

Brotzman, Ellis R., *Old Testament Textual Criticism: A Practical Introduction* (Grand Rapids, Michigan: Baker Books, 1994).

Brown, Raymond, *The Death of the Messiah* (London: G. Chapman, 1994).

Bruce, F. F., 'The History of New Testament Study', in Marshall, *New Testament Interpretation*, 21–59.

Bruns, Gerald L., *Hermeneutics Ancient and Modern* (New Haven: Yale University Press, 1992).

Bultmann, Christoph, 'Early Rationalism and Biblical Criticism on the Continent', in Sæbø, *Hebrew Bible/Old Testament*, II:875–901.

Bultmann, Rudolf, *Der Stil der paulinischen Predigt und die kynischstoische Diatribe* (Göttingen: Vandenhoeck & Ruprecht, 1910), 177–91.

—, 'Das religiöse Moment in der ethischen Unterweisung des Epiktet und das Neue Testament', *Zeitschrift für die neutestamentliche Wissenschaft und die Kunde der älteren Kirche*, 13 (1912).

—, *Die Geschichte der synoptischen Tradition* (Göttingen: Vandenhoeck und Ruprecht, 1921); ET: *History of the Synoptic Tradition'*, translated by John Marsh (Oxford: Blackwell, 1963).

—, 'Der religionsgeschichtliche Hintergrund des Prologs zum Johannes-Evangelium', in Hans Schmidt (ed.), *Eucharisterion: Studien zur Religion und Literatur des Alten und Neuen Testaments: Hermann Gunkel zum 60. Geburtstage*, 2 parts (Göttingen: Vandenhoeck & Ruprecht, 1923), 2:1–26.

—, 'Die Bedeutung der neu erschlossenen mandäischen und manichäischen Quellen für das Verständnis des Johannesevangeliums', *Zeitschrift für die neutestamentliche Wissenschaft und die Kunde der älteren Kirche* 24 (1925). Both essays reprinted in Bultmann, *Exegetica: Aufsätze zur Erforschung des Neuen Testaments* (Tübingen: J. C. B. Mohr (Paul Siebeck), 1967).

—, *Die Erforschung der Synoptischen Evangelien* (Giessen: Alfred Töpelmann, ¹1925, ²1930).

—, *Jesus and the Word* (New York: Charles Scribner's Sons, 1934).

—, *Theology of the New Testament*, translated by Kendrick Grobel, 2 vols. (London: SCM, 1952).

—, *Jesus Christ and Mythology* (London: SCM, 1958).

—, *Die Exegese des Theodor von Mopsuestia* (Stuttgart: Kohlhammer, 1984).

Bultmann, Rudolf and Kundsin, Karl, *Form Criticism: Two Essays on New Testament Research*, translated by Frederick C. Grant (New York: Harper & Row, 1934).

Buss, M. J., *Biblical Form Criticism in its Context* (Sheffield: Sheffield Academic Press, 1999).

Bussmann, Wilhelm, *Synoptische Studien*, 3 vols. (Halle: Buchhandlung des Waisenhauses, 1925–1931).

Carleton Paget, J. N. B., 'The Christian Exegesis of the Old Testament in the Alexandrian Tradition', in Sæbø, *Hebrew Bible/Old Testament*, I/1:478–542.

Carrington, Philip, *According to Mark: A Running Commentary on the Oldest Gospel* (Cambridge: Cambridge University Press, 1960).

Casalis, Georges, *Correct Ideas Don't Fall From the Skies* (Maryknoll, NY: Orbis, 1984).

Cassuto, Umberto, *La Questione della Genesi* (Florence: F. Le Monnier, 1934).

—, *The Documentary Hypothesis and the Composition of the Pentateuch*, translated by Israel Abrahams (Jerusalem: Magnes, 1961).

Catchpole, David R., 'Tradition Criticism', in Marshall, *New Testament Interpretation*, 165–180.

Chadwick, Henry, *Lessing's Theological Writings*, selections in translation with an Introductory Essay (London: Adam & Charles Black, 1956).

Chadwick, Owen, *The Victorian Church*, 2 parts (London: SCM, 1970–1972).

Childs, Brevard S., 'The Sensus Literalis of Scripture: An Ancient and Modern Problem', in H. Donner, R. Hanhart, and R. Smend (eds.), *Beiträge zur alttestamentlichen Theologie: Festschrift für Walther Zimmerli zum 70. Geburtstag* (Göttingen: Vandenhoeck & Ruprecht, 1977), 80–95.

—, *Introduction to the Old Testament as Scripture* (London: SCM, 1979).

—, *The New Testament as Canon: An Introduction* (London: SCM, 1984).

Chilton, Bruce, 'Traditio-Historical Criticism and Study of Jesus', in Green, *Hearing the New Testament*, 37–60.

Clements, Ronald E., *One Hundred Years of Old Testament Interpretation* (Philadelphia: Westminster, 1976).

Coats, George W., *Genesis, with an Introduction to Narrative Literature* (Grand Rapids: Eerdmans, 1983).

Coleman, Christopher B., *The Treatise of Lorenzo Valla on the Donation of Constantine: Text and Translation into English* (New Haven: Yale University Press, 1922).

Collini, Stefan (ed.), *Interpretation and Overinterpretation: Umberto Eco with Richard Rorty, Jonathan Culler, Christine Brooke-Rose* (Cambridge: Cambridge University Press, 1992).

Conzelmann, Hans, *Jesus* (Philadelphia: Fortress, 1973).

Cross, Frank M., 'The Contribution of the Qumran Discoveries to the Study of the Biblical Text', in Cross and Talmon (eds), *Qumran and the History of the Biblical Text*, 278–292.

—, *The Ancient Library of Qumran and Modern Biblical Studies* (Grand Rapids, Mich.: Baker, 1980).

Cross, Frank M. and Talmon, Shemaryahu (eds), *Qumran and the History of the Biblical Text* (Cambridge: Harvard University Press, 1975).

Crossan, John Dominic, *Four of The Gospels: Shadows on the Contours of the Canon* (Minneapolis: Winston-Seabury, 1985).

—, *The Cross That Spoke* (San Francisco: Harper & Row, 1988).

—, *The Historical Jesus: the Life of a Mediterranean Jewish Peasant* (Edinburgh: T & T Clark, 1991).

—, *Who Killed Jesus? Exposing the Roots of Anti-Semitism in the Gospel Story of the Death of Jesus* (San Francisco: HarperSanFrancisco, 1995).

—, *The Birth of Christianity: Discovering What Happened in the Years Immediately After the Execution of Jesus* (San Francisco: HarperSanFrancisco, 1998).

—, *Jesus: A Revolutionary Biography* (London: Harper Collins, 2009).

Crüsemann, Frank, *Das Widerstand gegen das Königtum: die altköniglichen Texte des Alten Testamentes und der Kampf um den frühen israelitischen Staat* (Neukirchen-Vluyn: Neukirchener Verlag, 1978).

Daniell, David, *The Bible in English: its History and Influence* (New Haven: Yale University Press, 2003).

Davies, G. I., 'Were there schools in ancient Israel?', in Day, Gordon, and. Williamson, *Wisdom in Ancient Israel*, 199–211.

Davies, Philip R., *Whose Bible is it Anyway?* (Sheffield: Sheffield Academic Press, 1995).

Davies, W. D. and Daube, D. (eds), *The Background of the New Testament and its Eschatology* (Cambridge: Cambridge University Press, 1954, 1964).

Davies, W. D. and Allison, Dale C., *The Gospel according to Saint Matthew*, 3 vols. Edinburgh: T & T Clark, 1988–1997).

Dawson, David, *Allegorical Readers and Cultural Revision in Ancient Alexandria* (Berkeley, Calif.: University of California Press, 1992).

Day, John; Gordon, Robert P.; Williamson, H. G. M. (eds), *Wisdom in Ancient Israel* (Cambridge: Cambridge University Press, 1995).

Delitzsch, Friedrich, *Die Lese- und Schreibfehler im Alten Testament nebst den dem Schrifttexte einverleibten Randnoten klassifiziert: ein Hilfsbuch für Lexikon und Grammatik, Exegese und Lektüre* (Berlin and Leipzig: Walter de Gruyter & Co., 1920).

Dibelius, Martin, *Die Formgeschichte des Evangeliums* (Tübingen: J. C. B. Mohr (Paul Siebeck), [1]1919, [2]1933). ET: Martin Dibelius, *From Tradition to Gospel*, translated by Bertram Lee Woolf (Cambridge: James Clarke, 1971).

—, *Die Geisterwelt im Glauben des Paulus* (Göttingen: Vandenhoeck & Ruprecht, 1909).

—, *Die urchristliche Überlieferung von Johannes dem Täufer* (Göttingen: Vandenhoeck & Ruprecht, 1911)..

Di Vito, Robert A., 'Tradition-Historical Criticism', in McKenzie and Haynes, *To Each Its Own Meaning*, 90–104.

Dodd, C. H., *The Parables of the Kingdom* (London: Nisbet & Co., 1935).

—, *Historical Tradition in the Fourth Gospel* (Cambridge: Cambridge University Press, 1963).

Donahue SJ, John R., 'Redaction Criticism: Has the *Hauptstrasse* Become a *Sackgasse?*', in Malbon and McKnight, *The New Literary Criticism and the New Testament*, 27–57.

Donfried, Karl P., 'Alien Hermeneutics and the Misappropriation of Scripture', in Braaten and Jenson, *Reclaiming the Bible for the Church*, 19–45.

Dozeman, Thomas B. (ed.), *Methods for Exodus* (Cambridge: Cambridge University Press, 2010).

Drewermann, Eugen, *Tiefenpsychologie und Exegese* (Zürich and Düsseldorf: Walter Verlag, [1]1984–1985, [5]1997–1998).

Dunn, James D. G., *The Evidence for Jesus: the Impact of Scholarship on our Understanding of how Christianity Began* (London: SCM, 1985).

—, *Jesus Remembered* (Grand Rapids, MI: Eerdmans, 2003)

Dunn, James D. G., and McKnight, Scot (eds), *The Historical Jesus in Recent Research* (Winona Lake, IN: Eisenbrauns, 2005).

Düsterdieck, Friedrich, *Kritisch Exegetisches Handbuch über die Offenbarung Johannis* (Göttingen: Vandenhoeck und Ruprecht, 1859). ET: Friedrich Düsterdieck, *Critical and Exegetical Handbook to the Revelation of John*, trans. from 3rd edn. of the German by Henry E. Jacobs (New York: Funk & Wagnalls, 1887).

Easton, Burton Scott, *The Gospel before the Gospels* (London: George Allen & Unwin, 1928).

Ebeling, Gerhard, 'Bedeutung der historisch-kritischen Methode für die protestantische Theologie und Kirche', *Zeitschrift für Theologie und Kirche* 47 (1950): 1–46; ET: 'The Significance of the Critical Historical Method for Church and Theology in Protestantism', in *Word and Faith*, translated by James W. Leitch (London: SCM, 1963), 17–61.

—, 'The Question of the Historical Jesus and the Problem of Christology', in *Word and Faith*, 288–304.

—, *Das Wesen des christlichen Glaubens* (Tübingen: J. C. B. Mohr (Paul Siebeck), 1959); ET: *The Nature of Faith*, trans. by Ronald Gregor Smith (London: Collins, 1961).

—, *Introduction to a Theological Theory of Language*, trans. by R. A. Wilson (London: Collins, 1973).

Egger, Wilhelm, *Methodenlehre zum Neuen Testament: Einführung in linguistische und historisch-kritische Methoden* (Freiburg im Breisgau: Herder, ³1987).

Ehrman, Bart D., 'Textual Criticism of the New Testament', in Green, *Hearing the New Testament*, 127–145.

Ehrman, Bart D. and Holmes, Michael W., *The Text of the New Testament in Contemporary Research: Essays on the Status Quaestionis* (Grand Rapids, Mich.: Eerdmans, 1995).

Eichhorn, Johann Gottfried, *Einleitung in das Alte Testament* (Leipzig: Weidmanns, 1780–1783).

—, *Johann Gottfried Eichhorns Urgeschichte*, edited with introduction and notes by Johann Philipp Gabler, 2 vols. (Altdorf and Nuremberg: Monath and Kussler, 1790–1792).

— , 'Über die drey ersten Evangelien: Einige Beyträge zu ihrer künftigen kritischen Behandlung', in Eichhorn, *Allgemeine Bibliothek der biblischen Litteratur* vol. 5 (Leipzig: Weidmann, 1793), 759–996.

Eissfeldt, Otto, *Hexateuch-Synopse* (Leipzig: J. C. Hinrich, 1922).

Elliott, J. K., *Essays and Studies in New Testament Textual Criticism*, 3 vols. (Cordoba: Ediciones el Almendro, 1992).

Elliott, J. K. and Moir, I., *Manuscripts and the Text of the New Testament: An Introduction for English Readers* (Edinburgh: T & T Clark, 1995).

Elliott, J. K., 'The Text of the New Testament', in Hauser and Watson, *A History of Biblical Interpretation*, 2:227–253.

Elliott-Binns, L. E., *Religion in the Victorian Era* (London and Redhill: Lutterworth Press, 1946).

Epp, E. J. and Fee, G. D. (eds), *New Testament Textual Criticism - its Significance for Exegesis: Essays in Honour of Bruce M. Metzger* (Oxford: Clarendon Press, 1981).

Epp, E. J. and Fee, G. D., *Studies in the Theory and Method of New Testament Textual Criticism* (Grand Rapids: Eerdmans, 1993).

Epp, E. J. and McRae, G. W. (eds), *The New Testament and its Modern Interpreters* (Philadelphia: Fortress, 1989).

Epp, Eldon Jay, 'Textual Criticism in the Exegesis of the New Testament, with an Excursus on Canon', in Stanley J. Porter (ed.), *Handbook to Exegesis of the New Testament* (Leiden: Brill, 1997), 45–97.

Evans, Craig A., *The Interpretation of Scripture in Early Judaism and Christianity: Studies in Language and Tradition* (London: T&T Clark, 2004).

295

Evans, G. R., 'Masters and Disciples: Aspects of Christian Interpretation of the Old Testament in the Eleventh and Twelfth Centuries', in Sæbø, *Hebrew Bible/Old Testament*, I/2:237–260.

Farmer, William R., *The Synoptic Problem: A Critical Analysis* (Dillsboro, North Carolina: Western North Carolina Press, 1976).

Farrar, Frederic W., *History of Interpretation* (London: Macmillan, 1886).

—, *The Life of Christ* (London: Cassell Petter and Galpin, 1872).

Farrer, A. M., *St. Matthew and St. Mark* (Westminster: Dacre, 1954).

Fascher, Emil, *Die formgeschichtliche Methode* (Giessen: Alfred Töpelmann, 1924).

Feyerabend, Paul, *Against Method: Outline of an Anarchistic Theory of Knowledge* (London: Verso, 1988).

Finegan, Jack, *Encountering New Testament Manuscripts: A Working Introduction to Textual Criticism* (Grand Rapids, MI: Eerdmans, 1974).

Fitzmyer, Joseph A., SJ, 'The Biblical Commission's Instruction on the Historical Truth of the Gospels', *Theological Studies* 25 (1964), 386–408.

—, *The Interpretation of Scripture: In Defense of the Historical–Critical Method* (New York/Mahweh, NJ: Paulist Press, 2008).

Floss, Johannes P., 'Form, Source, and Redaction Criticism', in J. W. Rogerson and Judith M. Lieu (eds), *The Oxford Handbook of Biblical Studies* (Oxford: Oxford University Press, 2010), 591–614.

Fohrer, Georg, *Introduction to the Old Testament*, trans. by David E. Green (Nashville: Abingdon, 1968).

Fortna, Robert Tomson, *The Gospel of Signs: A Reconstruction of the Narrative Source Underlying the Fourth Gospel* (Cambridge: Cambridge University Press, 1970).

Froehlich, Karlfried, 'Christian Interpretation of the Old Testament in the High Middle Ages', in Sæbø, *Hebrew Bible/Old Testament*, I/2:496–558.

Frör, Kurt, *Wege zur Schriftauslegung* (Dusseldorf: Patmos, 1963).

Frye, R. M., 'Literary Criticism and Gospel Criticism', *Today* 36 (1979), 207–219.

Fuchs, Ernst, *Zur Frage nach dem Historischen Jesus* (Tübingen: J. C. B. Mohr (Paul Siebeck), 1960); ET: *Studies of the Historical Jesus* (London: SCM, 1964).

Fuller, R. H., *A Critical Introduction to the New Testament* (London: Duckworth, 1966).

Fuller, Russell, 'The Text of the Tanak', in Hauser and Watson, *A History of Biblical Interpretation*, 2:201–226.

Funk, Robert W., 'The Watershed of the American Biblical Tradition: the Chicago School, First Phase, 1892–1920', *Journal of Biblical Literature* 95 (1976), 4–22.

Füssel, Kurt, 'The Materialist Reading of the Bible: Report on an Alternative Approach to Biblical Texts', in Norman K. Gottwald and Richard A. Horsley (eds), *The Bible and Liberation. Political and Social Hermeneutics* (Maryknoll, NY: Orbis, 1993; revised edn.), 116–127.

Gardner, Helen, *The Business of Criticism* (London: Oxford University Press, 1959).

Garton, Lloyd, *Horae Synopticae Electronicae: Word Statistics of the Synoptic Gospels* (Missoula, MT: Society of Biblical Literature, 1973).

Geddes, Alexander, *The Holy Bible*, vol. 1 (London: J. David, 1792).

—, *Critical Remarks on the Hebrew Scriptures*, vol. 1 (London: Davis, Wilks, and Taylor, 1800).

Gemser, B., 'The Rîb- or Controversy Pattern in Hebrew Mentality', in M. Noth and D. Winton Thomas (eds), *Wisdom in Israel and the Ancient Near East* (Leiden: Brill, 1955).

Gerhardsson, Birger, *Memory and Manuscript: Oral Tradition and Written Transmission in Rabbinic Judaism and Early Christianity* (Lund: C. W. K. Gleerup, 1961).

Gerstenberger, Erhard S., *Wesen und Herkunft des ,Apodiktischen Rechts'* (Neukirchen: Neukirchener, 1965).

—, *Psalms Part 1, with an Introduction to Cultic Poetry* (Grand Rapids, MI: Eerdmans, 1988).

—, 'Covenant and Commandment', *Journal of Biblical Literature* 84 (1965), 38–51.

Girgensohn, Karl, 'Geschichtliche und übergeschichtliche Schriftauslegung', in *Allgemeine Evangelisch-lutherische Kirchenzeitung*, 55 (1922).

—, 'Die Grenzgebiete der systematischen Theologie', *Greifswalder Reformgedanken zum theologischen Studium* (Munich, 1922).

Gore, Charles, (ed.), *Lux Mundi* (London: John Murray, 1889).

Goshen-Gottstein, Moshe H., 'The Rise of the Tiberian Bible Text', in Sid Z. Leiman (ed.), *The Canon and Masorah of the Hebrew Bible* (New York: Ktav, 1974).

Gottwald, Norman K., *The Tribes of Yahweh: A Sociology of the Religion of Liberated Israel, 1250–1050 BCE* (Maryknoll, NY: Orbis Books, 1979).

Graf, Karl Heinrich, *Die geschichtlichen Bücher des Alten Testaments* (Leipzig: T. O Weigel, 1866).

Grant, Robert M. with Tracy, David, *A Short History of the Interpretation of the Bible*, 2nd revised and enlarged edition (London: SCM, 1984).

Grayzel, Solomon, *A History of the Jews from the Babylonian Exile to the Present 5728–1968* (New York and Toronto: The New American Library, 1968).

Green, Joel B .(ed.), *Hearing the New Testament: Strategies for Interpretation* (Grand Rapids, Mich.: William B. Eerdmans, 1995).

Greenslade, S. L., 'English Versions of the Bible, 1525–1611', in S. L. Greenslade (ed.), *The Cambridge History of the Bible*, vol 3: *The West from the Reformation to the Present Day* (Cambridge: Cambridge University Press, 1963), 141–174.

Greer, Rowan A., *Theodore of Mopsuestia: Exegete and Theologian* (London: Faith, 1961).

Griesbach, J. J., *Synopsis Evangeliorum Matthäi Marci et Lucae una cum iis Joannis pericopis quae omnino cum caeterorum Evangelistarum narrationibus conferendae sunt. Textum recensuit* . . . J. J. Griesbach (Halle: Curtiana, 1776).

—, *Commentatio qua Marci Evangelium totum e Matthaei et Lucae commentariis decerptum esse monstratur*, 1789–90; reprinted in extended form in *Commentationes Theologicae*, ed. J. C. Velthusen, C. Th. Kuinoel, and G. A. Ruperti, Vol. I (1794), pp. 360ff.

Griffiths, Richard (ed.), *The Bible in the Renaissance: Essays on Biblical Commentary and Translation in the Fifteenth and Sixteenth Centuries* (Aldershot: Ashgate, 2001).

Gunkel, Hermann, *Die Sagen der Genesis* (Göttingen: Vandenhoeck & Ruprecht, 1901); ET: *The Legends of Genesis: The Biblical Saga and History*, translated by W. H. Carruth, introduction by William F. Albright (New York: Schocken, 1964).

—, *Zum religionsgeschichtlichen Verständnis des Neuen Testaments* (Göttingen: Vandenhoeck & Ruprecht, 1903).

—, 'Die israelitische Literatur', in *Die Kultur der Gegenwart*, 32 vols. (Leipzig: Teubner, 1905–1926), I.7:51–102.

—, 'Die Grundprobleme der israelitischen Literaturgeschichte', in *Reden und Aufsätze* (Göttingen: Vandenhoeck & Ruprecht, 1913), 29–38. ET: Hermann Gunkel, 'Fundamental Problems of Hebrew Literary History', in Hermann Gunkel, *What Remains of the Old Testament*, 57–68.

—, *What Remains of the Old Testament and Other Essays*, translated by A. K. Dallas (London: George Allen & Unwin, 1928).

—, *The Folktale in the Old Testament*, trans. by Michael D. Rutter (Sheffield: Almond Press, 1987).

Guthrie, Donald, *New Testament Introduction* (London: Tyndale, 1970).

Güttgemanns, Erhardt, *Offene Fragen zur Formgeschichte des Evangeliums. Eine methodologische Skizze der Grundlagenproblematik der Form- und Redaktionsgeschichte* (Munich: C. Kaiser, 1970, 2nd edn., 1971); ET: *Candid Questions concerning Gospel Form Criticism: A Methodological Sketch of Form and Redaction Criticism*, translated by William G. Doty (Pittsburgh, Penn.: Pickwick, 1979).

Habel, Norman, *Literary Criticism of the Old Testament* (Philadelphia: Fortress, 1971).

Haenchen, Ernst, *Der Weg Jesu* (Berlin: Alfred Töpelmann, 1966).

Hahn, Ferdinand, *Christologische Hoheitstitel: Ihre Geschichte im frühen Christentum* (Göttingen: Vandenhoeck & Ruprecht, ¹1963, ²1964); ET: *The Titles of Jesus in Christology*, translated by Harold Knight and George Ogg (London: Lutterworth, 1969).

Hahn, Ferdinand; Lohff, Wenzel; Bornkamm, Günther, *What can we know about Jesus? Essays on the New Quest*, translated by Grover Foley (Philadelphia: Fortress, 1969).

Halivni, David Weiss, *Revelation Restored: Divine Writ and Critical Responses* (London: SCM, 2001).

Hanson, R. P. C., *Allegory and Event: A Study of the Sources and Significance of Origen's Interpretation of Scripture* (London: SCM, 1959).

— 'Biblical Exegesis in the Early Church', in P. R. Ackroyd and C. F. Evans (eds), *The Cambridge History of the Bible*, vol. 1: *From the Beginnings to Jerome*, 307–77 (Cambridge: Cambridge University Press, 1970), 412–453.

von Harnack, Adolf, *Das Wesen des Christentums. Sechzehn Vorlesungen vor Studierenden aller Facultäten im Wintersemester 1899/1900 an der Universität Berlin gehalten* (Leipzig: J. C. Hinrichs'sche Buchhandlung, 1900); ET: *What is Christianity? Sixteen Lectures Delivered in the University of Berlin during the Winter-Term 1899–1900*, translated by Thomas Bailey Saunders (London: Williams and Norgate, 1901).

Harris, Robert A., 'Medieval Jewish Biblical Exegesis', in Hauser and Watson, *A History of Biblical Interpretation*, 2:141–171.

Harrison, R. K., *Introduction to the Old Testament with a Comprehensive Review of Old Testament Studies and a Special Supplement on the Apocrypha* (Grand Rapids: Eerdmans, 1969).

Harvey, Van A., *The Historian and the Believer: the Morality of Historical Knowledge and Christian Belief*, with a New Introduction by the Author (Urbana and Chicago: University of Illinois Press, 1966, 1996).

Hase, Karl, *Das Leben Jesu: Ein Lehrbuch zunächst für akademische Vorlesungen* (Leipzig: Johann Friedrich Leich, 1829).

Hauser Alan J., and Watson, Duane F. (eds), *A History of Biblical Interpretation*, 2 vols., vol. 1: *The Ancient Period*; vol. 2: *The Medieval through the Reformation Periods* (Grand Rapids, Mich.: William B. Eerdmans, 2003, 2009).

Hayes, John H. (ed.), *Old Testament Form Criticism* (San Antonio: Trinity University Press, 1974).

Hayes, John Haralson and Prussner, Frederick C., *Old Testament Theology: its History and Development* (London: SCM, 1985).

Hayes, John H., *Dictionary of Biblical Interpretation*, 2 vols. (Nashville: Abingdon, 1999).

—, 'Historical Criticism of the Old Testament Canon', in Sæbø, *Hebrew Bible/Old Testament*, II:985–1005.

Held, Heinz Joachim, 'Matthew as Interpreter of the Miracle Stories', in Bornkamm et al., *Tradition and Interpretation in Matthew*, 165–299.

Hendel, Ronald S., 'The Oxford Hebrew Bible: Prologue to a New Critical Edition', *Vetus Testamentum* 58 (2008), 324–351.

—, 'Assessing the Text-Critical Theories of the Hebrew Bible after Qumran', in Timothy H. Lim and John J. Collins (eds), *Oxford Handbook of the Dead Sea Scrolls* (Oxford: Oxford University Press, 2010), 281–302.

Herder, J. G., *Christliche Schriften*. Second Collection: *Vom Erlöser der Menschen. Nach unsern drei ersten Evangelien* (Riga: Johann Friedrich Hartknoch, 1796). Third Collection: *Von Gottes Sohn, der Welt Heiland. Nach Johannes Evangelium. Nebst einer Regel der Zusammenstimmung unserer Evangelien aus ihrer Entstehung und Ordnung*. Also in Herder's *Sämmtliche Werke*, ed. B. Suphan, 32 vols. (Berlin: Weidmann, 1877–1913), vol. XIX.

Herrmann, Willibald, *Der Verkehr des Christen mit Gott: Im Anschluss an Luther dargestellt* (Stuttgart: Cotta, 1886); ET: *The Communion of the Christian with God: A Discussion in Agreement with the View of Luther*, translated from the second thoroughly revised edition, with special annotations by the author, by J. Sandys Stanyon (London: Williams and Norgate, 1895).

Hidal, Sten, 'Exegesis of the Old Testament in the Antiochene School with its Prevalent Literal and Historical Method', in Sæbø, *Hebrew Bible/Old Testament*, I/1:543–568.

Hill, Robert C., *Reading the Old Testament in Antioch* (Leiden: Brill, 2005).

Hirsch, Emanuel *Geschichte der neuern evangelischen Theologie im Zusammenhang mit den allgemeinen Bewegungen des europäischen Denkens*, 5 vols. (Gütersloh: C. Bertelsmann, 1949–1954).

Holl, Karl, *Urchristentum und Religionsgeschichte* (Gütersloh: C. Bertelsmann, 1925); ET: *The Distinctive Elements in Christianity*, translated by N. V. Hope (Edinburgh: T & T Clark, 1937).

Hölscher, Gustav, 'Komposition und Ursprung des Deuteronomiums', *Zeitschrift für die alttestamentliche Wissenschaft* 40 (1922): 161–255.

Holtzmann, Heinrich Julius, *Die Synoptischen Evangelien: ihr Ursprung und geschichtlicher Charakter* (Leipzig: Wilhelm Engelmann, 1863).

Horbury, William, 'The New Testament', in Nicholson, *A Century of Theological and Religious Studies in Britain*, 51–134.

Hornig, Gottfried, *Die Anfänge der historisch-kritischen Theologie: J. S. Semlers Schriftverständnis und seine Stellung zu Luther* (Göttingen: Vandenhoeck & Ruprecht, 1961).

Hupfeld, Hermann, *Die Quellen der Genesis und die Art ihrer Zusammensetzung* (Berlin: Wiegandt und Grieben, 1853).

Iber, Gerhard, 'Zur Formgeschichte der Evangelien', *Theologische Rundschau* 24 (1957/58).

Jacob, Benno, *Das erste Buch der Tora: Genesis übersetzt und erklärt* (Berlin: Schocke, 1934); ET: Benno Jacob, *The First Book of the Torah, Genesis,* translated with commentary by B. Jacob (New York: Ktav Publishing House, 1974).

Jeanrond, Werner G., *Theological Hermeneutics: Development and Significance* (London: SCM, 1994).

Jowett, Benjamin, 'On the Interpretation of Scripture', in Temple (ed.), *Essays and Reviews*, 330–433.

Kahle, Paul, 'Untersuchungen zur Geschichte des Pentateuchtextes', *Theologische Studien und Kritiken* 88 (1915), 399–439; reprinted in *Opera Minor: Festgabe zum 21. Januar 1956* (Leiden: Brill, 1956), 3–37.

—, *The Cairo Geniza* (Oxford: Blackwell, 2ⁿᵈ revised edn. 1959).

Kähler, Martin, *Der sogenannte historische Jesus und der geschichtliche biblische Christus* (Leipzig: A. Deichert, 1892); ET: Martin Kähler, *The So-Called Historical Jesus and the Historic, Biblical Christ*, translated by Carl E. Braaten (Philadelphia: Fortress Press, 1964).

Kaiser, Otto, *Der Prophet Jesaja Kapitel 13–39* (Göttingen: Vandenhoeck & Ruprecht, 1973).

Käsemann, Ernst, 'Das Problem des historischen Jesus', in Ernst Käsemann, *Exegetische Versuche und Besinnungen*, vol.I (Göttingen, Vandenhoeck und Ruprecht, 1960), 187–214. ET: 'The Problem of the Historical Jesus', in Ernst Käsemann, *Essays on New Testament Themes*, translated by W. J. Montague (London: SCM, 1964).

—, 'Vom theologischen Recht historisch-kritischer Exegese', *Zeitschrift für Theologie und Kirche* 64 (1967), 259–281.

—, *Commentary on Romans* (London: SCM, 1980).

Kaufmann, J., 'Probleme der israelitisch-jüdischen Religionsgeschichte', *Zeitschrift für die alttestamentliche Wissenschaft* 48 (1930), 23–32; 51 (1933): 35–47.

Kaufmann, Yehezkel, *The Religion of Israel from its Beginnings to the Babylonian Exile*, trans. by M. Greenberg (London: Allen & Unwin, 1960).

Keil, Karl August Gottlieb, *Lehrbuch der Hermeneutik des neuen Testaments nach Grundsätzen der grammatisch-historischen Interpretation* (Leipzig: Friedrich Christian Wilhelm Vogel, 1810).

Kieffer, René, 'Jerome: His Exegesis and Hermeneutics', in Sæbø, *Hebrew Bible/Old Testament*, I/1:663–681.

Kierkegaard, Søren, *Concluding Unscientific Postscript to Philosophical Fragments*, translated and edited by Howard V. Hong and Edna H. Hong with Introduction and Notes, 2 vols. (Princeton: Princeton University Press, 1992).

—, *Philosophical Fragments/Johannes Climacus*, translated and edited by Howard V. Hong and Edna H. Hong with Introduction and Notes (Princeton: Princeton University Press, 1985).

—, *For Self-Examination and Judge for Yourself!*, translated and edited by Howard V. Hong and Edna H. Hong with Introduction and Notes (Princeton: Princeton University Press, 1990).

Kilpatrick, G. D., 'Western Text and Original Text in the Gospels and Acts', *Journal of Theological Studies*, xliv (1943), 24–36.

—, 'Western Text and Original Text in the Epistles', *Journal of Theological Studies*, xlv (1944), 60–65.

—, *The Principles and Practice of New Testament Textual Criticism: Collected Essays*, ed. by J. K. Elliott (Leuven: Leuven University Press,/Peeters, 1990).

Kippenberg, Hans G., *Religion und Klassenbildung im antiken Judäa. Eine religionssoziologische Studie zum Verhältnis von Tradition und gesellschaftlicher Entwicklung* (Göttingen: Vandenhoeck & Ruprecht, ¹1978, ²1982).

Kittel, Gerhard, *Die Probleme des palästinischen Spätjudentums und das Urchristentum* (Stuttgart: Kohlhammer, 1926).

—, (ed.), *Theologisches Wörterbuch zum Neuen Testament*, 10 vols. (Stuttgart: W. Kohlhammer, 1933–1979). ET: *Theological Dictionary of the New Testament*, trans. by Geoffrey W. Bromiley 10 vols. (Grand Rapids, Mich.: Eerdmans, 1964–1976).

Klein, Ralph W., *Textual Criticism of the Old Testament* (Philadelphia: Fortress, 1974).

Knierim, Rolf P. and Coats, George W., *Numbers* (Grand Rapids, MI: Eerdmans, 2005).

Knight, Douglas A., *Rediscovering the Traditions of Israel*, revised edn. (Missoula, Montana: Society of Biblical Literature and Scholars Press, 1975).

Koch, Klaus et al., *Amos: Untersucht mit den Methoden einer strukturalen Formgeschichte*, 3 vols. (Neukirchen-Vluyn: Neukirchener Verlag; Butzon & Bercker, 1976).

Koch, Klaus, *Was ist Formgeschichte? Methoden der Bibelexegese*, (Neukirchen-Vluyn: Neukirchener Verlag, ¹1974, ⁵1989). ET: *The Growth of the Biblical Tradition: The Form-Critical Method*, translated by S. M. Cupitt (London: Adam & Charles Black, 1969).

Koehler, Ludwig, *Das formgeschichtliche Problem des Neuen Testaments* (J. C. B. Mohr (Paul Siebeck), 1927).

—, *Hebrew Man*, translated by Peter R. Ackroyd (London: SCM, 1956).

—, 'Justice in the Gate', in *Hebrew Man*, 127–150.

Kooij, Arie van der, 'Textual Criticism', in Rogerson and Lieu (eds), *Oxford Handbook of Biblical Studies*, 579–590.

Köpf, Ulrich, 'The Institutional Framework of Theological Studies in the Late Middle Ages', in Sæbø, *Hebrew Bible/Old Testament*, II:123–153.

Kosellek, Reinhart, *Critique and Crisis: Enlightenment and the Pathogenesis of Modern Society* (Oxford, New York and Hamburg: Berg, 1988).

Krans, Jans, *Beyond What is Written: Erasmus and Beza as Conjectural Critics of the New Testament* (Leiden: Brill, 2006).

Kraus, Hans-Joachim, *Geschichte der historisch-kritischen Erforschung des Alten Testaments von der Reformation bis zur Gegenwart* (Neukirchen-Vluyn: Neukirchener Verlag, ³1982).

Krentz, Edgar, *The Historical–Critical Method* (Philadelphia: Fortress Press, 1975).

Kuhn, Thomas S., *The Structure of Scientific Revolutions* (Chicago: University of Chicago Press, ¹1968, ³1996).

Kümmel, Werner Georg, *The New Testament: the History of the Investigation of its Problems*, translated by S. McLean and Howard C. Kee (London: SCM, 1978).

Kundsin, Karl, *Topologische Überlieferungsstoffe im Johannes-Evangelium* (Göttingen: Vandenhoeck & Ruprecht, 1925).

Lachmann, Karl, *Novum Testamentum Graece* (Berlin: G. Reimer, 1831).

—, 'De ordine narrationum in evangeliis synopticis', in *Theologische Studien und Kritiken* 8 (Hamburg, 1835), 570–590.

—, *Novum Testamentum Graece et Latine*. Carolus Lachmannus recensuit, Philippus Buttmanus *Graece lectionis autoritates apposuit*, 2 vols. (Berlin: G. Reimer, 1842–50).

Laistner, M. L. W., 'Antiochene Exegesis in Western Europe', *Harvard Theological Review*, xl (1947), 19–32.

Leibniz, G. W., *New Essays on Human Understanding*, translated and edited by Peter Remnant and Jonathan Bennett (Cambridge: Cambridge University Press, 1996).

Lessing, G. E., 'On the Proof of the Spirit and of Power', *Lessing's Theological Writings*, selections in translation with an Introductory Essay by Henry Chadwick (London: Adam & Charles Black, 1956), 51–56.

— , 'New Hypothesis Concerning the Evangelists Considered as merely Human Historians', in Chadwick, *Lessing's Theological Writings*, 65–81.

— , 'The Education of the Human Race', in *Lessing's Theological Writings*, 82–98.

Liebing, Heinz, 'Historisch-kritische Theologie. Zum 100. Todestag Ferdinand Christian Baurs am 2. Dezember 1960', *Zeitschrift für Theologie und Kirche* 57 (1960), 302–317.

Lightfoot, R. H., *History and Interpretation in the Gospels* (London: Hodder and Stoughton, 1935).

— , *Locality and Doctrine in the Gospels* (London: Hodder and Stoughton, 1938).

Lim, Timothy H. and Collins, John J. (eds), *Oxford Handbook of the Dead Sea Scrolls* (Oxford: Oxford University Press, 2010).

Lohfink, Gerhard, *The Bible: Now I Get It! A Form-Criticism Handbook* (New York: Doubleday, 1979).

Lohmeyer, Ernst, *Die Offenbarung des Johannes* (Tübingen: J. C. B. Mohr (Paul Siebeck), 1926).

— , *Galiläa und Jerusalem* (Göttingen: Vandenhoeck & Ruprecht, 1936).

Louth, Andrew, *Discerning the Mystery: An Essay on the Nature of Theology* (Oxford: Clarendon, 1983).

Luther's Works: American Edition, 55 vols., vol. 54: *Table Talk*, edited and translated by Theodore G. Tappert (Philadelphia: Fortress, 1967).

Luz, Ulrich, *Matthew 8–20: A Commentary*, trans. by James E. Crouch (Minneapolis: Fortress Press, 2001).

Macquarrie, John, *Jesus Christ in Modern Thought* (London: SCM, 1990).

Maier, Bernhard, *William Roberston Smith* (Tübingen: Mohr Siebeck, 2009).

Maier, Gerhard, *Das Ende der historisch-kritischen Methode* (Wuppertal: Theologischer Verlag Rolf Brockhaus), 1974. ET: *The End of the Historical–Critical Method*, trans. by Edwin W. Leverenz and Rudolph F. Norden (Eugene, Oregon: Wipf and Stock, 1977).

Malbon, Elizabeth Struthers and McKnight, Edgar V. (eds), *The New Literary Criticism and the New Testament* (Sheffield: Sheffield Academic Press, 1994).

Malina, Bruce, *The New Testament World: Insights from Cultural Anthropology* (Atlanta: John Knox, [1]1981, [2]1993, [3]2001).

Manson, T. W., *The Servant-Messiah* (Cambridge: Cambridge University Press, 1953).

— , 'The Life of Jesus: Some Tendencies in Present-Day Research', in Davies and Daube (eds), *The Background of the New Testament and its Eschatology*, 211–221.

Marshall, I. Howard (ed.), *New Testament Interpretation: Essays in Principles and Methods* (Exeter: Paternoster, 1977).

Marxsen, Willi, 'Redaktionsgeschichtliche Erklärung der sogenannten Parabeltheorie des Markus', *Zeitschrift für Theologie und Kirche* 52 (1955), 255–271.

— , *Der Evangelist Markus* (Göttingen: Vandenhoeck & Ruprecht, [2]1959); ET: *Mark the Evangelist* (Nashville: Abingdon, 1969).

McCarter Jr., P. Kyle, *Textual Criticism: Recovering the Text of the Hebrew Bible* (Philadelphia: Fortress, 1986).

McKane, William, 'Early Old Testament Critics in Great Britain', in Sæbø, *Hebrew Bible/Old Testament*, II:953–970.

McKenzie, Steven L. and Haynes, Stephen R. (eds), *To Each Its Own Meaning: Biblical Criticisms and their Application*, revised and expanded edition (Louisville, KY: Westminster John Knox, 1999).

McKim, Donald K. (ed.) *Dictionary of Major Biblical Interpreters* (Downers Grove, Illinois: IVP Academic, ¹1998, ²2007).

McKnight, Edgar V., *The Bible and the Reader: An Introduction to Literary Criticism* (Minneapolis, MN: Fortress, 1985).

McKnight, Scot and Osborne, Grant R. (eds), *The Face of New Testament Studies: A Survey of Recent Research* (Grand Rapids, MI: Baker Academic, 2004).

Meeks, Wayne, *The Social World of the First Christians* (New Haven: Yale University Press, 1983).

—, *The Origins of Christian Morality* (New Haven: Yale University Press, 1993).

—, *In Search of the Early Christians: Selected Essays* (New Haven: Yale University Press, 2002).

Meier, John P., *A Marginal Jew: Rethinking the Historical Jesus*, 4 vols. (New Haven: Yale University Press, 1991–2009).

Mesguich, Sophie Kessler, 'Early Christian Hebraists', in Sæbø, *Hebrew Bible/Old Testament*, II:254–275.

Mesters, Carlos, 'The Use of Bible in Basic Christian Communities', in Sergio Torres and John Eagleson (eds), *The Challenge of Basic Christian Communities*, translated by John Drury (Maryknoll, NY: Orbis, 1981), 197–210.

—, *Por Tras das Palavras* (Petrópolis: Vozes, 1984).

Metzger, Bruce M., *The Early Versions of the New Testament: Their Origin, Transmission, and Limitations* (Oxford: Oxford University Press, 1977).

—, *A Textual Commentary on the Greek New Testament* (London, New York: United Bible Societies, ²1994).

Metzger, Bruce M. and Ehrman, Bart D., *The Text of the New Testament: its Transmission, Corruption, and Restoration* (Oxford: Oxford University Press, ⁴2005).

Meyer, Heinrich August Wilhelm, *Kritisch-exegetischer Kommentar über das Neue Testament*, 16 volumes (Göttingen: Vandenhoeck und Ruprecht, 1832–1859). ET: *Meyer's Commentary on the New Testament*, 20 vols. (Edinburgh: T. & T. Clark, 1873–1882).

Mill, John, *Novum Testamentum Graecum cum lectionibus variantibus* (Amsterdam, 1710).

Millard, Alan R., ' "Scriptio Continua" in Early Hebrew: Ancient Practice or Modern Surmise?' *Journal of Semitic Studies* 15 (1970), 2–15.

Minear, Paul S., *The Bible and the Historian: Breaking the Silence about God in Biblical Studies* (Nashville: Abingdon, 2002).

Moberly, R. W. L., *The Bible, Theology, and Faith: A Study of Abraham and Jesus* (Cambridge: Cambridge University Press, 2000).

Morgan, Robert, 'New Testament', in Rogerson and Lieu (eds), *Oxford Handbook of Biblical Studies*, 27–49.

Morgenstern, Julius, 'The Oldest Document of the Hexateuch', *Hebrew Union College Annual* 4 (1927), 1–138.

Mowinckel, Sigmund, *Psalmenstudien I–VI* (Kristiana: J. Dybwad, 1921–24).

—, *The Psalms in Israel's Worship*, 2 vols., trans. by D. W. Ap-Thomas (Nashville: Abingdon, 1961).

—, *Prophecy and Tradition: The Prophetic Books in Light of the Study of the Growth and History of the Tradition* (Oslo: J. Dybwad, 1946).

Muilenburg, James, 'Form Criticism and beyond', *Journal of Biblical Literature* 88 (1969), 1–18.

Nadler, Steven, 'The Bible Hermeneutics of Baruch de Spinoza', in Sæbø, *Hebrew Bible/ Old Testament*, II:827–836.

Nestle-Aland, 'Introduction', *Novum Testamentum* (Stuttgart: Deutsche Bibelgesellschaft, [26]1979).

Neuner SJ, J. and Dupuis SJ, J., *The Christian Faith in the Doctrinal Documents of the Catholic Church*, ed. by Jacques Dupuis, sixth revised and enlarged edition (New York: Alba House, 1996).

Nicholson, Ernest (ed.), *A Century of Theological and Religious Studies in Britain* (Oxford: Oxford University Press, 2004).

Nielsen, Kirsten, *Yahweh as Prosecutor and Judge: An Investigation of the Prophetic Law Suit (rîb-pattern)* (Sheffield: Journal for the Study of the Old Testament, 1978).

Nineham, D. E., 'Robert Henry Lightfoot', in D. E. Nineham (ed.), *Studies in the Gospels: Essays in Memory of R. H. Lightfoot* (Oxford: Basil Blackwell, 1955), vi–xvi.

Norris, Jr., Richard A., 'Augustine and the Close of the Ancient Period of Interpretation', in Hauser and Watson, *A History of Biblical Interpretation*, 1:380–408.

Noth, M. and Thomas, D. Winton (eds), *Wisdom in Israel and the Ancient Near East* (Leiden: Brill, 1955).

Noth, Martin, *A History of Pentateuchal Traditions*, trans. by B. W. Anderson (Englewood Cliffs, NJ: Prentice-Hall, 1972).

Ocker, Christopher, 'Scholastic Interpretation of the Bible', in Hauser and Watson, *A History of Biblical Interpretation*, 2: 254–279.

Oepke, Albrecht, *Geschichtliche und übergeschichtliche Schriftauslegung* (Gütersloh: Bertelsmann, 1931).

Oftesad, Bernt T., 'Further Development of Reformation Hermeneutics', in Sæbø, *Hebrew Bible/Old Testament*, II:602–616.

O'Neill, J. C., 'Biblical Criticism: History of Biblical Criticism', in David Noel Freedman (ed.), *Anchor Bible Dictionary* (New York and London: Doubleday, 1992), 1: 725–730.

Opitz, Peter, 'The Exegetical and Hermeneutical Work of John Oecolampadius, Huldrych Zwingli and John Calvin', in Sæbø, *Hebrew Bible/Old Testament*, II:407–451.

Overbeck, Franz, *Ueber die Christlichkeit unserer heutigen Theologie. Streit- und Friedensschrift* (Leipzig: Fritzsch, [1]1873; Leipzig: Naumann, [2]1903); ET: *On the Christianity of Theology*, translated and edited by John Elbert Wilson (San Jose, California: Pickwick 2002) and *How Christian is our Present-Day Theology?*, translated and edited by Martin Henry, with a foreword by David Tracy (London: T & T Clark/Continuum 2005).

—, *Christentum und Kultur. Gedanken und Anmerkungen zur modernen Theologie* (Basel: Schwabe 1919).

Palmer, N. H., 'Lachmann's Argument', *New Testament Studies* 13/4 (1967), 368–378.

Pannenberg, Wolfhart 'The Crisis of the Scripture Principle', in *Basic Questions in Theology*, trans. by George H. Kehm, 3 vols. (London: SCM, 1970–1973), 1:1–14.

Parker, D. C., *An Introduction to the New Testament Manuscripts and Their Texts* (Cambridge: Cambridge University Press, 2008).

Paulus, Heinrich Eberhard Gottlob, *Philologisch-kritischer und historischer Kommentar über die drey ersten Evangelien, in welchem der griechische Text, nach einer Recognition der Varianten, Interpunctionen und Abschnitte, durch Einleitungen, Inhaltsanzeigen und ununterbrochene Scholien als Grundlage der Geschichte des Urchristentums synoptisch und chronologisch bearbeit ist*, 3 vols. (Lübeck: Johann Friedrich Bohn, 1800–1802).

—, *Das Leben Jesu, als Grundlage einer reinen Geschichte des Urchristentums*, 4 vols. (Heidelberg: C. F. Winter, 1828).

—, *Exegetisches Handbuch über die drei ersten Evangelien* (Heidelberg: C. F. Winter, 1830–1833).

Peabody, David Barrett, *Mark as Composer* (Macon, GA: Mercer University Press, 1987).

Peake, A. S.; Black, Matthew; Rowley, H. H. (eds), *Peake's Commentary on the Bible* (Sunbury-on-Thames, Middlesex: Thomas Nelson and Sons, 1962).

Pedersen, Johannes, *Israel: Sjæleliv og Samfundliv* (Copenhagen: Pios, 1920); ET: *Israel: Its Life and Culture* (London: Oxford University Press, 1926).

Perrin, Norman, *Rediscovering the Teaching of Jesus* (London: SCM, 1967).

—, 'The Wredestrasse becomes the Hauptstrasse: Reflections on the Reprinting of the Dodd Festschrift', *Journal of Religion*, vol. 46, no. 2 (April 1966), 296–300.

—, *What is Redaction Criticism?* (Philadelphia: Fortress Press, 1969),

—, *A Modern Pilgrimage in New Testament Christology* (Philadelphia: Fortress Press, 1974).

—, Perrin, 'The Interpretation of the Gospel of Mark', *Interpretation* 36 (1976): 115–124.

Petersen, N. R., *Literary Criticism for New Testament Critics* (Philadelphia: Fortress Press, 1978).

Pfeiffer, R. H., 'A Non-Israelite Source of the Book of Genesis', *Zeitschrift für die alttestamentliche Wissenschaft* 48 (1930), 66–73.

—, *Introduction to the Old Testament* (New York: Harper & Brothers, 1941).

Pfleiderer, Otto, *Christian Origins* (London: Fisher Unwin, 1906).

Pitkin, Barbara, 'John Calvin and the Interpretation of the Bible', in Hauser and Watson, *A History of Biblical Interpretation*, 2:341–371.

Pius X, *Encyclical Letter ('Pascendi Gregis') of Our Most Holy Lord Pius X: On the Doctrine of the Modernists* (London: Burns & Oates, 1907).

Pontifical Biblical Institute, *The Interpretation of the Bible in the Church* (Rome: Libreria editrice vaticana, 1993).

Popper, Karl, *The Logic of Scientific Discovery* (London: Routledge, 1997).

Prior, Joseph G., *The Historical Critical Method in Catholic Exegesis* (Rome: Gregorian University Press, 2001).

Procopé, J. F., 'Greek Philosophy, Hermeneutics and Alexandrian Understanding of the Old Testament', in Sæbø, *Hebrew Bible/Old Testament*, I/1:451–477.

Pryke, E. J., *Redactional Style in the Marcan Gospel* (Cambridge: Cambridge University Press, 1978).

von Rad, Gerhard, *Die Priesterschrift im Hexateuch* (Stuttgart and Berlin: W. Kohlhammer, 1934).

—, *Genesis: A Commentary*, trans. by John H. Marks (Philadelphia: Westminster, rev. edn 1972).

Raeder, Siegfried, 'The Exegetical and Hermeneutical Work of Martin Luther', in Sæbø, *Hebrew Bible/Old Testament*, II:363–406.

Räisänen, Heikki, *Paul and the Law* (Tübingen: J. C. B. Mohr (Paul Siebeck), [1]1983, [2]1987).

—, 'Biblical Critics in the Global Village', in Räisänen et al., *Reading the Bible in the Global Village: Helsinki*, 9–28.

Räisänen, Heikki, et al., *Reading the Bible in the Global Village: Helsinki* (Atlanta: Society of Biblical Literature, 2000).

Reimarus, Fragments, edited by Charles H. Talbert, translated by Ralph S. Fraser (London: SCM, 1971).

Reitzenstein, Richard, *Die hellenistischen Mysterienreligionen* (Leipzig and Berlin: B. G. Teubner, 1910; 2nd revised edn. 1920); ET: Richard Reitzenstein, *The Hellenistic Mystery-Religions: Their Basic Ideas and Significance*, trans. by John E. Steely (Pittsburgh: Pickwick Publications, 1979).

—, *Das iranische Erlösungsmysterium: religionsgeschichtliche Untersuchungen* (Bonn: Marcus & Weber, 1921).

Renan, Ernest, *Vie de Jésus* (Paris: Michel Levy Frère, 1863); ET: *The Life of Jesus* (London: Trubner & Co., 1863).

Rendtorff, Rolf, *The Problem of the Process of Transmission in the Pentateuch*, translated by John J. Scullion (Sheffield: Sheffield Academic Press, 1990).

Rescher, Nicholas (ed.), *G. W. Leibniz's Monadology: An Edition for Students* (London: Routledge, 1991).

Reventlow, Henning Graf, *Epochen der Bibelauslegung*, 4 vols. (München: C. H. Beck, 1990–2001).

—, 'English Rationalism, Deism and Early Biblical Criticism', in Sæbø, *Hebrew Bible/Old Testament*, II:851–874.

—, 'Towards the End of the "Century of Enlightenment": Established Shift from *Sacra Scriptura* to Literary Documents and Religion of the People of Israel', in Sæbø, *Hebrew Bible/Old Testament*, II:1024–1063.

Riches, John K., *A Century of New Testament Study* (Cambridge: Lutterworth, 1993).

Richter, Wolfgang, *Exegese als Literaturwissenschaft: Entwurf einer alttestamentlichen Literaturtheorie und Methodologie* (Göttingen: Vandenhoeck & Ruprecht, 1971).

Riddle, Donald Wayne, *The Gospels: their Origin and Growth* (Chicago: Chicago University Press, 1939).

Riesenfeld, Harald, *The Gospel Tradition and its Beginnings: A Study in the Limits of 'Formgeschichte'* (London: Mowbray, 1957).

Ritschl, Albrecht, *Die christliche Lehre von der Rechtfertigung und Versöhnung*, 3 vols. (Bonn: Adolph Marcus, 1870–1874); ET: *The Christian Doctrine of Justification and Reconciliation: the Positive Development of the Doctrine*, translated by H. R. Mackintosh and A. B. Macaulay (Edinburgh: T. & T. Clark, 1900).

Roberts, Alexander and Donaldson, James (eds), *The Ante-Nicene Fathers: Translations of the Writings of the Fathers down to A.D. 325*, vol. IV (Grand Rapids: Eerdmans, 1971).

Roberts, Bleddyn J., *The Old Testament Text and Versions* (Cardiff: University of Wales Press, 1951).

—, 'The Textual Transmission of the Old Testament', in G. W. Anderson (ed.), *Tradition and Interpretation* (Oxford: Oxford University Press, 1979), 1–30.

Robinson, James M., *A New Quest of the Historical Jesus* (London: SCM, 1959).

Robinson, James M. and Cobb, John B. (eds), *The New Hermeneutic*, 2 vols. (New York: Harper & Row, 1964).

Rogerson, John W., *Anthropology and the Old Testament* (Oxford: Blackwell, 1978).

—, *The Bible and Criticism in Victorian Britain: Profiles of F. D. Maurice and William Robertson Smith* (Sheffield: Sheffield Academic Press, 1997).

—, *W. M. L. de Wette Founder of Modern Biblical Criticism* (Sheffield: Sheffield Academic Press, 1992).

—, 'Early Old Testament Critics in the Roman Catholic Church – Focussing on the Pentateuch', in Sæbø, *Hebrew Bible/Old Testament*, II:837–850.

—, 'History of the Discipline in the Last Seventy Years: Old Testament', in Rogerson and Lieu (eds), *The Oxford Handbook of Biblical Studies*, 5–26.

Rogerson, J. W. and Lieu, Judith M. (eds), *The Oxford Handbook of Biblical Studies* (Oxford: Oxford University Press, 2010).

Rohde, Joachim, *Rediscovering the Teaching of the Evangelists* (London: SCM, 1968).

Rollinson, Philip, *Classical Theories of Allegory and Christian Culture* (Pittsburgh: Duquesne University Press, 1980).

Rückert, L. I., *Commentar über den Brief Pauli an die Römer* (Leipzig: Hartmannsche Buchhandlung, 1831).

Rummel, Erika, 'The Renaissance Humanists', in Hauser and Watson, *A History of Biblical Interpretation*, 2:280–298.

—, 'The Textual and Hermeneutic Work of Desiderius Erasmus of Rotterdam', in Sæbø, *Hebrew Bible/Old Testament*, II:215–230.

Ryder, E. T., 'Form Criticism of the Old Testament', in Matthew Black and H. H. Rowley (eds), *Peake's Commentary on the Bible*, 91–5.

Sæbø, Magne (ed.), *Hebrew Bible/Old Testament: the History of its Interpretation*, 2 vols., vol. 1: *From the Beginnings to the Middle Ages (until 1300)*; vol. 2: *From the Renaissance to the Enlightenment* (Göttingen: Vandenhoeck & Ruprecht, 1996, 2008).

Sanders, E. P., *The Tendencies of the Synoptic Tradition* (Cambridge: Cambridge University Press, 1969).

—, *Paul and Palestinian Judaism: A Comparison of Patterns of Religion* (London: SCM, 1977).

—, *Paul, the Law and the Jewish People* (Philadelphia: Fortress Press, 1983).

—, *Jesus and Judaism* (London: SCM, 1985).

—, *The Historical Figure of Jesus* (Harmondsworth, Middlesex: Penguin, 1993).

Sanders, James A., *Torah and Canon* (Philadelphia: Fortress Press, 1972).

—, *From Sacred Story to Sacred Text: Canon as Paradigm* (Philadelphia: Fortress Press, 1987).

Sandys-Wunsch, John, *What Have They Done to the Bible? A History of Modern Biblical Interpretation* (Collegeville, Minn.: Liturgical Press, 2005).

—, 'Early Old Testament Critics on the Continent', in Sæbø, *Hebrew Bible/Old Testament*, II:971–984.

Schlatter, Adolf, *Der Evangelist Matthäus* (Stuttgart: Calwer, 1929).

Schleiermacher, F. D. E., *Hermeneutics: The Handwritten Manuscripts*, edited by Heinz Kimmerle, translated by James Duke and Jack Forstman (Atlanta, GA: Scholars Press, 1977).

Schmid, H. H., *Der sogenannte Jahwist* (Zürich: Theologischer Verlag, 1976).

Schmidt, Karl Ludwig, *Der Rahmen der Geschichte Jesu: literarkritische Untersuchungen zur ältesten Jesusüberlieferung* (Berlin: Trowitsch, 1919).

Schmithals Walter, 'Kritik der Formkritik', *Zeitschrift für Theologie und Kirche* 77 (1980), 149–185.

—, *Einleitung in die ersten drei Evangelien* (Berlin: de Gruyter, 1985).

Schniewind, Julius, *Euangelion. Ursprung und erste Gestalt des Begriffs Evangelium*, 2 parts (Gütersloh: 1927, 1931).

Scholder, Klaus, *The Birth of Modern Critical Theology: Origins and Problems of Biblical Criticism in the Seventeenth Century*, translated by John Bowden (London: SCM, 1990).

Schreiber, Johannes, *Theologische Erkenntnis und unterrichtlicher Vollzug. Dargestellt am Beispiel des Markusevangeliums* (Hamburg: Furche, 1968).

Schüssler Fiorenza, Elisabeth, *In Memory of Her: A Feminist Theological Reconstruction of Christian Origins* (New York: Crossroad, 1983).

—, 'The Ethics of Biblical Interpretation: Decentering Biblical Scholarship', first published in *Journal of Biblical Literature* 107 (1988), 3–17; reprinted in Räisänen et al., *Reading the Bible in the Global Village: Helsinki*, 107–123.

—, 'Biblical Interpretation and Critical Commitment', *Studia Theologica* 43 (1989), 5–18, reprinted in Yarchin, *History of Biblical Interpretation*, 385–397.

—, 'Defending the Center, Trivializing the Margins', in Räisänen et al., *Reading the Bible in the Global Village: Helsinki*, 29–48.

—, *Jesus: Miriam's Child, Sophia's Prophet. Critical Issues in Feminist Christology* (London: Continuum, 1994).

—, *Rhetoric and Ethic: The Politics of Biblical Studies* (Minneapolis: Fortress, 1999).

Schweitzer, Albert, *The Mystery of the Kingdom of God: the Secret of Jesus' Messiahship and Passion*, translated with an introduction by Walter Lowrie (New York: Dodd, Mead and Company, 1914). First published under the title of *Das Messianitäts- und Leidensgeheimnis: Eine Skizze des Lebens Jesu* as the second part of *Das Abendmahl im Zusammenhang mit dem Leben Jesu und der Geschichte des Urchristentums* (Tübingen and Leipzig: J. C. B. Mohr (Paul Siebeck), 1901).

—, *Von Reimarus zu Wrede: Eine Geschichte der Leben-Jesu-Forschung* (Tübingen: J. C. B. Mohr (Paul Siebeck), 1906); ET: *The Quest of the Historical Jesus*, 1st complete edition, edited by John Bowden (London: SCM, 2000).

Seal, Jr, Welton O., 'Norman Perrin and his "School": Retracing a Pilgrimage', *Journal for the Study of the New Testament* 20 (1984), 87–107.

Segovia, Fernando F. *Decolonizing Biblical Studies: A View from the Margins* (Maryknoll, NY: Orbis Books, 2000).

Seitz, Christopher R., *Word without End: The Old Testament as Abiding Theological Witness* (Grand Rapids: Eerdmans, 1998).

Sellin, Ernst, *Einleitung in das Alte Testament* (Leipzig: Quelle & Meyer, [5]1929).

Semler, J. S. 'Historische Einleitung in die dogmatische Gottesgelersamkeit', in S. J. Baumgarten (ed.), *Evangelische Glaubenslehre*, 3 vols. (Halle, 1759–60).

—, *Abhandlung von freyer Untersuchung des Canon*, 4 vols. (Halle: C. H. Hemmerde, 1771–1775); reprinted as *Abhandlung von freier Untersuchung des Canon*, ed. by Heinz Scheible (Gütersloh: Mohn, 1967).

Simon, Richard, *Histoire critique du Vieux Testament* (Rotterdam: Reinier Leers, [1]1678, [2]1685).

Smalley, Beryl, *The Study of the Bible in the Middle Ages* (Oxford: Basil Blackwell, [2]1952).

Smalley, Stephen S., 'Redaction Criticism', in Marshall, *New Testament Interpretation*, 181–195.

Smend, Rudolf, *Die Erzählung des Hexateuch auf ihre Quellen untersucht* (Berlin: G. Reimer, 1912).

Smend, Rudolf (Jr.), *From Astruc to Zimmerli*, translated by Margaret Kohl (Tübingen: Mohr Siebeck, 2007).

Soulen, R. N. and R. K., 'Form Criticism', *Handbook of Biblical Criticism* (Louisville, KY: Westminster/John Knox Press, 2001), 178–9.

Sparks, H. F. D., 'Jerome as Biblical Scholar', *Cambridge History of the Bible*, 1:510–540.

Sparks, Kenton L., 'Genre Criticism', in Thomas B. Dozeman (ed.), *Methods for Exodus* (Cambridge: Cambridge University Press, 2010), 55–94.

Spinoza, Baruch, *Tractatus Theologico-Politicus (Gebhardt Edition, 1925)*, translated by Samuel Shirley with an Introduction by Brad S. Gregory (Leiden Brill, 1989).

'Statement of the Ecumenical Dialogue of Third World Theologians', Torres and Fabella, *The Emergent Gospel*, 269–270.

Steck, Odil Hannes, *Old Testament Exegesis: A Guide to the Methodology*, translated by James D. Nogalski (Atlanta, GA: Scholars Press, 1995).

Stein, Robert H., 'The Proper Methodology for Ascertaining a Markan *Redaktionsgeschichte*', ThD Dissertation, Princeton Theological Seminary, 1968.

—, 'What is *Redaktionsgeschichte?*', *Journal of Biblical Literature* 88 (1969), 45–56; reprinted in Stein, *Gospels and Tradition*, 21–34.

—, 'The Proper Methodology for Ascertaining a Markan Redaction History', *Novum Testamentum* 13 (1971): 181–198; reprinted as 'Ascertaining a Marcan Redaction History', in *Gospels and Traditions*, 49–67.

—, *Gospels and Tradition: Studies on Redaction Criticism of the Synoptic Gospels* (Grand Rapids, Mich.: Baker Book House, 1991).

Steinmann, J., *Biblical Criticism* (London: Burns & Oates, 1959).

Steinmetz, David C., 'The Superiority of Pre-Critical Exegesis', originally published in *Theology Today* 37 (1980); reprinted in Yarchin, *History of Biblical Interpretation*, 322–332.

Stendahl, Krister, 'Biblical Theology, Contemporary', first published in *The Interpreter's Dictionary of the Bible*, 4 vols. (Nashville: Abingdon Press, 1962), 1:418–32; reprinted in Räisänen, Heikki et al., *Reading the Bible in the Global Village: Helsinki*, 67–106.

Stonehouse, N. B., *The Witness of Luke to Christ* (London: Tyndale, 1951).

Storr, Gottlob Christian, *Über den Zweck der evangelischen Geschichte und der Briefe Johannis* (Tübingen: Jakob Friedrich Heerbrandt, [1]1786, [2]1810).

Storr, Vernon F., *The Development of English Theology in the Nineteenth Century: 1800–1860* (London: Longmans, Green and Co., 1913).

Strauss, David Friedrich, *Das Leben Jesu, kritisch bearbeitet* (Tübingen: C. Osiander, 1835–36). ET: *The Life of Jesus, Critically Examined*, translated by Marian Evans (George Eliot) (London: Chapman Brothers, 1846).

—, *Das Leben Jesu für das deutsche Volk bearbeitet* (Brockhaus: Leipzig, 1864); translated as *A New Life of Jesus* (London: Williams and Norgate, 1865).

Strauss, Leo, *Die Religionskritik Spinozas als Grundlage seiner Bibelwissenschaft: Untersuchungen zu Spinozas theologisch-politischem Traktat* (Berlin: Akademie-Verlag, 1930). ET: Leo Strauss, *Spinoza's Critique of Religion* (Chicago: Chicago University Press, 1997).

Strecker, Georg, 'Redaktionsgeschichte als Aufgabe der Synoptikerexegese', in Georg Strecker, *Eschaton und Historie: Aufsätze* (Göttingen: Vandenhoeck & Ruprecht, 1979), 9–32.

Streete, Gail P. C., 'Redaction Criticism', in McKenzie and Haynes, *To Each Its Own Meaning*, 105–121.

Streeter, B. H., *The Four Gospels. A Study of Origins, Treating of the Manuscript Tradition, Sources, Authorship, and Dates* (London: Macmillan, 1924).

Stuhlmacher, Peter, *Historical Criticism and Theological Interpretation of Scripture: Towards a Hermeneutic of Consent*, translated by Roy A. Harrisville (London: SPCK, 1979).

Sugirtharajah, R. S., 'Critics, Tools and the Global Arena', in Räisänen et al., *Reading the Bible in the Global Village*, 49–60.

Sweeney, Marvin A., 'Form Criticism', in McKenzie and Haynes, *To Each Its Own Meaning*, 59–89.

—, *I & II Kings: A Commentary* (Louisville, KY: Westminster John Knox Press, 2007).

Talmon, Shemaryahu, 'The Old Testament Text', Ackroyd and Evans, *The Cambridge History of the Bible*, 1:155–199.

—, 'The Textual Study of the Bible – A New Outlook', in Frank M. Cross and Shemaryahu Talmon (eds), *Qumran and the History of the Biblical Text* (Cambridge: Harvard University Press, 1975).

Tan, Randall K. J., 'Recent Developments in Redaction Criticism: From Investigation of Textual Prehistory back to Historical-Grammatical Exegesis?' *Journal of the Evangelical Theological Society*, 44/4 (December 2001), 599–614.

Taylor, Vincent, *Formation of the Gospel Tradition* (London: Macmillan, 1933).

Temple, Frederick et al., *Essays and Reviews* (London: John W. Parker and Son, 1860).

Theissen, Gerd, *The First Followers of Jesus: Sociological Study of the Earliest Christianity*, translated by John Bowden (London: SCM, 1978).

—, *The Social Setting of Pauline Christianity: Essays on Corinth*, edited and translated with an introduction by John H. Schütz (Edinburgh: T & T Clark, 1982).

—, *The Shadow of the Galilean* (London: SCM, 1987).

—, *Social Reality and the Early Christians: Theology, Ethics, and the World of the New Testament* (Minneapolis: Fortress Press, 1992).

—, *The Gospels in Context: Social and Political History in the Synoptic Tradition*, translated by Linda M. Maloney (Edinburgh: T & T Clark, 1992).

Theissen, Gerd and Merz, Annette, *The Historical Jesus: A Comprehensive Guide*, translated by John Bowden (London: SCM, 1998).

Theissen Gerd and Winter, Dagmar, *The Quest for the Plausible Jesus: The Question of Criteria*, translated by M. Eugene Boring (Louisville, KY: Westminster/John Knox Press, 2002).

Thiselton, Anthony C., 'New Testament Interpretation in Historical Perspective', in Joel B. Green (ed.), *Hearing the New Testament: Strategies for Interpretation* (Grand Rapids, Mich.: William B. Eerdmans, 1995), 10–36.

Thompson, Mark D., 'Biblical Interpretation in the Works of Martin Luther', in Hauser and Watson, *A History of Biblical Interpretation*, 2: 299–318.

van Til, Cornelius, *The New Hermeneutic* (Nutley, NJ: Presbyterian and Reformed Publishing Co., 1974), esp. 1–18.

de Tischendorf, Constantinus, *Novum Testamentum Graece* (Leipzig: J. C. Hinrich, 1869–1872)

Tödt, H. E., *The Son of Man in the Synoptic Tradition* (Philadelphia: Westminster Press, 1965).

Torjesen, Karen Jo, *Hermeneutical Procedure and Theological Structure in Origen's Exegesis* (Berlin: de Gruyter, 1986).

Torres, Sergio and Fabella, Virginia (eds), *The Emergent Gospel* (Maryknoll, NY: Orbis, 1978).

Tov, Emanuel, *Textual Criticism of the Hebrew Bible* (Minneapolis: Fortress Press, 1992).

—, 'A Modern Textual Outlook Based on the Qumran Scrolls', *Hebrew Union College Annual* 53 (1982), 11–27.

Travis, Stephen H., 'Form Criticism', in Marshall, *New Testament Interpretation*, 153–164.

Trigg, Joseph Wilson, *Origen: The Bible and Philosophy in the Third-Century Church* (London: SCM 1984).

Troeltsch, Ernst, 'Über historische und dogmatische Methode in der Theologie', in *Gesammelte Schriften*, 4 vols. (Tübingen: J. C. B. Mohr, 1913, 1922), 2:729–53; reprinted in Gerhard Sauter, *Theologie als Wissenschaft* (Munich: C. Kaiser, 1971), 105–127; ET: 'Historical and Dogmatic Method in Theology (1898)', in Ernst Troeltsch, *Religion in History*, translated by James Luther Adams and Walter F. Bense with an introduction by James Luther Adams (Edinburgh: T & T Clark, 1991), 11–32.

—, 'Historiography', in James Hastings (ed.), *Encyclopaedia of Religion and Ethics* (New York: Charles Scribner's Sons, 1914), 6:716–723.

Tucker, Gene M., *Form Criticism of the Old Testament* (Philadelphia: Fortress Press, 1971).

Tuckett, Christopher, *Reading the New Testament* (London: SPCK, 1987).

Ulrich, Eugene, *The Dead Sea Scrolls and the Origins of the Bible* (Grand Rapids: William B. Eerdmans, 1999).

Van Seters, John, *Abraham in History and Tradition* (New Haven, CT: Yale University Press, 1975).

—, *Prologue to History: the Yahwist as Historian in Genesis* (Louisville, KY: Westminster/John Knox Press, 1992).

Vater, J. S., *Commentar über den Pentateuch* (Halle: Waisenhaus, 1802–1805).

Vatke, Wilhelm, *Die Religion des Alten Testaments nach den kanonischen Büchern entwickelt* (Berlin: G. Bethge, 1835).

Vermes, Geza, *Jesus the Jew: A Historian's Reading of the Gospels* (London: Collins, 1973).

—, *Jesus and the World of Judaism* (London: SCM, 1983).

—, *The Religion of Jesus the Jew* (London: SCM, 1993).

—, *The Passion* (London: Penguin, 2005).

—, *The Nativity: History and Legend* (London: Penguin, 2006).

—, *The Resurrection* (London: Penguin, 2008).

Via, Jr., Dan O., *Kerygma and Comedy in the New Testament: A Structuralist Approach to Hermeneutic* (Philadelphia: Fortress Press, 1975).

Viviano, Pauline A., 'Source Criticism', in McKenzie and Haynes (eds), *To Each Its Own Meaning*, 35–57.

Wallmann, Johannes, 'Scriptural Understanding and Interpretation in Pietism', in Sæbø, *Hebrew Bible/Old Testament*, II:902–925.

Waltke, Bruce K., 'The Samaritan Pentateuch and the Text of the OT', in J. B. Payne (ed.), *New Perspectives on the Old Testament* (Waco: Word, 1979), 212–239.

—, 'The Textual Criticism of the Old Testament', in Frank E. Gaebelein (ed.), *The Expositor's Bible Commentary* (Grand Rapids: Zondervan, 1979), 1:211–228.

Wansbrough OSB, Henry, 'History and Impact of English Bible Translations', in Sæbø, *Hebrew Bible/Old Testament*, II:536–552.

—, *The Use and Abuse of the Bible: A Brief History of Biblical Interpretation* (London: T & T Clark, 2010).

Watson, Francis, *Paul, Judaism and the Gentiles: A Sociological Approach* (Cambridge: Cambridge University Press, 1986); revised edn: *Paul, Judaism and the Gentiles: Beyond the New Perspective* (Grand Rapids, MI: William B. Eerdmans, 2007).

—, *Text and Truth: Redefining Biblical Theology* (Edinburgh: T. & T. Clark, 1997).

Wegner, Paul D., *A Student's Guide to Textual Criticism of the Bible: its History, Methods & Results* (Downers Grove, IL: InterVarsity Press, 2006).

Weingreen, J., *Introduction to the Critical Study of the Text of the Hebrew Bible* (Oxford: Clarendon, 1982).

Weiser, Artur, *The Old Testament: Its Formation and Development*, trans. by Dorothea M. Barton (New York: Association Press, 1961).

Weiss, Johannes, *Die Predigt Jesu vom Reiche Gottes* (Göttingen: Vandenhoeck & Ruprecht,1892; 2nd revised edition, 1900); ET: *Jesus' Proclamation of the Kingdom of God*, translated, edited and with an introduction by Richard Hyde Hiers and David Larrimore Holland (Philadelphia: Fortress Press, 1971).

Weisse, Christian Hermann, *Die evangelische Geschichte kritisch und philosophisch bearbeitet*, 2 vols. (Leipzig: Breitkopf and Härtel, 1838).

—, *Die Evangelienfrage in ihrem gegenwärtigen Stadium* (Leipzig: Breitkopf & Härtel, 1856).

Welch, Adam C., *The Code of Deuteronomy: A New Theory of Its Origin* (London: J. Clarke, 1924).

—, 'On the Present Position of Old Testament Criticism', *Expositor* 25 (1923), 344–370.

Wellhausen, Julius, *Das Evangelium Marci* (Berlin: Georg Reimer, 2 1909).

—, *Einleitung in die drei ersten Evangelien* (Berlin: Georg Reimer, 2 1911).

Wenham, David, 'Source Criticism', in Marshall, *New Testament Interpretation*, 139–152.

Wenham, Gordon J., *Word Bible Commentary, Vol. 1: Genesis 1–15* (Nashville: Thomas Nelson Publishers, 1987).

Wenham, J. W., 'Moses and the Pentateuch', in D. Guthrie and J. A. Motyer (eds), *New Bible Commentary Revised* (London: Inter-Varsity Press, 1970), 41–43.

Wernle, Paul, *Die synoptische Frage* (Freiburg im Breisgau: J. C. B. Mohr, 1899).

Westermann, Claus, *The Praise of God in the Psalms*, trans. by Keith R. Crim (Richmond: John Knox, 1965).

—, *Basic Forms of Prophetic Speech*, trans. by H. C. White (Cambridge: Lutterworth, 1991).

de Wette, Wilhelm Martin Leberecht, *Dissertatio critico-exegetica, qua Deuteronium a prioribus Pentateuchi libris diversum, alius suiusdam recentoris auctoris opus esse monstratur* (Jena, 1805)

—, *Commentar über die Psalmen* (Heidelberg: J. C. B. Mohr, 1 1811, 5 1856).

—, *Ueber die erbauliche Erklärung der Psalmen* (Heidelberg: J. C. B. Mohr, 1836).

—, *Lehrbuch der historisch-kritischen Einleitung in die kanonischen Bücher des Neuen Testaments* (Berlin: G. Reimer, 1826); ET: *An Historico-Critical Introduction to the Canonical Books of the New Testament*, translated from the fifth, improved and enlarged edition by Frederick Frothingham (Boston: Crosby, Nichols, and Company, 1858).

—, *Kurzgefasstes exegetisches Handbuch zum Neuen Testament*, 3 vols. (Leipzig: S. Hirzel, 1836–48).

Wettstein, Johann Jacob, *Novum Testamentum Graecum editionis receptae cum lectionibus variantibus*, 2 vols. (Amsterdam: Officina Dommeriana, 1751–52).

Whybray, R. N., *The Making of the Pentateuch: A Methodological Study* (Sheffield: JSOT, 1987).

Wicks, Jared, 'Catholic Old Testament Interpretation in the Reformation and Early Confessional Eras', in Sæbø, *Hebrew Bible/Old Testament*, II:617–648.

Wiles, Maurice and Santer, Mark (eds), *Documents in Early Christian Thought* (Cambridge: Cambridge University Press, 1975).

—, 'Origen as Biblical Scholar', *Cambridge History of the Bible*, 1:489–509.

Wilke, Christian Gottlob, *Der Urevangelist: Oder Exegetisch Kritische Untersuchung über das Verwandtschaftsverhältnis der ersten drei Evangelien* (Dresden and Leipzig: Gerhard Fleischer, 1838).

Windisch, Hans, *Der Hebräerbrief erklärt* (Tübingen: J. C. B. Mohr (Paul Siebeck), ²1931).

Wink, Walter, *The Bible in Human Transformation: Toward a New Paradigm for Biblical Study* (Philadelphhia: Fortress Press, 1973; reprinted with new preface, 2010).

Wrede, Wilhelm, *Das Messiasgeheimnis in den Evangelien: zugleich ein Beitrag zum Verständnis des Markusevangeliums* (Göttingen: Vandenhoeck & Ruprecht, 1901); ET: *The Messianic Secret*, trans. by J. C. G. Greig (Cambridge: James Clarke, 1971).

Wright, David F., 'Augustine: His Exegesis and Hermeneutics', in Sæbø, *Hebrew Bible/ Old Testament*, I/1:701–730.

Wright, N. T., *Jesus and the Victory of God* (London: SPCK, 1996).

Würthwein, Ernst, *The Text of the Old Testament: An Introduction to the Biblia Hebraica*, trans. by Erroll F. Rhodes (Grand Rapids, MI: William B. Eerdmans, ²1995).

Yarchin, William, *History of Biblical Interpretation: A Reader* (Peabody, MA: Henrickson, 2004).

Yeivin, Israel, *Introduction to the Tiberian Masorah*, translated and edited by E. J. Revell (Atlanta: Society of Biblical Literature, 1980).

Young, Frances M., *Biblical Exegesis and the Formation of Christian Culture* (Peabody, Mass.: Hendrickson, 2002).

—, 'Alexandrian and Antiochene Exegesis', in Hauser and Watson, *A History of Biblical Interpretation*, 1: 334–354.

Zaharopoulos, Dimitri Z., *Theodore of Mopsuestia on the Bible: A Study of His Old Testament Exegesis* (New York: Paulist Press, 1989).

Ziegler, Theobald, *David Friedrich Strauss*, 2 vols. (Strasbourg: Karl J. Trübner, 1908).

Zimmermann, Heinz, *Neutestamentliche Methodenlehre: Darstellung der Historisch-Kritischen Methode* (Stuttgart: Kath. Bibelwerk, 1966).

BIBLE REFERENCES

Old Testament
Genesis   107, 115–18, 145, 162, 202, 230
  1–11   145
  1.1–5.32   132, 134
  1–2   18, 131
  1.1–2.4a   50, 115, 131–4
  1.1   107
  1.3–4   50
  1.12–13   131
  1.14–18   50
  1.26–27   133
  1.26–28   134
  2.1   107
  2.4a   107
  2.4b–4.26   132, 134
  2.4b–3.24   ix, 50, 107–9, 131–4, 167–73, 198–202, **238–40**
  2.4b–25   115
  2.4b–9   199
  2.4b–7   169
  2.4b   107, 108, 131, 170, 272
  2.5   131, 169
  2.6   168
  2.7   133–4
  2.8–17   169
  2.8   168, 199
  2.9   168, 199
  2.10–14   168, 199
  2.10   168
  2.12   108–9
  2.15   131, 168, 199
  2.16–17   199
  2.17   170, 199, 201
  2.18–24   169
  2.18   200
  2.19   134

  2.21–24   170
  2.23   168, 169
  2.24   168, 170
  2.25   168, 199
  3.1–24   169, 171
  3.1–19   168, 200
  3.1–5   171
  3.1   168, 169, 200
  3.3   201
  3.5   170
  3.6   169
  3.7   168, 199
  3.11–13   170
  3.14–19   168, 170
  3.14   170
  3.16   170
  3.17–19   170
  3.17   168
  3.19a   168
  3.20   168
  3.21   168, 201
  3.22   171
  3.23   168
  3.24   168
  4.1–26   132
  4.1–16   200
  4.17   2
  4.17–22   132
  5.1–32   132–4
  5.1   132, 170
  5.2   170
  6–9   145
  6.1–4   171
  10.4   102
  10.9   146
  12–25   145
  12.10–20   125

14   145
15   117
17   145
19   145
19.26   146
20.1–18   125
26.1–13   125
27–35   145
29–31   145
32   145
33.18–20   146
34   146
35.9   146
38.11   146
Exodus   116, 117
 2   87
 4.24–26   146
 9.30   200
 21.17   147
 22.5   147
Leviticus   116, 117
Numbers   116, 117, 162
 21.14–15   113
Deuteronomy   115, 116, 117
 6.20–4   148
 8   87
 11.29   86
 12–26   116, 117
 12.5   86
 26.5b–9   148
 27.4   86
 34.5–8   2
Joshua-Kings   148
Joshua   117
 1   148
 10.12b–13a   113
 23   148
 24.2b–13   148
Judges   117
Ruth   44
Samuel-Kings   182, 210
Samuel   113
1–2 Samuel   117
1 Samuel
 10.27   266
 11.1   266
 12   148
 23.19–24.22   126
 26.1–25   126

2 Samuel
 1.19–27   113
 8.16–17   21
 9–20   119
 20.24–8   21
Kings   113, 124, 140, 194
1–2 Kings   117
1 Kings
 1–2   119
 4.3   21
2 Kings
 19.35   21
 22–3   116
 22.8–9   115
Chronicles   84, 113, 124, 140, 182,
    194, 210
 1 Chron. 1.7   102
Esther   44, 84
Job   126, 201
 32–7   119
Psalms   16, 30, 88, 144, 145, 146–7,
    149, 177–8, 183
 2   30
 2.11–12   94
 8   30
 22   30, 61
 44   30
 46   183
 47   183
 109   30
 148.13   107
Proverbs   16, 194, 201
 1–9   183
 10.8–9   201
 11.30   171
 13.12   171
 15   183
 15.4   171
Ecclesiastes   201
The Prophets   88
Isaiah   114
 1–39   114, 119, 269
 1.1   114
 6.1   114
 7.13   114
 11   119
 11.6–9   119
 11.10   119
 11.11–16   119, 269

21.1–10 269
37.36 21
40 114
45.1 269
47 269
52.7–12 269
53.4 129
53.7 30
Jeremiah
25.22 283
27.3 283
47.4 283
Ezekiel
28 283
28.11–19 170, 172
Daniel 27
Hosea 31
Joel 31
2.28 30
3.4 283
Amos 31, 160
Micah
5.2 61
Zechariah
9.1–4 283
The Writings 88

Apocrypha
Judith
2.28 283
Susanna 27, 29
1 Maccabees
5.15 283

New Testament
Matthew 63, 104, 113, 119, 120,
    122, 123, 124, 126, 128–30,
    134–7, 153, 179, 182, 183–4, 186,
    187, 189, 191, 192, 193, 197,
    208–9, 215
1.18–2.23 152
2.6 61
2.22 135
4.1–11 3
4.12 135
5–7 124, 184
5.3–10 140
5.17 140, 156
6.9–13 105–6

6.27 155
7.1–23 179
8.1–4 2
8.5–13 174, 176
8.8–9 113
8.11–12 209
8.13 174
8.14–17 2
8.16–17 128
8.22b 155
8.23–7 3, 189, 204
8.28 204
9.32–4 126
10.5–6 175–6
10.6 205
10.10 2
10.23 205
10.34–6 140, 156
11.21–2 135
11.21 283
12.22–4 126
12.34b 155
13.1–52 3
13.16–17 155
13.31–2 180
13.58 129–30, 203
14.13–21 126
14.13 135
14.22–33 59
15.1–20 204, 209
15.21–8 109–11, 134–7, 173–6,
    202–10, 241
15.21 135, 202–3, 204
15.22–4 203
15.22 109–10, 174, 203, 205
15.23–5 204
15.23 136, 204, 205
15.24 136, 137, 174, 204, 205
15.24b 136, 137
15.25 135, 174
15.26–7 134, 136
15.26 110–11, 174, 205, 206
15.27 111, 174, 206–7
15.28 135, 136, 174, 205, 207–8
15.32–9 126
16.16 183
18.15–17 156
18.21–2 156
18.23–35 156

21.23–7 113
21.28–31 156
21.33–46 2
21.40–1 2
21.43 209
23 140, 156
23.12 214
23.16–19 156
23.23–4 156
23.25–6 156
24.14 176, 209, 210
24.36 104
24.43–4 156
27.5 135
27.38 153
27.51 3
28.16–20 209, 210
28.16 190
28.19 176
Mark 63, 67, 113, 119, 120, 122,
    123, 124, 126, 128–30, 134–7,
    150, 153, 179, 182, 183, 184, 186,
    187, 189, 191–3, 197, 213, 214,
    283
1.29–31 2
1.34 128
1.40–5 2, 152
2.15 129
2.19 155
2.23–8 165
3.1–6 154
3.4 156
3.22 126
3.28–9 156
4.1–41 3
4.10 113
4.11–12 113
4.13 113
4.13–20 113
4.30–2 180
4.35–41 152, 154, 189
4.35–7 154
4.38 154, 204
4.39a 154
4.39b 154
4.41 155
5.1–20 152
5.21–43 152, 164

5.43 2
5.38–40 2
6.5–6 129–30, 203
6.7–31 164
6.8 2
6.35–44 152
6.45–52 152
7.15 156
7.24–30 134, 136, 202, 209
7.24 203
7.24a 206
7.24b 135, 137
7.25 135, 203
7.27 135, 136, 137, 204, 205
7.27–8 134, 136
7.31 104
7.32–7 152, 154
7.32a 154
7.32b 154
7.33–4 154
7.35 154
7.37 155
8.22–6 152
8.27–9 184
8.29 184
9.1 156
9.14–29 152
10.2–9 178
10.45 140, 156
11.27–33 113, 178
12.1–12 2
12.9 2
12.13–17 151
12.18–27 178
13.5–27 156
15.27 153
15.38 3
16.7 190
16.8 82, 120
16.9–20 82, 120
Luke 63, 95, 104, 113, 120, 122,
    123, 124, 126–7, 128, 129, 130,
    136, 153, 156, 179, 182, 186, 187,
    190, 192, 193, 197, 209, 214–15
1.1–2 113
1.5–2.40 152
2.1–2 3
2.41–9 152

3.16   104
4.1–13   3
4.16–30   209
4.23   155
4.25–7   209
5.29   129
6.20–7.35   124
6.24–6   156
7.6–7   113
7.11–16   152
7.41–3   156
9.3   2
9.57–13.34   124
9.60   155
10.7b   155
10.13   283
10.23–4   155
10.25–37   103
10.25–9   157
10.30–7   124, 157
11.2–4   105–6
11.5–10   156
11.15   126
12.25   155
12.35–8   156
13.18–19   180
13.31–5   190
14.11   214
15.11–24   156
16.16   190
16.19–31   157
17.7–10   156
17.20–1   156
17.23–4   156
18.1–8   156
18.9–14   156
18.14b   214
20.1–8   113
20.9–19   2
20.16   2
23.39–43   153
24.27   60
John   27, 55, 61, 62, 63, 68, 69, 95,
   100, 120, 123, 153, 186
1–8   100

7.53–8.11   82
14.31   125
15.1–17.26   125
15.1   125
18.1   125
18.10   153
18.31–3,   37–8, 95
20.30   125
21   125
Acts of the Apostles   55, 62, 100,
   190, 193
2.4–5   78
8.26–40   106
Romans   44, 72
3.25–6   126
15   44
15.8   176
16   44
1 Corinthians
11.23   113
15.3   113
Galatians   28
3.15–18   28
4   29
Ephesians   127
Philippians
2.6–11   126
Colossians   127
1.15–20   126
Pastoral Epistles   62, 105
1 Timothy   62
2 Timothy   62
Titus   62
Philemon   62
Hebrews   27, 55
James   55, 193
Peter   55
2 Peter   27, 113, 124
1 John
5.7–8   82
Jude   55, 113, 124
Revelation of St John   27, 55, 71, 95

Dead Sea Scrolls
4QSam^a   266

INDEX

Abbott, Walter M. 261
Adams, James Luther 244
advocacy interpretation 228–30
aetiology 145, 170, 171, 201
Africanus, Julius 27, 29
Age of Reason *see* Enlightenment
Aichele, George 286
Aland, Barbara 264, 267
Aland, Kurt 92, 264, 267
Albertus Magnus 33, 249
Albertz, Martin 150, 275
Albright, William F. 268
Aleppo Codex 84
Alexandrian family/recension 91, 99, 100, 104, 110
Alexandrians, the 29, 30–1, 55, 248
allegory, allegorical interpretation, allegorical exegesis 26–7, 29–31, 32, 33, 35, 36–7, 38, 247
Allison, Dale C. 80, 206–7, 264, 283
Alt, Albrecht 147–8, 274
Alter, Robert 15, 243
amplifications 128, 135
analogy 20–1, 22, 68
analysis 231
Anderson, Bernhard W. 285
Anderson, G. W. 264
Anglicanism 64
anomie 78
anthropological approaches 79
antinomianism 210
Antiochenes, Antiochene School 29, 30–1, 248, 249
anti-supernaturalism 22–3
aphorisms 175, 214
apocalyptic 65–6, 155–6, 177
apophthegms 153–4, 157, 158

aporia 217, 230
approximation process 221, 234
Aquila 87
Aquinas *see* Thomas Aquinas
Aramaic Targums 86
Aristeas, Letter of 28
Aristotle, Aristotelianism 32–3, 41
Ashton, John 272
Astruc, Jean 115
Augustine 28, 32, 119, 248
authenticity 98, 105–7, 217, 225
autographs 81

Babylonian Exile 54, 114, 118, 149, 202
Babylonian family/recension 99, 268
Babylonian Gemara 86
Bacon, B. W. 188, 280
Bailey, James L. 273
Bainton, Roland H. 250
Baird, J. A. 278
Baird, William 244, 246
Bampton Lectures 158, 187
baptism 69, 153
Bar-Kochba rebellion 86
Barr, James 4–5, 8, 94, 97, 114, 242, 246, 258, 267, 268, 269, 272
Barth, Gerhard 191, 280, 281
Barth, Karl 71–2, 226, 233, 259, 286
Barton, John 5–7, 10, 11–14, 16, 19–20, 26, 28, 186, 212, 230–1, 236, 242, 243–4, 245, 247, 248, 269, 273, 278, 279, 283, 286
Barton, Stephen C. 262
Bauckham, Richard 80, 263
Bauer, Georg Lorenz 50, 52, 253, 255
Bauer, Walter 71, 259

Baumgarten, Siegmund Jakob 42–3, 252
Baur, F. C. 62–3, 187, 245, 255–6, 280
Beardsley, Monroe 283
Beatitudes 155, 177
Bediako, Gillian M. 256
Bengel, Johann Albrecht 41, 90, 251, 267
Bense, Walter F. 244
Bentley, Jerry H. 250
Bentzen, Aage 268
Berger, Klaus 162, 277
Berndt, Rainer 249
Bertram, Georg 150, 275
Beza, Theodore 89, 267
Biblia Hebraica 88
Biblia Hebraica Quinta 88
Biblia Hebraica Stuttgartensia 83, 84, 88
biblical criticism 4, 5, 6–8, 12, 13–14
Biblical Interpretation: A Journal of Contemporary Approaches 76
biblical studies 4, 7–8, 218
Billerbeck, Paul 70, 258
Birdsall, J. N. 264
birth/infancy narratives 127, 129, 153
Black, C. Clifton 188, 192, 193, 213, 280, 282, 283
Black, Matthew 269
Blum, Erhard 79, 119, 149, 270, 275
Bodmer papyri 95
Boecker, Hans Joachim 275
Boff, Clodovis 222, 285
Boff, Leonardo 222, 285
Bohrmann, Georg 245
Bonner, Gerald 248
Book of Jashar 113
Book of the Wars of the Lord 113
Boorer, Suzanne 269, 278
Borg, Marcus 263
Bornkamm, Günther 73, 189–90, 191, 260, 280–1
Bossuet, J. B. 90
Bousset, Wilhelm 68–9, 258
Braaten, Carl E. 219, 284
Brecht, Martin 251
Brill 76
Brooke, George 85, 266

Brotzman, Ellis R. 264, 265
Brown, Raymond 75, 263
Bruce, F. F. 246
Bruns, Gerald L. 247
Bultmann, Christoph 252
Bultmann, Rudolf 25, 69, 71, 72, 73, 126, 149, 152–7, 159–60, 165, 176, 178, 179, 180, 187, 245, 248, 258, 259, 272, 275, 276, 280, 283
Buss, M. J. 269
Bussmann, Wilhelm 123, 271
Byzantine family 99, 100, 104, 106, 110

Caesarean recension 92
Cairo Genizah 83, 84, 265
Cajetan 35
Calvin 37, 250–1
Camerarius, Joachim 39, 251
Campbell, Jonathan G. 266
Canaanite 204
canon 44
canonical criticism/analysis 7, 80
Carleton Paget, J. N. B. 247
Carrington, Philip 188, 280
Casalis, Georges 285
Cassuto, Umberto 272
Catchpole, David R. 273
Catholic Modernism 74–5
causality 218
Chadwick, Owen 256
Chayyim, Jacob ben 88
Chester-Beatty papyrus 95
chiasmus 108
Childs, Brevard S. 18–19, 80, 217, 219, 220, 226, 244, 264, 284, 285
Chilton, Bruce 273
Christ *see* Jesus
Christianity 1, 41, 45, 47–9, 61, 62, 65, 67–9, 71, 79, 179, 209–10, 221
Christology 61–2, 137, 184, 191, 204
Chrysostom, St. John 29, 207
Church 18–19, 36, 41, 46, 48, 222
Church Fathers 26, 39, 92, 97–8
church rules 155, 156
clarifications 135
clarity/perspicuity of Scripture 25, 74, 89

Clements, Ronald E. 246
Coats, George W. 162, 172, 277, 278
Cobb, John B. 260
Codex Alexandrinus 96, 99, 100
Codex Beza Cantabrigiensis 100, 104
Codex Claromontanus 100
Codex Ephraemi rescriptus 96, 99
Codex Sinaiticus 92, 96, 99, 100, 103, 106, 109, 110, 111
Codex Vaticanus 92, 96, 99, 110, 111
coherence 218, 230, 231
Coleman, Christopher B. 249
Colet, John 35, 250
Collini, Stefan 243
Collins, John J. 266
composition 194–5
composition criticism 194–6
confessional approaches to the Bible 232
conjectural emendation 106–7
Constantinopolitan recension 91
contradiction(s) 27, 125, 131, 134, 138–9
controversy story 175, 178, 179
Conzelmann, Hans 73, 189, 190, 191, 260
Copernicus 38–9
correlation 22
Council of Trent 38, 74
Coverdale, Myles 36
creeds 148
criterion of antiquity 101
criterion of best witness 98, 110, 111
criterion of coherence 167, 179
criterion of dissimilarity 167, 179
criterion of genealogical relationship 99
criterion of geographical diversity 101
criterion of intrinsic probability 105, 107, 108–9
criterion of the most easily explainable reading 106, 108, 109
criterion of multiple attestation 167, 179–80
criterion of reliability 100–1, 110
criterion of transcriptional probability 101–2, 107, 108–9, 110, 111

criticism, critical 8–10, 14
Cross, Frank M. 99, 265, 268
Crossan, John Dominic 80, 193, 263, 282
Crüsemann, F. 79
Cynics 69
Cyrus 269

D (source) see Deuteronomic Code
Daniell, David 250
Daube, D. 276, 281
daughter translation 88
Davies, G. I. 283
Davies, Philip R. 218, 284
Davies, W. D. 206–7, 276, 281, 283
Dawson, David 247
Day, John 283
Dead Sea Scrolls 79, 83–4, 85, 87, 266
decolonialization 78
deconstructionism 79
Deism 41, 45
deliberate alterations 104
Delitzsch, Friedrich 268
demythologization 72
Descartes 39, 40
Deutero-Isaiah 119
Deuteronomic Code (D) 116, 117–19, 149
Deuteronomic History 119, 148
development 55–6, 58, 60, 64, 70, 118
dialectic 62
Dibelius, Martin 69, 143, 144, 149, 150–3, 154, 157, 159–60, 165, 178, 180, 268, 273, 275
differentiation 153
Dilthey, Wilhelm 73
Dinkler, E. 269
Diodorus of Tarsus 29
Dionysius of Alexandria 27
disappearing redactor 212
dittography 103
Divine Word see Word of God
Divino afflante Spiritu 75
Di Vito, Robert A. 273
doctrine see dogma
documentary hypothesis 116, 118, 119, 149
Dodd, C. H. 157, 158, 190, 276

dogma, dogmatics, dogmatic
theology 42, 52, 54, 56, 59, 66, 67
Donahue, John 185, 191, 279
Donaldson, James 247
Donation of Constantine 35
Donfried, Karl P. 284
doublets *see* duplications
Dozeman, Thomas B. 269, 273, 278
Drewermann, Eugen 216, 219, 225,
   284, 285
Driver, Samuel Rolles 64
Dunn, J. D. G. 80, 263
duplications 125–6, 132, 168
Dupuis SJ, Jacques 260, 261
Düsterdieck, Friedrich 56, 254

E (source) *see* Elohist, Elohistic source
Easton, B. S. 141, 144, 273, 274
Ebeling, Gerhard 25, 73, 244, 245,
   259, 260
eclecticism 92–3
Eco, Umberto 17
Eden 168, 170, 199
Edwards, Richard 191
Egger, Wilhelm 269, 273, 278
Egyptian family/recension 99, 268
Ehrman, Bart D. 264, 265
Eichhorn, Johann Gottfried 50–1, 52,
   115, 121, 253, 269, 271
Eissfeldt, Otto 118, 270
Eliot, George 63, 255
Elliott-Binns, L. E. 256
Elliott, J. K. 265, 266
Elohim 133, 200
Elohist, Elohistic source (E) 115, 116,
   117–18, 149, 202
Engnell, I. 149
Enlightenment 25, 26, 37, 38–52, 53,
   223
Ephraem Syrus 29
Epictetus 69
Epp, E. J. 246, 264, 265
Erasmus 35, 89, 92, 250, 266, 267
Ernesti, Johann August 42, 234, 252
error 102–4
Esau 145–6
eschatology 65, 69, 177
Essays and Reviews 64, 256

ethics, ethical *see* morality
Eudamidas 221
Eusebius of Caesarea 247, 248
Eusebius of Emesa 29
Evans, Craig A. 247
Evans, G. R. 249
evolution *see* development
Ewald, H. 116, 270

Fabella, Virginia 285
facts 13, 20, 59
faith 48, 73, 176, 207–8, 221, 222
fallacy of imitative form 10
families, textual 90, 99
Farmer, William 123, 272
Farrar, Frederic W. 30, 65, 246, 248,
   249, 257
Farrer, A. M. 188, 280
Fascher, Emil 143, 274
Fee, G. D. 264, 265
feeling 219
feminism, feminist theology 7, 77, 78,
   79, 80, 230
Feyerabend, Paul 243
Finegan, Jack 264
First Vatican Council 74
First World War 71
Fitzmyer, Joseph A. 75, 261
Flacius Illyricus, Matthias 38, 39, 251
Floss, Johannes P. 160, 277
Fohrer, Georg 118, 270
form and content 141, 142, 160, 178,
   226
form criticism 11–12, 23–4, 134,
   140–80, 181, 182, 189, 195, 196,
   197, 198, 204, 214, 273, 278–9
form history 143, 144
Formgeschichte 143, 158
Formkritik 143
forms *see* form criticism
Fortna, Robert Tomson 272
foundational source *see Grundlage*
four-document hypothesis 123
fragmentary hypothesis 115
fragmentation 214, 217–18, 230–1
Francke, August Hermann 41–2
Free Church of Scotland 64
Freedman, David Noel 246

Friedberg Genizah Project 265
Fries, Jakob Friedrich 54
Froehlich, Karlfried 249
Frör, Kurt 278
Frye, R. M. 192–3, 213, 214–15, 282,
    283
Fuchs, Ernst 73, 259, 260
Fuller, R. H. 167, 277
Fuller, Russell 265
Funk, Robert W. 80, 229, 286
Füssel, Kurt 229, 286

G (source) see Grundlage
Gabler, Johann Philipp 50, 51–2, 253
Gaebelein, Frank E. 268
Galileo 39
Gardner, Helen 217, 284
Gaston, Lloyd 192, 282
Gattungskritik 165
gay interpretation 79
Geddes, Alexander 115, 269
Gemser, B. 274–5
gender theory 80
genealogies 99
genizah 84
genre 3, 5, 6, 12, 18, 141, 145, 161, 162,
    165–6, 170–1, 173, 177, 183, 196
genre criticism/analysis 141, 143, 144,
    162, 165
Gentiles 136, 175–6, 206, 207,
    209–10
Gerhardsson, Birger 179, 278
Gerizim 86–7
Gerstenberger, E. S. 119, 271, 274
Gesenius, Wilhelm 87
Girgensohn, Karl 72, 259
God 11, 22, 47, 49, 133, 201, 220
Good Samaritan 4, 103, 106, 157, 166
Gordon, Robert P. 283
Gore, Charles 64, 256
Goshen-Gottstein, Moshe H. 265
Gospels 5, 60, 61, 62, 63, 64, 67, 99,
    100, 105, 119, 158, 184, 210–11
Gottwald, N. K. 79, 286
Graf, Karl Heinrich 117, 270
Grant, Frederick C. 157
Grant, Robert M. 30, 246, 247, 249,
    257

Grayzel, Solomon 265
Green, Joel B. 246, 262, 264, 273
Greenslade, S. L 250
Greer, Rowan A. 248
Gressmann, Hugo 79
Griesbach, Johann Jakob 91, 120, 271
Griffiths, Richard 250
Grimm, Jakob and Wilhelm 144
Grotius, Hugo 39
Grundlage 118
Gunkel, Hermann 68, 79, 142, 144–7,
    171, 172, 258, 273, 274, 277
Guthrie, Donald 272
Güttgemanns, Erhardt 159, 273, 276,
    278

Habel, Norman 269
Haenchen, Ernst 195, 282
Hahn, Ferdinand 191, 281
Halivni, David Weiss 260
Hanson, R. P. C. 247, 249
haplography 103
Harnack, Adolf von 64, 256
Harris, Robert A. 249
Harrison, R. K. 272
Harvey, Van A. 21, 22, 244
Hase, Karl 55, 254
Hauser, Alan J. 246, 247, 248, 249,
    250, 251, 265
Hausrath, Adolf 67, 258
Hayes, John Haralson 246, 252, 272
Haynes, Stephen R. 269, 273, 278
Heb. 24,570 84
Hebrew University Bible Project 84
Hegel, Hegelianism 58, 60, 62, 63,
    70, 117, 118
Heidegger, Martin 72
Held, Heinz Joachim 191, 280, 281
Hendel, Ronald S. 85, 266
Henry of Ghent 34
Herder, Johann Gottfried 121–2, 271
hermeneutics 56, 57, 194
    theological 232
Herrmann, Willibald 64, 256
Hesiod 50
Hexapla 86, 87
Hexateuch 148
Heyne, Christian Gottlob 49–50, 51

Hidal, Sten 248
higher criticism 23, 85, 114
hilasterion 126
Hill, Robert C. 248
Hirsch, Emanuel 245
historical consciousness 11
historical–critical method, historical
    criticism 1, 4, 5, 7–20, 22, 23,
    25, 26, 27, 65, 72, 74–5, 76, 77,
    216–37, 242, 245
historical Jesus 45, 63, 66, 67, 79–80,
    137, 158, 187, 188
historical sense *see* sense, historical
historicism 6, 17, 223, 225–6, 232,
    235
historiography 26
history 1, 5–6, 7, 47–9, 65, 66, 72,
    73, 219, 220, 221
History of Religions 67–70, 79
Holl, Karl 71, 259
Holmes, Michael W. 265
Hölscher, Gustav 270
Holtzmann, Heinrich Julius 122,
    271
Holy Spirit 28, 30, 37, 42
Homer 50, 115
homoioarcton 103
homoioteleuton 103
Horbury, William 246
Hornig, Gottfried 245
Horsley, Richard A. 286
Hort, John Anthony 64, 92
Hugh of St Victor 32
Hupfeld, Hermann 116, 270

Iber, Gerhard 158–9, 276
ideology 77, 223–30, 232–3, 235
idolatry 233–4
Iliad 115
imperial text 100
inconsistency(ies) 6, 27, 134, 138,
    228, 230
individualization 153
inspiration 23, 45, 56, 64
intended sense *see* sense, intended
intention, authorial 16, 33, 211
intentional fallacy 16, 211
interpretation 234–5

interruptions 125, 131
introduction 40, 45, 51
intuition 12–13, 14
I-sayings 140, 155, 156, 178
Itala 88

J (source) *see* Yahwist
Jacob 145–6
Jacob, Benno 272
Jeanrond, Werner 255
Jenson, Robert W. 219, 284
Jeremias, Joachim 191
Jerome 27, 28, 31, 35, 88, 247, 248
Jesus 1, 2, 29, 30, 41, 46, 48–9, 52,
    57, 61, 62, 64, 65, 66, 140, 150,
    151, 152, 154, 155, 175–6, 186,
    208–9
Jesus Seminar 80
Joachim of Fiore 33, 49
Johannine comma 82
John Paul II 75
Josephus 3, 242
Josiah 115, 116
Jowett, Benjamin 64, 223, 226, 227,
    236, 256, 285, 286
Judaism 1, 43, 54, 68, 70–1, 82, 176,
    179, 210
Julian of Eclanum 31
Junilius Africanus 31, 247
justification by faith 25, 73

K (source) *see* Kenite source
Kahle, Paul 87, 265, 266
Kähler, Martin 66–7, 257
Kaiser, Otto 119, 271
Käsemann, Ernst 25, 73, 126, 245,
    260, 272
Kaufmann, J. 270
Kaufmann, Yehezkel 272
Keil, Karl August Gottlieb 56, 254
Kelber, Werner 191
Kenite source 118
Kenotic Christology 66
Kepler 39
kerygma 152, 188, 233
Kieffer, René 248
Kierkegaard, Søren 220–1, 234,
    284–5

Kilpatrick, G. D. 264
Kimmerle, Heinz 255
kingdom of God 66, 151, 155
Kittel, Gerhard 70, 71, 259
Kittel, Rudolf 84, 88
Klein, Ralph W. 266
Klippenberg, Hans G. 262
Knierim, Rolf P. 162, 277
Knight, Douglas A. 273
Koch, Dietrich-Alex 255
Koch, Klaus 160, 177, 277, 278
Koehler, Ludwig 142, 275
Koine 100
Kompositionsgeschichte 195
Kooij, Arie van der 265
Köpf, Ulrich 249
Kosellek, Reinhart 8, 242
Krans, Jans 267
Kraus, Hans-Joachim 245, 246, 260
Krentz, Edgar 26, 245, 246
Kuhn, Thomas 13, 243
Kümmel, Werner Georg 246, 251,
    252, 254, 257, 258, 259, 267,
    271, 275
Kundsin, Karl 157, 187, 276, 280

L (Lucan special source) 123
L (Pentateuchal source) *see* Lay source
Lachmann, Karl 63, 91, 122, 256,
    267, 271
Laistner, M. L. W. 31, 249
Lamentibili 74
law 147, 210
    apodictic 147
    casuistic 147
law of biographical analogy 152
law of the single perspective 156
Lay source (L) 118
lectio brevior lectio potior 105, 107,
    112
lectio difficilior lectio potior 105,
    110–11, 112
legal sayings 155, 156
legends 144, 145–6, 152–3
    ceremonial 146
    ethnological 145
    etymological 145–6
    geological 146

Leibniz, G. W. 46–7, 252, 253
Leiman, Sid Z. 265
Leningrad collection 84
lesbian interpretation 79
Lessing, G. E. 45–9, 120–1, 252, 253,
    271
Liberal Protestantism 65–6
liberation exegesis/theology 7, 77–9,
    80, 222, 230
Liebing, Heinz 245
Lieu, Judith M. 262, 277
Life of Jesus 55–6, 58–9, 65, 66, 137,
    184
Lightfoot, John 39–40
Lightfoot, Joseph Barber 64
Lightfoot, R. H. 157–8, 187–8, 276
Lim, Timothy H. 266
literal sense *see* sense, literal
literalism 18
literary approaches/criticism/
    theory 76–9, 114, 161, 193, 194,
    211, 214, 269
liturgy 175, 177–8, 204
local-genealogical method 92
Locke, John 41
logocentrism 225
Lohfink, Gerhard 273
Lohmeyer, Ernst 71, 187, 259, 280
Loisy, Alfred 74
Lord, Lordship 69, 204, 207, 208
Lord's Prayer 104, 105–6
lost ending of Mark 120
Louth, Andrew 10–13, 243
lower criticism 23, 81, 85, 114–15
    see also textual criticism
Luther, Martin 36, 37, 250
Lutheranism 25, 41
Lux Mundi 64, 256
Luz, Ulrich 204, 283
Lyons, William John 266

M (Matthaean special material) 123
Macquarrie, John 59, 255
McCarter, P. Kyle 105, 264, 268
McKane, William 269
McKenzie, Steven L. 269, 273, 278
McKim, Donald K. 246
McKnight, Edgar V. 78, 262, 279

McRae, G. W. 246
Maier, Bernhard 256
Maier, Gerhard 9, 10, 216, 222, 242, 285
majuscules 96
Malbon, Elizabeth Struthers 279
Malina, Bruce 79, 262
Manson, T. W. 158, 276, 279
manuscripta ponderantur non numerantur 98
Marcion 44
Markan hypothesis 187, 188, 280
Markan priority 63, 122, 130, 197
Marshall, I. Howard 246, 273
Marxism 79, 229
Marxsen, Willi 185–6, 188, 189, 191, 214, 279, 280, 281
Masoretes, Masoretic edition 83, 84, 86, 87, 88, 98, 99, 107, 108–9, 265, 266, 268
materialism 79
Matthaean priority 123
meaning 14, 15, 16, 20, 76, 211, 225, 236–7
  existential 72
  historical 29, 76–7, 220
  intended 56, 76, 227
  literal 29, 32, 34, 36, 37, 77
  objective 226–8
  original 76–7
  spiritual 27, 37
  stable 226–8, 236
  textual 223, 226–8
  theological 219, 220, 233
Meeks, Wayne 79, 262
Meier, John P. 80, 263
Merz, Annette 263
Mesguich, Sophie Kessler 250
messiah, messiahship 55, 186–7, 209
messianic secret 67, 208
Mesters, Carlos 222–3, 285
metaphor 18, 33
metathesis 102
method 10–14, 20, 23–4, 40, 213, 222, 224, 227, 235
Metzger, Bruce M. 264, 265, 267

Meyer, Heinrich August Wilhelm 56–7, 254
Michaelis, Johann David 43, 45, 120, 252
Middle Ages 32, 36
Mill, John 90, 91, 267
Millard, Alan R. 268
minatory sayings 156
Minear, Paul S. 220, 284
minorities 78
Minuscule 33 96, 99
Minuscule 1739 96
minuscules 96, 100, 110
miracles 47–8, 55, 59, 152, 154, 155, 160, 174–5, 178, 186, 208
Mishnah 86
misspellings 102
Moberly, R. W. L. 233, 286
Moir, I. 265
monasteries 32
de Moor, J. C. 286
morality 40, 46, 49, 59, 64, 65, 66, 77–8
Morgan, Robert 262
Morgenstern, Julius 118, 270
Mosaic religion 54
Moses 2, 50, 86–7
Motyer, J. A. 272
Mowinckel, Sigmund 16, 146–7, 274
Muilenburg, James 161, 277
mystery religions 67, 69
myth 49–52, 58, 60, 61, 69, 71, 144, 145, 170–1, 178, 187, 200, 201, 226
  evangelical 60
  faded 171, 172, 173, 200
  historical 50, 51, 60
  philosophical 50, 51
  poetic 51
  pure 60

N (source) *see* Nomadic source
Nadler, Steven 251
Nag Hammadi Library 79
narrative criticism 79
National and University Library of Jerusalem 84
Nestorianism 31

Neuner SJ, J. 260, 261
New Criticism 76, 123, 214
New Hermeneutic 73
Nicholson, Ernest 246
Niebuhr, Barthold Georg 53, 62, 115
Nielsen, Kirsten 275
Nimrod 146
Nineham, Dennis 157–8, 276
Nomadic source 118
nominalism 33, 34
non-confessional approaches to the
    Bible 232
Norris, Richard A. 248
Noth, Martin 16, 118, 148, 189, 270,
    275
novellas *see* tales

O'Neill, J. C. 246
objectivism 232
objectivity, objective truth 11, 13, 77,
    223
Ocker, Christopher 249
Odyssey 115
Oepke, Albrecht 259
Oftestad, Bernt T. 251
Old Latin 88
Olshausen, Hermann 58–9
omissions 102, 129, 135–6, 197, 199
Opitz, Peter 250
oppression 77, 80, 229
Origen 27, 28–9, 31, 33, 47, 86, 87,
    92, 186, 236, 247, 249
original sense *see* sense, original
Osborne, Grant R. 246
other, the 78
Overbeck, Franz 65, 257
Oxford English Dictionary 8, 225
Oxford Hebrew Bible Project 88

P (source) *see* Priestly source
P[38] 100
P[45] 95
P[46] 95
P[47] 95
P[48] 100
P[52] 95
P[66] 95
P[75] 95

Palestinian family/recension 99, 268
Palestinian Gemara 86
Palmer, N. H. 256
Pannenberg, Wolfhart 25, 245
papyri 95, 96
Parable of the Mustard Seed 180
parables 129, 155, 156, 157, 166, 178,
    180
paradigm shift 13
paradigms 151, 152, 157, 158
paresis 126
Parker, D. C. 93, 267
parousia 151, 190
Pascendi dominici gregis 67, 75, 260
Passion Narrative 61, 150, 153
past, the 20, 21, 47, 53, 171, 219, 220
Paul 28, 29, 55, 56, 62, 68, 79, 95, 96,
    113, 123, 126, 127
Paul of Nisibis 31
Paulinus 27
Paulus, Heinrich Eberhard
    Gottlob 55, 58–9, 254
Payne, J. B. 265–6
Peabody, David Barrett 192, 282
Pedersen, Johannes 270
Pentateuch 5, 7, 12, 16, 28, 50, 54,
    79, 86, 99, 115, 116, 117–18, 119,
    139, 148–9, 217, 230
Perrin, Norman 167, 184, 186–7, 188,
    190, 191, 193, 194, 195, 210,
    214, 277, 279, 280, 281, 282, 283
Peshitta 88, 107
Petersen, Norman R. 76, 261
Pfeiffer, R. H. 118, 270
Pfleiderer, Otto 67–8, 258
philology 35, 41–2, 43
Pietersen, Lloyd K. 266
Pietism 41–2, 76
Pitkin, Barbara 251
Pius X 67, 74, 260
Pius XII 75
Platonism 32
Plutarch 221
pneumatic exegesis 72
politics 77
Pontifical Biblical Commission 75
Pontifical Biblical Institute 75, 261
Popper, Karl 13, 243

Porter, Stanley J. 265
positivism 63, 224, 235
postcolonialism 78
Postmodern Bible 228, 286
postmodernism 76, 211
poststructuralism 7, 8, 228
Pratensis, Felix 88
praxis 220-3, 234-5
prayer 204, 208
present, the 11, 20, 21, 47, 53, 171, 219, 220, 233
Priestly source (P) 116, 117-19, 134, 149, 202
primal Gospel 120-2
printing 35, 81
Prior, Joseph G. 261
probability 20, 22
Procopé, J. F. 247
Prodigal Son 4, 156
progress 46, 219
pronouncement stories 157, 158, 175
prophetic sayings/speech 155, 164
prophets 117, 140, 147, 149
Protestantism, Protestants 74, 76, 89
Proto-Luke 123
proverbs 155, 175, 206
Prussner, Frederick C. 246
Pryke, E. J. 192, 282
Pseudo-Heraclitus 26, 247
psychological criticism 79
Ptolemy I 28

Q, Quelle 122, 123, 124, 126, 130-1, 153, 180, 186
quest of the historical Jesus 73, 79-80, 188
Qumran 84, 85

Rabbinic Bibles 88
Rabbis 82-3, 97, 98, 179
Rad, Gerhard von 16, 134, 148, 189, 230, 270, 272
Raeder, Siegfried 250
Räisänen, Heikki 78-9, 258, 261, 262, 263, 284
Ranke, Leopold von 53
Rashi 32

rationalism 42, 46, 55, 58-60, 223, 224-5
reader, the 76, 228
reader-response criticism 7, 8, 79
reason 10, 25, 42, 47, 49, 55, 224
Received Edition 88
received text see textus receptus
redaction 164, 173, 176, 181-2, 194-5, 213, 279
redaction criticism 23-4, 80, 173, 181-215, 278
Redaktionsgeschichte 182, 185, 189, 191
Redaktionskritik 185
redemption 69
Reformation 25, 26, 35-8, 82
Reformers, the 19, 36-7
regnal reports 140
Reimarus, Hermann Samuel 45-6, 186-7, 252
Reischle, M. 258
Reitzenstein, Richard 68-9, 258
Renaissance 26, 34-5, 36
Renan, Ernest 65, 257
Rendtorff, Rolf 149, 280
repetitions 132, 214
Reuchlin, Johann 35
revelation 9-10, 47, 49, 64, 72, 226
Reventlow, Henning Graf 42, 50, 51, 144, 246, 250, 251, 252, 253, 254, 269, 274
rhetorical criticism 7, 8, 79, 161
Riches, John K. 246, 258
Richter, Wolfgang 119, 141, 160, 165, 185, 189, 194, 269, 272, 273, 277, 278, 279, 280, 282
Riddle, Donald Wayne 157, 276
Riesenfeld, Harald 179, 278
Ritschl, Albrecht 64, 66, 256
Roberts, Alexander 247
Roberts, Bleddyn J. 264
Robertson Smith, William 64, 256
Robinson, James M. 73, 260
Rogerson, John W. 79, 253, 256, 260, 262, 277
Rohde, Joachim 188, 193, 278, 280, 282
Rollinson, Philip 247

Roman Catholicism, Roman Catholic
  Church 36, 38, 62, 74–5, 76, 90
Rowley, H. H. 269
Rückert, Leopold Immanuel 56, 254
Rummel, Erike 34, 249, 266
Ryder, E. T. 269

S (source) *see* Southern source
Sæbo, Magne 246, 247, 248, 249,
  250, 251, 252, 260, 269
sagas 144, 145, 171
salvation history 190
Samaritan Pentateuch/Torah/
  Bible 85–7, 99, 102, 107, 108
Sanders, E. P. 79, 80, 178, 263, 278
Sanders, James A. 80, 264
Sandys-Wunsch, John 246, 252
Santer, Mark 248
Sassoon 507 84
Sassoon 1053 84
scepticism 25, 73
Schlatter, Adolf 187, 280
Schleiermacher, F. D. E. 57, 59,
  234–5, 255
Schmid, Hans Heinrich 119, 270
Schmidt, Hans 259
Schmidt, Karl Ludwig 149–50, 153, 275
Schmithals, Walter 159, 277
Schnackenburg, Rudolf 75
Schniewind, Julius 70, 259
Scholder, Klaus 245
Schreiber, Johannes 187, 280
Schüssler Fiorenza, Elisabeth 77, 79,
  193, 216, 227, 229, 236–7, 258,
  261, 262, 282, 284, 286, 287
Schweitzer, Albert 46, 66, 252, 257
science, scientific, (natural)
  sciences, scientific world view,
  scientism 11, 13, 22–3, 40, 64,
  222, 223–4, 226, 229, 235
scriptio continua 103
Seal, Welton O. 191
Second Vatican Council 75, 261
secular, secularity, secularism 6, 9,
  10, 219, 224, 232
Segovia, Fernando 75–6, 78, 216, 217,
  228, 236, 261, 262, 284, 286
Seir source *see* Southern source

Seitz, Christopher 9, 242
Sellin, Ernst 270
Semler, Johann Salomo 43–5, 62, 245,
  252
sense (of Scripture) 14–20
  sense, grammatical 37, 38
  sense, historical 17–18, 19, 37
  sense, intended 15–17, 19
  sense, literal 18–19, 29, 31, 33, 35,
    37, 38, 232
  sense, original 14–15, 19
  sense, plain 19–20
Septuagint 82, 85, 86, 87, 88, 99, 107
Sermon on the Mount 124, 129, 184
Severianus 29
Shechem 86
signs 228
signs source 123
Simon, Richard 74, 89–90, 245, 260,
  267
sin 10, 200
Sitz im Leben 70, 141–2, 143, 145,
  148, 155, 158, 161, 164, 166, 172,
  175–6, 177, 179, 191, 192, 197,
  201, 204, 209–10, 228
Smalley, Beryl 31, 32, 249
Smalley, Stephen 190, 195, 212, 278,
  281, 282, 283
Smend, Rudolf 247, 270
social-scientific approaches 79
sola scriptura, Scripture alone 25, 37,
  38, 74, 82, 89
Soulen, Richard K. 269
source criticism 8, 11–12, 13, 23–4, 55,
  113–39, 144, 163, 166, 167, 181,
  182, 186, 189, 196, 197, 198, 214
Southern source (S) 118
Sparks, H. F. D. 248
Sparks, Kenton L. 273
Spener, Philipp Jacob 41
Spinoza, Baruch 40, 89, 245, 251, 267
spirit 60, 62
Sprachereignis 73
Stähelin, J. J. 116, 270
Statement of the Ecumenical Dialogue
  of Third World Theologians 222,
  285
Stäudlin, Carl Friedrich 57

Steck, Odil Hannes 78, 160–1, 189, 262, 269, 273, 277, 278
Stein, Robert H. 181, 189, 191–2, 213–14, 276, 278–9, 280, 281–2
Steiner, George 10, 243
Steinmann, J. 260
Steinmetz, David C. 236/237, 286/287
Stendahl, Krister 70, 258
Stephanus 89
Stonehouse, N. B. 188, 280
Storr, Gottlob Christian 120, 271
Storr, Vernon F. 256
Strauss, David Friedrich 58–62, 63, 144, 187, 224, 255, 285
Strauss, Leo 245
Strecker, Georg 278
Streete, Gail P. C. 278
Streeter, B. H. 92, 123, 267
structuralism 7, 79, 160, 228
Stuhlmacher, Peter 76, 261
style 126–7, 128, 135, 139
subjectivity, subjective truth 11
subtilitas applicandi 234–5
subtilitas explicandi 234–5
subtilitas intelligendi 234–5
Succession Narrative 119
Sugirtharajah, R. S. 229, 258, 286
supernatural, supernaturalism 6, 43, 58–60, 63, 64
supplementary hypothesis 116
Sweeney, Marvin A. 273
symbol 59–60
Symmachus 87
synonymous parallelism 170
synopsis 120
Synoptic Apocalypse 156
Synoptic Gospels 55, 63, 120–3, 124, 131, 153, 154, 155, 186, 193, 198
Synoptic Problem 130
synthesis 231
Syrian text 92
Syro–Phoenician 204

T & T Clark 56, 254
Talbert, Charles H. 252
tales 151–2, 154

Talmon, Shermaryahu 99, 264, 265, 268
Tan, Randall K. J. 195, 212, 282, 283
Tappert, Theodore G. 250
Targum Neofiti 107
Taylor, Vincent 157, 275
Temple, Frederick 256
Temptation Narrative, Jesus' temptation 3, 33, 51–2, 178, 186
tendency, tendency criticism 53, 63
Testimonium spiritus sancti internum 37
textual criticism 11–12, 23, 81–112
textus receptus 89, 90, 91, 92
Theissen, Gerd 79, 80, 159, 262, 263, 277
Theodore of Mopsuestia 29–31, 248
Theodoret 29
Theodotion 87
theological interpretation 72, 235
theology 11, 46, 65, 66, 126–7, 139, 188, 218–19, 226
  biblical 52
  dogmatic 52
  of history 218
theory 13
Thiselton, Anthony C. 246
Thomas Aquinas 33, 249
Thompson, Mark D. 250
Tiberias 83
van Til, Cornelius 260
Tindal, Matthew 41
Tischendorf, Constantin von 92, 267
Tödt, Eduard 191, 281
Toland, John 41
Torjesen, Karen Jo 247
Torres, Sergio 285
Tov, Emanuel 85, 99, 264, 266, 268
Tracy, David 30, 246, 247, 249, 257
tradition criticism 162, 166, 173, 176, 273
tradition history 143, 148, 273
Traditionsgeschichte 166
transfiguration 153
translations 97
transposition 102
Travis, Stephen H. 273

Trigg, Joseph Wilson 247
Trinity 82
Troeltsch, Ernst 21–2, 26, 244, 245, 246
Trollope, Anthony 243–4
truth 53
  contingent 47, 48
  correspondence theory of 226
  divine 57
  eternal 57
  necessary 47, 48
Tucker, Gene M. 272
Tuckett, Christopher 264, 269, 273, 278
Turretini, Jean Alphonse 42, 252
two-document hypothesis 122–3, 179, 186
Tyndale, William 36
typology 29–30
Tyre and Sidon 104, 135, 202–3, 204
Tyrell, George 74

Überlieferungsgeschichte 166
Ulrich, Eugene 85, 266
uncials 96, 100
understanding 11, 12, 13, 43, 231
universals 32–3
universities 32
Urevangelium see primal Gospel
Usteri, Leonhard 56

Valla, Lorenzo 35, 249–50
Valle, Pietro della 86
Van Seters, John 118–19, 270
Vater, Johann Severin 115, 269
Vaticinia ex eventu 156
Vatke, Wilhelm 58, 60, 117, 255
Vermes, Geza 80, 263
Via, Dan O. 214, 283
virtue *see* morality
Viviano, Pauline A. 269
vocabulary 126–7, 139
Vulgate 34, 35, 36, 74, 88

Wadi Murabba'at 86
Wallmann, Johannes 251
Waltke, Bruce 105, 265, 268

Wansborough OSB, Henry 247, 250
Watson, Duane F. 246, 247, 248, 249, 250, 251, 265
Watson, Francis 79, 232, 263, 286
Wegner, Paul D. 265
Weingreen, J. 264
Weiser, Artur 268
Weiss, Johannes 65–6, 257
Weisse, Christian Hermann 63, 256, 280
Welch, Adam C. 270
Wellhausen, Julius 117–18, 119, 186, 279
Wenham, David 269
Wenham, Gordon J. 108, 268
Wenham, J. W. 272
Wernle, Paul 279
Westcott, Brooke Foss 64, 92
Westermann, Claus 149, 275
Western family/recension 91, 100, 104, 110
de Wette, Wilhelm Martin Leberecht 53–5, 59, 116, 144, 253, 254, 270, 274
Wettstein, Johann Jakob 90–1, 267
Whybray, R. N. 119, 271
Wicks, Jared 250
Wiles, M. F. 247, 248
Wilke, Christian Gottlob 63, 122, 256, 280
William of Ockham 34
Williamson, H. G. M. 283
Wimsatt, William 283
Windisch, Hans 71, 259
Wink, Walter 216, 218, 220, 222, 225, 227, 228, 236, 284, 285, 286, 287
Winter, Dagmar 263
Winton Thomas, D. 275
wisdom 155, 172, 175, 177, 183, 201
Word of God 19, 43–4, 71, 72, 73, 75, 219, 222, 232, 237
Wordsworth, William 17
works-righteousness 73
Wortgeschehen 73
Wrede, Wilhelm 66, 67, 137–8, 186, 187, 188, 257, 279, 280

Wright, David F. 248
Wright, N. T. 80, 212, 263
Würthwein, Ernst 264, 266, 268
Wycliffe, John 36

Yahweh 133, 134, 200
Yahwist , Yahwist source 115,
    117–19, 134, 148, 149, 172, 173,
    201, 202

Yarchin, William 247, 261, 262
Yeivin, Israel 265, 266
Yemen 88
Young, Frances 31, 247, 248, 249

Zaharopoulos, Dimitri Z. 248
Ziegler, Theobald 58, 255
Zimmermann, Heinz 264, 269, 272,
    278